D1532854

RIVALS!
MU VS. KU

A CLASSIC SPORTS MATCH-UP, SINCE 1891

Edited by David Smale

KANSAS CITY STAR BOOKS
Kansas City, Missouri

MISSOURI
vs
KANSAS

November 25, 1937

25c

RIVALS!
MU VS. KU

A CLASSIC SPORTS MATCH-UP, SINCE 1891

KANSAS CITY STAR BOOKS
Kansas City, Missouri

RIVALS!
MU VS. KU

A CLASSIC SPORTS MATCH-UP, SINCE 1891

EDITED BY DAVID SMALE

*From the archives of
The Kansas City Star,
University of Missouri
and University of Kansas*

DESIGN BY BRIAN GRUBB

*Photographs of artifacts by
Rebecca Friend, Kansas City Star*

KANSAS CITY STAR BOOKS
Kansas City, Missouri

Published by Kansas City Star Books,
an imprint of *The Kansas City Star*
1729 Grand Blvd.
Kansas City, Missouri 64108

All rights reserved
Copyright 2005 by The Kansas City Star

No part of this book may be reproduced, stored in
a retrieval system, or transmitted in any form or by
any means, electronic, mechanical, photocopying,
recording or otherwise, without the prior consent
of the publisher.

*To order copies, call StarInfo (816-234-4636
and say "operator.") www.TheKansasCityStore.com*

*First edition, first printing. Printed in the United States of America
by Walsworth Publishing Co., Inc. Marceline, Missouri*

ISBN: 0-9764021-3-0

CONTENTS

Acknowledgements

When I first started this project, I knew it would be difficult to narrow the choices of events to cover. This rivalry goes so far back I knew it would be impossible to include every significant event. I had no idea.

Speaking to legends like Max Falkenstein and Norm Stewart, I heard about decades of heroic battles between the Jayhawks and Tigers. Every year's battles could have been included, because there never was an insignificant football or basketball game between the two universities.

What follows is a chronological account of the men's football and basketball histories between the two schools. The textual content is primarily gleaned from the archives of *The Kansas City Star* and *Kansas City Times*, with stories reprinted exactly as they appeared in the newspapers – headlines and all. In some cases, stories were tightened for length.

Because the most history – and vast media and public attention since the late 1800s – has centered on the men's football and basketball programs, this book does not attempt to explore other sports, including women's sports. The exception: Chapter Eleven looks at the burgeoning rivalry in women's basketball ... though even in 2005, sources on both sides agree that the rivalry doesn't yet have the heat of the men's programs. This was not done to exclude ... every program, men's or women's, likely has a compelling history. But time and resources limited us to this focus.

Finally, the history of the rivalry runs very deep – back before the Civil War. We asked Donna Martin, a Kansas City writer and editor who has overseen a number of *Kansas City Star* Books' history projects, to explore in detail this historic context of this other "war between the states." She's done so in Chapter One.

I want to thank Coach Stewart, Gary Link and John Kadlec from the Missouri side, and Falkenstein, Tom Hedrick, Bill Mayer and Don Fambrough from the Kansas side for spending time with me and helping me decide which events best flavored this rivalry. Their friendliness and cooperation was exceeded only by their passion for their teams.

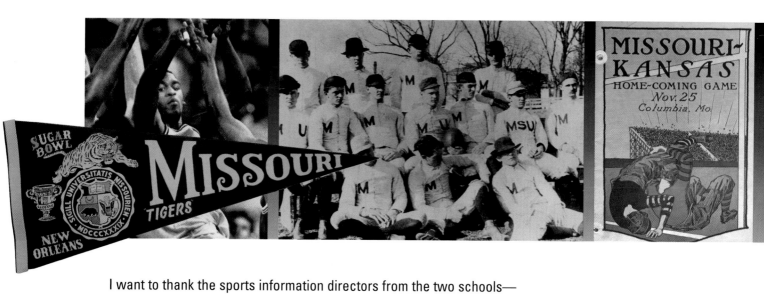

I want to thank the sports information directors from the two schools—Chris Theisen of Kansas and Chad Moller of Missouri—for their assistance in locating personalities, as well as photographs.

I want to thank the university archivists—Greg Cox of Missouri and Rebecca Schulte of Kansas—for their assistance in finding many of the artifacts pictured in this book. I want to thank Rebecca Friend of *The Kansas City Star* for taking those photographs. I also want to thank the staff of *The Star* archives for helping me with microfilm and old photographs.

I want to thank Jim Chappell of Chappell's Bar and Grill in North Kansas City, Mo., for supplying some unique memorabilia seen on the pages of this book.

I want to thank my Mom, Carol, for typing the stories from the photocopies of microfilm, and her and my Dad, Ray, for helping with the proofreading. Dad, who passed away during the preparation of this book, was the best proofreader I ever had. I will miss him greatly, for many more reasons than that.

I want to thank Doug Weaver of *The Star* books division for having faith in this Kansas State Wildcat to be fair, balanced and positive in the presentation of the stories of these two prestigious universities.

Finally, I want to thank Brian Grubb for his outstanding work on the design of this book. He made the pages come to life, and in the process, became a friend.

- David Smale

CHAPTER 1

BORDER LORE

AN INTRODUCTION

FANS DISPLAY ALLEGIANCES WITH PRIDE

The two highways are a few miles apart. But that imaginary dotted line between U.S. 69 in Kansas and U.S. 71 in Missouri makes all the difference in the world.

How big is the Kansas-Missouri rivalry? How important is athletic competition to the fans of the two schools? How big is the sky?

Long-time Missouri basketball coach Norm Stewart did his part to perpetuate the strong feelings between Kansas and Missouri.

"I decided I was not going to spend my good Missouri money in Kansas," Stewart said. When the Tigers would play at Kansas, he would bus his team to Kansas City—Missouri, not Kansas—to spend the night. He would then take his team to breakfast in Missouri and then head to Lawrence. After the games, he would bus back into Missouri for the team meal.

He did it once and the story made the papers. He decided that it wasn't a bad creed to live by. "When you have something that motivates your team, you use it," he said.

Not to be outdone, broadcaster Tom Hedrick, who was at the microphone for Kansas for 17 years, refuses to stop in Columbia when driving through.

"My wife and I were driving back to Lawrence from Indiana and we approached Columbia around noon," Hedrick said. "My wife said, 'Are we going to stop for lunch in Columbia?' I just kept driving. As the options started to diminish, she said again, 'We aren't going to stop for lunch in Columbia, are we?'

"If Norm won't spend money in Lawrence, I won't spend money in Columbia. We ended up eating in Emma. It's still in Missouri, but it's not Columbia."

Kansas City Star writer Ivan Carter took a trip down 69, and then back up 71 and found that there's a lot more difference than being just two numbers apart. Carter's whimsical, yet accurate portrayal of the animosity between the two universities appeared as the teams, and their Big XII counterparts, prepared for the 2003 Big XII Basketball Tournament in Dallas.

Here's how it appeared in the March 9, 2003, *Star*

FORT SCOTT, KAN. — The shelves of the J&W Sports Shop, here in the heart of the tiny downtown district, are stocked with all things collegiate.

There are hats, T-shirts, key chains, you name it. They carry the image of the Jayhawk, Willie the Wildcat, even the puckered mug of the Pittsburg State Gorilla.

But the one thing you won't find, the one thing that's nowhere in the store, is this: a Missouri Tiger. No ballpoint pens, no hats, nothing.

"We don't carry anything like that here," owner Lisa Stephan said. "No need for it. We have some Nebraska hats and I think we have some things from Oklahoma and Oklahoma State ... but nothing from Missouri.

"That stuff," Stephan said, chuckling, "doesn't sell over here."

And yet just outside her door, no more than a few miles and a brisk walk away, is the state of Missouri. "It doesn't make sense," Stephan continued. "You would think we would have MU fans coming over because we're so close, but I guess things kind of stop at the border."

And that about says it all.

This is where the Border War battle lines are drawn, where the term is more than a fancy moniker – it defines a

Nevada High student Tara Kiest may go to school and work in Missouri but she proudly wears her KU hat even though she is surrounded by Tigers fans.

Curtis Long may live in Paola, Kan., but his heart - and basement - belong to the Tigers. He graduated from MU in 1986.

geographical war zone.

Go ahead. See for yourself. Spend an afternoon taking the Border War pulse. Head south down U.S. 69 on the Kansas side, weaving in and out of small towns along the way. Then dart east on U.S. 54 from Fort Scott to Nevada, Mo., and back north on U.S. 71.

Stop and talk to the good people in some of the towns on this journey. Visit the grocery stores, the shops. Along the way, get a taste of what today's latest installment of the Border War is all about.

PAOLA, KAN.

Curtis Long grew up in Butler, Mo., a small town just off U.S. 71 between the towns of Rich Hill and Adrian.

Tiger country.

But since 1986, Long has lived in Paola – enemy territory. He's surrounded by Kansas and K-State fans, but that hasn't stopped Long and his wife, Becky, from compiling one of the coolest collections of Mizzou memorabilia this side of Columbia.

When Long's smack-talking KU buddies step into his basement to catch a game, they find themselves surrounded by Missouri photos, jerseys, newspaper clippings, helmets, buttons, cups, game programs and autographed balls.

Some of the material dates back to the early 1900s, and most of it contains two words: Beat Kansas.

When friends step up to Long's bar to pour a drink – in an MU cup, of course – they do so while standing on an MU logo. They even have to walk between a replica of the famous Missouri columns to get to Long's couch.

The motivation for compiling such an impressive collection?

"Basically, we wanted to make our KU friends suffer when they come over," said Long, who graduated from Missouri in 1986. "Living over here with so many KU fans all around us really makes the rivalry fun."

Long said he still remembers the frustration he felt that day he walked out of Allen Fieldhouse in 1992. Anthony Peeler memorably ripped Allen's nets for 43 points, but the Tigers still lost.

"My head was ringing walking out of that place," Long recalled. "I still think that was the loudest I've ever heard a crowd."

So, given his disdain for KU, would Long trade a couple of regular-season losses against the Jayhawks for a single Missouri national championship?

"Wow, that's a tough one," Long said, pausing to gather his thoughts. "Of course, you'd have to take the national championship, but man, it's really hard losing to Kansas.

"I hate losing to Kansas."

BUTLER, MO.

Not everyone along the border views today's game – or any game, for that matter – as a matter of life and death.

Check out the Outback bar, for example. It's Wednesday night, and the game between Missouri and Iowa State is about to get started.

In here, the focus is on something else: the weekly pool tournament.

"Normally we have the game on, but tonight's pool night," the bartender says. "But you'll see some people coming in to watch the game."

As Mark Daniels and a buddy warmed up for the pool tournament by playing a couple of quick games, basketball seemed to the furthest thing from anyone's mind.

But even Daniels conceded that, today, the antenna will be up a bit higher.

"When they play Kansas, that's kind of when everyone pays attention – even people who aren't big into sports," Daniels said. "Everybody likes to see them beat Kansas."

BUCYRUS, KAN.

Jerry Rutherford has owned "The Shirt" for 30 years and, like Stephan's store down the road in Fort Scott, you won't find anything with a Tiger on his racks.

Oh, you can pick up a K-State T-shirt making fun of the Jayhawks or a Kansas shirt bashing the Wildcats – heck, you can even pick up an anti-Osama bin Laden shirt – but no MU.

"No need for 'em," Rutherford says. "Don't sell."

Not that Rutherford himself is especially taken by this rivalry.

"There's some of that, sure, but it's not like people hate each other around here," Rutherford said. "That's more a media-driven thing in my opinion.

"People used to kill each other in wars. Now, they put different colors on people and watch them beat each other's heads in. It's more fun than anything else."

PAOLA, KAN.

How serious are Steve and Mary Miller about their Jayhawks? Well, consider that they have been basketball season-ticket holders for nearly 30 years and that their oldest son is named Tyson Jay.

As in Jayhawk.

Mary Miller almost had to choose between KU and her husband.

But to hear Mary Miller tell it, Steve almost ruined the relationship – the one with his wife, not the one with the Jayhawks - years ago. You see, not long after graduating from Kansas in 1970, the young couple had Tyson Jay and finances were tight.

Steve thought he'd save some money by not renewing his season tickets. Being the good, devoted spouse that she was, Mary did the only reasonable thing: She hired a lawyer.

"Oh yeah, I sat right over there in my lawyer's office and told him that if he didn't get those tickets back, I was going to divorce him," Mary said, no hint of humor or sarcasm in her voice. "I was going to do it, too."

Steve got the tickets back.

That's the kind of passion you'll find along the border.

Some of the Millers' favorite memories have been tied to this series, to the Border War. When the Tigers visited Allen Fieldhouse back in February, the Millers turned around and noticed a familiar face.

Norm Stewart.

Now, Stewart wasn't exactly the favorite son of KU fans back in his coaching days. But he's out of the coaching ranks now, and Miller figured she'd ask him for an autograph.

Stormin' Norm signed Mary's ticket stub and even added this line: "Go Jayhawks."

Norm Stewart expressing love for the Jayhawks? What's next, Hootie Johnson and Martha Burk getting married?

Actually, the display of class helped Stewart score major points with Kansas fans who spent so many years telling him to take a seat.

"Without Norm, there would be no basketball tradition at Missouri," Steve said. "He built that program from the ground up. You have to respect that.

"Even though we never liked him."

NEVADA, MO.

Patrick Brophy is not a sports fan, but as the curator of the Bushwhacker Museum, he knows about the attitudes that were shaped by the battles that once raged in the border region.

These days, folks settle their scores by shooting hoops - not guns - but there was a time when this section of country featured more violence than a Steven Seagal movie.

When the Kansas-Nebraska Act was passed in 1854, the Kansas territory was opened up to white settlement for the first time but residents of the area were left with the choice of allowing slavery or not.

Missourians bent on maintaining the peculiar institution crossed over the border to help "encourage" a vote for slavery. Some Kansans, along with abolitionists who poured into the state, opposed them.

And that, you could say, is when the real Border War began.

Over the course of the next 30 years, skirmishes, raids, massacres and out-and-out wars took place between Kansans dubbed "Jayhawkers" and Missourians dubbed "Bushwhackers."

One of them is commemorated on the other side of the state line, just north of Fort Scott in Kansas.

In 1858, a Missouri man named Charles Hamelton was driven from that spot. He returned with around 30 Missouri men, captured 11 Kansans and lined them up for an execution. Five of the men died, five were wounded and another escaped by faking his death.

The incident would become known as the Marais Des Cygnes Massacre, and a memorial just off U.S. 69 tells the tale.

"There is a strong cultural fault line that runs along that border," said Susan Flader, University of Missouri history professor. "It goes back years and years to a time when the Missouri/Kansas border was the center of a political war. In some ways, that area was more at the heart of the Civil War than places in the deep south.

"It would make sense that those feelings have been passed down from generation to generation."

Anymore, though, people look for new ways to express their emotions.

Sports has become one of them.

"I guess you could say that choosing a team and feeling that it represents you is kind of like warfare – just far more harmless," Brophy said.

Which would explain why Nevada High School senior Tara Kiest can walk around her Missouri town wearing Kansas blue and red.

"Most of the people around here are big Missouri fans, but I've always liked the Jayhawks," Kiest said. "Sometimes people will give me a hard time but then I say something like: 'What, is your KU shirt dirty today?' "

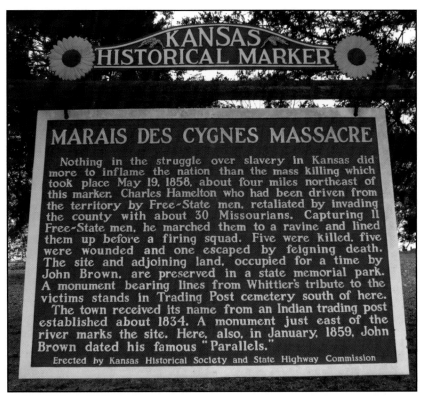

A historical marker along U.S. 69 tells of the Marais des Cygnes Massacre, part of the real Border War between Missouri

MORE THAN A RIVALRY

A HISTORY BORN OF THE CIVIL WAR

By Donna Martin

Their rivalry may well have been born in the epic struggle between their states. Even their team names reflect the pugnacity of their citizens. The Tigers were named for the Columbia Tigers, a local vigilante group established during the Civil War. The Jayhawks were named for the Jayhawkers, the free-soil guerrillas in Kansas and Missouri during the border disputes in the decade beginning in 1854. Perhaps the extremist history incited a fiercer competition. The vicious conflicts between Border Ruffians and Jayhawkers, said historian James McPherson, in *Battle Cry of Freedom,* produced a form of terrorism that exceeded anything else in the war.

The westward expansion of the country had made slavery an explosive issue. In 1820, trying to deal with the issue as it affected the Louisiana Purchase, Congress had enacted the Missouri Compromise, in which slavery was allowed only below the latitude of 36º 30´; north of that latitude, slavery was not allowed, with the exception of Missouri, which was admitted as a slave state (as part of the Compromise).

The collision course between Missouri and Kansas was set into motion by the Kansas-Nebraska Act of May 1854. That act, McPherson says, may have been the most important single event pushing the nation toward civil war. Stephen A. Douglas (renowned later for the Lincoln-Douglas debates), chairman of the Senate committee on territories, pushed through a bill organizing two territories—Nebraska west of Iowa and Kansas west of Missouri—and explicitly repealing the absolute ban on slavery north of the latitude of 36º 30´. President Franklin Pierce signed the act, which allowed the territorial legislatures to decide whether they would admit the institution of slavery. Nebraska was widely expected to enter as a free state and Kansas as a slave state.

In the same year as the Kansas-Nebraska Act, however, the Massachusetts legislature chartered the New England Emigrant Aid Company, formed by financier Amos Lawrence to promote free-soil settlement of Kansas. New Englanders did not respond widely to the call, but the company also aided free-soil farmers from Midwestern states who began to move into Kansas. The importance of Amos Lawrence was recognized in the naming of the town that would become the free-state headquarters in the territory.

Meanwhile, Missourians from just across the border were determined that Kansas would not enter the union as a non-slave state. Nearly 5,000 of them cast illegal ballots to elect a territorial legislature in Lecompton consisting almost exclusively of pro-slavery men. This group, later known as the Bogus Legislature, retroactively legalized the Border Ruffian ballots by not requiring residence in Kansas to vote.

By the fall of 1855, however, free-soil Kansans outnumbered pro-slavery settlers and had no intention of recognizing the Bogus Legislature. They called a convention of their own in Topeka and drew up a free-state constitution. At the beginning of 1856 Kansas had two territorial governments—one in Lecompton and one in Topeka.

In the spring of 1856, a posse of 800 Missourians laid siege to Lawrence and demolished its two newspaper offices, burned a hotel and otherwise raised havoc. The "Sack of Lawrence" was widely decried in the North, and its Republican press began to refer to the territory as Bleeding Kansas, a name that tragically would endure.

Hearing of the attack on Lawrence, abolitionist John Brown, who had organized a free-state militia in the guerrilla conflict, went into a rage. Deciding that pro-slavery forces had killed at least five free-soilers in Kansas, Brown, with two of his sons and three other men, forced five pro-slavery settlers who had nothing to do with those murders from their cabins along Pottawatomie Creek in Kansas and hacked them to death with broadswords. The eye-for-an-eye atrocities at Pottawatomie Creek escalated the bushwhacking battles in Kansas.

The "Sack of Lawrence" was widely decried in the North, and its Republican press began to refer to the territory as Bleeding Kansas, a name that tragically would endure.

After much contention, the U.S. Congress rejected the Lecompton constitution in April 1858. The Buchanan administration supported a compromise in which Kansans would vote again on acceptance or rejection of Lecompton with the carrot of adjusting the size of the land grant customarily offered with statehood. Rejecting the land grant would defer statehood for at least two years. Kansans saw the subterfuge and soundly defeated the measure.

In 1859, free-state Kansans organized a Republican party and elected two-thirds of the delegates to a new constitutional convention. Kansas finally entered the Union as a free state in June 1861.

But the violence begun in 1854 continued along the Kansas-Missouri border. The battles between Border Ruffians and Jayhawkers escalated dramatically after the secession of the Southern states from the Union in1861, gaining sanction from the Confederate and Union governments. William Clarke Quantrill and other guerrilla chiefs raided several Kansas border

---

The battles between Border Ruffians and Jayhawkers escalated dramatically after the secession of the Southern states from the Union in 1861.

---

towns, slaughtering unarmed civilians. The guerrillas sought sanctuary in the countryside, forcing civilians to choose sides.

Meanwhile, hardened abolitionists were determined to destroy slaveholding society by any means necessary. Jayhawkers plundered and killed their way across western Missouri.

Although William Quantrill was the son of an Ohio schoolteacher and had no ties to the South or slavery, he apparently thrived on the violence he could inflict on behalf of the Confederacy in Missouri. Quantrill was awarded a captain's commission in the Confederate army. When Quantrill was later declared an outlaw by federal authorities, a number of wives and children of his guerrilla band were arrested and held in Kansas City, and five died when a building collapsed.

Inflamed by a passion for revenge, Quantrill assembled several hundred men and made plans for an attack on Lawrence.

William Clarke Quantrill

Among those who joined him were the psychopathic Younger brothers and Frank James. As they headed for Lawrence, they murdered several farmers they encountered along the way.

Approaching at dawn on August 21, 1863, Quantrill ordered his followers to kill every male and burn every house. One witness said, "The events of the next three hours had no parallel outside the annals of savage warfare." Heavily armed, they attacked the unsuspecting community, robbing buildings and shooting the occupants, then setting torch to the town. When it was over, more than 180 men and boys had been murdered and 185 buildings in Lawrence had been burned.

While Quantrill's raid horrified the nation, Confederate General Sterling Price praised him. Price was convinced by guerrilla chieftains that Missourians would welcome an invasion of the state by the Confederate army. Price met his first setback on September 27, 1864, in Pilot Knob, Mo., where a Union force under General Thomas Ewing held a fort under assault from the Confederate troops.

Price headed for Jefferson City, expecting to install a Confederate governor who had accompanied him. Learning of strong defenses in Jefferson City, however, Price turned westward toward Boone County, whose inhabitants were terror-stricken. Business in the county seat at Columbia ground to a halt. Every able-bodied man was drafted into a local military organization dubbed the Columbia Tigers. The Confederates, probably forewarned, didn't go to Columbia, but continued along the south bank of the Missouri to Westport, now a part of Kansas City. They were soundly defeated at Westport, ending organized Confederate resistance in Missouri.

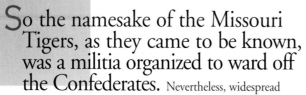

So the namesake of the Missouri Tigers, as they came to be known, was a militia organized to ward off the Confederates. Nevertheless, widespread belief in the disloyalty of Boone County, and the university in particular, would cause serious problems for the university for years to come.

Founded in 1839, the University of Missouri was the first state university established west of the Mississippi. The first constitution of Missouri required the General Assembly to fund a university. It was taken for granted that the state university, like the capital, would be located in Missouri river country near the geographic center of the state. When Columbia was laid out in 1821, 10 acres were donated by the land syndicate as an inducement for the state university to be located there. In 1833, the citizens of Columbia secured a charter for Columbia College.

In competition with other counties in the region, Boone raised the highest subscription of cash, and Columbia was designated for the location of the university in 1839.

The bulk of Boone County's residents had come from Virginia, Tennessee, North Carolina, and especially Kentucky. Although Boone County's residents were predominantly slaveholders, the first president selected for the university, John Lathrop, was a "Yankee," born in central New York of New England stock. He served the university with distinction. Unfortunately, partisan politics intervened in 1849, and the Board of Curators, dominated by the extreme pro-slavery wing of the Democratic Party, forced the resignation of Lathrop.

Lathrop was succeeded in 1850 by James Shannon, an Irishman who had migrated to Georgia, where he became a Baptist preacher and later a professor at the University of Georgia. When the Board of Curators tapped Shannon, he was president of Bacon College in Kentucky, but his first love was preaching. It was Shannon's habit, once installed as MU's president, to travel the state giving a popular lecture on the Biblical justification of slavery.

In the mid-1850s he defended the Missouri invasion of Kansas for pro-slavery voting purposes. He even participated in a student meeting in June 1855 to sign volunteers for the Kansas invasion. Shannon was induced to resign that year and was succeeded by William Hudson, a slaveholder.

The death of Hudson in 1859 precipitated a crisis. It was widely believed in the state that Boone County, and especially the university, was closely aligned with the state sovereignty and pro-slavery position of the South. A new Board of Curators was elected by the state legislature, and although the members of the Board differed widely on secession or union, they seemed determined to put the university back on sound footing.

After the national election of 1860 and the formation of the Confederacy, Missouri had to decide what course it would pursue. A majority of state officials believed the state was ready for secession. They called for a state convention, and an act was passed by the General Assembly in January 1861 for the election of delegates to a convention.

The first meeting of the convention clearly indicated that a large majority of the delegates opposed secession. A second session was called and by that time the governor and many state officials, as well as a majority of the members of the General Assembly had gone over to the side of the Confederacy. The governors and other officials who'd gone over to the Confederacy were then suspended. A third session of the convention required a stringent loyalty oath, not only of state officials but also of the Board of Curators of the university.

At the outbreak of the Civil War in the spring of 1861, charges of disloyalty to the Union were persistently leveled against the university and the community. When classes resumed in October 1861, attendance was greatly reduced. Shortly after school started, a detachment of state troops favoring the South camped near the town and confiscated horses and feed. In December, a company of federal soldiers established temporary living quarters in the university building and in January set up permanent headquarters there.

A new Board of Curators, less familiar with the university than the old group was, closed the university on March 1862. Frank F. Stephens in his *History of the University of Missouri* calls the period from November 1862 to June 1865 a period of convalescence for the university. During this period, John Lathrop returned to the university and again became president. Lathrop called attention to the importance of the Morrill Act.

In July of 1862, Congress had passed the Morrill Act, which would establish a system of land-grant colleges and universities throughout the country. It gave to each state 30,000 acres of government land for each of the state's senators and representatives. The receipts of the land sales were to be an investment fund to support at least one college whose leading object was to teach branches of learning related "to agriculture and the mechanic arts" in order to "promote the liberal and practical education of the industrial classes in the several pursuits and professions in life."

In April 1865, during Lathrop's tenure, the surrender of Lee at Appomattox was celebrated in Columbia. When Lincoln was assassinated shortly thereafter, appropriate eulogies were delivered and the columns of the courthouse and the university building were draped in mourning for thirty days.

After Lathrop's death in 1866, the Board chose Daniel Read of the University of Wisconsin to succeed him. Western born and educated (in Ohio), Read thoroughly identified with the Northern cause in the Civil War. He had lost a son and two brothers in that war.

Nonetheless, Boone County had acquired the reputation of being a "rebel" county. Three-fourths of the Board were anti-slavery Radicals and were hostile to the university. To meet the arguments of disloyalty of university graduates, records were produced to show that of 182 graduates since 1862, 73 were Union men in the war, and only 28 were rebels.

Gradually, the university was rehabilitated. Joseph Viles, in his *The University of Missouri: A Centennial History*, says that the successful development of the university was assured only in 1870, when the Assembly located in Columbia the College of Agriculture and Mechanic Arts provided for in the Morrill Act.

The University of Kansas never succeeded in getting the designation as land-grant institution provided for by the Morrill Act. KU opened its doors on September 12, 1866, more than 25 years after the opening of MU. Even then, it had only a name, a charter (1864) and a faculty.

During the territorial period of the 1850s, both pro-slavery and free-state forces wished to create a public university, but each group sought its own institution and the conflict between them cancelled out their efforts. Even after Kansas became a state in 1861, fierce competition among several towns delayed the creation of a university for two more years and ultimately chopped up the university into three parts.

Interestingly, the pro-slavery faction was the first to propose a university for Kansas. After President Franklin Pierce signed the Missouri-Nebraska Act in 1854, the Bogus Legislature of Lecompton chartered a territorial university to be located in the town of Douglas, several miles upriver from Lawrence. The territorial university never materialized. The constitution produced by the free-staters in Topeka only "permitted" a university. That never materialized either.

Congress admitted Kansas as a state on January 29, 1861. The Kansas legislature of 1861 hotly contested the location of various state institutions—the capital, the university and the penitentiary. Leavenworth was pleased to get the penitentiary. In Manhattan, Bluemont Central College—a Methodist institution—was offered to the state in return for its becoming the state university.

After Kansas voters chose Topeka as capital on November

permission. The Kansas legislators continued their debates, seemingly without end.

Then, in July 1862, when President Lincoln signed the Morrill Act, the federal government made it possible to satisfy all contenders. On January 14, 1863, Governor Thomas Carney called attention in his inaugural address to the Morrill Act. The Kansas legislature accepted Bluemont College in Manhattan as the state agricultural college. Lawrence won the university site in

"Me" Kicks Goal.
Missouri 3 Kansas O

15, 1861, the town of Lawrence redoubled its efforts to get the university. Amos Lawrence had pledged more than $10,000 for a state university in 1856, but he couldn't rustle up any other investors and withdrew his offer.

In the legislature of 1862 Manhattanites renewed their offer of Bluemont College and a small bid also came from Emporia. A group of Lawrence men offered a cash bid—mostly made up of the funds Amos Lawrence had earlier offered, but without his

February, and in early March Emporia got a normal school, as teacher's colleges were called at the time.

By 1868 the University of Kansas did appear in Lawrence. It had a building, three full-time faculty members, and in its first semester, 55 students. Yet Clifford S. Griffin, in his *University of Kansas: A History*, says that during the university's early years its most remarkable characteristic was that it existed at all.

The funds promised by local men to endow the university

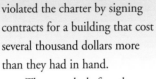

were withdrawn after Quantrill's raid. Fortunately, Amos Lawrence was induced to renew his contribution. And in 1865 a subscription of relief bonds raised in St. Louis for victims of Quantrill's raid was given to the university. Further money for Quantrill victims was raised in Boston.

In 1865, the university also secured the rights to the land and abandoned foundation of a Presbyterian institution to have been called Lawrence University. Shortly thereafter, the regents violated the charter by signing contracts for a building that cost several thousand dollars more than they had in hand.

Three weeks before the opening in September 1866, the regents ran out of money, but by then, the building was mostly finished. In 1866 and 1867, the board transformed the barren Hogback Ridge, where the university was located, into a lovely park, setting out some 500 trees. Mount Oread was born.

Some 25 years would elapse between the end of the Civil War and the first football game between the universities of Missouri and Kansas. Perhaps it is just as well that those who opposed each other on a playing field were a generation removed from the direct combatants between the states. Football in its early days, played without helmets, was known to be a brutal game.

Intercollegiate football was introduced on the MU campus in the fall of 1890. MU played its first intercollegiate game against Washington University in St. Louis on Thanksgiving Day 1890. The Missouri team was routed 28-0, but the enthusiasm for football only grew. KU also played its first intercollegiate game in 1890 with Baker University, which also wrecked the Kansas debut. But football's future at Kansas was secure.

In 1891, the first game between Missouri and Kansas was played in Kansas City. Although each team played a number of regional colleges and universities, almost from the beginning the big game for each was the Kansas-Missouri game.

Don Fambrough, head football coach at KU from 1971 to 1974 and again from 1979 to 1982, still lives in Lawrence and is known to hate MU. Most years, he gives the pre-game pep talk to the KU football team before they play Missouri. It is said that he usually wraps up his talk with a discussion of Quantrill and all he did "to our fair city.

"And you know what?" he adds, "Quantrill was a Missouri grad." No one believes it, of course.

Or, given the nature of the competition, perhaps they do.

CHAPTER 2

The Rivalry Takes the Shape of a Football

STILL EVEN AFTER ALL THESE YEARS

When Kansas dominated Missouri 31-14 November 20, 2004, in Columbia—to end the regular season, at least for the Jayhawks—the Crimson and Blue evened their series with their most hated rival. The oldest football series west of the Mississippi River is squared at 52-52-9 after the win by Kansas.

The 2004 match-up was the 113th in the series, and each team has taken its turn to dominate, but never for too long. Neither team has won more than seven games in any decade, and the longest winning streak by either team is five. Kansas won five straight between 1930 and 1934, while the Tigers won five in a row between 1938 and 1942.

It seemed that when one team was the strongest, the other would jump up and bite them. The best example of this was in 1960, when the Tigers came into the final game of the season at 9-0 and ranked No. 1 in the country. Final score: Kansas 23, Missouri 7.

Kansas has won or shared five conference championships: 1908 (Missouri Valley), 1930 (Big 6), 1946 (tied for Big 6), 1947 (tied for Big 6) and 1968 (tied for Big 8).

Missouri has won or shared 12: 1909 (Missouri Valley), 1913 (tied for Missouri Valley), 1919 (tied for Missouri Valley), 1924 (Missouri Valley), 1925 (Missouri Valley), 1927 (Missouri Valley), 1939 (Big 6), 1941 (Big 6), 1942 (Big 6), 1945 (Big 6), 1960 (Big 8) and 1969 (tied for Big 8).

HERE'S A RUN-DOWN OF THE DECADES:

1890s **Kansas, 7-2**

1900s **Kansas, 6-2-1**

1910s **Missouri, 4-3-2**

1920s **Missouri, 6-3-1**

1930s **Kansas: 5-3-2**

1940s **Missouri, 7-3**

1950s **Missouri, 6-3-1**

1960s **Missouri, 7-2-1**

1970s **Kansas, 6-4**

1980s **Even**

1990s **Kansas, 6-4**

2000s **Even**

FROM LEFT TO RIGHT; TOP TO BOTTOM
Faurot
Fambrough
Powers
Onofrio
Mason
Widenhofer
Pinkel
Mangino

ROCK! CHALK! JAYHAWK! K. U.

THE KANSAS UNIVERSITY ELEVEN DEFEATS MISSOURI'S FOOTBALL TEAM

RIVAL KICKERS MEET AT EXPOSITION BALLPARK AND A LIVELY GAME PLAYED — THE MISSOURIANS OUTPLAYED AT EVERY POINT — SCORE 22 TO 8

The end of the Civil War was less than 30 years old and the tension between the citizens of the states of Kansas and Missouri was still very real. The field of athletic competition provided a way for representatives of the state universities to match wits in an orderly fashion.

The year was 1891 and Kansas and Missouri started their football rivalry that has become the oldest rivalry west of the Mississippi River. The game was played in Kansas City, and *The Kansas City Star* covered the game. There were no sidebars, but it was clear that the rivalry had found a new venue for exercise.

Here's how it appeared in the November 2, 1891, *Star* (Note that "touch downs" were worth four points and "goals" [extra points] were worth two. Also, note the unique spelling of several common sports terms):

Exposition Base Ball park was the scene of a foot ball match Saturday between rival elevens representing the Missouri and Kansas state universities. It resulted in a well earned victory for the Jayhawkers by a score of 22 to 8. The Kansans scored five touch downs and a goal, while the Missourians made but two touch downs during the game. In fact the Missourians had the hot end of the game after the first ten minutes of play and did not shake off the trance they fell into until the closing quarter of an hour, when they seemed to realize their advantage of weight for the first time.

The audience was rather mixed, being somewhat evenly divided between collegians, society people and base ball "fans." The latter, of course, were not up to the points of the game, but the enthusiasm of the college youths seemed contagious and everybody warmed up to the game as it progressed, and as the uninitiated began to "catch on" to the merits of the plays, they became as wildly hilarious as the hundreds of young men who sported the crimson of Kansas or the orange and black of Missouri.

The game was witnessed by a crowd of about 3,000 people. The Kansans were first on the ground and the delegation of enthusiastic "rooters" from Lawrence promptly took possession of the west bleachers which were just opposite the center, the goals being placed almost directly north and south from the left field fence to the east end of the covered stand. The west bleachers became one waving mass of crimson bunting and completely overshadowed the more subdued orange and black of the Missourians. Before the game the college cries of the rival universities filled the air, and the lung power of the Kansans rang out particularly strong. They yelled themselves hoarse with their cry of "Rock Chalk Jay Hawk! K. U!" Just previous to the call of time, the Missourians were reinforced by a delegation of the university alumni with Tom Oaiuce, Tom Crittendeu, jr., Will Cowherd, Joseph Denny and others at its head. This party had resurrected a lot of horns that had been expected to do duty for the late lamented Blues at the close of the base ball season, and they made good use of them. Their appearance was the occasion for a grand rallying cry and "Rah! Rah! M. S. U! Missouri University, Rah, Ray, Rue!" was given with a lusty good

RIVALS!
MU VS. KU

KU:22
MU:8

FOOTBALL
OCTOBER 30, 1891

will followed by a continuous tooting of horns that drowned out the Jayhawkers for a few moments.

THE BATTLE BEGINS

Captain Hill of the Missourians won the toss, selected the south goal and his team started off with strong play. The Kansans, notwithstanding the fact that Captain Kinzie was disabled and unable to play and his position was filled by Sherman who was also a cripple, were strong favorites before the game, but the Missourians started off so well that their supporters began to have some hopes of their winning.

As soon as the ball was put into play it was passed to Bradley and he carried the ball clear into the Kansans' territory at the first attempt, and they held their ground on the next down. Shawhan, the other half back, was then given a chance and lost ground, but on the next play succeeded in getting around the left end and by a beautiful run evaded the Kansans and scored a touch down. Shawhan's run and Briegleb's blocking were the features of the play. The Kansans were surprised, while the Missourians cheered lustily. This gave the orange and black a free kick for goal, but Anderson made a sorry attempt, kicking too low.

Hogg then kicked down the field, and though Shawhan fumbled Bradley gathered the ball and made some ground. Shawhan made another effort to get around the end, but the Kansans had tumbled to the play and Dobson downed him. This was followed by hard work by Williamson, Champlin, Sherman and Hogg of the Jayhawkers and Hill, Shawhan and Lamotte of the Columbias. Champlin's work outshone the rest, however, and by dint of steady, persevering work he was finally carried

through the Missouri line for a touch down, tieing the score. Hogg's failure to kick a goal left the game a tie.

The Kansans had now recovered

University of Kansas Archives

confidence and forced the work. Champlin was again set to work and repeatedly broke through the line. Sherman was given several opportunities. Though his weak ankle left him at the mercy of the Missouri tacklers, he finally succeeded in getting through for a touch down, giving the Kansans the lead by a score of 8 to 4.

HOGG KICKS A GOAL

This was followed by punting in which the Kansans excelled, Hogg kicking the ball over the line and after a brush for it in the corner, Coleman secured the ball for a touch down and Hogg kicked a goal, the only one of the game, leaving the score 14 to 4.

After another brief play time was called and probably prevented the Kansans from another touch down on a sharp play by Sherman, Williamson and Mendall. The score was 14 to 4 in favor of Kansas and the west side bleachers

was one mass of waving streamers of bloody hue, while the Kansas university cry filled the air.

After ten minutes' rest play was

resumed. Champlin, who by this time has a beautiful mouse over his left eye, is again set at work and lively times ensue. Scrimmage follows scrimmage, until Terrill comes out from under a pyramid with a sprained ankle and Hodge takes his place at the left end for Missouri.

The Kansans again continued their rushes, Champlin and Sherman alternating in efforts to crowd through the Missourians. Champlin almost got clear when LaMotte downed him. Hogg then took the play and by a clever run round the left end scored another touch down, making the score 18 to 4 in favor of Kansas.

Hogg again distinguished himself a few minutes later, making a neat running catch off Anderson's punt. He feinted and while the Missourians settled for a catch off the expected kick he sailed down the side line and scored another goal, increasing Kansas' lead four more points.

CHAPTER TWO

15

1893

CROWN OLD MISSOURI

HER FOOTBALL TEAM FINALLY DOWNS THE HAUGHTY KANSANS

IT WAS A GREAT GAME, TOO

THE JAYHAWKERS SEEMINGLY OUTPLAYED AT EVERY POINT

A TIE IN THE PENNANT RACE

COLUMBIA'S FOLLOWERS GO WILD OVER THE TEAM'S VICTORY

ENTHUSIASM AT THE PARK

*

Thirteen years before the formation of the NCAA, an organization that would regulate the rules of football to protect the players, the game of football already was becoming a rough one. As Kansas and Missouri prepared for their 1893 game, there was talk about outlawing the sport because of too many injuries and even a few deaths. But this was a sport that could not be stopped. There was just too much fan interest.

It didn't take long in the Missouri-Kansas rivalry for the annual Thanksgiving day football game to become an event, in many cases with the game being an afterthought.

In 1893, the two schools each sent 400 students to Kansas City for the game. The *Lawrence Daily Journal* and *Evening Tribune* reported that the game "was witnessed by the biggest crowd ever gathered for an athletic event in the west." While that may have been an exaggeration, *The Kansas City Times* reported that the city was "taken by storm" by fans of both teams.

Missouri won the game 12-4, the Tigers' first victory in the three games played by the two schools.

Here's how it appeared in the December 1, 1893, *Times:*

RIVALS!
MU VS. KU

MU:12
KU:4

FOOTBALL
NOVEMBER 30, 1893

Something like 5,000 people assisted in the digestion of their Thanksgiving day dinners yesterday by stomping on the seats at Exposition park and yelling vociferously and oft in concert at the foot ball elevens of the Missouri and Kansas universities, while the Missourians scored 12 points to the Kansans 4.

The game was hard fought, and the winning team played the finest foot ball ever seen in the city.

For the first time in the series of games which the orange and black and the red-legged Jayhawkers have fought here, the orange and black won, and won like winners, out-playing their opponents along the line and back of it. Their magnificent work was a surprise both to the cheering populace and to the Kansans. The contest was one of team play against individual work. Team play won.

Only one man was injured so that he had to leave the field. Center Rush Coleman of the Kansas eleven hurt his nose in the last half. It was broken in the Kansas-Michigan game Saturday, and in a scrimmage the newly-set bones were unjointed again.

Barring a little fistic dispute between Platt and Pauley in the last half, the game was reasonably free from slugging.

Messrs. Fred Turner, umpire, and Herbert Doggett, referee, performed their duties to the satisfaction of both elevens and the spectators.

The management of the grounds and the crowd were good. Mr. Hal. W. Reed had this matter in charge, assisted by a force of local policemen and a squad under Captain Mahady of the Pinkerton patrol.

Crown old Missouri with the historic wreath of laurel and lay all the other glittering gew-gaws at her feet! She is entitled to all honor, for she has administered a crushing defeat to the strongest aggregation of foot ball players that troubled Kansas can produce.

The story of yesterday's memorable function is nothing more or less than a detailed account of all that was said and done hereabouts in the hours that come between dawn and midnight. From the field, and after that the celebration by the victors and the lamentations of the vanquished.

The events and incidents of the day will linger for many moons in the memories of about every man, woman and child dwelling in this sport-loving community. In point of fact the foot ball people literally took the town by storm. They wouldn't let you think of anything but the game. Every other fellow you met on the street was a walking advertisement for the show. Corridors of the hotels and the places where men congre-

University of Missouri Archives

'Crown old Missouri with the historic wreath of laurel and lay all the other glittering gew-gaws at her feet! She is entitled to all honor.'

break of day until long after high noon those who participated in the "festival of the gridiron" were busy preparing for the struggle. Then came the two hours devoted to the actual struggle on the gate were bubbling over with color, life and excitement. Almost everybody sported either a crimson rosette or a gold and black streamer. The city was literally stained with the tints of the rival universities.

CHAPTER TWO

17

But don't imagine for a lonely instant that the picture was a study in "still life." It was just the reverse, for the riot of conflicting colors didn't begin to compare with the riot of noise and revelry. This town never endured such a prolonged and terrific chorus of finely assorted yells since the day it was incorporated. It seemed for a time as though 90 percent of the population had developed emotional intensity.

But all this preliminary shouting of the morning was like unto a vault of silence when compared to what occurred during the afternoon and evening. The 400 students who got in from Columbia about noon, and the 400 Jayhawkers who came down from Lawrence an hour or two before noon contributed to the vocal pyrotechnics exploded during the morning. But when that composite crowd began to gather at Exposition park, shortly after 1 o'clock, the full strength and volume of a college yell was sprung. And what a crowd it was. Picture in your mind the big grand stand draped in bunting and filled with a restless, good-natured throng of thousands. They divided this humanity into five sections and dealt out a distinctive yell for each section. Have all these varied shouts rise and blend, in a deafening cyclone of noise. Flavor it with snatches of popular songs and the blare of tin horns. Do this and the result will be tolerably accurate reproduction of yesterday's chorus.

Viewed from the field the stand seemed like a huge bank of rainbow colors. At the extreme left the posts and railing were enshrouded in the dark blue of Yale. There are a dozen different shades of blue, but the blue of Yale is the most effective for decorative purposes. Every man and every woman in that section was decked out with blue ribbons. Bands of blue were wound about

the canes of the men and the waists of the women. In the adjoining section everything was crimson, the color dear to the hearts of old Harvard's many sons. The display was every bit as effective as that of Yale. Many of the men wore red cravats and all of them sported crimson badges. The little girls in red looked as pretty as the girls in blue, and that is paying them the most florid of compliments.

The section just north of Harvard was set aside for Princeton, but there are few Princeton men in Kansas City, and as a result the announcement of the result of the game on Manhattan field did not create the enthusiasm that might have been expected.

What space that was left in the grand stand and the rows of bleachers on either side of it was occupied by the friends and followers of the contesting teams. Missouri had a great turn-out, and as a matter of course lost no oppor-

that it was grand weather for foot ball. In the first place, it was cold. There was more than a suggestion of winter in the air, and the zephyrs that rioted over the field and through the stand was anything but gentle. And so it came to pass that when the populace gathered around the field the men turned up the collars of their top coats and the women readjusted their furs and wraps. But despite these and kindred precautions the crowd shivered and shook like so many aspen leaves. It was hard on the men and harder on the women. The former stamped their feet and shouted with an energy born of the occasion, but dainty femininity had to take it out in smiles and shivers.

It was under these conditions that the members of the rival team pulled off their sweaters and made ready for the struggle.

It was not until the men appeared on the "gridiron" that the real serious

---

A MISSOURIAN WAS DOWN AND A KANSAN WHO WAS A-TOP OF HIM, ACCORDING TO PAULEY, USED UNNECESSARY VIOLENCE. PAULEY INTERFERED, THEN PLATT INTERFERED. PAULEY SAYS PLATT STRUCK HIM. THE FIRST SPECTATORS SAW OF IT, PLATT AND PAULEY WERE ON THEIR FEET, PAULEY WAS SWINGING FOR THE KANSAN'S JAW, AND PLATT WAS "LAYING FOR A KNOCKOUT." NO DAMAGE WAS DONE.

---

tunity to flaunt the gold and black in the faces of the foe. Bleeding Kansas brought out her entire stock of all crimson and the effect was most impressive. Out in right field were groups of carriages, tally-hos and various other kinds of vehicles.

Right at this stage of the proceedings it is proper to say something about the weather. Truth to tell, the day was not over-pleasant for ordinary mortals, despite the fact that the critics insisted

work of the small army of shouters began. All that had been done before was simply infantile compared to the roar that crushed through the wintry atmosphere when the players appeared. It began with the "Rock, Chalk, Jayhawk, K. U." of Kansas, and even as this mystic slogan was in its youth, the "Rah, Rah, Rah, Missouri," and the "Tiger, Tiger, M. S. U." of Missouri rang out from a thousand throats. It was like and yet unlike the opening measures

THE RIVALRY TAKES THE SHAPE OF A FOOTBALL

RIVALS!
MU VS. KU

MU:12
KU:4

FOOTBALL
NOVEMBER 30, 1893

of orchestral symphony. The shrill scream of the Jayhawkers and the Tigers being backed by the aged shout of Yale, the "Tiger-Sis-Boom-ah;" of Princeton, and the sonorous notes of Harvard's string "Rahs."

When all these vocalists had got down to business the result was a composite yell that sounded something like this:

"Rock, Rah, Sis, M. S. U. , Hi Rah, Hawk, Princeton, Yessirree, Yale, Niversitee, Tiger, Harvard, K. U., Rah, Rah, Rah, Boom, Missouri, Rah, Rah, Rah, Hoorah, Tiger, Chalk."

During all this noise and clatter the leading actors in this blending of farce and tragedy never cracked a smile or paid the slightest attention to what was going on in the stand. They "lined up" for the struggle as calmly as though the glory of two States was not trembling in the balance. They listened attentively to the final instructions of their coaches, and made a final examination of shoe laces and the other sections of their attire. Then the referee placed the whistle to his lips and the composite yell died as quickly as it had begun. The silence was simply nerve-straining. For a lonely instant the men stood in their tracks as motionless as though they were stone images. The Jayhawks had the ball, the "Tigers" were ready. There was a "flying wedge," a collision of the two groups of bone and muscle, and then a confused jumble of flesh and blood. A yell came from the stand, a thousand bits of colored cambric were waved, and the big Thanksgiving day game was on.

As the two teams struggled for the mastery and the sorely abused pig-skin was carried forward and back over the chalk-traced field the excitement increased. Missouri's first touch-down plunged all Missouri into a state of unqualified bliss. Again and again did

they hoarsely intone their war-whoop. But every yell was answered by the opposition. The Yale, Harvard and Princeton contingents shouted, too, but theirs were the critical plaudits of unbiased critics, who could gaze at the struggle and not take leave of their senses.

As the battle aged and the tide turned in Missouri's favor men on both sides lost their temple, and the work grew fast and rough.

Captain Young came out of one of the tangles with a beautifully colored eye and an upper lip that was twice its natu-

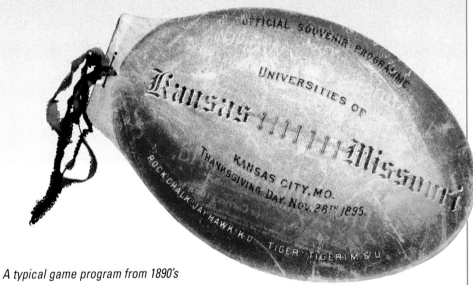

A typical game program from 1890's
University of Kansas Archives

ral size. Robinson wrenched his knee and Harrison followed suit. Coleman got a nasty thump on his damaged nose, and Mattson's left eye collided with the shoulder of an adversary. But despite all this "rough" work there was only one scrimmage that might be dignified by the name of "slugging."

It happened this way, as near as the truth can be had out of the tangle. A Missourian was down and a Kansan who was a-top of him, according to Pauley, used unnecessary violence. Pauley interfered, then Platt interfered.

Pauley says Platt struck him. The first spectators saw of it, Platt and Pauley were on their feet, Pauley was swinging for the Kansan's jaw, and Platt was "laying for a knockout." No damage was done. After it was all over Pauley claimed that Platt had deliberately struck him while he was on the ground. Platt insists that he didn't do anything of the sort, and that Pauley's assault was unprovoked. The episode created considerable comment at the time.

When Missouri's men realized that their team had really won they seem to

take leave of their senses. With incoherent yells they rushed on the field, throwing their hats high in the air and embracing each other like so many brothers. Captain Young was carried from the field on the shoulders by his followers. The sight of Young's bruised and battered form as it showed above the throng inspired groups of Missourians to pick up the other members of the team and carry them to the tally-ho.

THE OFT REPEATED STORY

KANSAS WAS WEAK, MISSOURI STRONG, BUT THE JAYHAWKERS WON

THE TIGERS FOUGHT HARD, BUT LOSING TEAMS ALWAYS BATTLE THAT WAY — ONLY THE SCORE WILL COUNT IN THE FUTURE

Nothing has changed in 100 years. Expectations often fail to materialize.

Coming into the 1907 game, Kansas had experienced a mediocre season with a 4-3 record but having lost three straight games. After seasons of 8-1-1, 10-1 and 6-2-2 in Coach A.R. "Bert" Kennedy's first three years, 1907 was a disappointment.

Missouri, meanwhile, came in 7-1 and already guaranteed its best record since 1899 when the Tigers went 9-2. The Tigers had scored at least 27 points on five occasions, with the high-water mark being a 70-6 victory over Tarkio.

In other words, Coach W.M. Monilaw's squad was supposed to have little trouble handling the "Jayhawkers." But defense ruled on this day, as Kansas earned its first ever conference victory, 4-0.

Here's how it appeared in the November 29, 1907, *Times:*

Kansas Citians who witnessed the football game between Missouri and Kansas in St. Joseph yesterday say that the struggle was a pretty contest to watch, interesting, exciting, frequently spectacular, but always hard fought. Kansas won, to be sure, but that was according to the necessary course of human events. Who expected Missouri to win? Of course the rah rah children from Columbia could not see defeat for their team. They never can. Perhaps an ardent Missouri supporter here and there in the crowd and elsewhere looked for victory to perch in the Tiger escutcheon. But that was all. Missouri fought hard. Have you ever noticed that the losing eleven usually fights hard? But Kansas carried off the wampum. It is ever thus – against Missouri. And now the famed Tiger eleven of '95 and the victorious Washerites of the "Oughty-one" are backed into the dim past of still another year.

To the casual observer of football it appeared that if Missouri was ever to whip the Kansans again this was the year to turn the table. The Kansas schedule had been a severe one, no denying, but the Kansas team has been the weakest turned out at the Lawrence

> TO THE CASUAL OBSERVER OF FOOTBALL IT APPEARED THAT IF MISSOURI WAS EVER TO WHIP THE KANSANS AGAIN THIS WAS THE YEAR TO TURN THE TABLE. THE KANSAS SCHEDULE HAD BEEN A SEVERE ONE, NO DENYING, BUT THE KANSAS TEAM HAS BEEN THE WEAKEST TURNED OUT AT THE LAWRENCE SCHOOL IN RECENT YEARS. THE PLAYERS WORKED HARD AND THERE WAS NO LACK OF SPIRIT, BUT THE MATERIAL WASN'T THERE.

RIVALS!
MU VS. KU

KU: 4
MU: 0

FOOTBALL
NOVEMBER 28, 1907

school in recent years. The players worked hard and there was no lack of spirit, but the material wasn't there. Kennedy searched in vain for men of the Donald Brunner type. Failing to find them the eleven Jayhawker mentor

and were fast. Their schedule was easy with one exception, Iowa. The team became known as one of the best Missouri had ever had. It would beat Kansas, the students said. The Tigers journeyed to St. Joseph and tore some

few holes in the Jayhawkers' line and plowed down the field with some energy. But the Jayhawkers won. And victory is the goal they were fighting for – not yards gained. Perhaps sometime Missouri will repeat the deal of '95 and the turn of "oughty-one."

THE TEAM BECAME KNOWN AS ONE OF THE BEST MISSOURI HAD EVER HAD. IT WOULD BEAT KANSAS, THE STUDENTS SAID. THE TIGERS JOURNEYED TO ST. JOSEPH AND TORE SOME FEW HOLES IN THE JAYHAWKERS' LINE AND PLOWED DOWN THE FIELD WITH SOME ENERGY. BUT THE JAYHAWKERS WON. AND VICTORY IS THE GOAL THEY WERE FIGHTING FOR – NOT YARDS GAINED. PERHAPS SOMETIME MISSOURI WILL REPEAT THE DEAL OF '95 AND THE TURN OF "OUGHTY-ONE."

The game program served a dual purpose in the early years of the rivalry, allowing fans to keep score.

University of Kansas Archives

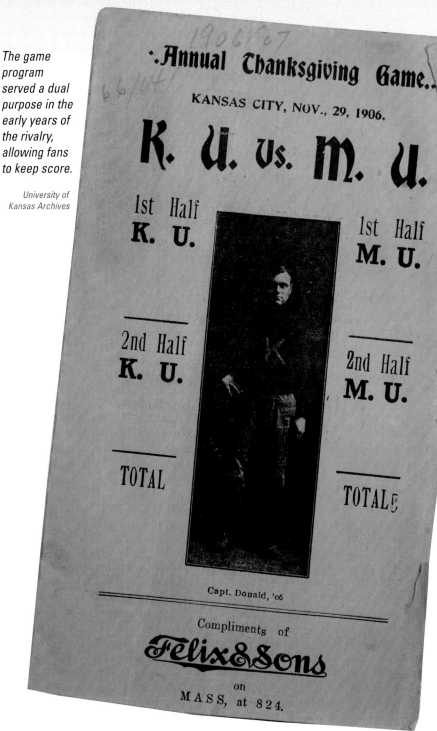

.'.Annual Thanksgiving Game..
KANSAS CITY, NOV., 29, 1906.
K. U. Vs. M. U.

1st Half K. U.   1st Half M. U.

2nd Half K. U.   2nd Half M. U.

TOTAL   TOTAL

Capt. Donald, '06

Compliments of
Felix&Sons
on
MASS, at 824.

went to work with the material on hand. Taking advantage of one man whose kicking ability made him the only player of any real talent on the eleven, Kennedy rounded out a good eleven; good enough to beat Missouri, at any rate. And that one representative of real football talent won the seventeenth annual game from the Tigers.

On the other hand W. J. Monilaw rounded out a trim eleven at Columbia. The Tiger material was fairly good, better than the average at Missouri. The Tigers mastered the forward pass

A TIGER TRIUMPH AT LAST

A 12 TO 6 GAME WITH MISSOURI ON THE WINNING END

THE JAYHAWKERS FOUGHT HARD, BUT WERE OUTPLAYED BY THEIR LIGHTER OPPONENTS — HACKNEYS GREAT KICKING A BRILLIANT FEATURE

Only once in the 112 years that Kansas and Missouri have faced each other have both teams entered the game with undefeated records. In 1909, Missouri entered the game at 6-0-1, with only a 6-6 tie at Iowa State blemishing the record. The Tigers owned three shutouts.

Kansas, meanwhile, was 8-0, with only two opponents having scored on the "Jayhawkers." Coach A.R. "Bert" Kennedy's squad shut out Emporia State, St. Mary's, Oklahoma, Washington (Mo.), Washburn and Nebraska. Kansas State scored three points and Iowa scored seven.

Missouri had not beaten Kansas in eight years, so when the Tigers pulled out a 12-6 victory in Kansas City, the city braced for a celebration. The "story" was more about how the Missouri faithful reacted to the victory than the events of the game itself.

Here's how it appeared in the November 27, 1909, *Times:*

The Missouri Tiger, proud beast of the football jungle, has come into his own. At last the Kansas Jayhawk has been put to flight. For nineteen years this Tiger animal has been emerging from his retreat, and for thirteen of these years he has been sorely wounded as he slunk away to the denseness of his lair. Twice has the Tiger kept the Jayhawk at bay, and only four times has he tasted the sweetness of victory – four times in all these nineteen years – but yesterday was the fourth, and now the Tiger, Missouri's fighting Tiger, is mounted high on the pedestal of triumph, and the Jayhawk, wounded unto death, has flown back to Kansas. It was a great battle. The Tiger won, 12 to 6.

The men of Roper – great is Coach Roper – outplayed the men of Kennedy and Mosse. Each eleven scored a touchdown on straight football and each eleven rose and hurled the enemy back when a second touchdown was imminent. The hefty right leg of Hackney, and Coy of Missouri, gave the Tiger team the first six points of the game by toeing drop kicks, the first of which sailed over the Kansas cross bar scarcely three minutes after the game started. All the scoring was done in the first half, which saw the Roper machine playing better ball than the Kennedy-Mosse eleven, with Hackney's great kicking giving a still greater advantage to the Missourians. The second half was fought without a score and was fairly even, both teams being within a few yards of touchdowns, but unable to ram the oval over the hostile line.

RIVALS!
MU VS. KU

MU:12
KU:6

FOOTBALL
NOVEMBER 26, 1909

THE FIRST VICTORY IN EIGHT YEARS

It was the first victory Missouri has won since 1901 and the first time since that 18 to 12 triumph that the eleven from Columbia has crossed the goal line football machine when Captain Ristine's team appeared. It was a football eleven, well coached, in excellent physical condition, with classy plays and a fighting spirit. It was strange to the great majority of Tiger followers, that never quit, ever charging demon spirit those athletes of

The Missouri rooters met the appeal. In a might volume of lungings, the cheering M-I-S-S-O-U-R-I-I-I was sent echoing across the field. The Tiger team heard and heaved the Jayhawks back. That touchdown was averted. That was the Roper spirit, the spirit that

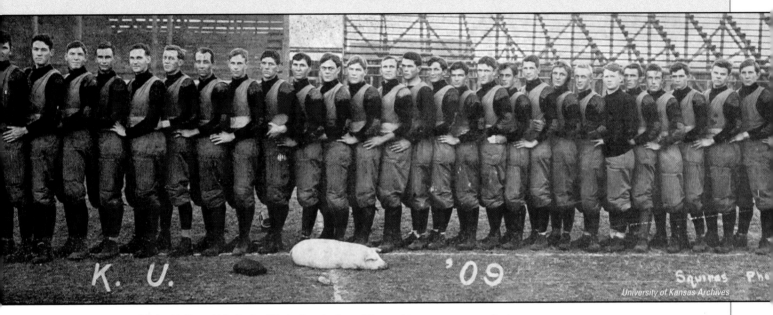

Not even a real "pigskin" could help the '09 Jayhawks beat Missouri to preserve a perfect season.

of the team from Lawrence. The Kansas eleven was far heavier than the Missouri machine and it looked it on the gridiron, but the Tiger forwards outcharged their heavier opponents. It was this speedy charging of the Missourians that caused the many Jayhawker fumbles in the first half. The mighty Bluck and the powerful Gilchrist led the Tiger line in ramming through the Jayhawker line. Time after time Bluck lunged through the Lawrence line, his broad shoulders brushing the Jayhawkers out of the way. The backfield would not have time to get started before the Missouri forwards would be tearing through. This caused the fumbling and the Kansas coaches say fumbling was the chief cause of the Kansas defeat.

Missouri rooters saw a fighting

Roper displayed. Roper, there's the name that will be embellished in letters of gold in Missouri's hall of fame. Roper, "Bill" Roper, the man from Princeton, is given the credit for the great showing of the Tiger team. It was the Roper spirit, a new spirit at Missouri, that kept those fighting boys ever up and at the foe. Once in the second half when the Tiger line was in danger silence settled deep over the Missouri section. Roper raved at the yell leaders. That was sufficient. The cheer boys screamed through their megaphones:

ROPER MADE THEM ROOT

"Roper says you're quitters, Roper says you're quitters. Come on, let's show him."

has given the University of Missouri an undefeated football team for the season of 1909, a team that defeated Kansas, robbing the Jayhawkers of a third ever-victorious eleven and an eighteenth straight victory.

After the game the Missouri crowd broke through the wires and swarmed over the gridiron. Never has Association Park, the staid old home of second division ball clubs been the scene of a wilder, more hilarious demonstration. One of the goal posts was pulled up and at the top was crucified a black hen, the nearest thing to a Jayhawk that frantic Missourians could find. Lifting this Jayhawk effigy aloft, the Tiger rooters fell in behind the Missouri band and

THE RIVALRY TAKES THE SHAPE OF A FOOTBALL

paraded around the gridiron. The Missouri student rooters, a thousand strong, cheered until their throats were dry and their lips were parched. Missouri alumni fought their way through the crowd and joined the marching ranks. Missouri followers from everywhere throughout the state, Missourians who never before had seen a Tiger team beat Kansas, fell in with the gay paraders. Around the field marched the regiment of rooters, hats were in the air, canes with streaming ribbons of old gold and black were tossed high, wild-eyed Columbians beat the backs of those in front and took insane delight in pounding derby hats into fragments. For an hour after the game this made confusion lasted. It was Missouri's first football victory over Kansas in nine years and the fourth in nineteen; it was a Missouri Valley championship for the Tiger team. Missouri had come to Kansas City to root, why shouldn't Missouri root? Missouri did root.

WHEN THE TIGERS ARRIVED

When the train carrying the Tiger team arrived at the park from Excelsior Springs the big crowd, some 15,000 persons, was eagerly awaiting the arrival of the teams. The word went out that the Missouri team was outside the park and immediately the Tiger rooters banked in the north bleachers shouted a gladsome welcome. The officials walked across the field and were cheered. The K. U. student band marched on to the field and along the front of the Kansas bleachers. The K. U. rooters wafted their welcome. The battle of the rooters was on. The yell leaders were on the job. The voice skirmish that precedes every Turkey day battle was launched. The Kansas coaches appeared and Arthur St. Leger Mosse, the light haired chap of the long kicks, sauntered out and dug his heel into the soil of the

gridiron. Then – it was just ten minutes after 2 o'clock – the Tigers darted through an opening from the Missouri section and spread out on the field for kicking practice. What a conglomerated volume of voice culture pierced the atmosphere. The Tiger rooters rose and stormed applause for their favorites. Every Tiger yeller had a megaphone and every Tiger yeller waved a Missouri pennant. The Columbia section was just a sea of billowy pennants.

NOISE FOR THE JAYHAWKERS, TOO

In another five minutes the squad from Kansas, the big red team, ran on to the field and down the side lines. The rooters from Lawrence were not to be outdone by their cheering foemen across the battleway and they greeted their brawny heroes as only faithful rooters can rise and sing the praises of battle scarred heroes. Kansas megaphones and K. U. pennants were as plentiful as those of Missouri. The rival elevens began to run signals up and down the field.

Kansas had two teams on the field and the second eleven seemed even larger than the regulars. Many a Missouri heart beat slower as he compared the size of the two elevens. How could Missouri beat that weight? was a line that surged through many a Tiger rooter's brain. Some fifteen thousand persons stood and watched the rival elevens "warming up." It was a pretty spectacle, that football crowd of many colors gathered about the gridiron in the Tebeau Amphitheater. Nor was the crowd confined to the park. Boys and men, hundred of them, sat on housetops along Prospect Avenue and Twentieth Street and looked down on the fight ground. Referee Masker's whistle sounded and Hackney's toe lunged into the oval and the struggle was on.

IT WAS THE TIGER'S NIGHT

A BONFIRE IN THE STREET ONE MISSOURI FOOTBALL CELEBRATION

IN FRONT OF KANSAS HEADQUARTERS A "JAYHAWK" WAS BURNED AMID YELLS, WHILE KANSAS SUPPORTERS LOOKED ON — A PARADE AND MUCH YELLING.

Kansas City was turned over to the Tiger rooters last night. Anything a Missourian wanted he got, for he had beaten Kansas at football 12 to 6 before 15,000 persons. If it wasn't given to him he took it. All over the business part of the city happy Tigers wandered, cheering continually. They paraded, then they broke up into disorganized crowds, then they paraded some more.

The piece de resistance of the evening – these imported terms go great in the college stories – was the parade of the Tigers which ended in front of the Coates House. At the Jayhawker headquarters the invaders built a bonfire on the street car tracks in front of the hotel and before the very eyes of the heartsore Kansans plunged them into horrible humiliation by burning a turkey that was labeled "Jayhawk."

MU:12
KU:6

FOOTBALL
NOVEMBER 26, 1909

RIVALS!
MU VS. KU

FROM THE KANSAS CITY TIMES, 1909

Before the "Jayhawk" was consumed the fire department sprinted around the corner and extinguished the fire and drove Tiger and Jayhawker in a wild rush into the safety and dryness of the hotel.

KANSAS STILL HAD YELLS LEFT

The Kansas men did not seem to be angry because the victors taunted them. The Lawrence men yelled and the Missourians yelled and the supporters of both teams smiled – some triumphantly, some sadly.

The celebrators were not all college men. Many were men whose only claim to the college class was that they once had had their hair cut at a barber college. These took advantage of the night of joy. There were more of these persons than usual on Thanksgiving nights.

Hundreds of Kansas City men who had no personal interest in either team, were so proud of the fact that a team bearing the name of the state in which they live had won a game that they considered themselves bound to sing a few verses of "Here's to Jolly Old Roper."

There were no disturbances, except minor ones, caused by too much cheer and too much cheering. The Kansans seemed glad to show that they were sportsmen and they proved that they were good losers by cheering for their team just as often as the Missourians cheered for the Tigers.

KANSANS WERE PHILOSOPHICAL

"They deserve to celebrate," was the Kansas opinion. "They beat us fairly."

When the Kansans talked about what would have happened if – they were in small groups, away from the victors.

The Missourians tried hard to makeup for past Thanksgiving nights.

"We've had these yells bottled up

AT THE JAYHAWKER HEADQUARTERS THE INVADERS BUILT A BONFIRE ON THE STREET CAR TRACKS IN FRONT OF THE HOTEL AND BEFORE THE VERY EYES OF THE HEARTSORE KANSANS PLUNGED THEM INTO HORRIBLE HUMILIATION BY BURNING A TURKEY THAT WAS LABELED "JAYHAWK."

---

for a long while," laughed a Missouri graduate as he apologized to a hotel clerk who was holding his ears, "so you'll have to excuse us for this one night."

"Oh, I haven't anything against you," said the clerk. "If it wasn't you it would be that Kansas bunch. Go ahead."

THE HOTELS TOOK PRECAUTIONS

Five minutes after the timekeeper blew his whistle and ended the game Frank P. Ewins, owner of the Savoy Hotel, was at one end of a telephone wire. At the other end was Frank F. Snow, chief of police.

"I've ordered the bartenders to close the Savoy bar at once," said Mr. Ewins, after he had told the score, "and I'll have the doors of the hotel locked unless you send me a squad of police."

Thomas Keys, Samuel Crowley, John Williams and James O'Rourke, patrolmen, were sent to the Savoy to see that the boys from M. S. U. did not become too boisterous in celebrating their victory. Two more patrolmen joined them an hour later. Five men were stationed at each theater. Six men were sent to the Hotel Baltimore at the request of D. J. Dean, the proprietor. The men at the hotels were in charge of Peter McCosgrove, a sergeant. One-half of the day force of police worked until 11 o'clock last night. Many men were brought in from outside stations to assist in districts No. 1 and No. 4. The force working from police headquarters was almost doubled.

The Coates House bar was closed for an hour last night. Between 8:30 o'clock and 9 o'clock, when the Missourians were having their bonfire, the overflow from the street wandered into the large barroom of the Coates House. The crowd there became so large and so noisy that it was thought best, for the comfort of the guests of the hotel, to intimate to the students that it would be an accommodation to the hotel if a few of them would take their yells outside. The students made no objection.

WILL THE GAME COME BACK?

FOR TWENTY YEARS THE TIGERS AND JAYHAWKERS HAVE BATTLED HERE

ALUMNI OF THE TWO SCHOOLS BELIEVE THAT THE ANNUAL GAME SHOULD BE PLAYED IN KANSAS CITY — SOME GREAT BATTLES IN THE PAST

✳

Today it seems like it has been this way forever. But in 1911, when the Missouri-Kansas game was switched to campus sites, it was shocking news. The first piece listed here asked the question on everyone's mind: Is this a permanent switch? It was for the next 33 years, then, after two years in Kansas City, has become the norm.

Here's how it appeared in the November 23, 1911, and November 24, 1911, *Times:*

Columbia, Mo., Nov. 22

For the second time in twenty years of athletic relations between the state universities of Missouri and Kansas, the annual Tiger-Jayhawker football clash will not be played in Kansas City, and for the second time in that period the game will not be played on Thanksgiving Day. Will the change prove satisfactory? Will the two schools have to return again to Kansas City and to the turkey day game? Columbia business men are doing their utmost to make the event here Saturday a success from the standpoint of the visitors.

It will take a burden of proof to convince members of the alumni of the two schools that the change is desirable, for college men hang on to cherished tradition and the tradition of a fifth of a century calls for the playing of the game at Kansas City and on Thanksgiving Day.

TIGERS 3, JAYHAWKERS 3

WITH FOUR MINUTES TO PLAY, SHUCK'S FIELD GOAL TIED THE SCORE

A DROP KICK BY DELANEY GAVE KANSAS A LEAD OF THREE POINTS IN THE THIRD QUARTER — KANSAS NEAR A TOUCHDOWN AT THE START

Columbia, Mo., Nov. 23

Missouri's ill-fated Tiger of 1911, wounded near unto death, scarred and maimed, emerged from its lair with a mighty roar today and fought the powerful Jayhawk to a standstill. The final count was 3 to 3, the second tie game the rival universities have played to in as many years. The erudite toe of Carl Delaney, left end of the Kansas eleven, sent his team into the lead late in the third quarter, 3 to 0, and the well trained toe of Captain Shuck of Missouri enabled the Tigers to make the twenty-first annual battle of the gridiron a draw just four minutes before the final whistle sounded this afternoon.

The football teams that waged war

RIVALS!
MU VS. KU

KU:3
MU:3

FOOTBALL
NOVEMBER 23, 1911

this afternoon for the glory of Kansas and Missouri were as nearly evenly matched as two rival elevens possibly could be. The score tells the story of the game. It was a drop kick that placed Kansas in front, and it was a drop kick that enabled Missouri to fight its way back to even terms. The field was muddy, making the footing very insecure. The athletes slipped and slid in the thawing mushy soil of the gridiron and neither eleven could gain consistently from scrimmage. The ends got down the field with spectacular speed, but frequently skidded in the marshy loam just when ready to drag down the man with the ball. Considering the condition of the gridiron the playing of the ends, both Missouri and Kansas, was one of the remarkable features of the struggle.

A Missouri jersey and cap from the early years.

TIGER DEFENSE WAS GREAT

The greatest piece of work in all the game came shortly before the end of the first period. It was the marvelous defense of the Tiger eleven under the very shadow of its goal line. A forward pass, Heil to Brownlee, the first of the game, worked perfectly for a gain of twenty-one yards, and Kansas had the ball just two yards from the Missouri goal line and three trials to take it over. Every Tiger heart sank low, although the student rooters shouted the old "hold that line" plea to their valiant lads so hard pressed. The rooters of the crimson and the blue stood and stormed their faith in the ability of the men of Ammons to lug the oval over the Tiger line. Perhaps the Missouri linesmen heard those cries, for the stand they made will go down in history as one of the gamest exhibitions of defense ever made by a team fighting for the old gold and black. The voice of Captain Shuck rang out over the field as he exhorted his men to throw the hated Jayhawks back. It sent a galvanizing current through the beings of those linesmen, crouching there, shoulder to shoulder, welding them into a mighty wall of defense.

THREE TIMES THEY CHARGED AND FAILED

Three times did the charging Kansans hurl themselves into the Tiger team and three times the Missourians rose and threw them back. The wonderful Ammons failed to pierce the Missouri line, the darting Coolidge tried and was dragged down without a gain. Then the diminutive Heil tried to sneak across the Tiger line by skirting Missouri's right end. He was felled when he reached the scrimmage line. It was Missouri's ball on its 2-yard line and Mills dropped far back on his goal and booted the ball out of danger. It was a remarkable bit of football, saving the game for Missouri. It was the chance of the Kansans and they failed in the hour of trial. Yet, it was not so much the bad play of the Jayhawkers as it was the heroic stand of the Tigers. Missouri's followers went wild and the Kansans shook the wooden bleachers as they, too cheered prowess of their ancient foe.

When Missouri flashed that defense the wise ones predicted a no-score game. The heaviness of the field also led to this conclusion. But it was not to be. Delaney, the great Kansas kicker, was not in the game in the first half, but he was inserted in the third period and his dropkick in this quarter near the end gave Kansas the points that destined to win the game. Kansas had the ball in Missouri territory when Delaney was sent in to replace Price. Demon rushing by Captain Ammons, the star of the Kansans, carried the ball for a first down and seven more yards placed the oval on Missouri's 28-yard line. Delaney fell back to the 35-yard line for his first attempt at dropkicking. The pass was accurate.

DELANEY'S KICK WAS PERFECT

With coolness the Kansas kicker dropped the ball and sped his toe into the oval as it rose from the ground. Low, just over the Tiger line, sailed the oval, and across the bar of the goal posts by a scant half foot. Many thought the goal had been missed, but the jubilant shouts of the Jayhawkers as they darted back up the field told the trueness of Delaney's kick better than words. Three minutes later the quarter ended. Kansas had a 3 to 0 lead, a lead that looked good for the victory.

But Missouri came back in the fourth quarter. Wounded the Tiger may have been, scarred by many defeats, it is true, but there was no yellow in the eleven that defended Missouri today, and fight, fight, fight was the spirit the Tigers displayed in the final fifteen minutes of the game. And it won them a draw when all seemed lost. Hall, Missouri's punter, had been called into

a forward pass from Blees for a gain of twenty-five yards, but the Missouri leader slipped in the mud and a Kansan pounced on him before he could recover.

A FORWARD PASS THAT COUNTED

Twice Kansas broke up forward passes from the Tiny Blees, but it was an onward flip from Blees to Right End Hall that gave Shuck his opportunity to tie the score. It was a long pass of six-

ty-six yards and the Tigers were raging close to the Kansas lines. The Missouri rooters massed solid in the concrete stand, arose as one and bellowed forth their faith in Shuck's men to take it over and to hurry. Pixlee gained a yard and Dexter twisted through for four. It was third down and five yards to travel. Nothing to do but kick. Captain Shuck dropped back from his position on the Missouri wing, back to the Kansas 22-yard line. Missouri hopes were low.

Captain Shuck isn't a sure drop kicker, but nobly he met the emergency and the ball rose gracefully, soared high over the crossbar and dropped downward into three points for the fighting Tigers. Then it was Missouri's time to cheer, and Tiger rooters raged mad with joy at the turning of bitter defeat into an even break. There were only four minutes left to play and every one of the eight thousand spectators realized that the game would end a tie unless a fluke play occurred.

The Kansans came back with a furious

University of Missouri Archives

Missouri 3 Kansas 0

The football game was the place to be for Missouri's high society in 1911.

battle. Time after time he booted the ball down the field and the Tiger captain was there to drag the Kansas safety man down or fall on the ball in case of a fumble. But no fumble came and Missouri grew desperate with the passing of the minutes. Onside kicks and forward passes followed one another in quick succession, but the men of Brewer could not get away. Once Captain Shuck caught

teen yards. The elongated Hall reached high in the air and pulled the oval down. Tucking the leather under his arm he headed for the Kansas goal at full speed. Only Heil stood between Missouri and victory. But Heil was enough – the salvation of the Jayhawkers. The little safety player tumbled the Tiger runner to the ground. But the play had netted Missouri twen-

assault. A forward pass from Heil to Coolidge netted ten yards and a first down. Heil dashed around a Missouri end for fifteen yards and another first down. Two plunges into the splendid Missouri line were repulsed and Ahrens the Kansas center, fell back to Missouri's 38-yard line for an attempt at place kick. The ball fell twelve yards short and Hall raced it back ten yards before being downed out of bounds. That was the last chance for the Jayhawkers.

RIVALS!
MU VS. KU

KU:3
MU:3

FOOTBALL
NOVEMBER 23, 1911

THEN MISSOURI CAME AGAIN

With two minutes left to go the Tigers began to tear through the Kansas line. Knobel ripped twelve yards and a first down off the left side of the Kansas line. Pixlee darted through a hole for six yards, the catapultic Dexter tore off three and the final whistle blew the end of a hard fought and, at times, brilliantly waged struggle of the gridiron.

The first half closed with Kansas having a slight shade in the play, although the wonderful defense of the Tiger team on its 2-yard line caused many of the

advantage than the Kansas forwards, although Baird opened up some big holes on his side. The Missouri backfield classed above that of the Kansas team. Coach Brewer had three men in his backfield who could lug the ball, while Coach Sherwin had only one. Lemire, Wilder, Knobel, Dexter and Pixlee gained yardage for Missouri and gave promise of what they might have done on a fast field. For Kansas, Captain Ammons was the one bright star of the backfield, just as he was the greatest of all the Jayhawker ground gainers in the game against Missouri at the Gordon and Koppel field in Kansas City last year.

BLEES, THE MIDGET GOT HIM

Fast down the field went Ammons, gaining in speed at each step. Across several lines of lime he raced, tearing down on Missouri's mite of a quarter like a mighty Gulliver running into a brownie. Would Blees get him? Missouri said yes, Kansas answered no. Missouri was right. Blees threw himself into the powerful Kansan and toppled him to dirt after a run of thirty-six yards. Ammons arose and ran back to his position, but Blees failed to get up. He had defended the Missouri goal with valor, but was badly bruised. Time was taken out and a substitute quarter raced up and down the sidelines, ready to go in if needed. But Blees went back to his post after a 2-minute rest. The Tiger rooters were not slow in shouting their praises to the little chap.

ALL IN ALL, SUMMED AND WEIGHED IN THE BALANCE, NEITHER TEAM DISPLAYED ANY SUPERIORITY. FIRST ONE ELEVEN WAS FORCING THE OTHER BACK AND THEN THE SITUATION WOULD BE REVERSED. EACH TEAM FOUGHT HARD FOR EVERY INCH OF GROUND. WHO WILL SAY THAT MISSOURI WAS BETTER THAN KANSAS, OR THAT KANSAS WAS GREATER THAN MISSOURI?

football experts to call the half a draw, as the score indicated. Kansas outplayed Missouri in the third period, when Delaney kicked his goal. Then Missouri came back in the last quarter, tied up the game and had the Jayhawkers on the run when Umpire Curtis whistled the battle into history. All in all, summed and weighed in the balance, neither team displayed any superiority. First one eleven was forcing the other back and then the situation would be reversed. Each team fought hard for every inch of ground. Who will say that Missouri was better than Kansas, or that Kansas was greater than Missouri?

TIGER LINE THE STRONGER

The Tiger line appeared to better

Woodbury seldom got beyond the line of scrimmage when carrying the ball. Coolidge, the other half, did little better than his running mate, but the doughty captain of the Kansans always was good for a gain. And time and time again he was called on to pack the oval. His off-tackle smashes gained many yards for the Kansas offense. Frequently he carried Tigers' tacklers with him for several yards. The splendid physique and the fighting spirit of the Kansas captain was a potent factor in the game. Once he broke away off Missouri's right tackle and dashed for the Tiger goal. He passed every safety man of the Missouri defense and only the wee Blees, a mere minute of a football player, stood between the husky Jayhawker and the coveted goal line.

The brilliant play of the Kansas ends, Brownlee and Price, and the splendid charging down the field of the Missouri wing men, Shuck, Mills and Hall, was a remarkable feature of the sixty minutes of turmoil, especially when the heavy condition of the field is considered. The Kansas ends outflashed the Tiger ends, but the stellar work of Captain Shuck brought him cheer after cheer from the Missouri section.

Heil, the Kansas quarterback, played his usual dashing game in returning kicks. Frequently the K. U. midget was compelled to dig into the mud after skidding punts or run back after kicks that bounded over his head, but he was the right man at the right place and seldom did he fail to lug the ball back from three to twelve yards. On the other hand, Blees was unable to help Missouri by returning kicks.

KANSAS THE VICTOR

HUMBLED THE INVADING TIGER, 15 TO 9, IN ANNUAL THANKSGIVING DAY CLASSIC

TWENTY THOUSAND THERE

*

WERE MASSED IN NEW STADIUM WHILE OTHERS WATCHED FROM THE HILLS ABOVE

A CHEERING FRENZIED MAELSTROM, THEY SAW ONE OF GREATEST VALLEY GRIDIRON BATTLES

*

K. U. OFFENSE A SURPRISE

CARRIED A DRIVE WHICH MISSOURI, CONFIDENT OF WINNING, WAS UNABLE TO STEM WITH SUCCESS

Kansas opened Memorial Stadium, a tribute to the students and faculty who gave their lives in the World War (remember, there was only one World War, so it wasn't called World War I until after World War II), with a game against another rival, Kansas State. The second game in the gleaming new stadium was against the hated rivals from Missouri.

The Tigers had every reason to believe that they would spoil things for Kansas. They came in with a 6-1 record, losing only to Kansas State. The Jayhawks were just 3-3.

But with 20,000 spectators present, a huge crowd for that era, Kansas held off a late Missouri charge to win 15-9. The Tigers let this one slip away.

And no, Max Falkenstein did not call the game for the KU radio network.

Here's how it appeared in the November 25, 1921, *Times:*

RIVALS!
MU VS. KU

KU:15
MU:9

FOOTBALL
NOVEMBER 24, 1921

(By a Staff Correspondent)

Lawrence, Kas., Nov. 24

Twenty thousand persons gathered here this afternoon to spur to greater efforts from a Jayhawk and a Tiger in their annual dispute.

On the one side of the K. U. stadium sat the guests, the Missourians, who sniffed the air, their nostrils tuned to catch the savor of well done jaybird. On the other, the hosts who pitted their winged defender against the jungle beast from Columbia.

And the maelstrom of enthusiasm which issued from the throng, the avalanche of cheering which echoed and re-echoed about Mount Oread, furnished a setting to be enshrined forever in the hearts of those twenty thousand spectators.

A CHASTENED TIGER

Along the by-ways of Lawrence tonight a tiger, meek and humble, chastised and contrite, was being bustled back into his cage by Keeper James Phelan and crated for his journey to familiar and more friendly surroundings.

Tonight Lawrence celebrates. Tonight the jaybird struts like a peacock. He is supreme. He has turned back the 4-footed foe. He has twisted the tiger's tail, bruised him and humiliated him.

The score was 15-9.

school days remained. Those stands became a melting pot where all bonds of conventionality were broken.

The game was worth its place in the spectacle. It brought its surprises; not many would have dared anticipate such a burst of offensive power as was

---

TONIGHT LAWRENCE CELEBRATES. TONIGHT THE JAYBIRD STRUTS LIKE A PEACOCK. HE IS SUPREME. HE HAS TURNED BACK THE 4-FOOTED FOE. HE HAS TWISTED THE TIGER'S TAIL, BRUISED HIM AND HUMILIATED HIM.

THE WEATHER WAS GOOD

The gods of football lent the sun to the picture today. A crisp but friendly wind swept the glistening white ribbed lines which stretched between the goal posts, the one draped in the Crimson and Blue, and the other in the Old Gold and Black.

Everyone was there. There was the yearling and the officious upper classmen, the grads, some of the days so long ago that only dim remembrances of their

shown by Kansas early in the game nor quite such a sturdy defense.

M.U. MISSED TWO CHANCES

Followers of the game admitted after the contest almost to a person that Missouri passed up its two great chances.

One came in the first quarter when the Tigers had rushed the spheroid to the Kansas 2-yard line, had felt the foundation of the Jayhawker defense stand firm and unyielding, and had

University of Kansas Archives

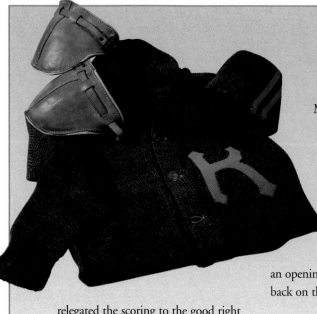

relegated the scoring to the good right foot of "Chuck" Lewis, playing his last game in a Tiger uniform. Lewis made the 3 points good, but the Tigers stood an equal chance of bucking through for the necessary distance and a touchdown.

The other was in the last quarter when the Columbians commenced a campaign directed at the Crimson and Blue line which brought the oval to the 12-yard line. Here once more Missouri advertised her fear of the Kansas line. Lewis grounded a forward pass and soon Kansas punted out of danger.

SPECTATORS EVERYWHERE

When the two teams took the field for their annual battle the stadium, which never had felt the thrill of the Missouri-Kansas conflict, presented a solid mass of cheering, madly cheering, spectators. On the north and the south the temporary bleachers rocked with their burden while the hill overlooking the gridiron was dotted with less fortunate spectators.

Spurgeon, Kansas fullback, whose weighty plunges stood forth in the day's play, kicked off far down the gridiron, over the freshly chalked lines to Lewis, who ran back the boot twenty yards.

THE GAME WAS ON!

Tiger backs were hurled against the red forward. Plunges were attempted.

Missourians diving headlong into that Kansas line. But it held firmly and Lewis was forced to kick.

Then Kansas took the ball and tested the flexibility of her opponent's defense. With intrepid zeal the Jayhawkers strove to pierce an opening. But McAdams was called back on the fourth down for the punt.

ON K.U.'S 5-YARD LINE

The quarter had not aged when Missouri suddenly found herself in possession of the ball on K. U.'s 5-yard line. A bad pass from Saunders, Kansas center, bounded past the receiver, and Storms, Missouri left guard, broke through and fell on the pigskin.

It was the first break. Missouri

LET LEWIS KICK

Plainly the Tigers were in a quandary. Should they take a chance on making the two yards? Should Lewis attempt a short kick with every chance at success? They decided in favor of the latter plan and the Tiger quarter booted squarely and true over the cross bar, putting his team in a 2-point lead.

A forward pass started Kansas on her way a few minutes later. And an aerial flip resulted in the touchdown. With the ball on Missouri's 40-yard line, Wilson hurled to McAdams for a 10-yard gain. Krueger and Spurgeon broke through left tackle twice, worked a fake criss-cross and amid the din from all sections of the stadium brought the ball to the 5-yard line from where Wilson shot a pretty accurate pass to McAdams, who clutched the ball over the Tigers' last line.

THE SUN WAS HIDDEN BY THIS TIME AND THE GRIDIRON WAS SHROUDED IN SHADOWS. WITH THIS GENIAL WARMTH LOST THE WIND MADE ITSELF QUICKLY FELT. JAYHAWKERS WERE PREPARING THEIR CRY OF VICTORY, WHILE THE WEARERS OF THE GOLD AND BLACK MOURNFULLY SEARCHED FOR ALIBIS TO HIDE THEIR CHAGRIN.

---

hearts were beating high and they loosened a roar of triumph which shook the hills. Kansas hearts were running the gamut between hope and fear.

Kershaw – "Red" they call him – tucked the sphere under his arm and essayed a sprint around right end. It failed. Lincoln spurred his mates with a plunge through center, which netted two yards. Three yards and two downs to make them in. The Tigers circled in consultation while Hardin, who had been injured on the play, received medical aid. Then Lewis was called upon, but his dash around right end proved fruitless.

For the first time this season Wilson failed to kick the goal, his effort striking the cross bar.

K.U. HAD A WALLOP

But that didn't matter so much. The Crimson and Blue had unpacked its wallop and it had gone over big. It had sent the jungle warriors reeling back, bewildered.

Soon the period ended, Kansas having the ball on her own 30-yard line.

The Tiger line was weak; woefully weak. It had been outcharged by the Kansans. The secondary defense had

RIVALS!
MU VS. KU

KU:15
MU:9

FOOTBALL
NOVEMBER 24, 1921

not aided as it should have done. And once again, this time in the second period, Kansas was heading for Missouri's goal line.

The march started after Lewis had punted after his team had been held for downs. McAdams caught the kick and was downed on the Tiger 48-yard line. Then Spurgeon and Wilson split open the Missouri line with plunges. McAdams shot a 10-yard pass to Krueger, and the ball was on Missouri's 10-yard line. It was on the fourth down that Wilson went over, negotiating a distance of two yards. This time Wilson kicked the goal.

GLOOM ON M.U. SIDE

Ah, then there was gloom on the west side of the stadium. The bitter look of defeat flitted across the faces of those Tiger rooters who pulled themselves together and with cheers sought to rouse their warriors. But such a turn of affairs was unlooked for and it was hard to realize.

Two spectacular runs dazzled the crowd before the half had ended. Once "Chuck" Lewis broke away on an end run for fifteen yards. And then Krueger intercepted a pass from Lewis and sprinted sixty-five yards to Missouri's 5-yard line.

Another score seemed imminent, but on this occasion Missouri held and Lewis had punted out of danger after Kansas had been halted on the 1-yard line. The period ended.

During the intermission the various rival organizations vied with each other. The bands struck up blatantly. A boxing ring was erected in the center of the grid-iron on which a Tiger and a Jayhawker engaged in a 2-round exhibition, which ended with the latter being counted out. In the first stanza of this affair the promoters had kindly permitted the Missourian to be pummeled considerably, but he retaliated with a "clean" knockout in the second round.

And then the marching was halted. The bands resumed their places, the teams lined up and the game was on again.

TIGERS IN A COMEBACK

The snarl from those Tigers was ominous. M. U. rooters sensed it in the stands and were encouraged. It drifted across the gridiron to Jayhawkers and chilled their cries of victory.

Shortly after the third period had gotten under way Missouri scored. Humes, Lincoln and Lewis alternated in carrying the ball. They bored savagely into the Red wall and it yielded. A forward pass, Packwood to Lewis, advanced the oval to the 36-yard line and a line smash by Lincoln and an end run by Lewis found it nestling one yard inside the 10-yard limit.

On the first down Lewis went over. But Lewis, usually reliable, missed the goal.

Once again in that quarter Missouri threatened but merely succeeded in raising a fright among the Jayhawkers.

So tonight the Tiger slinks away from Lawrence, leaving the Jayhawker flushed, happy and victorious.

University of Kansas Archives

"Stadium" was the location for the game in 1921.

TO "OLD MIZZOU"

Derry, Waldorf and Dills the Combination Making Touchdown That Defeats K. U.

A PASS AND IT'S 7 TO 0

Quarter Catches Captain's throw for the Score After Half Races 33 Yards

The Ball Keeps Moving. But Bausch-less Jayhawks Lack Punch to Put It Over

31,500 IN THE STANDS

Thrills and Frenzy of Contest Make Them Forget Cold and Gloomy Skies

✳

The Missouri Valley Conference was no more and the Big Six—the predecessor to the Big Seven, the Big Eight and the Big XII—had arrived. In the first Big Six Conference game between the two schools, Missouri defeated Kansas at Memorial Stadium for the first time.

It was a low-scoring affair, 7-0, with Mizzou scoring on a first-quarter touchdown by fleet but tiny receiver Russell Dills, who weighed only 145 pounds. A sprinter for the Tigers' track team, Dills outran the Kansas secondary for the lone score of the game.

As *The Star* article said, "Kansas went sour on Missouri's pickles. We mean Dills."

Here's how it appeared in the November 24, 1929, *Star*:

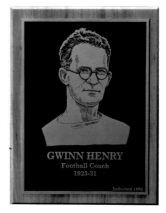

Gwinn Henry's Hall of Fame plaque

RIVALS!
MU VS. KU

MU: 7
KU: 0

FOOTBALL
NOVEMBER 23, 1929

By a Member of the *Star's* Staff

Lawrence, Kas., Nov. 23

Tradition has been smashed, custom overturned and in thousands of houses of University of Missouri students tonight there is nobody home but father. The reason is that the Missouri Tigers rose up in their angry might here this afternoon and turned back the Kansas Jayhawkers in the thirty-eighth annual football game between the two universities, 7 to 0.

The tradition side of the matter comes through the fact that today was the first time the Jayhawkers ever had lost to their old Gold and Black rivals in their new stadium, flanked by the sacred Mount Oread and the generally profane Kaw. The custom angle to affairs is attributable to the same source. A crowd of 31,500 roaring spectators saw the game and got enthused enough over its heated moments that they forgot the gray of the sky and the chill of the weather.

DUE TO DILLS' FLEETNESS

The twinkling feet and stout heart of Russell Dills, the 145 pounds of greased lightning that cavorts in the Tiger backfield in the fall and on the Missouri track team in the spring, provided the scoring punch that enabled the Bengal hordes to turn back the Jayhawkers. Dills is a pest supreme to Kansas. Last year on his own gridiron at Columbia he made a neat little length-of-the-field 100-yard run that virtually folded up the Crimson and Blue cause and made its cohorts say: "Oh, what's the use?" Today at Lawrence, he scored the only touchdown of the hard-fought game and then, just to show he still could run he romped right through the Kansas team afterwards for the added

point. Kansas hopes that if Mr. Dills ever marries and has children they will matriculate at Vassar or Wellesley.

The game opened with Missouri winning the toss and defending the north goal, Kansas thus getting the kick-off. Up and down the field the two teams plowed, with neither getting a particular advantage until, about at the middle of the quarter, Missouri had the ball on its own 42-yard line.

DERRY IS SLOWED ENOUGH

Then Louis Derry – a halfback from Poplar Bluff, who proved a constant thorn in the Jayhawks' side and often carried the ball for two or three plays at a time, found a hole in the Kansas line and started sprinting goalward as though in time to that song that goes "I've got a great big date with a little bit of girl."

Derry seemed on his way for keeps when Floyd Ramsey, Kansas end in a frantic grabbing gesture clawed at the Tiger's back long enough to sort of tag him down. Derry got right back up and started away again but the time he had lost in the spill enabled George Atkeson, Jayhawker tackle, to charge up and get in for the kill.

It was the Tigers' ball on the Jayhawkers' 19-yard line then and the Missouri stands began shrieking frantically:

"Touchdown! Touchdown! We want a touchdown!"

Dills fumbled on the first play as though to show the Kansans he wasn't to be feared particularly, but cannily

MU managed to hang on to a 7-0 victory.

picked up the ball and lost no ground in the play. Johnny Waldorf, the Tiger captain, then plunged one yard out of bounds and the ball was moved out to the middle of the field. Derry lugged it three yards through center on a fake kick formation and then Waldorf dropped back and hurled a long forward pass over to the sidelines to Dills.

DILLS WAITING FOR IT

The Tiger sprinter was waiting for it – grabbed it out of the air and also out of the arms of a Kansan or two, who were not too far away, and then cut back toward the center of the field and went over the goal line standing up. He only actually ran three yards on the play but he could have gone another quarter mile if he had desired to. In fact, he kept stepping on the try for goal after touchdown – circling the Kansas end and going across the line again standing up. That was all of the scoring for the day. It was enough.

The remainder of the game, for the greater part, found the Kansans threatening the Missouri goal more or less constantly and achieving nothing except the reputation that a man gets who does a lot of threatening. Down into Missouri territory they would charge – only to be thrown back. Down into the Tiger domain again they would go – only to be repulsed once more. They threw forward passes and threw forward passes – particularly in the latter half – until even the ball would have had a right to complain – but they couldn't get over that goal line.

Missouri coach Gwinn Henry's Tigers scored a touchdown in the first quarter and then held on for a 7-0 victory.

JAYHAWKS LACKED FINAL PUNCH

For instance, immediately after the Missouri touchdown, the Jayhawkers started a drive that, aided by some good ball lugging by Stewart Lyman, the Crimson and Blue captain, and Forrest Cox, the fullback from Newton, and also by a 15-yard penalty clamped on the Tigers for unnecessary roughness, found the men of Hargiss standing on their opponents' 34-yard line, with the goal seeming not too far away.

Lyman stepped and dodged nine yards around right end. Schmidt picked up five more at right tackle.

"Get 'em, Kansas! It won't be long now!" the Crimson and Blue stands shrieked, but it was long – much too long.

Campbell, Missouri end from Odessa, who spent a busy afternoon spilling Jayhawker backfield men when he wasn't punting, and punting when he wasn't spilling Jayhawker backfield men, smashed through a field of Crimson jerseys and carried Lyman back for a 5-yard loss. Paul Fisher, K. U. quarter, regained two of them, then dropped back to try a forward pass.

If he had made it, it would have been just too bad for Missouri, but he didn't make it – not by three charging Tiger linemen, who were on him at the same time.

CHANCE FOR ODESSA CELEBRATION

When the pile-up was piled off, every jubilant Columbia athlete on the field tried to pat Leonard McGirl, Missouri guard, on the back at the same time, he being the leader of the three who upset Mr. Fisher's plans. Just

RIVALS!
MU VS. KU

MU:7
KU:0

FOOTBALL
NOVEMBER 23, 1929

another boy from Odessa strutting his stuff! Lafayette County should hold a public celebration some time next week.

The second quarter found the ball going up and down the field with a kaleidoscopic quickness that made it difficult to follow. Just when Kansas had Missouri backed deep into Tiger territory, the irrepressible Mr. Dills made a 38-yard toe dance back into the Kansas domain – actually stopping before some harassed tacklers once to poise himself and decide a new direction in which to shoot. That took the edge off most of the Kansas attack for the remainder of the period and the half found substitutes going in for each team so fast the press box was dazed and welcomed the timer's pistol.

The third quarter found Art Lawrence, the Olathe flash, going into the Kansas backfield and when Lawrence comes out of one wing into a football stage, forward passes come out of the other. There would be a successful pass and the one that was not so successful – but what color Mr. Lawrence's goings-on provided for the spectators. The Kansas stands were shrieking at him to get hotter and the Missouri stands yelling for him to cool off.

EASY TO SPOT THAT THROWER

He wore a large No. 11 on his back and was as conspicuous on the field as a blackface comedian would be at a performance of "Aida." And he always was throwing, throwing, throwing.

Just before the quarter ended, Lawrence must have gotten a sore arm for a minute but the ball was handed to Lyman for a play and the latter fumbled the ball – Campbell recovering for the Tigers on the Kansas 26-yard line. To the 8-yard line the Gold and Black

plunged, and then Waldorf, with three yards to go on a fourth down, hit an immovable Kansas wall and the Jayhawkers took the ball on downs. Lawrence then, just to show that he

> DOWN INTO THE TIGER DOMAIN AGAIN THEY WOULD GO – ONLY TO BE REPULSED ONCE MORE. THEY THREW FORWARD PASSES AND THREW FORWARD PASSES – PARTICULARLY IN THE LATTER HALF – UNTIL EVEN THE BALL WOULD HAVE HAD A RIGHT TO COMPLAIN – BUT THEY COULDN'T GET OVER THAT GOAL LINE.

could run when he was not throwing, sprinted forty yards to the middle of the field as the pistol sounded for the close of the third quarter.

The final period found Kansas still threatening – but never quite making good the threats. Down into Missouri territory they would go and right back up the field the ball would return. Passes that went for gains in the mid-field territory were grounded or went awry when disaster for the Tigers threatened. Every play contained plenty of punch because the Jayhawker team and its followers had the constant hope that just one would get away and bring them a possible tie score – with victory just around the corner. The Missouri men stayed in there, though – kept hurling themselves at throwers and receivers and batting frantically at the ball when it was in the air – and they won the game. They had the scoring punch at that big moment when the punch was needed. Kansas did not.

BUT BAUSCH DIDN'T GO IN

There was a hectic moment at the middle of the fourth quarter, when the Jayhawkers were driving close toward

the Tiger goal, and Jim Bausch – their battering ram ace – started to race back and forth on the sidelines in a warming-up gesture. The Missouri athletes cocked a weather eye at him, and taking

no chances, repelled the Kansas invasion before the "big shot" could get in. Coach Hargiss then wisely kept him on the bench the remainder of the game. With a situation demanding one game-tying plunge never actually at hand, there was no use in taking a chance of making a sick man sicker.

Perhaps the absence of Bausch from the Kansas lineup was the margin that helped Missouri to its victory. Certainly the Kansas team was weakened without the "big train" in there. The Jayhawkers had said Bausch was sick and probably would not play. He did not. The Tigers had said Johnny Waldorf, their "spark plug captain," was sick and probably would not play." He did.

Still, if you ask us, Missouri's victory today had the better team winning as the better team should – and not because Waldorf, a gallant athlete, who got a justly-deserved hand when he limped off the field late in the fourth quarter, played for them and Bausch was lost to the Kansans. A horde of Old Gold and Black fighting athletes produced more punch in the pinch than their hard-scrapping Crimson and Blue adversaries. Kansas went sour on Missouri's pickles. We mean Dills.

'SHOULD HAVE WON'

DON FAUROT, MISSOURI PILOT, COMMENTS ON THE SCORELESS BATTLE WITH JAYHAWKERS

COACH TAKES THE BLAME

INSTEAD OF A PLUNGE, TIGERS SHOULD HAVE TRIED SECOND PLACE KICK, HE SAYS LINDSEY PROUD OF HIS BOYS

The Goal Line Stand by the K.U. Eleven in Last Minute is Praised by Mentor

✳

In today's sporting culture, coaches get fired for decisions like the one Missouri coach Don Faurot made that cost his team a possible victory versus Kansas in 1937. The Tigers had the stronger team but failed to take advantage of numerous scoring opportunities, and the game ended in the only 0-0 tie in series history.

It came down to fourth-and-goal at the KU 1-yard line late in the game. Mizzou had tried to punch it in on three previous downs, but to no avail. Faurot contemplated trying a field goal, but instead tried one more running play.

After the game, Faurot second-guessed himself for not trying the kick, but placekicking was anything but certain during this era. Kansas coach Ad Lindsey said he agreed with Faurot's decision.

Here's how it appeared in the November 26, 1921, *Times:*

BY A MEMBER OF THE *STAR'S* STAFF

Lawrence, Kas., Nov. 25

"Tell, it looks as thought they'll have to give the tom-tom back to the Indians," bawled Ad Lindsey, coach of the Kansas Jayhawkers, in the dressing room after the game. "Boys, I'm shaking hands with everybody."

Pride in his players shone in the face of the K.U. coach. In the Missouri dressing room, Don Faurot was forcing a smile. "We should have won," he exclaimed. "They handed the game to us on a silver platter, and we wouldn't take it. When we got that break on a penalty Mondala should have kicked. I blame myself for that. I should have sent in another quarterback to make sure the kick was tried."

RIVALS!
MU VS. KU

MU:0
KU:0

FOOTBALL
NOVEMBER 25, 1937

Ad Lindsey was all smiles after his Jayhawkers preserved a tie with a goal-line stand.

THE COACHES DISAGREE

"We only had a yard to go, but when you try a running play you're taking a chance. Much more of chance than if we had let Mondala try a kick. That boy can make place kicks. That one he missed was close."

Coach Lindsey viewed the situation differently. "All I can say," he said, "is that if Missouri had let me name the way they would try to score from the 1-yard line, I would have said kick the ball. Why, goodness sakes, they only

---

"Anyway, it was a pretty swell game. While we think we should have won we didn't. And if you get the breaks and can't utilize them the other team should get some credit."
—Don Faurot

---

had one yard to go. A kick always is a gamble from any place.

"But I'll say it was quite a game and I'm glad this season is over. When we started we thought by the time the Thanksgiving day game rolled around we'd have the wolves on our doorsteps. But we got by. I want to say this for my boys: They didn't lack fight. We had plenty of that. If you saw that goal line stand they had you'll know that.

"The trouble with us was every time we threw the ball, Missouri caught it. If that last forward pass we threw with about seven minutes left to play hadn't been intercepted we might have won. At least we would have had a chance. After that it took every thing we had to stop them."

"And when they got that ball on the 1-yard line, I wanted to close my eyes," shouted Mike Getto, line coach. "Boy that was bad."

A CLEAN HARD FOUGHT GAME

To Chester Brewer, former athletic director at Missouri, the game was the cleanest fought of any Missouri-Kansas game he has seen. "That Kansas bunch played fine and clean football," he praised. "I enjoyed watching it."

To Gwinn Henry, K.U. athletic director, the game was a lot of fun. "I don't know when I've ever had so much fun," said Henry as he entered the Missouri dressing room to compliment Coach Faurot and the Tigers.

While the Tigers were berating themselves for failing to take advantage of the opportunities, the Jayhawkers were in high glee.

"Well, we had the chance, but didn't take it," moaned one of the Tigers. "You

can't ask for more than a chance."

"And they didn't gain on that play," exulted one of the Jayhawkers. "Boys, did we stop 'em or did we stop 'em."

But the subject of the tom-tom was uppermost in the mind of Coach Lindsey.

"I feel awful sorry about that there thing," he said. "It was to go to the winning team and it seems there wasn't a winning team. After thinking it over, I guess the Indians will have to take it."

None of the players suffered other than minor bruises and sprains and both squads praised the sportsmanship tactics of the other. In the words of Coach Faurot:

"Anyway, it was a pretty swell game. While we think we should have won we didn't. And if you get the breaks and can't utilize them the other team should get some credit."

—Ernest Mehl

Don Faurot was gracious about the tie, but felt his Tigers should have won.

TIGER V-3 CLICKS

JAYHAWKS ARE SHATTERED BY JIM KEKERIS, 273-POUND LINEMAN SHIFTED TO FULLBACK

SCORE IS M. U.-28, K. U.-0

SA CROWD OF MORE THAN 20,000 PERSONS FILLS EVERY SEAT IN RUPPERT STADIUM

MISSOURI'S "SECRET WEAPON" CRASHES FOR SIXTEEN YARDS TO SIGNAL THINGS TO COME

*

Sometimes in rivalry games, you have to do something to surprise your opponent. They have seen your team and your plays for years, and it's just a matter of who executes better. That sneak play, if run correctly, can make the difference in victory or defeat.

In 1944, Missouri had such a surprise for Kansas, when tackle Jim Kekeris took some snaps at fullback. A huge player in that day, Kekeris weighed 273 pounds. Kansas did not have an answer for Kekeris.

The score was 28-0, so one player hardly dictated the outcome of the entire game. But a bruising fullback pounding into and through the line play after play certainly demoralized the Kansas defense.

Here's how it appeared in the November 24, 1944, *Times:*

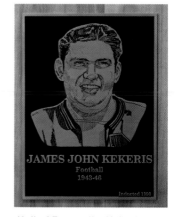

JAMES JOHN KEKERIS
Football
1943-46

Inducted 1990

Hall of Famer Jim Kekeris

BY C. E. MCBRIDE
(THE *STAR'S* SPORTS EDITOR)

How would you like to have a 273-pound human battering ram bouncing through, over and off you all afternoon?

There is only one answer and the boys of the University of Kansas football team thoroughly agree with you. It wasn't much fun and when it was all over Missouri was on the winning end of a 28 to 0 score in the fifty-third annual football game with Kansas.

With his stellar back, Bill Dellastatious, out with a lame ankle, Coach Chauncey Simpson of the Missouri Tigers announced that his team might make use of a new and secret V-3 trick by way of revenge on the Kansas Jayhawkers for that unexpected 7 to 6 defeat at Lawrence a year ago.

RIVALS!
MU VS. KU

MU:28
KU:0

FOOTBALL
NOVEMBER 23, 1944

Jim Kekeris was menacing enough as a lineman. When he switched to fullback for the Kansas game, the Kansas defenders knew they were in for a long day.

TOTAL OF 19,969 PAYS

Kansas and the crowd of 19,969 cash customers (others pushed the total above 20,000) at Ruppert stadium in this city yesterday afternoon knew what the coach's secret weapon was when the Missouri team took the field, with the giant lineman, Jim Kekeris holding down the fullback position. All season Mr. Kekeris, 6 foot 1 inch, 273-pound sophomore from McKinley high of St. Louis has been a Tiger forward bulwark as well as a sureshot Deadwood Dick in place-kicking for the extra point after touchdown.

No sooner had Missouri come into possession of the ball which incidentally was as soon as Kansas had six plays than Mr. Kekeris gave a line on why he was out there playing fullback and why Coach Simpson had spoken of him as a secret weapon.

The first four plays when Missouri came into possession of the ball saw the mammoth 20-year-old St. Louisan carrying the ball and he wasn't trying any end runs. He was just crashing his way through the Kansas forward wall, a wall that has done right well by itself all season. Mr. Kekeris went for three and he went for five, he went for two and he went for six and that was just a starter.

If any one of Kansas' sympathizers is in need of an alibi he can ring in Mr. Kekeris. He simply rocked the Jayhawkers back on their heels and then the other Tigers went on to deal the lethal punches although from time to time as play ran along, Mr. Kekeris went back to his secret weaponing, nearly always with success.

Kansas never had a chance in the first game of the classical series played in this city since 1910. The Tigers were in control all the way even though they led by the scant margin of a touchdown,

KANSAS NEVER HAD A CHANCE IN THE FIRST GAME OF THE CLASSICAL SERIES PLAYED IN THIS CITY SINCE 1910. THE TIGERS WERE IN CONTROL ALL THE WAY EVEN THOUGH THEY LED BY THE SCANT MARGIN OF A TOUCHDOWN, 7 TO 0, AT THE HALF. THE JAYHAWKERS, WEAKENED BY THE POUNDING THEY HAD RECEIVED, WERE EASIER PICKING IN THE LAST HALF, THE TIGERS SCORING A TOUCHDOWN IN THE THIRD PERIOD AND TWO IN THE FOURTH WHEN KANSAS, DESPERATE FOR A SCORE, STARTED PASSING DEEP IN ITS OWN TERRITORY AND ALERT TIGERS INTERCEPTED.

7 to 0, at the half. The Jayhawkers, weakened by the pounding they had received, were easier picking in the last half, the Tigers scoring a touchdown in the third period and two in the fourth when Kansas, desperate for a score, started passing deep in its own territory and alert Tigers intercepted.

FINE DAY FOR CROWD

The day was ideal for football, a cheery sun smiling on the crowded bleachers on the north side of the field. The game was a sellout, the total receipts amounting to approximately $45,000. The victory was Missouri's seventh in the last eleven years but left Kansas with an edge of four games in the full series of fifty-three.

The first touchdown came within three or four minutes of the end of the first quarter and it was a 32-yard run by Mr. Kekeris that laid the runway for the counter. Collins, who shared with his giant teammate, ball-lugging honors, had run a Kansas punt back twenty yards and was nine yards into Kansas territory when Kekeris found a hole in the center of the Kansas line. Quickly he found himself far down in the Jayhawker secondary. He probably was quite surprised at that but he jugger-

nauted his way for thirty-two yards, running over K. U.'s Moffett and finally being dragged down by Robison.

The ball was on the Kansas six and it took four plays to carry it over, showing the determined defense of the Kansans against unstoppable power. Kekeris took it over from the 1-foot line and place-kicked his first of four extra points for a 7 to 0 lead that stood through a scoreless second period.

Kansas rooters were hopeful through the twenty-three minutes of intermission while bands and service units conducted interesting and entertaining activities on the field. Hopeful was about all, however, as the Missouri defense had been superb and the Tiger offense a pounding, driving force that gave indication of further development in the second half.

The second half was only four minutes old when Columbia's Paul Colins, the Tiger captain, clever senior ball manipulator of the T-formation plays, intercepted a Kansas forward pass and ran sixty-five yards to plant the inflated pigskin in pay dirt.

KU:28 FOOTBALL
MU:0 NOVEMBER 23,1944

Ruppert Stadium, which later became Municipal Stadium, was the home of minor league and Negro Leagues baseball. It also hosted the MU-KU game in 1944 and 1945.

POWER WINS FOR MU

KANSAS, STUBBORN FOR A HALF, FINALLY YIELDS TO SHARP RUNNING ATTACK AND PASSES, TO LOSE FIFTY-FOURTH RENEWAL OF CLASSIC, 12 TO 33

TITLE IN VICTORY

IN SUBDUING MT. OREAD RIVAL THE TIGERS CAPTURE BIG SIX CHAMPIONSHIP

MISSOURI FIRST TO SCORE

BRINKMAN SMASHES OVER AFTER A 71-YARD MARCH, BUT JAYHAWKS QUICKLY TIE IT

VICTORS COME BACK IMMEDIATELY, FORGE AHEAD AND BREAK AWAY IN THIRD QUARTER

The last Kansas-Missouri game in Kansas City took place in 1945. Once a tradition in Kansas City, the game had moved to campus sites in the century's second decade, much to the delight of local merchants in the college towns. But World War II restrictions on travel meant the game returned to the neutral site "halfway" between the two schools for the 1944 contest.

The following year, the war was over and the restrictions were lifted, but the game still remained in Kansas City. But it was the last time. The crowd of more than 21,000 saw the Tigers dominate. The Tigers held a 12-6 advantage at halftime, and then pulled away in the second half.

The victory clinched the Big Six Conference championship for Missouri, the Tigers' third in five years and last until 1960.

Here's how it appeared in the November 25, 1945, *Times*:

BY DAN PARTNER
(A MEMBER OF THE *STAR'S* SPORTS STAFF)

The mighty Tigers of Missouri mixed a respectable passing attack with synchronized power off the deceptive T formation yesterday, and defeated a gallant Kansas squad 33 to 12, before 21,494 customers in Ruppert Stadium.

Held to a 1-touchdown lead at the half, 12 to 6, the Columbia combination clicked off fourteen points in the third quarter and added seven more in the final fifteen minutes to take the Big Six conference championship from the Oklahoma Sooners.

RECORD AMOUNT IS PAID

The crowd paid $32,164—a record figure for the stadium—to witness the fifty-fourth game between the two universities and was rewarded with a contest that contained not one dull moment.

Until Missouri's man-power became unbearable in the second half, the Jayhawkers did themselves proud in choking off the quick-scoring Tiger plays in a manner superior to the efforts of both Nebraska and Oklahoma, and gave the Missouri patrons more than a few anxious moments during the interesting, cleanly played game.

The fine Missouri line, led by Jumbo Jim Kekeris, found a respectable opponent in the Kansas forwards, who fought the Tigers to a standstill in the first half. The smooth-moving Missourians weren't to be denied in the last thirty minutes, however, and finished their last season under Coach Chauncey Simpson undefeated in conference competition.

GLORY TO "SUB" COACH

The Tigers dropped nonleague clashes with Minnesota and Ohio State of the Big Ten conference and 7 to 14 to Michigan State this season. It was a great victory for Simpson, who resumes his role as first assistant to Don Faurot next fall.

A 7-yard Bob Hopkins to Lloyd Brinkman pass and a 17-yard scamper by North Kansas City's Leonard Brown highlighted the 73-yard touchdown drive engineered by the Tigers for their initial touchdown mid-way in the opening period.

Brinkman zig-zagged twenty yards with a Kansas punt to plant the ball on the Missouri 27 and from that spot, with Hopkins the spearhead, the Tigers moved forward in an unstoppable manner.

It was Hopkins at right tackle for four, Brinkman at left guard for four and Brinkman eight more after Fullback Jack O'Connell was stopped cold. That was the power pattern until the Tigers reached the Kansas 34, from where Hopkins flipped to Brinkman with the 9-yarder and later crashed five more yards to the 20. K.U.'s 7-man line allowed O'Connell only two yards.

Trips at Goal Line

Then Brown faked to Hopkins, looped back and sliced past the Jayhawk left tackle and was touchdown bound until he was tripped a yard away from the end zone. Brinkman plunged over for the score. Kekeris' kick was wide to the right and Missouri led 6 to 0.

This display of ability should have convinced the Jayhawkers they were overmatched, but Coach Henry Shenk's athletes hadn't come along for the ride.

The Tigers had that touchdown look in their eyes later in the period but Hopkins muffed the ball at the Missouri 25 and Norman Pumphrey, end, recovered for Kansas. Five plays later the score was locked at 6-6. Frank Pattee, Kansas halfback, found a gaping hole in the left side of the highly regarded Missouri line and went for five before the Missouri secondary got him. Then he fired a pass to Halfback Dick Bertuzzi on the Missouri 10. The pass catcher was knocked out of bounds. Fullback Leroy Harmon picked up four yards in two thrusts at center as the quarter ended.

SCHMIDT OVER UNTOUCHED

On the first play of the second quarter, Kansas shifted off the T into a single wingback to the right and observers, who had watched the Jayhawks in previous games knew what was coming. That "what" was Dave Schmidt on an end-around play and the left wingman went across untouched to score for the fourth time this season on that maneuver.

Schmidt, a naval trainee from Milwaukee, made the play look easy as he cut inside the wide playing Missouri left end for the tally. LeRoy Robinson, Kansas fullback, sidelined because of a broken collarbone, came in for the conversion, but his kick went awry.

Missouri attempted to get underway after Brinkman returned the kickoff seventeen yards to the Tiger 24, but an offside penalty and a 15-yard fine for an intentionally grounded pass cooled its efforts. Kansas was on the march again after Bertuzzi rushed back sixteen yards with a punt to the Missouri 46. Pattee and Harmon alternated at punctuating the Tiger tackles until the 35-yard line was reached and Coach Simpson rushed an entire new Missouri team into the fray.

JAYHAWK PASS TO M.U.

Pat Green, K.U.'s sophomore halfback, greeted the Missouri varsity with a 5-yard gain at right tackle, but on the next play, Pattee's pass went astray. O'Connell took it on the Missouri 22 and finally was stopped on the Missouri 25.

From that point on, the Tigers moved to touchdown No. 2—sixty-five yards in eight plays, including a 29-yard pass tagged with an 18-yard run. This aerial, with Bill Dellastatious throwing, provided end Roland Oakes with the ball on the Kansas 32 and he went to the 14 before being run off the field.

Brown, Brinkman and O'Connell made it first down two yards out and Dellastatious bent left tackle for that deficit and the touchdown. Again Kekeris kicked too far to the right and the half ended with Missouri in front 12 to 6, but only after Kansas had moved to the Tiger 12 where the gun ended activities.

FROM THE KANSAS CITY TIMES, 1945

A PEAK GRID DAY

CROWD OF 21,494 PAYS $52,160 TO SEE M. U. BEAT K. U. HERE, 33 TO 12

GAY THRONG FOR CONTEST

OLD GRADS AND NEW BOBBY SOXERS AND MANY SERVICEMEN IN THE STANDS

RECORD TOTAL AT GATE

RECEIPTS PROBABLY LARGEST EVER FOR A COLLEGE SPORTS EVENT IN STATE

A crowd of 21,494 football fans yesterday afternoon packed into Ruppert stadium and left $52, 160 at the ticket windows, probably the largest box office total ever rolled up at a college sports event in Missouri.

Beneath a golden autumn sun the crowd saw the Missouri Tigers bear out pre-game predictions with a 33 to 12 defeat of the fighting underdogs, the Kansas Jayhawks. The game marked the end of the profitable 2-year vacation of the annual gridiron battle from the university stadiums. Next year's contest will be held at Columbia, Mo.

A GAY, COLORFUL THRONG

Never was there a gayer or more colorful sports spectacle in Kansas City. Bobby-soxers cheered alongside women in fur coats and galoshes. Young men with battle stars and service ribbons slapped the backs of men who came prepared for the worst with blankets and great coats with fur collars.

Every seat in the stands was sold before game time. Hundreds packed the embankment at the east end of the park. Others found vantage points in the fenced area in the northwest corner of the park.

RIVALS!
MU VS. KU

MU:33
KU:12

FOOTBALL
NOVEMBER 24, 1945

Missouri and Kansas students occupied temporary bleacher seats on the north side. Kansas, which was the "home" school, had 1,500 student seats and Missouri 1,000. The overflow crowd banked around the student section.

FOR TOP SEATS, $3.80

Top seat prices were $3.80 and the standees shelled out $1.60 to enter on a catch-as-catch-can chance of getting a view of the annual gridiron event between the two state universities. There have been more persons in the park, but never before has there been rolled up such a total in cash at the box office of the 22-year-old baseball park, according to H. Roy Hamey, president of the Kansas City Baseball club.

Kansas City's 2-game taste of Big Six football yielded the school athletic funds close to $100,000 before deductions for expenses. Last year the schools agreed to play here because of restrictions on travel, and 18,483 fans paid

$44,000. The schools split 50-50 on receipts at both games.

The first period had all the thrills of an upset when the smaller Kansas team surged back in the opening moments of the second quarter to tie the score at 6 and 6. They held the Tigers to a 1-touchdown lead at the half and were threatening to even the score again just before the second period ended. In the second half the fans saw the heavier Missouri line taking its toll.

BIG COMMERCE TRUST PARTY

Biggest seat buyer at the game was the Commerce Trust company, which purchased 750 for visiting bankers here as guests at a bankers' forum. William J. Slack, agent for the Metropolitan Life Insurance company, bought thirty hot dogs and explained he had bought that many tickets for his salesmen.

Holders of the reserved seats did not start surging into the stadium until

about thirty minutes before game time. General admission ticket buyers who were admitted to the bleachers and the west side embankment were lined up before 12 o'clock.

Many an overseas veteran was there for his first football game in a long time. Marine Sergt. Robert Philippi, 5917 Grand avenue, back from two years in the Pacific, brought his son, Robert Philippi Jr. The sergeant was in uniform.

Among the early arrivals was Shannon Douglass, lawyer and holder for years of track records at M. U. Robert B. Caldwell, Jack Cannon, Carson Cowherd, John Moberly, Fred Bellemere, Clif Langsdale, James Nugent and Jerome Walsh were among other members of the legal profession with grandstand tickets.

CHAPTER 3

A Brand New Battleground

HOOPIN' IT UP

Heading into the 2004-2005 basketball season, Kansas was 1,825-764 all-time. The 1,825 wins ranks the Jayhawks third all-time behind only Kentucky (1,876) and North Carolina (1,827).

The Jayhawks have won 47 conference championships, including 13 in the Missouri Valley Conference (1908-28), 12 in the Big 6 (1929-47), five in the Big 7 (1948-58), 13 in the Big 8 (1959-96) and four in the Big XII (1997-present).

It only seems natural that the Jayhawks would be a national power in basketball. In the fall of 1898, just seven years after he nailed the first peach basket on a wall inside a gymnasium in Springfield, Massachusetts, Dr. James Naismith became the first coach of an intercollegiate basketball team at Kansas. Ironically, he's the only coach in the school's 106-year history to own a career mark lower than .500.

Naismith was 55-60 in nine seasons. The nine men who have followed have lived up to the tradition started by the bespectacled man who said, "You don't coach basketball, you play it." The most revered of the bunch is Dr. Forrest C. "Phog" Allen, who coached at Kansas for 39 seasons and compiled a 590-219 record.

Fifteen men have earned the title of head coach at the University of Missouri, where the all-time record stands at 1,362-962. The most notable is Norm Stewart, who played under Wilbur "Sparky" Stalcup from 1953-56 and then coached for 32 seasons (1967-99), compiling a 634-333 record.

The Tigers have won 15 conference championships, including four in the Missouri Valley, three in the Big 6 and eight in the Big 8.

RIVALS!
MU VS. KU

FROM LEFT TO RIGHT: TOP TO BOTTOM
Stalcup
Allen
Harp
Self
Owens
Stewart
Williams
Brown
Snyder

49

1907

TIGERS WON AT BASKET BALL

MISSOURI BEAT THE JAYHAWKERS LAST NIGHT BY A SCORE OF 34 TO 31

✳

The football rivalry had turned Sweet 16 by the time the two schools faced each other for the first time in basketball. Kansas, under coach James A. Naismith, who invented the game, was in its ninth season of competition. Missouri and coach Dr. Isadore Anderson were in their first year. Naismith brought his "Jayhawks" into Columbia for a contest that barely warranted mention in *The Kansas City Times*. In the original March Madness game between the now-familiar combatants, the Tigers gained the upper hand, in overtime, a precursor to the next century of hard-fought games between the two schools.

Here's how it appeared (barely) in the March 12, 1907, *Times*:

University of Missouri Archives

Columbia, Mo., March 11

The Jayhawkers sprung something of a surprise on the Tigers to-night and sent them into extra time in order to win the first of two basket ball games by a score of 34 to 31. The Kansans put up a fast and furious game and in the first ten minutes took a lead of six points. The Tigers succeeded in getting within reach of their opponents and the score stood 12 to 11 in favor of the Jayhawkers at the end of the first half. When time was called in the second half each team had 31 points to its credit. In the extended time the Tigers got a foul throw, followed by a basket which won the game. The Jayhawkers excelled in team work while the Tigers evened things up by locating the basket with more accuracy. The two teams play again to-morrow night.

FIRST GAME TO KANSAS

THE MISSOURI BASKET BALL TEAM LOST LAST NIGHT, 28 TO 25

✳

The first half ended with the score 15 to 9 in favor of Kansas. Better team work and the ability to hit the goal gave the Jayhawkers the lead. The nine points for the Tigers came as the result of nine free throws from ten fouls made by Kansas.

In the second half, the Missourians improved in team work and kept Kansas to a three point lead most of the period. John Cheek, former Kansas City Central High School star, and Capt. "Snooks" Bernet played the leading role for the Tigers, while Captain Sproull and Greenlees did stellar work for the Jayhawkers. Weaver, the big Kansas center, was disqualified by Umpire Green and put out of the game. In the second period the Tigers displayed team work and ability to hit the baskets, scoring their five field goals of the game.

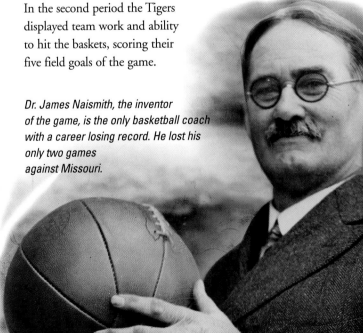

Dr. James Naismith, the inventor of the game, is the only basketball coach with a career losing record. He lost his only two games against Missouri.

1914

RIVALS!
MU VS. KU

MU: 34
KU: 31

BASKETBALL
MARCH 11, 1907

In 1908, Kansas replaced Dr. James Naismith with Dr. Forrest C. "Phog" Allen as head coach. Naismith, who remains the only coach in Kansas history with a career losing record, finished his reign at 42-44. He reportedly told Allen, "You can't coach basket ball, Forrest, you play it."

Allen proved Naismith wrong very quickly, winning Missouri Valley Conference championships in each of his first two years. Allen was replaced for the next 10 years by W. O. Hamilton, and Hamilton picked up where Allen left off, winning the next three titles, before a down year in 1912-13.

But 1913-14 proved once again to be Kansas' year, as the "Jayhawkers" went 17-1 and claimed the MVC title once again. The lone loss was at Kansas State, while Kansas defeated Missouri all four times the teams squared off. The first two were in Columbia.

Here's how the first game appeared in the February 12, 1914, *Times* and how the second game appeared in the February 13, 1914, *Times:*

KANSAS BEAT MISSOURI AGAIN

THE TIGERS LOST BASKET BALL GAME TO JAYHAWKERS, 21 TO 27

❋

Columbia, Mo., Feb. 12

Kansas paved the way to a Missouri Valley championship claim in basket ball by defeating Missouri again tonight, 27 to 21. The Missourians had a 5-point lead all through the game, but in the latter part of the second period, with Captain Bernet and Palfreyman out of the game, the Tigers weakened. Captain Bernet and Palfreyman of Missouri and Weidlein and Greenlees of Kansas were taken out of the game on personal fouls.

The first period ended with Missouri in the lead, 11 to 6. It was distinctly a Missouri half. The Tigers played a better defensive game and landed three field goals to one by the Jayhawkers. John Cheek, a Kansas City lad, and Captain Bernet starred for Missouri.

From here the Kansas five goes to St. Louis to meet the Washington University team, while the Tigers travel to Ames to meet the Iowa Aggies for a return engagement.

University of Kansas Archives

KANSAS OUT OF THE RACE

VICTORY FOR TIGERS, 24 TO 20, ENDS JAYHAWKERS' CHANCES

AFTER A GOOD START, THE HAMILTON FIVE DROPPED OUT OF THE LEAD AND NEVER GOT IT AGAIN – PLAY AGAIN TODAY

There's nothing more satisfying to Missouri fans than a Tigers win—unless it's a Kansas loss. When the Missouri win is against Kansas, it's that much sweeter. When the Missouri win knocks Kansas out of the championship race, as it happened in 1917, well, that's as sweet as it gets.

Kansas had won the Missouri Valley Conference championship five of the seven years that W.O. Hamilton had been the coach. They entered the 1916-17 season coming off their first losing season in 10 years, and that was a 7-8 mark under Dr. James Naismith in 1906-07. But the 1915-16 season saw them drop to 6-12, their worst record ever in 18 years of competition.

The 1916-17 season saw renewed optimism, and when the Jayhawkers arrived in Columbia, they still had a chance for another conference crown. But that ended quickly with a 24-20 loss in Columbia. For good measure, the Tigers won big the next night, 38-15.

The wins set up a head-to-head competition with Kansas State the following weekend and things didn't turn out well for the Tigers. But the following year saw MU win its first league crown, a feat the Tigers duplicated in four of the next five years.

Here's how the first game appeared in the February 22, 1917, *Times* and how the second game appeared in the February 23, 1917, *Times*:

Columbia, Mo., Feb. 21

Missouri University eliminated Kansas from the Missouri Valley basket ball championship race tonight, defeating the Jayhawkers 24 to 20. Kansas led by a few points during the first few minutes of play, but toward the last of the first half Missouri got started, never after that period letting Kansas get dangerously near.

The same teams will meet again on the court of Rothwell Gymnasium in an afternoon game tomorrow. Missouri is within two games of a Valley championship now, the single game with Kansas, the two next week with the Aggies and the two with Washington being all that are left on the Tiger schedule.

TIGERS DOWN KANSAS AGAIN

SEVERE WALLOPING GIVEN JAYHAWKER FIVE BY A 38 TO 15 COUNT

Columbia, Mo., Feb 22

Missouri basket ball quintet gave Kansas another drubbing on the Rothwell gymnasium court this afternoon, the final count being 38 to 15, in favor of the Tigers. Captain Williams, the Kansas City boy who captains the Tiger team, led in the scoring by shooting nine goals from the field. The Tigers will play the Aggies in a series that means the title March 8 and 9.

1923

VALLEY TITLE TO KANSAS

JAYHAWKERS DEFEATED MISSOURI LAST NIGHT, 23 TO 20

VICTORY BROUGHT FOR THE LAWRENCE CAGERS THE DISTINCTION OF HAVING FINISHED THE SEASON WITHOUT A CONFERENCE DEFEAT

The 1922-23 season promised to be a good one for Kansas and Missouri. The two teams tied for the Missouri Valley Conference title the previous year—the fourth in five years for Missouri. The Jayhawks also won the Helms Foundation national title in 1922.

Both teams were strong again in 1923, and that showed in the records. As they approached their second contest of the season, Kansas was undefeated in conference play at 15-0. Missouri was just one game back at 14-1, with the lone loss coming at home to Kansas. With a victory in Lawrence, Missouri would again tie for the conference crown.

But Kansas would have nothing to do with that. They raced, a relative term by today's standards, to a 20-11 lead before Missouri put on a charge, getting as close as 20-18. The final score was 23-20 and Kansas had turned in the first undefeated conference season since the MVC was founded in 1907.

The Tigers finished in second, a very respectable 14-2. They would not win another conference crown until 1930.

Here's how it appeared in the March 1, 1923, *Times:*

Lawrence, Kas. Feb 28

The Kansas Jayhawk owns the whole blooming valley tonight. If you don't believe it ask the three thousand madly milling Jayhawk students whose cries of victory rent the crisp moonlit February air. The old Kansas Jayhawk sure possesses the valley entirely, has a cinch on it by virtue of a 23 to 20 victory over the ancient enemy, the Missouri Tiger tonight, owns the valley because the Crimson and Blue warriors of Coach F. C. Allen went through a strenuous season of Missouri Valley basket ball with sixteen victories and no defeats in the conference.

For forty minutes of soul racking basket ball three thousand spectators, those fortunate souls who got in, held onto their seats and let their hopes rise or fall depending upon whether it was a Jayhawk shot or a Tiger flip toward the basket that went sailing through the air. There were two records established at this exciting fray tonight, one was made when Kansas won and set up a clean slate in the conference. For an entire season, the first time such a thing has been written into the records since the conference was established back in 1907.

CHAPTER THREE

●

53

University of Kansas Archives

1923

KU tasted plenty of success in Robinson Gym before moving to Hoch Auditorium.

● A BRAND NEW BATTLEGROUND

A RECORD BREAKER CROWD

The second record breaker was the crowd itself – at least three thousand. But now to the game itself, the actual battle that the fighting men of Captain Paul Endacott of Kansas and Captain Bun Browning of Missouri waged through forty minutes of milling in which they gave their all. All glory must go to Kansas, for Kansas won by right of superior play and perhaps superior condition. But it was a close margin and the Missouri Tigers fought from behind with a tenacity that kept the result of the game concealed until the final gun crack turned loose a bedlam of Jayhawk victory screams.

The fray started with Wulf getting the tip from Bunker the ball was going to Ackerman. But Bowman played hard, was given a foul and Browning then opened the festivities of the evening and a thousand Tiger throats with a free toss. Then Faurot fouled and Ackerman missed the free toss. Kansas was again fouled and Browning tossed in two more free throws and his team lead, 3 to 0. Kansas hearts were stand-ing still, but they immediately raced into action when Wulf laid one in from under the basket. Soon Hays was caught fouling and this time Ackerman tied up the score at 3 all with a free throw. Then Bowman heaved a long shot for a pretty basket and Kansas led.

TIGERS LED FOR A WHILE

Wheat tossed in two field goals a bit later, the only baskets Missouri got in the half and Missouri led for a time with the score 9 to 8. However, 9 points was all the Tiger scoring for the half and the Jayhawkers drew away for a 5-point lead, 14 to 9, at the end of the first period.

The second half was a thriller and Kansas early ran up a 20 to 11 lead. Then the Tigers braced and it was some brace. Wheat dropped in two field goals and Bunker one, while the Kansas score stood still. Browning added a free throw and the score was 20 to 18 for Kansas. Kansas played a passing game and did not worry about getting down for shots for a time, then a Missourian fouled and also a Kansan, Ackerman, making the free toss and Browning missing.

Kansas revived her play and Bowman put in a thriller from well behind the free-throw line.

Kansas led, 23 to 18, and the Jayhawk part of the crowd breathed easier. The irresistible Wheat got under his basket again, however, unguarded for a minute and Browning fed him a beauty. The ball sped in, the gun cracked and Kansas found herself the landlord of the valley, 23 to 20.

EVERY KANSAN SCORED

To whom should honors go for the battling in this historic fray? That's easy – all honors to the five Jayhawkers who fought all the way and to the six Missourians who did duty for the Tiger. They were all stars. Every man on the Kansas squad scored. Wheat and Browning did most of Missouri's scoring, with Bunker, counting one field goal.

Wheat was high man of the evening with five goals. Browning, the leading scorer of the Valley got only one field goal, but made six free throws out of nine attempts. Perhaps the brightest star of Kansas was Captain Endacott.

54

RIVALS!
MU VS. KU

KU:23
MU:20

BASKETBALL
FEBRUARY 28, 1923

He bulldogged the ball, was always on it from the rebound and broke through for two field baskets. The game was the last for Endacott, Wulf and Bowman of the Kansas squad. And what a game, and what a record they wrote for their farewell to Jayhawker basket ball activities. Wulf, long center, was there on the tipoff and he caged three necessary field baskets. Bowman also caged two baskets and delivered them on long shots when they were needed to keep the Jayhawkers ahead.

BLACK A WHIRLWIND

Charley Black, the other Kansas guard, was a whirlwind on dribbling down the court, and to Ackerman, the other forward, must go credit for shooting

The 1923 Jayhawkers, with Allen and Naismith (with glasses) in suits. Adolph Rupp, legendary Kentucky coach, was in the back on the left.

Dr. Naismith (left) handed things over to Dr. Allen.

in seven out of eleven free throws and also credit for playing a fighting floor game that stood out. Bunker of Missouri, in floor work was the mainstay of the Tigers. Faurot at guard, was another Missourian whose work meant much to the Tigers. He was replaced late in the first half by Vanice, but he came back for the whole of the second half. The low count in baskets of the Kansas forwards also pays tribute to the work of Hays, veteran Tiger guard.

Special reason for the Kansas victory, aside from condition and superior playing through most of the game, might be found in the ability of every man on the Kansas team to score baskets.

On defense Missouri played an erratic game. For the first five minutes Kansas could not crack it and did not get a shot. Then the Missouri wall seemed to crack and the Jayhawkers were never troubled long at a time thereafter to get through for their shots. The Kansas defense was strong throughout, with the exception of a failing for letting Wheat get down under the basket in several occasions for set-ups.

1928

M.U. IS WINNER

KANSAS BOWS TO OLD FOE IN BASKET BALL OPENER IN CONVENTION HALL

THE SCORE IS 38 TO 31

HARRY WELSH, FORMER WESTPORT STAR, SETS PACE FOR TIGERS WITH 10 GOALS

THE JAYHAWKERS OVERCOME LEAD IN SECOND HALF BUT FAIL TO HOLD MARGIN

*

The Missouri Valley Conference was no more, to the chagrin of the Kansas basketball team, which had won six of the final seven conference championships. The new Big Six Conference—the predecessor to the Big Seven, the Big Eight and today's Big XII—had arrived.

Though the exhibition game at Kansas City's Convention Hall was a non-conference game, it was the first of three contests that season between Kansas and Missouri.

The Tigers jumped out to an early lead behind local star Harry Welsh. The Jayhawks managed to stay close, and even took a lead in the second half, before Missouri rode Welsh's shoulders to victory.

Here's how it appeared in the December 23, 1928, *Star*

issouri University's basket ball team vindicated every pre-season prediction of being a formidable entry in Big Six competition this season by beating the Kansas University quintet 38 to 31 last night in Convention Hall before a large crowd. The game was listed as a non-conference attraction.

Although the game failed to come up to the expectations of the more discriminating court fans, it was not without the usual thrills and excitement akin

to a meeting between these two rivals.

The play of the Jayhawkers was excellent at times, yet the offense of the Crimson and Blue lacked the necessary drive and punch and the passing and floor play was loose and sloppy.

K.U. RALLIES IN SECOND HALF

Missouri held the upper hand in the scoring throughout the contest, with

the possible exception of the opening minutes of play and once in the middle of the second half when the Jayhawkers rose to the occasion and staged a rally that perished at the zenith of an 8-point lead.

A preponderance of glory goes to Harry Welsh, former Westport High School Star, and Ruble, the veteran forwards who were potent factors in making the evening miserable and quite uncomfortable for the Jayhawk players.

RIVALS!
MU VS. KU

MU: 38
KU: 31

BASKETBALL
DECEMBER 22, 1928

> THE PLAY OF THE JAYHAWKERS WAS EXCELLENT AT TIMES, YET THE OFFENSE OF THE CRIMSON AND BLUE LACKED THE NECESSARY DRIVE AND PUNCH AND THE PASSING AND FLOOR PLAY WAS LOOSE AND SLOPPY.

It was Welsh, especially, who shot many one-handers and close shots from all angles until a majority of the gathering lost count of the goals. By the finish the brilliant forward had made 10 goals.

The scoring ace of the Tigers drew first blood of the game when he netted a shot through the basket on an out of bounds play and followed a second later with a pot shot.

BISHOP GETS "HOT"

Bishop duplicated Welsh's feat for the Lawrence crew a few minutes later with a tip in shot and a clean basket from the side court.

The terrific pace set in the opening minutes of play was in no way lessened as the game progressed. Team speed, however, detracted somewhat the teams' efficiency and awry shots and wild flings at the basket were not infrequent.

After two free throws by Maney, Kansas surrendered the scoring lead to Missouri and was not regained except for one brief minute in the second half. Welsh and Ruble continued their disastrous work, the former tossing in one-handers and dizzy counters in a manner marvelous to behold. Cox and McGuire kept the Crimson and Blue within scoring distance of the Tigers, and abetted by a free throw by Hauser and a pretty basket by Plumley, the Kansas squad sliced the Missouri lead to six points as the half ended, 20 to 14.

BAKER A TIGER STAR

An outstanding feature in the play of the Edwards men in the first half was the work of the elongated Baker, M.U. center.

Excitement was churned into the festivities with the improvement of the Jayhawkers in the second half. After a ponderous Huhn, who had furnished a few smiles in the first half by his nervous though willing endeavors, succeeded in dropping two charity tries, Plumley sent a side shot through the hoop as clean as a hound's tooth. Angle shots by Cox and McGuire brought the Lawrence cagers within two points of the Tigers and the entire assemblage to its feet.

A JAYHAWK RALLY

Missouri veterans were rushed into the line-up as quickly as possible to prevent the Kansas players from doing anything dangerous. But Kansas was not to be stopped at this junction. Paden, after getting a rebound, let fly an unconscious one over his head that found its way through the basket and Cox followed up with a goal a few seconds later from the free throw line to give the Jayhawkers a momentary advantage.

The Welsh-Ruble combination threw a wet blanket on the flaming Kansas hopes. A shot under the basket was registered by Welsh on a pass from Ruble, and after a few wild scrambles under the Kansas basket Welsh broke through the Jayhawk defense to tally again and establish a lead that never was threatened again.

University of Kansas Archives

M. U. STOPS K. U.

JAYHAWKERS LOSE FIRST GAME IN BIG SIX, BOWING TO TIGERS, 18 TO 29

HUHN IS HIGH POINT MAN

THE FLASHY MISSOURI FORWARD SCORES SEVEN FIELD GOALS TO LEAD ATTACK

VICTORY ADVANCES WINNER TO ONE-HALF GAME BEHIND LEADING LAWRENCE FIVE

❋

University of Kansas Archives

The brand new Brewer Fieldhouse, which cost a whopping $225,000 to build, was dedicated in grand fashion, as the Missouri Tigers ended a two-game skid with a resounding victory over the arch-rival Kansas Jayhawks.

The Jayhawks came into the contest at 13-0, 7-0 in the Big Six, while the Tigers had suffered back-to-back losses on the road to Kansas State and Nebraska, both bottom tier teams in the conference.

It was back home and time to break in a new building for MU, and the Tigers did it in style. Behind 14 points by Charlie Huhn, the Tigers jumped out to an early lead and never looked back. Huhn almost single-handedly outscored the Jayhawks, as the final tally was 29-18.

Here's how it appeared in the February 22, 1930, *Times:*

(BY THE *STAR'S* OWN SERVICE)

Columbia, Mo., Feb. 21

Four thousand University of Missouri basket ball followers, mad men in ecstasy, saw their basket ball team, twice beaten by conference underdogs a week ago, rise to unprecedented heights tonight and turn back the erstwhile undefeated University of Kansas five, 29 to 18. It was a Missouri night almost from the start, the Tigers overcoming an early Kansas lead in the first six minutes of play, and holding the advantage for the remainder of the contest. At half time the Missourians led, 14 to 8.

An auspicious occasion it was – the night of the dedication of Brewer field house, new $225,000 home of Missouri indoor sports, and nowhere in all the books could there have been found an observance of the occasion more acceptable in the Tiger lair.

Frank B. Rollins, president of the Stadium Building Corporation, Stratton Shartel, attorney general, and George C.

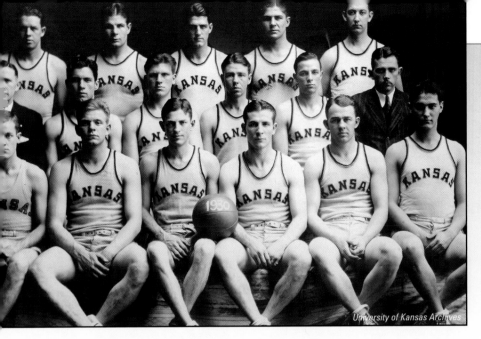

University of Kansas Archives

Willson of St. Louis, all paid tribute to the efforts of C. L. Brewer, Missouri director of athletics, and to the university alumni, whose efforts made possible the building of the field house.

A TIGER LEAD IN CRAIG'S GOAL

From the moment Huhn slipped under the basket to tie the score at 3-all and Captain Craig followed with a long shot that gave the Tigers the lead, Missouri held the winning hand. It was a pageant of careful, cautious basket ball by Missouri, and frantic, but futile attempts by Kansas to head the Tigers and settle down to the type of basket ball the Kansans wished to play.

"Long Charley" Huhn was far too deadly under the basket. His fourteen points brought him individual scoring honors with almost twice as many counters as Cox, star K. U. guard, could compile for second place. He worked perfectly under the basket, with his performance on rebound shots accounting for no small share of the Tiger strength.

With the advantage of the tip-off, Missouri adopted the slow break before a point had been scored and the Kansans were struggling for the ball throughout the first five minutes of the contest, which netted exactly two points, first a free throw for Page and then a free throw for Waldorf. Then Jim

Bausch dropped in a field goal to take the lead, but his failure to count a pair of free throws which came to him on Baker's foul held the Jayhawk margin to two points.

Huhn slipped under the basket to knot the count for Missouri, and when Craig immediately dropped in another counter from well out on the floor to give Missouri a lead of 5 to 3, Kansas took time out. Huhn scored again, taking a rebound from Baker's shot for the counter, and when he and Cox each counted from the floor the score was 9 to 5 in Missouri's favor, with Welsh's free throw bringing the Missouri count to ten.

M. U. AHEAD AT HALF, 14-8

Cox sank another long one, but Craig answered with the Tigers still playing their slow-moving game, with now and then a thrust under the basket. A final basket by Huhn and a free throw by Cox sent the teams out for the intermission, with Missouri leading 14 to 8.

An epidemic of Missouri fouls aided the Kansans in a determined rally with which they launched the second period, and one charity counter by Cox and a pair by Bishop, coupled with a shot by Bishop, who found himself wide open under the basket, brought the Kansans to within one point of the Tiger total before Missouri broke back into the scoring with a field goal by Huhn. The Kansas rally was still on, however, for Cox sank a long one from away out on the floor, and the Missouri lead was again a single point.

Welsh went out; Collings went in for Missouri, and Huhn and Collings each dashed under the basket for field goals in brilliant scoring thrusts that checked the Kansas assault and put the Missouri scoring machine once more under way. Gradually the Missourians crept ahead, until, with four minutes to play, the Tiger lead assumed comparatively safe proportions.

The Missouri victory tonight served notice that the Tigers were once more decidedly in the race for the Big Six championship. The Jayhawkers still hold the conference lead with six victories in seven starts, while Missouri has won six out of eight, and can now tie the Jayhawkers for the title by winning from Oklahoma here next Saturday and from the Kansans at Lawrence, March 5. If the Tigers turn those two tricks and Kansas should stumble, either against Iowa State or Nebraska, the undisputed championship would go to Missouri.

> AN AUSPICIOUS OCCASION IT WAS – THE NIGHT OF THE DEDICATION OF BREWER FIELD HOUSE, NEW $225,000 HOME OF MISSOURI INDOOR SPORTS, AND NOWHERE IN ALL THE BOOKS COULD THERE HAVE BEEN FOUND AN OBSERVANCE OF THE OCCASION MORE ACCEPTABLE IN THE TIGER LAIR.

CHAPTER THREE

K. U. IS HUMBLED

AMAZING MISSOURI OFFENSIVE CRUSHES JAYHAWKS UNDER A 55 TO 30 SCORE

CLINCH A TIE FOR TITLE

THE TRIUMPHANT TIGERS, LED BY KEIRSEY, BOMBARD GOALS ALL THE WAY

A CAPACITY CROWD OF MORE THAN 5,000 PERSONS SEES CRUCIAL BIG SIX GAME

AT THE HALF, IT'S 29-11

AND BENGALS NEVER ARE THREATENED THEREAFTER — OFFICIAL SCORER LOSES A POINT

It had been nine years since the Missouri Tigers had raised a conference championship banner. Over the previous 17 years, it had happened only once. But when the Tigers finally claimed another championship, they did it in grand fashion, trouncing the defending league champion Jayhawks, 55-30.

The victory clinched at least a share of the Big Six title for the Tigers with Oklahoma. The Sooner won their final two games to earn the tie for the conference crown.

The Tigers led 29-11 at halftime and cruised through the second half. They dominated the boards to put an end to Kansas' three-year run as conference champions. Harlan Keirsey led all scorers with 14 points.

Here's how it appeared in the March 3, 1939, *Times:*

RIVALS!
MU VS. KU

MU: 55
KU: 30

BASKETBALL
MARCH 2, 1939

(BY THE STAR'S OWN SERVICE)

Columbia, Mo., Feb. 21

The University of Missouri hoisted its first Big Six championship pennant since 1930 here tonight with a smashing victory, 55 to 30, over the title-defending University of Kansas Jayhawkers. The Tigers took the lead after a minute and twenty seconds of play and never surrendered the advantage. At the half Missouri led, 29 to 11.

The Missourians, playing before a capacity crowd of more than 5,000 persons, dominated every department of the game, but it was their complete control of the ball on rebounds, both on offense and defense, that put the Kansans out of the running almost from the first whistle.

Whether the Missourians shall rule the Big Six cage roost alone, or whether they shall share the title with Oklahoma depends on the outcome of two games which the Sooners have yet to play – with Kansas State and Nebraska. Oklahoma must win both of those games to tie Missouri for the championship.

ATTACK IS BEWILDERING

The magnitude of the victory left the Missouri fans almost speechless. They had been hopeful of victory over Kansas before the doors opened, but nowhere could there have been found a Tiger follower so ardent that he would have predicted the Bengals would set a two-to-one pace most of the way.

But the Missourians were not too speechless to stand and cheer for several minutes when Harlan Keirsey, veteran forward, left the game for the last time in the final three minutes of the second half. It was Keirsey's last game for

THE SECOND HALF WAS PRETTY MUCH A REPETITION OF THE FIRST, SAVE THAT THE JAYHAWKERS BEGAN TO FIND THE BASKET WITH OCCASIONAL LONG SHOTS BY LYMAN CORLIS AND ALLEN, WHO BETWEEN THEM GATHERED IN THIRTEEN OF THE NINETEEN POINTS WHICH KANSAS SCORED IN THE SECOND HALF. THE TIGERS PUSHED THEIR FAST BREAK RELENTLESSLY, WITH HARVEY TAKING THE SCORING LEAD FOR THE BENGALS.

Missouri and he celebrated by taking individual scoring honors – fourteen points. One other Missourian, Hal Halsted, guard, played his final game tonight. All of the other members of the Tiger squad will be available next year.

The game was not without its comedy spots. Early in the second half the official scorer lost a point which Capt. John Lobsiger scored when he hit a free throw after being fouled by Loren Florell. And so the official record stands. 54 points for Missouri instead of the 55 which every score book in the press box showed.

ONLY FOUR K. U. MEN ON COURT

Then, later in the contest, officials permitted play to be resumed after a time out with only four men playing for Kansas. Bob Allen, son of Dr. F. C. Allen, the K. U. coach, had left the game on personal fouls, and before his daddy got Wayne Nees into the struggle to replace him, Arch Watson, Tiger forward, had gathered in a free throw, and play was going ahead at a furious pace. Sideline whistles finally halted the battle long enough for Nees to get into the game.

Ralph Miller gave the Jayhawkers a 2-point lead with a long shot in the first thirty seconds of the game, but Blaine Currence's free throw and Bill Harvey's rebound shot less than thirty seconds later put Missouri in front 3 to 2.

Howard Engleman knotted the count with a free throw, but Captain Lobsiger sent Missouri in front again with a field goal from long range. Missouri led then, 5 to 3, with a minute and twenty seconds of the game gone, and Missouri led from then on.

ONCE LED BY 19 POINTS

Kansas points came at intervals of about five minutes during the first half while Keirsey, Clay Cooper and Halsted pounded the basket for goal after goal from the field and Haskel Tison contributed four successive free throws for a lead that reached nineteen points at one time, and which stood 29 to 11 at the intermission.

The second half was pretty much a repetition of the first, save that the Jayhawkers began to find the basket with occasional long shots by Lyman Corlis and Allen, who between them gathered in thirteen of the nineteen points which Kansas scored in the second half. The Tigers pushed their fast break relentlessly, with Harvey taking the scoring lead for the Bengals.

In the last five minutes, the Kansans, who had spurned defensive tactics in the back court earlier in the game, went out after the ball, but the Missouri margin was too big then for any change in offense or defense to make any difference.

1940

VICTORY TO K.U.

MISSOURI IS DEFEATED IN CRUCIAL BIG SIX CONFERENCE BATTLE, 42 TO 40

SHOT BY EBLING WINS GAME

Decisive Point Comes From the Free Throw Line Near Finish of Battle

RALPH MILLER AND HAROLD ENGLEMAN SHARE SCORING HONORS, EACH WITH 10 POINTS

LOBSIGER PACES TIGERS

TRIUMPH BOOSTS KANSAS INTO FIRST PLACE, WITH ONLY SOONERS ON SCHEDULE

✳

The Kansas Jayhawks didn't take kindly to Missouri taking away their conference championship in 1939, and the Jayhawks returned to familiar surroundings at the top of the Big Six in 1940. After defeating the Oklahoma Sooners in a conference playoff, the Jayhawks went to the NCAA tournament—the second year of the tournament's history —where they were national runners-up.

This was not an easy victory for Kansas. Don Ebling broke a 40-40 tie with a free throw with four and half minutes remaining. Kansas held the ball for the final two minutes, and Dick Harp's free throw with no time on the clock provided the final margin.

The Jayhawks outscored the Tigers 10-4 from the line, to make up for a two-basket edge for the Tigers from the field.

Here's one other note of interest from this game story: two of Kansas' stars that night later went on to long, successful coaching careers. Dick Harp, who later succeeded Dr. Allen as Kansas coach, was the star of the game, according the writer of the Times story. And Ralph Miller, who went on to a very successful coaching career at Oregon State University, was one of two leading scorers.

RIVALS!
MU VS. KU

KU: 42
MU: 40

BASKETBALL
MARCH 1, 1940

Dick Harp, who later succeeded his coach, Dr. Forrest "Phog" Allen as KU's head coach, was a star on the 1940 team.

Lawrence, Kan., March 1

"Rock Chalk, Jayhawk," rolled off Mt. Oread and down the Kaw valley as an inspired squad of Kansas university basketeers outlasted the University of Missouri Tigers to win an important Big Six conference game here tonight, 42 to 40.

The victory, coming amidst the din provided by approximately 4,300 screaming spectators, moved Kansas to the top spot in the standings with eight victories in nine starts and shoved the Tigers into second place with the Oklahoma Sooners, the only remaining conference opponent on the Jayhawk schedule.

The outcome of that K. U.-Oklahoma game to be played in

University of Kansas Arch

Hoch Auditorium looked more like a church than a basketball arena, but visitors found it to be an unholy place to play the Jayhawks.

The 1940 runner-up trophy

University of Kansas Archives

Norman March 8 either will slice the title into three parts with Oklahoma, Missouri and Kansas sharing alike or will give Coach Phog Allen's athletes undisputed possession.

A FREE THROW DECIDES IT

A free throw by Forward Don Ebling with four and one-half minutes remaining gave Kansas the victory tonight and Dick Harp converted another charity shot after the gun had sounded as an anti-climax to a tingling final five minutes of play which saw Kansas hang on to the ball for the last two minutes.

Kansas actually won the contest from the free throw line for Missouri outscored the Jayhawkers from the field 18 to 16. But Kansas converted ten times from the free throw line as Missouri committed eighteen fouls. Only seven fouls were charged against K. U. and of these free chances Missouri took advantage only four times.

It was the twentieth consecutive victory for Kansas on the Hoch auditorium floor in a dramatic setting sprinkled with the thrills provided by both good and bad play, spectacular shots and rough action.

Both teams traded punch for punch throughout the first half with Missouri landing the last blow to lead, 25 to 24 at the rest period. Ahead 12 to 11 after ten minutes, the Jayhawkers stretched their advantage to 20 to 11 as the Missouri machine started missing when Coach George Edwards inserted substitutes. The Tigers after weathering a cold streak, started finding the range with four minutes left and bombarded the netting in a rally which gave them a 1-point lead at the intermission.

SCORING HONORS TO LOBSIGER

Capt. John Lobsiger took scoring honors with six field goals for twelve points

RIVALS!
MU VS. KU

KU:42
MU:40

BASKETBALL
MARCH 1, 1940

The 1940 Jayhawks fell one game short of the goal, but they still had a great season.

with Ralph Miller and Harold Engleman, Kansas forwards, next in line with ten points each.

The individual star of the game was common knowledge as the crowd pushed its way out of the auditorium for the name of Dick Harp, Kansas guard, became a household word early in the fray. The former Rosedale high school player blocked shots, recovered rebounds, covered the tall Missouri centers – Blaine Currence and Haskell Tison – and played the entire forty minutes without rest.

Coach Allen turned on the power valve at the start of the second half and his usually deliberate offensive tactics were transformed into scorching fast-breaking thrusts which gave K. U. a 40 to 33 lead with eleven minutes gone. Currence and Clay Cooper scored for Missouri to provide the only scoring for the next four minutes with the former deadlocking the count at 40-all with five minutes to play.

PASS UP FREE SHOTS

From that point there are numerous versions as to what happened. The official scorer's book testifies to the fact that Ebling cashed his game winning free throw after being fouled by Mills and that both Bobby Allen and Engleman missed charity shots when the officials whistled down Cooper and Lobsiger for roughness.

With a 1-point lead and two minutes to play, Kansas elected to keep the ball and three times Allen chose the out-of-bounds play instead of taking free throws when Currence, Harvey and Cooper fouled in desperate attempts to gain possession. Currence committed his fourth foul of the game in the form of a hard tackle around Harp's waist as the gun sounded and the Kansas guard converted his gift shot as the spectators jammed the floor.

K. U. IN OVERTIME

BIG SIX BASKETBALL GAME IS LOST BY MISSOURI IN COLUMBIA, 44 TO 47

LONG SHOTS DECIDE IT

KISSELL AND BUESCHER CONNECT FROM FAR OUT IN COURT IN EXTRA PERIOD

THE VICTORIES TO NINE

CHAMPION JAYHAWKS KEEP RECORDCLEAN IN CONFERENCE CAGE RACE

Overtimes are not uncommon in the Kansas-Missouri rivalry. No one who has followed the series in recent years can forget the double-overtime thriller in Columbia in 1997. The 1943 contest was no less thrilling, but not because of the high-scoring nature of latter years.

The teams traded leads in the first half, then Missouri stormed to a seven-point advantage in the second half. Kansas then went on a 10-1 run to claim a two-point edge. Missouri tied it, then Kansas grabbed two more two-point leads only to see Missouri tie it up. The final tie knotted the game at 43-all at the end of regulation.

The Jayhawks hit the only two field goals in the overtime and Missouri only managed a lone free throw.

The Jayhawks claimed their fourth straight conference title with the victory.

Here's how it appeared in the March 3, 1943, *Times*:

(BY THE *STAR'S* OWN SERVICE.)

Columbia, Mo., March 2

A pair of long looping shots by John Buescher and Max Kissell in an overtime period kept the University of Kansas' slate clean in the Big Six conference and gave the Jayhawkers victory, 47 to 44, over the University of Missouri here tonight.

The Tigers had dogged the Kansas champions through the first half, trailed them by only two points at the intermission, and then forged into a lead early in the second period to set the pace through three-quarters of that stanza. Then the two teams pounded into a

KU:47
MU:44

RIVALS!
MU VS. KU

BASKETBALL
MARCH 2, 1943

slam-bang final five minutes of the regularly allotted time to wind up all even, 43 to 43.

KISSELL AND BUESCHER BREAK IT UP

First Kissell, and then Buescher, pitching from far out in the court, scored 2-pointers in the first three minutes of the overtime and then the Jayhawkers went into successful keep-away, with a free throw by Thornton Jenkins Missouri's only contribution to the extra period scoring.

Despite the fact the Tigers paced the Kansans through three-fourths of the second period, the Missourians had to come from behind to tie the count and force the battle into an extra five minutes. It was a shot by Capt. Earl Stark from outside the free-throw circle that did the trick with fewer than forty-five seconds of the second half remaining.

Kansas forged ahead at near the end of the nip-and-tuck first half with an even more spectacular trade of long shots. With fifteen seconds of the period remaining, Stark of Missouri connected from outside the free-throw circle to knot the count at twenty, but Buescher, from about the center of the court, heaved one of his loopers from almost off the floor to bring the score 22 to 20 in favor of K. U. with fewer than ten seconds of the half left to play.

MISSOURI IN LEAD, 36 TO 29

Ed Matheny scored for the Tigers in the first minute of the second half, and Jim Austin led an almost single-handed Missouri attack for the next six minutes. Thornton Jenkins joined the scoring, and the Tigers advanced to a 7-

Dr. Allen with three of his stars: Charlie Black, Ray Evans and John Buescher.

point lead, 36 to 29, which was the widest margin either team ever achieved in the hectic game.

Otto Schnellbacher, Buescher and Kissell launched a Kansas rally then, and in seven minutes the Kansans had forged ahead, 39 to 37. Jenkins hit to tie the count at 39, and when Schnellbacher scored again Jenkins tallied once more for a 41-all deadlock. Free throws by Schnellbacher and Buescher and Stark's last-minute goal from the field produced the third consecutive tie at 43 to push the game into its extra minutes.

The first half was even tighter than the second. The Jayhawkers shot ahead

at the start, with a free throw by Harold McSpadden and a goal by Ray Evans, but Matheny and Austin equaled that for a 3-3 tie, and the score was tied five times after that, in the first half, with a momentary K. U. lead of four points, the widest margin of the period.

GAME DECIDED ON FREE THROWS

The overtime goals by Buescher and Kissell brought the deciding points, but Kansas really won on free throws, for the two teams broke even on field goals with 18 each.

CHAPTER 4
Moving On Campus

1946

SPORTING COMMENT

TWO PLAYS WILL LINGER IN THE MEMORY OF KANSAS-MISSOURI FOOTBALL FANS.... THE FIRST SELL-OUT CROWD IN THE FIFTY-FIVE YEARS OF THE SERIES....A LOT OF UNBELIEVABLE THINGS, BUT THEY HAPPENED

✳

After playing the series in Kansas City and on other neutral sites for most of the first 55 years of the rivalry, the schools saw the series move to campus sites for good in 1946. The first such contest took place in Columbia, where the "Jayhawkers" edged the Tigers 20-19 to complete the season 7-2-1. The only losses came at Tulsa and at home against Nebraska. Missouri finished 5-4-1.

Kansas looked to be in trouble in the first half, but some "unbelievable" plays helped them come from behind. On the first play of the second quarter, Ray Evans completed a 63-yard touchdown pass to Marvin Small.

The ball sailed 40 yards in the air, with Small running the final 23. That gave Kansas a 7-6 lead.

Then, on the final play of the quarter, Evans ran 54 yards for another go-ahead touchdown. The conversion attempt was no good, but the Jayhawks still led 13-12 at the half. Each team scored one touchdown in the second half, and the Jayhawks prevailed.

Here's how it appeared in the November 29, 1946, *Star:*
BY C. E. McBRIDE
(THE *STAR'S* SPORTS EDITOR)

Columbia, MO., Nov. 29

The first play of the second quarter of yesterday's 20 to 19 Kansas triumph over Missouri and the last play of that quarter.

Long will those two plays linger in the memories of the only sellout crowd in the fifty-five years of the annual game between the Jayhawkers and Tigers.

The first play and the last play of the second period of the fifty-fifth game between Missouri and Kansas. If you saw the game or listened to any of the several radio reports you know all about them.

"Story book plays" was the consensus in the post-game buzzing bees here last night and again this morning.

THEY WERE 'UNBELIEVABLE' PLAYS

"Unbelievable plays," commented Paul Hamilton, Kansas City police commissioner and a former Missouri football captain. "Absolutely unbelievable."

Unbelievable, of course, because of their setting and the manner of their execution. Ray Evans was the hero of both plays. Or the villain, according to the lights in which you viewed the game and continue to replay it.

Both plays have been duly recorded, of course, but in the light of the marvelings that are a subsequent part of every great game they would seem to bear repeating.

The fact that these Frank Merriwell plays marked the beginning and the end of one quarter of the game would seem to make them all the more remarkable.

K. U.'s Baker had just found a hole outside Missouri's right tackle and had slithered through for ten yards and a first down on the 37 when the gun ended the first quarter. The teams changed goals. Kansas had the ball on its own 37 and a first down, but chances are no one in the stadium-packed crowd and we might add, no one on the playing field, gave a thought to a possible score from that point.

University of Missouri Archives

THE LONG PASS FROM EVANS TO SMALL

Yet, that's when and from where the first play of the second quarter started. You know about the play. Evans threw a long-range pass to Marvin Small who had succeeded in getting behind the Tiger defender of that territory. The pass was forty yards and Small ran the remaining distance to cover sixty-three yards on the play.

"At that stage Missouri had the game won, you might say," said a football man in commenting on the sudden twist. "Not won, of course, but Missouri had outplayed the Kansans and held a 6 to 0 lead so you might say the Tigers had the game won. It was the same way with the last play of the quarter. Again Missouri apparently had the game sewed up, but once again came the unbelievable."

So we jump to that final play of the second quarter. Again Missouri has the game won. If for the moment you wish to look at it that way. Anyway you look at it Missouri was leading 12 to 7 and there were only seven seconds left in the half. That meant that the Tigers would carry a 12 to 7 lead to the dressing quarters. Kansas would have to come from behind in the second half.

FACE TASK OF COMING FROM BEHIND

But the game wasn't to be written that way. Instead, Missouri was destined to go to the locker room in arrears, facing the task of coming from behind in the second period.

You wouldn't believe it if you hadn't seen it or heard it over the air. Even then it was almost unbelievable.

Kansas had the ball on its own 46-yard line. Fifty-four yards away from pay dirt and only one play left. We have no way of computing the odds as to the possibility of a play such as happened, but we know those odds would be prohibitive. It couldn't be in the cards for a touchdown play on the last play of the half, but you know what happened.

It was the Ray Evans solo flight that started to one sideline, went to the other and over the goal line.

Unbelievable. Yes, positively, but it happened. Time ran out as Evans swifted his way down field and the half was over with the place kick attempt.

THY WERE DOOMED BUT DIDN'T KNOW

Instead of going to their dressing room, trailing a 7 to 12 score, the Jayhawkers carried with them a 13 to 12 lead that augured the finish by a similar margin, although no one dreamed it then.

Unbelievable plays starting and ending a quarter.

Yet it had been that way with Kansas through an unbelievable season.

Unbelievable. Well, maybe, but not when the 1946 Jayhawkers and Ray Evans are concerned.

GRIFFITH A STAR

LEE'S SUMMIT PLAYER WHO SCORED WINNING TOUCHDOWN HAS GREAT BIG SIX FUTURE

CAN SEE THE FAUROT SIDE

SOME 40,000 FANS UNDERSTAND NOW WHY MISSOURI COACH WANTED THE FINE FULLBACK

PRAISE FROM A TIGER

HI SIMMONS, CHIEF SCOUT, CALLS JAYHAWKS THE MOST VERSATILE TEAM HE HAS SEEN

Things were starting to heat up when Kansas faced Missouri in Lawrence in 1947. Besides the intense rivalry between the two states, two excellent teams met on the football field that Saturday.

The Jayhawks came into the game ranked 17th in the nation. All Kansas had to do was win the game to advance to its first bowl game in history, the 1948 Orange Bowl. Missouri had been to four bowl games in its history, including the Cotton Bowl following the 1945 season.

Bill Mayer, the longtime sports editor of the *Lawrence Journal-World,* was a student at KU at the time. He notes that the 40,000 who watched the game (with a seating capacity of 38,000) was the largest crowd ever to watch a Big 6 football game in person.

Tom Hedrick, who later went on to be the Voice of the Jayhawks for 17 years, was a 10-year-old lad who was able to walk the sidelines with his uncle. He recalls the winning touchdown.

"There was a minute left when KU lined up on the 1-yard-line. If they score, they go to the Orange Bowl," he said. "Forrest Griffith ran through a hole you could drive a truck through. I may live to be 100, but I will always be able to see that like it was yesterday."

KU won the game, 20-14, with Griffith's late touchdown. They defeated Arizona the next week (one of the few seasons in which the KU-MU game didn't conclude the season) and finished the regular season 8-0-2. They went on to play 10th ranked Georgia Tech on January 1, 1948 (a 20-14 loss).

Here's how it appeared in the November 23, 1947, *Star:*

By C. E. McBride
(THE STAR'S SPORTS EDITOR)

Lawrence, Kas., Nov. 22

Now more than 40,000 football fanatics know why Don Faurot, head master of gridology at the University of Missouri, tried so valiantly to obtain the ball running services of Forrest Griffith, the Lee's Summit lad who this cold, gray afternoon plunged across the goal line to beat the Tigers in a hard fought and brilliant 20 to 14 Kansas victory.

The capacity crowd in the Memorial stadium here saw the Griffith boy turn defeat into victory with only a minute left to play. They saw him do it in four successive stabs at a Missouri defense that was superb in the shadows of its goal line and didn't surrender until the final plunge.

The beautifully-driving Kansas team started the winning drive on its own 6-yard line where it had held the surging Tigers for downs. That was the turn of the tide. As the offensive drove steadily toward Missouri terrain, it was a 26-yard gain on a forward pass from Ray Evans to Otto Schnellbacher that arranged the scenery for the Griffith plunges.

FOUR HARD PLUNGES

It was K. U.'s ball on the Missouri 8-yard line, and so begrudging was the Tiger defense that Griffith still was a yard away from pay soil at the end of his third straight stab at the Tiger line. Then on the fourth and final down of the sequence he found a hole and sped through, standing up. Then and there the crowd had license to sympathize with Don Faurot on losing that lad and to congratulate George Sauer on obtaining him. He ought to be quite a footballster next year.

The game fought before the biggest crowd in the history of Big Six conference play, was a thrilling game to watch, filled with stern defensive stands and studded with gems of offense. Kansas was the better team, the smoother, the more versatile. It never ran up the white flag even toward the finish when the Tigers were carrying the play deep toward the Jayhawker goal. And then when they stopped that charge, the Kansans had the courage and the stuff to travel ninety-four yards without surrendering the ball.

"It's the best team I've seen this year, a beautiful team," said Hi Simmons, the chief Missouri scout, as he visited in the press box after the game. "I've seen some of the best teams this season – Duke, Georgia Tech – but this Kansas team that beat us today comes close to being the best. It's smooth, with a hard, smart line and fast backs, and it is versatile. Maybe that's the greatest asset of the team. It's versatile. When the defense spreads, it can run; when the defense moves up, it can pass."

Forrest Griffith strapped the Jayhawks on his back and carried them past MU.

RIVALS!
MU VS. KU

KU:20
MU:14

FOOTBALL
NOVEMBER 22, 1947

EVANS IS A POWER

The game had the customers on their feet many times. Ray Evans, as always, played well. Defensively, he was a rugged power. Without Evans as a last-stand tackler, the Jayhawkers might have lost the game by a touchdown or possibly two. Once when it looked as if Kansas City's Nick Carras was through the Kansas secondary, Evans charged in to bust him down.

Carras, by the way, probably was the outstanding offensive star of the Missouri team that the Jayhawkers found very hard to trample – even with its backfield star, Loyd Brinkman, and its stellar end, Mel Sheehan, on the sidelines with injuries. Several times Carras sped through quick openings in the Kansas line, made by his forwards, or sliced outside tackle for spectacular gains that found the Kansas secondaries, quite frequently Evans, coming in to stop him.

The Kansas defense did not mass along the scrimmage line to stop the Missouri ground game as consistently as did the Oklahomans, but at times they punched tacklers along the line to meet the Tiger runner almost as he took the handoff.

Harold Entsminger, the Missouri quarterback and a master of the T-formation's speedy handoffs, may well be proud of the game he played, although he had plenty of help.

The Tigers showed their stout hearts by coming back after the Jayhawkers had moved to the game's first touchdown, with Missouri having the ball only once and then so deep that Bill Day had to punt from his end zone.

TEAMS EVENLY MATCHED

Probably the detail of the scrimmage plays tells the story of the closeness of the competition as well as any factor which one's fancy might cite. In the first quarter, after a slow start, Missouri pulled up on the Kansans, to compile eighteen plays from scrimmage to K. U.'s nineteen. In the second quarter Missouri got the one play deficit back, running twenty to K. U.'s nineteen. That gave each team a total of thirty-eight plays from snapback in the first thirty minutes.

The Jayhawks gained on the Tigers in the last thirty minutes, their final touchdown drive from their own goal line shadows giving them a 6-play edge in the last half. The third quarter, scoreless, saw the Tigers running seventeen plays from scrimmage, the Jayhawkers eighteen. Missouri fell behind in the fourth quarter as the Kansans marched steadily to their victory. The Tigers held the ball from scrimmage plays only seventeen times in this stanza. Kansas ran off nineteen plays. That made thirty-one for Missouri in the last thirty minutes, thirty-seven for Kansas.

The Jayhawkers totaled seventy-five plays in the hour of rugged battling, the Tigers sixty-nine and the game was that close all the way.

The 1947 KU football yearbook
University of Kansas Archives

THE CAPACITY CROWD IN THE MEMORIAL STADIUM HERE SAW THE GRIFFITH BOY TURN DEFEAT INTO VICTORY WITH ONLY A MINUTE LEFT TO PLAY. THEY SAW HIM DO IT IN FOUR SUCCESSIVE STABS AT A MISSOURI DEFENSE THAT WAS SUPERB IN THE SHADOWS OF ITS GOAL LINE AND DIDN'T SURRENDER UNTIL THE FINAL PLUNGE.

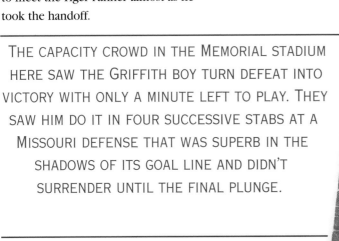

SPORTING COMMENT

YESTERDAY WAS A BAD DAY ANYWAY YOU LOOK AT IT FOR MR. CONSENSUS, WHO HAS SKIPPED TOWN FOR THE TIME BEING...IT WAS THE MISSOURI LINE WHICH MADE THE DIFFERENCE AS THE TIGERS UPSET THE DOPE... A NEW YEAR'S GAME BID FOR MIKE MCCORMACK

The one thing both sides agree on was that it was cold.

The Thanksgiving Day game in Columbia in 1950 is remembered less for the events of the game than the conditions in which the game was played. Let's hear from some of the participants.

Don Fambrough, who played for the Jayhawks in 1946 and '47, served as an assistant for head coach J.V. Sikes in 1950. "We left Lawrence on Wednesday and it was pleasant. We spent the night in Moberly, Mo. A blizzard hit overnight and I woke up with snow on my bed," Fambrough said. "Since it was Thanksgiving Day, nothing was open and we couldn't buy any warm-weather gear.

"The MU equipment manager said he didn't care if we froze to death, he wasn't giving us anything. We had to park the bus on the track behind the bench and players sat on the bus when they weren't in the game."

Not so fast, if you listen to John Kadlec, a member of the 1950 Missouri squad and now the color analyst on the Missouri radio network. "We didn't have the right gear either, because the snow storm surprised us, too," he said. "We had to go to Park's Department Store to buy long underwear. We bought all they had."

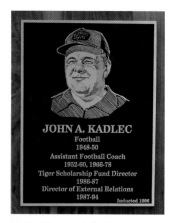

Hall of Famer John Kadlec

The favorites from Kansas fumbled six times in the game played in a wind-chill of near 10 degrees, and Missouri claimed a 20-6 victory.

Here's how it appeared in the November 24, 1950, *Star:*

By ERNEST MEHL
THE STAR'S SPORTS EDITOR

Columbia, MO, Nov 24

Who is this guy, Consensus, who picked the Kansas Jayhawks to beat the Missouri Tigers here yesterday? What's he look like? Where did he get his information?

A smug lot of Missourians would

like to know. These Missourians haven't thawed out yet but the process is a pleasurable one. And so far as the Tigers themselves are concerned, they can thaw out next weekend in Miami where they close their season.

It's a season which opened on a low note and closes on a high no matter what is the outcome of the Miami scrap. A victory over Kansas was the

prime objective and that's what the Bengals achieved.

Such a triumph has a dulling effect on the memory. Who cares what happened against Clemson and Southern Methodist or other uninteresting and criticism-provoking chapters along the way?

Came the big game and the payoff and there were the Tigers kicking the

RIVALS!
MU VS. KU

MU:20
KU:6

FOOTBALL
NOVEMBER 24, 1950

dope bucket around with a savage boot.

Yeah, just who is this guy Consensus? How did he happen to pick Kansas in the first place? What logic did he use for a basis of such a selection?

Mr. Consensus can't be located. He's completely disappeared and doesn't intend to show up until next year, by which time he hopes all this will have been forgotten. He is a craven character at the moment and would rather forget all about this 20 to 6 triumph of the Tigers, their superior line play, their commendable alertness.

Good-bye, Mr. Consensus. You made a fool of yourself, didn't you? Never will learn, will you?

THE JAYHAWKS' TURN TO FUMBLE

Last year at Lawrence the Tigers were the ones who made the fumbles although they still managed to win. Yesterday the Jayhawkers were the victims of loose ball-handling and the Jayhawker supporters will contend, perhaps that but for these errors they might have roped one or two more touchdowns.

The fact is true that in the first quarter and for part of the second, the Tigers largely were confined to their own half of the field, almost constantly in danger. The fact also is true that whenever the Kansans had to be stopped by other means than the recovery of a fumble Missouri managed the means.

The blue-nosed and chap-lipped spectators waited with mingled feelings for the time when Charlie Hoag or Wade Stinson would break loose with the sort of runs they had made against all other opposition this season. But their mates didn't supply them with much blocking. Their mates weren't tackling well in contrast to the Tigers.

> MR. CONSENSUS CAN'T BE LOCATED. HE'S COMPLETELY DISAPPEARED AND DOESN'T INTEND TO SHOW UP UNTIL NEXT YEAR, BY WHICH TIME HE HOPES ALL THIS WILL HAVE BEEN FORGOTTEN. HE IS A CRAVEN CHARACTER AT THE MOMENT AND WOULD RATHER FORGET ALL ABOUT THIS 20 TO 6 TRIUMPH OF THE TIGERS, THEIR SUPERIOR LINE PLAY, THEIR COMMENDABLE ALERTNESS.

Kansas coaches may search for the reason or they may know it. Perhaps the Jayhawkers didn't take this game seriously enough, maybe the Tigers were in the better mental fettle.

Whatever it was you can put it down, this victory that is, as the result of unlooked for fine play on the part of a Tiger line. You could name a half dozen or more Missouri forwards who exceeded their past season's efforts.

That was the real reason why a team, picked as the underdog by at least seven points, and in some quarters fourteen, scored a decisive victory.

John Kadlec has been part of the MU program since the 1940's.

MISSOURI 20, KANSAS 19

WIN IN FRENZIED FINISH

Interception Deep in K. U. Territory Sets Up Winning Touchdown in Fourth Quarter As Tigers Take Second Place in Big Seven

BIDS ARE HALTED

Fessler Knocks Bogue Loose From Touchdown Pass With Only 35 Seconds Left.

FIELD GOAL ATTEMPT FAILS

With Fourteen Seconds Remaining Reich Tries Boot but It Is Short of Mark

MISSOURI HOLDS A 14-6 LEAD AT HALF BUT LOSES IT IN THIRD – HOAG, REICH INJURED

✳

It's been a characteristic of the Kansas-Missouri rivalry for its entirety. When one team has a clear advantage in talent and is the heavy favorite heading in, the other team usually rises up and makes it a tight contest if not an upset.

This was the case in 1952, when Kansas came into the season-ender at 7-2 and still with a shot to tie for the conference title. Missouri, meanwhile, was 4-5 with only the hope of a .500 season. Kansas clearly had the advantage in talent, especially in the backfield where Charlie Hoag toted the ball for the Jayhawks.

But Hoag was injured on his first carry and missed the rest of the game. His back-up, Gil Reich, was injured with four minutes left in the second quarter. Missouri managed to keep the game close, trailing only 19-14 heading into the fourth quarter.

That's when the Missouri defense stepped up, picking off a Jerry Robertson pass deep in KU territory. Four plays later, Tony Scardino plunged over from the 1 and the Tigers were up 20-19. Kansas had two other chances to score, but an interception in the end zone with less than three minutes left, and a missed field goal in the final minute snatched victory from the Jayhawks.

MU: 20
KU: 19

RIVALS!
MU VS. KU

FOOTBALL
NOVEMBER 22, 1952

Here's how it appeared in the November 23, 1952, *Star:*

By Bob Busby.
(A Member of The *Star's* Sports Staff)

Columbia, Mo., Nov. 22

Missouri's Tigers, the so-called Cinderella Kids of Big Seven football, today finished like alert champions, upsetting the Kansas Jayhawkers, 20 to 19, on a fourth quarter pass interception and a rugged defensive stand.

The victory, which gave Missouri uncontested claim to second place and dumped Kansas into a fourth-place tie with Colorado, followed the thrilling pattern of the series. It was a breathless fourth quarter and a photo-finish in the waning minutes.

The lid really blew off midway in the final period, when Missouri, trailing 14 to 19, intercepted a Jerry Robertson pass. The Jayhawk quarterback, with the ball on the K. U. 13, cocked his arm and threw. Almost before it reached the line of scrimmage, Jack Hurley, an end, deflected the ball and latched onto it. As he was being downed he lateralled back to Bob Bauman who was nailed on the K. U. 13.

TIGERS ARE UNDAUNTED

A holding penalty set the Tigers back to the 24, but Tony Scardino passed for twelve yards to Jim Jennings and nine more to Jim Hook. With the ball on the 1, Scardino couldn't find Nick Carras for the handoff so the tiny Tiger signal-caller kept it and neatly slid over for his first touchdown of the season. Paul Fuchs missed his first kick of the day, but Mizzou was in front, 20 to 19, with 6:40 to play.

Kansas eying the clock, began a drive from its own 31, that carried, largely on Robertson's passes to the M. U. 45 for a first down. Then Robertson uncorked a home-run pitch aimed for Paul Leoni and Harold Thomeczek intercepted for Missouri on the Tiger 4. The Hawks were stalled again and as M. U. took over there was 2:35 left.

The Tigers could pickup only two yards and Bill Fessler was called on to punt on third down. It went high, bounced around and dead on the M. U. 35. Less than a minute and a half remained and the crowd of 26,000 arose and began a roaring chorus.

Kansas naturally took to the air. Robertson beaded one to Bob Brandberry good to the 21. Then another from Robertson to Brandberry, down to the 16. On each completion K. U. called time, thus stretching out the drama.

FESSLER IS INJURED

Finally, with thirty-five seconds left, Robertson arched one to Bogue in the end zone, who took it on his chest, but a jarring, last-ditch tackle by Fessler, playing his first defense of the year, knocked Bogue loose from the ball. That was a big one for the Tigers. Fessler was injured and removed on the play.

There were fourteen seconds left when Kansas elected to try a field goal with the ball held on the 22. Gil Reich, who retired from the game with a broken finger on his right hand, tried the boot.

President and Mrs. Truman enjoyed the football game in Columbia.

University of Missouri Archives

It was short and to the left.

That was it, nine seconds left and Scardino ran one sneak before the victory bedlam erupted.

This action-packed final six minutes overshadowed what had taken place before, but those earlier moments had their thrills. Missouri approached the game with great hustle on both offense and defense while Kansas sputtered too often and suffered from loss of key personnel.

Charlie Hoag, K. U. senior offensive star, fumbled the ball and was injured on his first carry, the second offensive play of the game, and never returned. Reich, who filled in well for him at the left side, saw his last action with four minutes left in the second quarter.

JAYHAWKS STRIKE FIRST

Kansas was first to score, pulling a 64-yard parade on thirteen plays with 4:10 elapsed in the second. It hinged on a 20-yard pass from Reich to Jerry Taylor and good running by Brandeberry. The pay off was a pass from Robertson to Reich, who lateralled off to Brandeberry, good for ten yards, Reich's attempted placement was blocked by Terry Roberts, who was all the way one of Missouri's finest defensive performers.

Thirty seconds later the Tigers were in front, 7-6. On the first play after the kick-off, Bill Rowekamp exploded between the Kansas right guard and tackle for an 82-yard touchdown run. He outdistanced his two pursuers, Bogue and Hal Cleavinger. It was Missouri's longest offensive thrust of the campaign.

Missouri then missed another good scoring opportunity when Brandeberry fumbled the kick-off, after being jarred

by Ray McMichael, and Don Rutter recovered for the Tigers on the K. U. 31. But the K. U. defense stiffened and the Tigers had to turn over the ball on the Hawk 22.

With a little more than a minute to play Missouri cashed in again, on a 60-yard 10-play offensive. Jim Hook's 19-yard run and his 16-yard pass to Jennings highlighted the drive. From the 2-yard line it was Nick Carras, finishing out his career, who smashed for the score and Fuchs added the point to make it 14-6.

DOMINATE THIRD PERIOD

Kansas came to life in the third to control the ball most of the way and pick up two more touchdowns.

After snuffing a 38-yard Tiger sortie, the Hawks took over on their own 22 and moved steadily. Robertson was the key as he ran from the so-called optional "keeper" play made famous by the split T formation which Coach Don Faurot of Missouri fathered.

Robertson, fittingly enough, sneaked over with the ball from the 1-yard line and Reich added the point to pull the Jayhawks to within one point, 13-14. A fraction more than ten minutes had gone by in the third.

A clipping penalty on Missouri that pushed the Tigers back to their 1 opened the gates again. Fessler's punt

was downed on the K. U. 48. Robertson tried two passes without connecting, but on the third he found Taylor, who had gotten behind Jerry Schoonmaker, on the 20 and the Kansas

---

IT WAS THE FINAL BLOW IN A SEASON WHICH STARTED IN HIGH EXPECTATION. THERE WAS TALK OF A CHAMPIONSHIP AND POSSIBLY A BOWL BID. BUT ALL THAT WAS EARLIER. THE SCYTHE OF INJURY CUT DOWN KANSAS HOPES AND REACHED ITS CULMINATION HERE TODAY.

---

end tucked it in and was off to score.

Charles Phillips deflected Reich's attempted kick that might have led to a tie game. There were only forty seconds left in the third when Kansas tallied. It was 19-14, Kansas.

EVEN ON FUMBLES

Loss of fumbles were about evenly distributed, K. U. losing three and Missouri two. Kansas let two passes be intercepted and Missouri permitted one to stray.

Even though it was a tasty Tiger victory, Don Faurot was the first to face realities. In a visit to the press box after his players had gone, he had this to say:

"We are happy to win, but it's no discredit to Kansas. The Jayhawks lost Hoag and Reich, and that hurt. If we had lost Rowekamp and Hook from our backfield, picture our position."

RIVALS!
MU VS. KU

MU:20
KU:19

FOOTBALL
NOVEMBER 22, 1952

FROM THE KANSAS CITY STAR, 1952

Sikes Praises Team, but Mounting Injury List Cost Jayhawks in Loss

BY ED GARICH
(A MEMBER OF THE *STAR'S* SPORTS STAFF)

Columbia, Mo., Nov. 22

Through the dull silence of defeat which hung heavily on the Kansas dressing room the voice of Jules Sikes was clearly audible.

"I'm proud of you boys, you really fought."

The words fell on ears which were stunned and not too attentive. It was so quiet you could hear every drop from the showers hit the cement floor. No voices were heard, just the sound of shoes hitting the floor heavily as the athletes undressed.

HIGH HOPES EARLIER

It was the final blow in a season which started in high expectation. There was talk of a championship and possibly a bowl bid. But all that was earlier. The scythe of injury cut down Kansas hopes and reached its culmination here today.

Out of action was Charlie Hoag after one play. Then Gil Reich went out in the early second half with a broken finger. Late in the game with Kansas fighting its heart out to pull even, Bob Brandeberry went out after catching a pass. Then Warren Woody was injured and pulled out.

That, of course, was the telling difference here today, although Sikes did not seek refuge in excuse.

"Missouri has a fine team and played a good game against us," Sikes said. And he went on to say that he was proud of his boys.

BOYS PLAED HARD

"They played as hard as they could right up to the last minute," he said. "You can't ask for anything more than that."

As the game ended the Kansans were knocking on the door. A pass was almost completed but dropped in the end zone. Then on the final play a field goal attempt failed.

That play was one of the two choices Sikes had. He had to go for a play which would take it all the way. Kansas was on the M. U. 16. It was either a home run pass or the field goal.

Sikes said the K. U. comeback in the last quarter was a tribute to his patched up team.

He called John Hurley's deflection of Jerry Robertson's pass attempt in the fourth quarter and the ensuing Missouri touchdown the turning point of the game.

"It was just one of those things," Sikes added. Hurley hit the pass as it left Robertson's hand, caught it, then lateralled to Bob Bauman who got to the K. U. 13. Tony Scardino hit two passes then went over on a sneak when a planned hand-off to Nick Carras missed connections. That, it turned out, was the ball game.

SPIRITS ARE LOW

The visitors to the Jayhawks dressing room, many of them fathers of team members, tried valiantly to lift those sagging spirits. But they, too, knew how many hopes lay buried on the sod outside.

They did their best. Most frequent of the comments was, "you boys played a good game."

But the answer of one player, in a barely audible voice, pretty much summed it up for the defeated Kansans.

"It just wasn't good enough."

A victory over Kansas is always cause for celebration.
University of Missouri Archives

SAFETY FELLS K. U., 15-13

CHUCK MEHRER, SENIOR TACKLE, SPILLS BOBBY ROBINSON IN END ZONE WITH 39 SECONDS LEFT TO GIVE MISSOURI HECTIC TRIUMPH IN DON FAUROT'S FINAL GAME AS COACH

WILD FINISH TO FRAY

GOAL POST COME DOWN BEFORE THE GAME IS OVER — TIGERS OVERCOME THEIR OWN MISTAKES TO GAIN STIRRING VICTORY

❋

There was no way the Missouri Tigers would let their legendary coach go out on a losing note, and a big defensive play made sure he didn't. Don Faurot was going to retire at the end of the 1956 season, and, as usual, the final game was against Kansas. That made the victory even more important.

While it was Missouri's goal to send Faurot out on a winning note, Kansas was the team that may have assured the result. The Jayhawks ran a double-reverse in their own end zone with less than a minute to play in a tie game. Missouri tackle Chuck Mehrer knifed through the line and tackled Bobby Robinson for a safety.

Missouri was going for the victory in more traditional fashion when Ken Clemensen's pass was intercepted in the end zone. KU got the ball on the 20, but lost 16 yards on a sack on the first play. The reverse on the next play helped Missouri overcome sure heartbreak.

The Tigers had tied the score with just over three minutes left on an 18-play drive, but missed the extra point. That set the stage for a late rally, more heartbreak and final elation.

University of Missouri Archives

Here's how it appeared in the December 2, 1956, *Star*:

BY BOB BUSBY
(A MEMBER OF THE *STAR'S* SPORTS STAFF.)

Columbia, Mo., Dec. 1.

Don Faurot's last game as Missouri football coach ended on a hectic, though victorious, note today with 39 seconds left on the clock.

The name of Chuck Mehrer, senior left tackle on the M. U. alternate unit, and a product of Kansas City Hogan high school, will be etched in Faurot's mind. Mehrer speared through to nail Bobby Robinson, Kansas halfback, in the end zone for a 2-point safety and a 15-13 triumph for the Tigers over the Jayhawks.

What started out as a listless, dull contest between the two rivals, who were meeting for the 65th time, finished as a wild, frantic affair. Some of the 28,000 home-coming fans became so overstimulated by the safety that they

RIVALS!

MU VS. KU

MU:15
KU:13

FOOTBALL
DECEMBER 1, 1956

After Chuck Mehrer's heroics, the Tigers carried Don Faurot off the field after winning the last game of his coaching career.

stormed the north goalpost and ripped it down.

FANS ARE ENTHUSIASTIC

Twenty-three seconds were left as the lumber went in all directions. It was the first time anyone could recall of post going before the game ended.

Missouri's victory came the hard way. The Tigers, in gaining third place in the Big Seven standings and squaring the series with K. U. at 29-29-7, had to overcome a string of mistakes, including two pass interceptions and two lost fumbles.

But Mizzou today had what it took to come from behind twice and give Faurot a career record over K. U. of 13 victories, four losses and two ties.

The clinching sequence came following a Kansas offensive that carried from the Jayhawk 25 to the K. U. 32.

On fourth down, and needing two yards, Homer Floyd tried to sweep Missouri's left flank only to be hauled down by Joe Wynn and Bill McKinney.

PASS GOES AWRY

Missouri took over, and on the first play Ken Clemensen tried a long aerial that was intercepted in the end zone by Wally Strauch, Jayhawk quarterback. Putting it in play on his 20, Strauch went back to pass and had to eat the ball for a 16-yard loss to the 4.

Then came Robinson's futile attempt to run and Mehrer's game-winning tackle.

With only 3:12 left in the ball game, Missouri had tied the score at 13-all after a 73-yard sortie that required 18 plays. And then came a heartbreak. Charlie Rash, a good point-kicker, got a low pass from center. The opportunity for a 1-point edge didn't have a chance to materialize.

It was a 14-yard pass from Dave Doane to end Larry Plumb that brought the deadlock.

Kansas broke into the scoring column first with 45 seconds left in the first half, climaxing an 11-play, 89-yard punch featuring the sharp running of Charlie McCue.

AN AERIAL CLICKS

Strauch passed 22 yards to McCue

U. 17. Glen St. Pierre made a great catch of a pass down the middle from Doane to make it first down by inches on the Jayhawk 13. Rash kicked the point to put Mizzou in front by 7-6.

Kansas countered by taking the kick-off and rolling 77 yards in 15 plays, the payoff being a 3-yard flip down the middle from Strauch to Jim Letcavits. Strauch's kick made it 13-7 with 10:20 left in the fourth period. The march was helped along by a 15-yard penalty against Missouri for roughing Strauch on a pass throw. It placed the ball on the Tiger 41.

TIGERS ARE TOUGH

Just as surely and as steadily Missouri took the kickoff that followed and rolled to the tying marker. The Doane to Plumb pass was one of the finest of the day. Doane was swarmed and looked helplessly lost, but he got it away. Then Plumb, just as badly

U. 42, steamed to the Tiger 11, there to expire as Floyd, on third down, was held to no gain and then Hank Kuhlmann reached in to deflect a pass from Strauch to Letcavits.

Strauch, in pitching 12 passes, completing two for touchdowns and 79 yards gained, wrested the aerial title from Missouri's Jimmy Hunter, leader most of the year. Strauch has completed 33 for 596 yards, Hunter 42 for 567.

James of M. U. snared two passes for 21 yards to win receiving honors. He has caught a total 30 for 362 yards.

HUNTER LEAVES GAME

Hunter, the Big Seven's all-star quarterback, had to leave the game with about two minutes to play in the second quarter. First report said he suffered a pinched nerve in his left arm.

McCue, playing the best game of his career, picked up 17 yards on 17 carries, and caught two passes for 28 yards. Kuhlmann was Missouri's top carrier with 59 yards on six attempts.

Kansas held a slight total offense edge at the half, but finished by outrushing the Jayhawks 263-297.

The game was played in sunny, 43-degree conditions, good for the spectators, but not altogether for the players. The frozen turf of the field thawed enough to make it slippery and the footing poor.

And in all the confusion toward the end, the man running the scoreboard credited the safety to Kansas. Howls corrected it to put a dizzy top on the whole affair.

MIZZOU TODAY HAD WHAT IT TOOK TO COME FROM BEHIND TWICE AND GIVE FAUROT A CAREER RECORD OVER K. U. OF 13 VICTORIES, FOUR LOSSES AND TWO TIES.

---

for the touchdown. Strauch's kick attempt went awry.

The Tigers went ahead with 2:15 remaining in the third as Doane slanted over from the 4 to cap a 14-play, 58-yard revival. Sonny Stringer, Charley James and Doane stayed on the ground to pick up their yardage.

The key play in the sequence came with fourth down and four on the K.

hemmed in, jumped up to make a good outfielder's grab of a high fly.

Both teams, their offenses sputtering, missed scoring chances in the first quarter. Missouri went from its 38 to the K. U. 3 to watch James fumble. The ball was recovered by Ervell Staab, Kansas guard, on the K. U. 8.

Kansas, after Wynn had fumbled and Paul Swoboda recovered on the K.

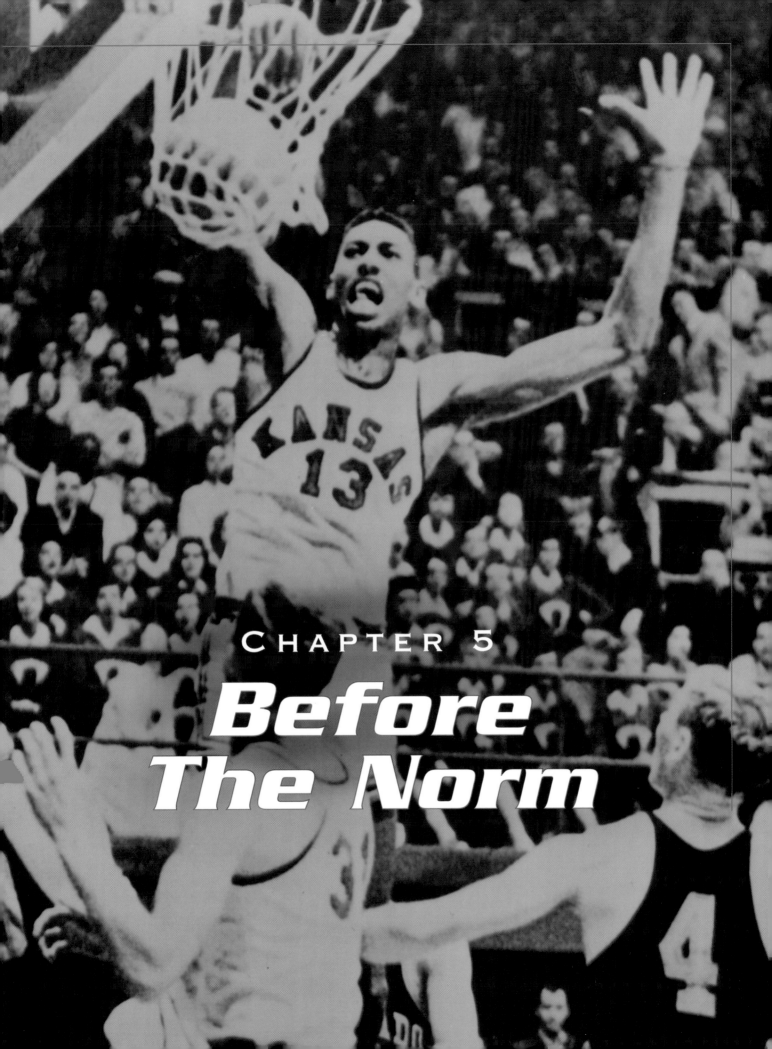

CHAPTER 5
Before The Norm

BULGING CROWD IN ARENA BEGINS UPROAR AFTER FOUL BY CLYDE LOVELLETTE.

One of the greatest examples of the rivalry between MU and KU occurred in 1951 in the pre-season Big Seven Basketball Christmas Tournament. A potentially volatile situation erupted between the two schools, then was dispelled when one of the coaches took control.

Kansas center Clyde Lovellette stepped on the stomach of Missouri guard Win Wilfong after a shot under the basket. A fight nearly broke out, but the referees were able to stop it, partly by ejecting Lovellette.

"Clyde stepped on Wilfong," recalls Max Falkenstein, who was broadcasting the game for Kansas. "Was it accidental? That's always been subject to debate. The Missouri players didn't think so, and neither did the fans."

Once the officials were able to resume the game, it went on without incident. But the fans still were hot. Several minutes after the game, despite repeated pleas on the public address system, the crowd was still ready to "get it on."

"Sparky Stalcup calmed them," Falkenstein said in his matter-of-fact style. Stalcup, the MU coach, grabbed the microphone and told the MU fans to stop whining. He said he believed that it was an accident. Just that quickly, things calmed down.

"Doc Allen said, 'If I ever doubted that Sparky was a friend, that proved that he was,'" said Bill Mayer, long-time sports editor of the Lawrence Journal-World.

Here's how it appeared in the December 30, 1951, Star:

FUSE IN LATE MINUTES

Tremendous Clamour Breaks Out When Big Center Steps On M. U. Guard.

It was a dramatic and uproarious conclusion last night to the most successful and spectacular Big Seven pre-season basketball tournament ever held.

The championship game between the University of Missouri and the University of Kansas went along smoothly and expertly until the last three minutes. Then an incident, which in a less spirited contest might have been considered trivial, resulted in a concerted chorus of booing, yelling and shouting rarely heard in the big Arena.

M. U. PLAYER FOULED

It all happened after Clyde Lovellette, K. U.'s star center, stepped on the stomach of Winfred Wilfong, Missouri guard. Lovellette attempted a shot, Wilfong bumped into him and fell to the floor. Lovellette

RIVALS!
MU VS. KU

KU:75
MU:65

BASKETBALL
DECEMBER 29, 1951

turned around, placed his right foot on Wilfong's mid-section and walked away.

The towering All-American immediately was ejected from the game. Missouri players swarmed around him and it appeared momentarily that a mass altercation might result.

But things quickly quieted down on the floor and play resumed. The crowd of 9,787 paying customers, however, did not quiet down. There were boos the remaining three minutes of the game – which K. U. won, 75 to 65.

Then came the time to award the championship trophy to the Jayhawks.

Bruce Drake, University of Oklahoma coach, was to present the championship emblem, a huge gold basketball. He stepped onto the floor with the trophy. Meanwhile, Lovellette went from the Kansas bench to the Missouri bench, apparently to apologize to Wilfong.

SPARKY STALCUP INTERCEDES

But Wilbur (Sparky) Stalcup, the M. U. coach, greeted him instead. He shook hands with the big center.

"Let's forget all about it," Stalcup said. He gave Lovellette a friendly slap on the back.

The booing continued.

Reaves Peters, the executive secretary of the Big Seven, stepped to the microphone.

"I hope everyone here will remember where you are," he said to the crowd. Every person in the place was on his feet.

"This is America; not Russia," Peters continued.

That also was greeted with boos.

Then Drake tried to quiet the throng.

"In a basketball game like this," the Oklahoma coach said, "you are bound to have tensions…

"Please, please," he pleaded as the refrain of boos continued.

"I know no one regrets this any more than Clyde," Drake added.

"If you could be as close to this boy as I am now, you could see the tears streaming down his face."

The towering All-American immediately was ejected from the game. Missouri players swarmed around him and it appeared momentarily that a mass altercation might result. But things quickly quieted down on the floor and play resumed.

Wilbur "Sparky" Stalcup

Stalcup managed to calm the crowd and trun the boos to cheers.

Almost spontaneously then, the M. U. players swarmed to the Kansas bench and began shaking hands with the Jayhawk contestants. Wilfong and Lovellette ended up hugging each other. There were no fights and the booing seemed to cease as the players joked with one another.

Then Drake quoted a verse from the Bible.

LAUDS THE RIVALRY

Stalcup next went to the microphone. He said the rivalry between the University of Kansas and the University of Missouri always has been the finest.

"The University of Missouri enjoys this rivalry with the University of Kansas. Doc Allen is a great coach," Stalcup concluded. He was referring to Dr. Forrest C. Allen, the K. U. Coach.

Almost spontaneously then, the M. U. players swarmed to the Kansas bench and began shaking hands with the Jayhawk contestants. Wilfong and Lovellette ended up hugging each other. There were no fights and the booing seemed to cease as the players joked with one another.

Drake presented the trophy to Allen and the spectators cheered. The disturbance seemed to end abruptly.

Before the unfortunate incident on the court, all in the game had gone well. Kansas maintained a lead throughout the contest, but Missouri never gave up. In fact, Missouri played a better and closer game than many observers had expected.

PACK DOWNTOWN AREA

The downtown area, immediately after the game, was jammed with the spectators who poured from the big Auditorium. Many fraternity and sorority parties were in progress. It was one of the most active post-Christmas week ends in years.

On Twelfth street, between Baltimore avenue and Wyandotte street, some pedestrians got soaked with water. The practice of dropping bags filled with water from hotel windows was undertaken by a few overzealous celebrators. Streamers and confetti also were apparent.

Hotels have been filled to capacity. Persons dining out often experienced long periods of waiting before they could be seated in the jammed restaurants.

Merchants also have been doing a heavy volume of business with many shoppers going to stores to exchange Christmas presents and others cashing in store gift bonds.

Traffic, normally heavy at this time of year, has been even more congested in the evenings during the basketball tournament as thousands of fans, many from out of town, moved toward the Municipal Auditorium for each night's games.

K. U. WINS ON LATE GOAL

Kansas was on its way to a Big Seven Conference championship and an NCAA championship when the Jayhawks rolled into Columbia with an 11-0 record in January 1952. Nobody expected the Tigers to give them much of a contest. The main intrigue was whether there would be any retribution against Kansas center Clyde Lovellette.

Lovellette had been ejected from the teams' previous game in the Big Seven holiday tournament when he stepped on Missouri guard Win Wilfong late in the game.

But the Tigers overcame a 14-point half-time deficit and took a one-point lead when Wilfong sank a shot in the closing minutes. Lovellette missed a shot that would have reclaimed the lead and Mizzou tried to hold the ball. A traveling violation gave the ball back to Kansas. Dean Kelley hit the game-

winner with 30 seconds left, and Kansas improved to 12-0.

An interested spectator in the crowd was Shelbyville, Mo., high school senior Norm Stewart, who was in Columbia on his official visit.

Here's how it appeared in the January 13, 1952, Times:

Guard Dean Kelley's Long Shot From the Corner in Final 30 Seconds Sinks Missouri, 60 to 59

CAN'T HOLD BALL

Tigers Try to Play Keepaway, but Traveling Violaton Gives Jayhawks Possession

AHEAD ON WILFONG'S GOAL

The Freshman Star Dumps in Basket From the Side to Put Bengals Out in Front.

Clyde Lovellette Collects Twenty-Three Points Before Leaving the Game Late

BY J. P. HAMEL
(THE *STAR's* M. U. CORRESPONDENT)

Columbia, Mo., Jan 11.,

Dean Kelley, Kansas guard, dropped in a long shot from the far corner to give the Jayhawkers a 60-59 victory over Missouri and wipe away a gallant Tiger rally which had swept the Missourians into a 59-58 advantage over the unbeaten Jayhawkers with only three minutes to play.

It was a spectacular rally for the Missourians who were ice cold at the start, hitting only 20 percent of their shots in the first half and coming up to the inter-mission at the short end of a 33-19 score.

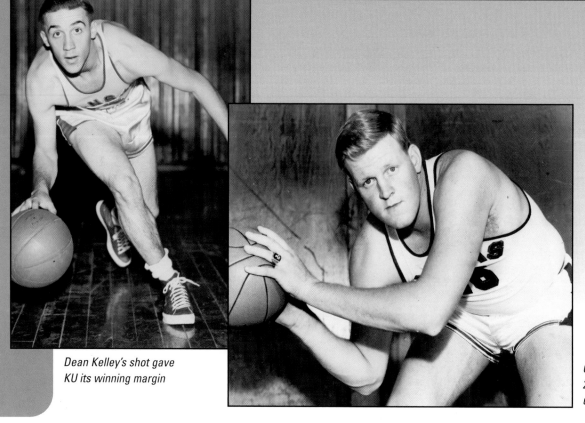

Dean Kelley's shot gave
KU its winning margin

Clyde Lovellette scored
23 points for the
unbeaten Jayhawks.

Freshman Art Helms and Veteran Bill Stauffer led the steady Missouri climb through the second stanza. The Tigers outscored the Jayhawkers, 21 to 15, in the third quarter, and 19 to 12, in the final frame.

TIGERS STAY CLOSE

As the game moved into its final five minutes, the Bengals several times pulled within three points of the Jayhawkers. Then it was two, then it was one, as Gene Landoldt scored from the field for Missouri with three and a half minutes to play.

Freshman Win Wilfong, with a basket from the far corner, produced the goal that put Missouri in front, 59 to 58, and the Tigers started playing keepaway.

Big Clyde Lovellette missed a shot that could have put the Jayhawkers ahead, and when Missouri took time with a minute and 45 seconds to play, Lovellette went to the bench, with John Keller replacing him.

The Tigers were playing keepaway,

and the Jayhawkers were battling desperately to break it up. A violation gave them the ball, and Kelley's long shot with thirty seconds to go decided the game.

LOVELLETTE IS TOP SCORER

Lovellette was the high scorer with twenty-three points, while Stauffer led the Missouri attack with seventeen. Each man played dogged defense against the other.

Missouri gave Lovellette a lot more cordial reception than some people

knocked Missouri's Win Wilfong down and stepped on him. Only a mild chorus of boos met Lovellette, and the Missouri crowd was generally better behaved than usual. Lovellette played all but one minute and forty-five seconds of the game.

The crowd – 5,800, which taxed the Missouri fieldhouse capacity – went wild in the final minutes when Missouri overcame its early 18-point deficit and momentarily pulled away.

Despite the victory, which kept his team at the top of the league and pulled

It was a spectacular rally for the Missourians who were ice cold at the start, hitting only 20 percent of their shots in the first half and coming up to the intermission at the short end of a 33-19 score.

expected, in view of the fact that he was bounced out of the Missouri-Kansas game in the Big Seven tournament at Kansas City three weeks ago after he

him a step closer to his goal of 700 college basketball victories, Dr. F. C. Allen, the Kansas coach, was anything but gracious when the game was over.

RIVALS!
MU VS. KU

KU:60
MU:59

BASKETBALL
JANUARY 12, 1952

He was unhappy because Chauncey Simpson, a Missouri football coach who was keeping time, ruled that a Kansas field goal at the end of the first half did not count because it was shot after time ran out.

box for some unprintable comments about Simpson.

The Tigers, who hit only 20 percent of their shots in the first half, were hot enough to run their game average to 39 per cent, their best mark of the season.

just before the intermission and came out of the first half as the game's leading scorer, with five goals for ten points in the first twenty minutes.

Missouri gave Lovellette a lot more cordial reception than some people expected, in view of the fact that he was bounced out of the Missouri-Kansas game in the Big Seven tournament at Kansas City three weeks ago after he knocked Missouri's Win Wilfong down and stepped on him. Only a mild chorus of boos met Lovellette, and the Missouri crowd was generally better behaved than usual.

Allen first had a sharp exchange over the matter with Missouri's football coach, and then made his way to the press

Kansas hit 39 per cent.

Lovellette got away to a slow start, but he rallied with three quick baskets

University of Kansas Archives

The 1952 KU team claimed the NCAA Championship and brought home the James St. Clair trophy.

University of Kansas Archives

1955
K.U. STRING ENDS

Hoch Auditorium, the home of Kansas basketball from 1927 through 1955, was going to be replaced by Allen Fieldhouse, named after the Kansas coach who had been involved in the program since his collegiate playing career in 1905.

Though it was not the last game in the old auditorium, the game against Missouri in early January 1955 was a must-win for the Jayhawks.

Missouri had other ideas, however, and came away with a resounding 76-65 victory. It ended a 33-game home winning streak The Jayhawks would lose three more times at home that season, before concluding the year with a victory against Kansas State to close the building.

Norm Stewart, who was a junior on that Missouri squad, remembers what it was like playing in Hoch as a visitor.

"They conveniently placed the band behind the visiting team's bench," he said. "It was so loud in there that you couldn't hear your coaches. At halftime of one game, we came into the locker room and somebody had raised the windows. There was snow on the floor."

It didn't stop Missouri on this night.

Here's how it appeared in the January 5, 1955, Times:

Missouri Hands Jayhawks First Loss in Last 34 Games in Lawrence, 76-65

TIGERS ARE SMOOTH, COOL

Kansas Provides No Real Threat and Gets No Closer Than 8 Points in Second Half

Victory is First for Tigers Since 1948 in Hoch Auditorium - Reiter Hits 21

By Ed Garich
(A Member of The Star's Sports Staff)

Lawrence, Kas., Jan 4

Smooth as the glass off which they ricocheted their shots, Missouri's Tigers started their Big Seven season tonight by handing Kansas' mistake-haunted Jayhawks the first defeat the Kansans have suffered on their home floor in the last thirty-four games. The score was a convincing 76-65.

The last time Kansas lost at home was in the next to last game of the 1951 season when Oklahoma took home a 61-59 triumph on a late shot.

BEFORE THE NORM

90

KU:76
MU:65

RIVALS!
MU VS. KU

BASKETBALL
JANUARY 4, 1955

The Tigers, winners of the Big Seven pre-season tournament during the holidays, shook off an early Kansas threat and went ahead 23-22 with half the first period played. They flashed to a 10-point halftime lead and went on to win without strain.

NO REAL K. U. THREAT

Kansas threatened only mildly in the last half, creeping to within eight points several times, the last occasion when the Jayhawks got to a 60-68 position with a little more than four minutes to go.

But Missouri was too smooth, too clever, too experienced and too cool for the Kansans. Each time the Jayhawks threatened the Tigers pulled away again. Coach Sparky Stalcup used his reserves in the last minute or two.

Not since 1948 had Missouri won in hostile Hoch auditorium, and only four times since the formation of the old Big Six conference have the Tigers managed to win in the stronghold of the Jayhawks.

A crowd of about 3,500, close to capacity, watched the game.

Bob Reiter, Missouri's 6-9 center, led the scoring with twenty-one points. Med Park hit twenty, Redford Reichert twelve and Gary Filbert, ten. Only Norm Stewart and Lionel Smith of the Tiger starters failed to dent double figures.

Stewart, the Missouri scoring ace over the season with 17.9 average, was shadowed by Gene Elstun, Kansas sophomore from Shawnee Mission high school, and got only three buckets. Only one was a good shot, a tribute to Elstun's hawking.

EARLY KANSAS LEAD

Kansas, after missing its first two shots, roared into the lead, 6-4, after two minutes of play, then had the Tigers down 16-8 after five minutes. Dallas

Kansas threatened only mildly in the last half, creeping to within eight points several times, the last occasion when the Jayhawks got to a 60-68 position with a little more than four minutes to go. But Missouri was too smooth, too clever, too experienced and too cool for the Kansans. Each time the Jayhawks threatened the Tigers pulled away again. Coach Sparky Stalcup used his reserves in the last minute or two.

Dobbs, Elstun and Larry Davenport were the ringleaders.

Missouri, led by Park, climbed to a 17-18 spot, then got the lead at 23-22 with ten minutes gone. Kansas tied at 23-all but Reiter got two and Park one goal to pull the Missourians away. They threw dust in the Jayhawker eyes the rest of the way.

At halftime the lead was 41-31 and the gap stayed at eight to ten points until Missouri pulled away in the last five minutes. The widest Missouri lead was 76-61 with two minutes left.

Kansas outrebounded the Tigers, 51 to 42, despite the Missouri height superiority. Dobbs had eighteen points, Lew Johnson sixteen and Elstun thirteen in the losing cause.

Again as in the pre-season tournament, Missouri's offense opened up the Kansas defense for easy lay-ups. The Tigers converted 38 per cent of their field shots, Kansas 36.9.

Reiter led both clubs in rebounding with twenty-four. Elstun got fourteen for Kansas.

Missouri won the last game between the two schools in the band box called Hoch Auditorium.

University of Kansas Archives

TIGER BALANCE RIPS KANSAS

Dr. Forrest C. "Phog" Allen had an arena named after him. The Kansas coach, who was retiring at the end of the 1956 season, was coaching in his "own" building. His Jayhawks won their first seven games in the new fieldhouse, and revenge was on their minds as the Missouri Tigers came to town.

The Tigers had ended a 33-game home winning streak the previous season and had started the Jayhawks on a skid that ended up giving them a season record of 11-10.

Missouri started quickly and opened up a 28-9 lead during the first half. Kansas finally got untracked and cut the halftime lead to 10, but never got closer than seven points in the second half.

Senior forward Norm Stewart was one of the scoring leaders for Missouri, which claimed its fourth win in the last five games against the Jayhawks.

"I had a teammate named Bill Ross, who had a big rivalry with Gene Elstun," Stewart said. "In that game, Gene accidentally hit Bill in the eye. Bill's father tried to get on the floor and our assistant coach grabbed him by the leg.

"Bill's first free throw was like one of my putts, about a foot short and a foot to the left."

Here's how it appeared in the February 7, 1956, Times:

This 4-inch Jayhawk was given to fans entering the fieldhouse before the first game.

University of Kansas Archives

All Five Missouri Starters Score in Double Figures to Hand Jayhawks Their First Defeat in Allen Field House, 85 to 78.

BIG EARLY LEAD STANDS UP

Bengals Shatter K. U. Zone and Roll Up 28-9 Margin in First Half

RIVALS!
MU VS. KU

KU:85
MU:78

BASKETBALL
FEBRUARY 6, 1956

BY BILL SIMS
(A MEMBER OF THE STAR'S STAFF)

Lawrence, Kas., Feb 6.

Missouri's Tigers, who seem to be making a habit of ending Kansas university winning streaks, handed the Jayhawks their first loss in Allen field house, 85 to 78, here tonight as all five Tiger starters scored in double figures.

The Tigers last year snapped the longest Jayhawker home winning streak in history at thirty-three games. Since the Kansans moved into their new field house they had posted seven straight triumphs before running into the pesky Tigers again.

A crowd of about 10,000 saw the game.

Missouri forged a wide margin early in the game before the Jayhawks could get any sort of offensive to jell and then held off several spirited rallies to even their conference record at 3-3. The loss also gives the Jayhawks a 3-3 mark and a tie with the Tigers for fourth place in the Big Seven.

SLOW START BY JAYHAWKS

How much the loss of Dallas Dobbs, captain and top scorer, was felt showed clearly in the early minutes of the opening half as the Jayhawks played extremely raggedly. Actually, it wasn't until after the halfway mark in the first period that Kansas seemed to be able to become organized.

At that point the line-up consisted of Gene Elstun, Lew Johnson, Maurice King, John Parker and Eddie Dater. This same unit played most of the rest of the game and made it a battle after finally starting to roll in the last six minutes of the first half.

The Jayhawks started with a zone defense but the Tigers bombed them out of it after four and a half minutes with Lionel Smith and Bill Ross pushing the Tigers to a 12-2 lead. The man-for-man plan didn't work with too much success at first and Missouri moved out in front, 28-9, about halfway through the period.

The Tigers built their widest gap at 33-13 before the Jayhawks cut the margin to ten points, 45-35 at intermission.

Johnson, Elstun and Dater sparked a drive which carried Kansas to within seven points, the closest they could get, at 49-42. But the Tigers stayed in front and maintained a spread of about twelve points until the last three and a half minutes.

HOLD SMITH IN SECOND HALF

Smith, who tallied fourteen points in the first half for Missouri, was completely shackled in the second half and managed to add only four free throws, all in the final two minutes. But Stewart, Ross and Denny kept hitting from the field to carry the Tigers to victory. Denny took game scoring honors with twenty-three points. Stewart had twenty, Smith eighteen, Ross twelve and Rodger Egelhoff ten.

Allen got to coach one season in the building named for him.

University of Kansas Archives

Elstun was top scorer for Kansas with twenty-two but Dater, who hit ten of eighteen shots, chipped in with twenty-one to give Jayhawk fans some hope that an adequate replacement has been found for Dobbs.

The Tigers hit a hot 47.4 per cent of their shots, eighteen of thirty-eight, in the first half and wound up with an overall mark of thirty-one out of seventy-four for 41.9 per cent.

The Jayhawks connected on fourteen of forty-five in the first half for 31.1 and finished with thirty-five of eighty-six for a game average of 41.1.

Kansas had a slight superiority in rebounding with a 46-41 edge. Elstun was tops for the night with thirteen and Smith grabbed twelve for Missouri.

Allen Fieldhouse was in the middle of nowhere when it was first erected.

K.U. SPEEDS PAST TIGERS

There was little doubt that KU earned a huge advantage over the Tigers when Coach Dick Harp signed prep star Wilt Chamberlain out of Philadelphia. Both Kansas and Mizzou were in the running for "the Stilt," and for good reason. The 7-footer was as agile as he was tall and he could dominate at both ends of the floor.

The Tigers got their first taste of Chamberlain on January 5, 1957 in Lawrence, as the Jayhawks downed the Tigers, 92-79. The return engagement took place in Columbia about six weeks later and Chamberlain really flexed his muscles.

Despite sitting out much of the second half, he scored 32 points and pulled down 20 rebounds, as the Jayhawks manhandled the Tigers, 91-58. The 32 points were the most ever by an opponent in Brewer Fieldhouse. Missouri did everything it could to stop the dominant big man in the game—and we mean everything.

"After the game, Chamberlain was talking with the press," said Bill Mayer, the longtime sports editor of the Lawrence Journal-World. "He said, 'I know they're a bunch of Tigers, because one of them bit me.' Then he showed us the teeth marks."

Tom Hedrick, the long-time Voice of the Jayhawks who then was a student reporter for the KU paper, said, "After he showed us the teeth marks, he said, 'It made my arm black and blue...well, at least blue.'"

Norm Stewart, who feels fortunate to have graduated the year before so he didn't have to play against Chamberlain, was a graduate assistant for Coach "Sparky" Stalcup. He disputes the biting story, in typical Norm Stewart fashion.

"I don't think it really happened, though he probably said it did," Stewart said. When asked why he would doubt it, he replied, "I don't recall anyone getting close enough to bite him. If they did, that was the only damage we inflicted on him all night."

The Kansas City Star did not mention the biting incident, but there was no lack of praise for the performance of Chamberlain and his mates.

Here's how it appeared in the February 17, 1957, Star:

The Stilt Hits a Record 32 Points as Jayhawks Roll On Toward Big Seven Title With 91-58 Triumph

SUBS IN ACTION

Easy Victory Lets Coach Dick Harp Use His Entire Squad

No Threat By Mizzou

Visitors Spring Into 43-27 Halftime Lead – Ron Loneski a Star

RIVALS!
MU VS. KU

MU: 91
KU: 58

BASKETBALL
FEBRUARY 16, 1957

Columbia, Mo., Feb. 16.

Kansas double-timed past Missouri here tonight by a whopping 91-58 to build its record for the season to 14-1.

Wilt Chamberlain picked up 32 points, another record for the 7-foot wizard, since it marked the most points ever scored by a visiting player in Brewer field house.

The Kansas subs also got some experience after a string of tough contests which had kept the K. U. regulars busy most of the season.

> *The issue never was in doubt here before 6,000 fans, a capacity throng. Missouri was ahead once, 6-5, 2 minutes into the game. Maurice King's driving jump shot and John Parker's poke made it 9-6 for the Big Seven leaders and from then on the Tigers made futile chase.*

ALL JAYHAWKS PLAY

Coach Dick Harp used all 12 of his men in racking the largest score ever for these two long-time rivals in this field house. Missouri had a 90 total in a 1955 game here.

The previous high for an individual opponent on the Missouri court was 29 by Clyde Lovellette of Kansas in 1950. Norm Stewart of Missouri retained his record for the field house, though, at 36.

Chamberlain sat out the final seven and a half minutes while Ron Loneski

and Ron Johnson, both sophomores, shared the post duties for the remainder of the game. Loneski, who started at forward, was an able No. 2 punch for the Jayhawks, hitting 14 points and getting 16 rebounds.

Chamberlain got 20 rebounds. He and Loneski got within one of Missouri's

total as the Jayhawks took a huge 67-37 edge in saves.

BRIEF TIGER LEAD

The issue never was in doubt here before 6,000 fans, a capacity throng. Missouri was ahead once, 6-5, 2 minutes into the game. Maurice King's driving

University of Kansas Archives

Wilt Chamberlain revolutionized college basketball with his unique combination of size, strength and athleticism.

jump shot and John Parker's poke made it 9-6 for the Big Seven leaders and from then on the Tigers made futile chase.

By halfway through the first period Kansas had built a 9-point lead, then with Chamberlain and Loneski laying them in like homing pigeon eggs, the Jayhawks spurted late in the half with 10 points in less than two minutes for a 43-27 half-time edge.

Loneski got all his 14 points in the first half, Wilt had 15 in the period.

Guarding Chamberlain, a tough way to make a living, claimed its first victim five minutes into the second half when sophomore Al Abram picked up personal No. 5 and departed.

Chamberlain sat out the final seven and a half minutes while Ron Loneski and Ron Johnson, both sophomores, shared the post duties for the remainder of the game. Loneski, who started at forward, was an able No. 2 punch for the Jayhawks, hitting 14 points and getting 16 rebounds.

Charlie Duren, No. 1 Mizzou middle man, already was gone, having sprained an ankle in the early part of the first half, so that left John Stephens to cope with the Stilt the remainder of the time Wilt was in there. Stephens picked up four personals doing his job.

Missouri was 15 back early in the second and from that point on never was closer than 17 in arrears.

Both teams relied on the zone defense. Chamberlain blocked five shots to run his string to 113 for the year.

Chamberlain was the center of attention during his seasons as a Jayhawk.

RIVALS!
MU VS. KU

MU: 79
KU: 75

BASKETBALL
MARCH 11, 1961

MIZZOU RUINS K.U. HOPE

It was one of the most frightening scenes in college basketball history. Players from Missouri and Kansas fought each other on the court, surrounded by dozens—in some estimations, hundreds—of fans.

Kansas broadcaster Tom Hedrick said he was fearful for his life as the announcer for the visitors. "I didn't think the fight would end before somebody got really hurt," he said.

Norm Stewart, who was an assistant coach at Mizzou at the time, said the hostilities had been building for several months. In the fall, Kansas' football team had come into Columbia and knocked off undefeated and No. 1-ranked Missouri, ending any chance at a national title.

The Jayhawks later had to forfeit the game because running back Bert Coan had accepted a plane ticket. How was that discovered? In the eyes of KU fans, somebody at Missouri snitched.

"When we played at KU, the booing was so loud that they could not play the national anthem," Stewart said. "They were booing everything about Mizzou, because they blamed us.

"When they came to Columbia, the refs tried to prevent things from getting out of hand. They did for a while, but then the fight happened."

Wayne Hightower of Kansas and Charlie Henke of Missouri were the first to throw punches, but
it wasn't long before everyone was involved.

"There were 300 people on the court, and they weren't exchanging pleasantries," Stewart said. "Everybody got hit. It's like bullets. They don't put names on them."

Missouri won the game, 79-76, ending Kansas' chances at tying for the Big 8 Conference title.

Here's how it appeared in the March 12, 1961, Star:

In a Wild, Fighting, Scrambling Big 8 Basketball Game, Tigers Knock Kansas Out of Chance for Title Tie

BOTH LOSE ACE

Henke and Hightower Thrown Out After Melee Interrupts Second Half

Charlie Turns Trick

Before Going Out, He Triggers 44-39 M. U. Advantage – Tigers Go Into Delay

By Sid Bordman
(A Member of The Star's Sports Staff)

Columbia, Mo., March 11.

Any hope Kansas owned for a Big Eight championship tie was demolished this afternoon in as wild a battle as ever has been staged on a basketball floor.

A wild scramble – both teams cleared the bench, punching, wrestling and kicking – put a damper on the tense duel, which swung to Missouri, 79-76.

Before the free-for-all, which lured hundreds of fans from the stands, Wayne Hightower of Kansas and Missouri's Charlie Henke opened the gates with a fist-swinging bout under the Jayhawks' goal.

Although the actual combat spanned only about three minutes, it was at least ten minutes before the sluggers returned to shooting and rebounding.

TV AUDIENCE ON HAND

In addition to a crowd of about 3,500, a national television audience witnessed the clash, which resembled a pressure chamber from the very start.

Not only did the Tigers foil K. U.'s chances for a title deadlock with Kansas State, but they also erased the Jayhawks' 10-game hold on them, which began in 1959. Coach Dick Harp's perfect record against M. U. also went up in air.

After the "mess" was over, both Henke and Hightower were chased to the showers, and each charged with a "flagrant" foul – a 2-shot situation.

Until his forced exit, Henke turned in a sparkling job in his farewell game for Mizzou.

During a 3-minute, 27-second span, winding up the first and starting the second half, Henke chucked in 11 of his 20

> *Before the free-for-all, which lured hundreds of fans from the stands, Wayne Hightower of Kansas and Missouri's Charlie Henke opened the gates with a fist-swinging bout under the Jayhawks' goal. Although the actual combat spanned only about three minutes, it was at least ten minutes before the sluggers returned to shooting and rebounding.*

points to trigger the Tigers to a 44-39 advantage.

When the brawl erupted with 14:49 remaining, Mizzou was nursing a 48-44 lead.

From that point, the Tigers refused to wilt; Kansas appeared to lose its momentum and poise.

Wayne Hightower was one of the combatants who started a melee that lured hundreds of fans onto the floor.

RIVALS!
MU VS. KU

MU: 79
KU: 75

BASKETBALL
MARCH 11, 1961

GARRETT DOES TOP JOB

Through the opening half, sophomore Howard Garrett prevented Kansas from winning the backboards by a landslide, and he also turned in a sharp defensive job on Hightower, although the tall Jayhawk punched in 12 of his 14 counters before the turn.

But Garrett did most of his deeds after the fracas. He fired in nine of his 15 tallies, captured four of his 11 rebounds, intercepted three passes and blocked several shots.

With Joe Scott at the helm, the Tigers switched to a delay game with a 67-58 bulge and 5:30 to play.

Garrett drilled in a one-hander from the top of the circle, sophomore Lyle Houston popped a jumper in from the side, followed with four consecutive free throws and Garrett dumped in a crisp shot off a fast break to pull Missouri to a 75-62 position.

Allen Correll cut loose for nine points for the Jayhawks during the "mad-dog" closing three minutes, but they served only as scare cards.

Kansas, which whipped the Tigers, 88-73, in Lawrence Kas., broke from the barrier in a rush, forging a beachhead on both boards.

Bill Bridges, the Hawks' fluid, 6-5 jumping jack, needed only five rebounds to sack his third consecutive Big Eight championship in that department. It took him only 1:30 to turn the trick.

K.U. CAN'T SHAKE LOOSE

But the apparent domination failed to shake the Jayhawks loose as they couldn't score on tips and the percentage shots.

Missouri cashed in most of its opportunities, clicking for 58.6 percent from the field in the first half on its way to a 42.4 log. Kansas, 40.5 before intermission, recorded 41.4, but the figure is misleading as the Jayhawks' fattened up

Not only did the Tigers foil K. U.'s chances for a title deadlock with Kansas State, but they also erased the Jayhawks' 10-game hold on them, which began in 1959. Coach Dick Harp's perfect record against M. U. also went up in air.

on Correll's late gunning.

On the backboard Kansas built a 61-47 margin as Bridges pulled off 20 rebounds and Hightower 21.

Henke, who hit on 9-of-12 shots from the field, had too much variety for Hightower, his assigned guard. The Kansan played him tight because of his hooking ability. Then Henke would drive.

Most of the feeds to Henke came from Scott, who chalked only 12 points on a 4-for-16 day from the field. With Nolen Ellison (6-1) and Dee Ketchum (5-11) working on Scott, the Tigers tried to pull the jumpshooting ace inside to take advantage of his 6-4 size. He scrambled for eight points in the first half, but Ketchum then put the handcuffs on him.

Scott then turned to feeding and running the delay game.

KU broadcaster Tom Hedrick was fearful for his life as the fight escalated.

INCIDENT IS PREVIEW

A preview of the "unscheduled" fight took place at the end of the first half when Scott was charged with a technical foul for roughing. Had the move occurred before the buzzer, Scott would have been tagged with a personal.

Thus, Kansas received a free throw and the ball at the center line to start the second half.

CHAPTER 6
Dynamic Years

RIVALS!
MU VS. KU

MU:67
KU:66

FOOTBALL
JANUARY 16, 1968

MISSOURI ACCEPTS ORANGE BOWL BID AFTER SUFFERING FIRST DEFEAT

The 1960 game between Missouri and Kansas marked the only time in series history that either of the teams entered the game ranked No. 1 in the country. That team was Missouri, and at 9-0 the Tigers had a legitimate shot at a national championship. Kansas was no slouch either, entering the game ranked 11th. But Kansas prevailed 23-7 in a game both teams' media guides claim as a victory.

The Kansas defense was so dominant that Missouri did not muster a first down until late in the third quarter. But Kansas used a running back named Bert Coan (who later played for the Kansas City Chiefs) in the game. Coan later was ruled ineligible because he had accepted a plane ticket to attend a college all-star game.

Kansas fans cried foul, because they believed that Missouri coach Don Faurot was the one who turned in the Jayhawks. Some even believe that Faurot had something to do

with the infraction; you might call it a set-up. But Kansas' guide lists the Jayhawks at 7-2-1, with two games later forfeited, and Missouri's guide lists the Tigers at 11-0, including that 7-23 "victory" against Kansas.

There's no dispute, however, that Jack Mitchell's Jayhawks were prepared that day, and the Tigers left the field with their tails between their legs.

Here's how it appeared in the November 20, 1960, Star

BY BOB BUSBY
(ASSISTANT SPORTS EDITOR OF THE *STAR*)

Columbia, Mo., Nov. 19

In one of the finest games of this ancient football series, Kansas defeated Missouri today, 23-7, before a record-breaking crowd of 43,000.

It was such a game that no apologies could be offered from either side. The Jayhawks simply out-defensed the Tigers with their souped-up 9-man line and managed to get the majority of points.

Nevertheless, as was expected, the Tigers, ranked No. 1 nationally last week on the strength of their 9-0 record, received and accepted a bid to play in the Orange Bowl game in Miami January 2. There was a report the Bengals may play Duke.

Kansas, even though it wins the Big Eight conference title, is barred from the Miami trip because of an NCAA penalty.

Even so, Coach Jack Mitchell's Jayhawks had the elements it took to wrap up the game. They had demonstrated their potential earlier and today displayed it in fine fashion.

Not even the most partisan Missouri fan could deny that the better team on the field in this classic came away with the heavy end of the score. It was so completely convincing there was nothing to look back upon as a turning point.

Kansas scored 10 points in the third quarter and 13 in the fourth. The Tigers finally got into the scoring column in the fourth quarter on a sparkling forward pass from Ron Taylor to Mel West. The sequence carried 36 yards on nine plays.

Bill Tobin booted his 22nd consecutive extra point to keep the Tigers out of the doghouse.

So well did Kansas align its defense that Missouri did not make a first down until 9:06 remained in the third quarter. As it turned out, KU rolled up 186 yards on the ground to Missouri's 61. Each team went 53 yards by air.

Fumbles plagued both teams in the early part of the game. Kansas lost three in the first quarter and Missouri gave up two in the second.

The Jayhawks missed several early scoring chances, but mainly because Missouri's rugged defense took advantage of every miscue. Twice in the second quarter Kansas blew opportunities. The Jayhawks punched to the Tiger 3 only to see John Hadl stopped to no gain. On the next sequence the Jayhawks took a puny Danny LaRose punt on the MU 38 and moved it to the 12 before giving up possession.

Finally the drought was broken early in the third quarter when K.U.'s long-ball kicker was called into action.

Roger Hill, who had tried two field goals this season, connected from 47 yards out to give the Jayhawks a 3-0 lead.

BOBBLE PAVES WAY

Then came the big punch, Norris Stevenson fumbled and Gib Wilson recovered for K.U. on the Tiger 19. On the third play from there, Hadl passed 19 yards to Bert Coan for the TD. John Suder kicked the point and it was 10-0 with 9:25 to go in the third.

The Jayhawks seeking their first conference title since 1930, barged ahead 17-0 on a 13-play sortie that carried from the KU 31. It involved Coan in his second touchdown from two yards out. Suder banged the point. Kansas iced the cake with 37 seconds left in the fourth when Doyle Schick intercepted a pass from Missouri's Taylor on the MU 24. The Tigers were getting tough, but K. U. dented to the two. Rodger McFarland, in at

Bert Coan (23) helped KU beat No. 1 Missouri, but couldn't elude controversy, causing KU to forfeit the game.

RIVALS!
MU VS. KU

KU:23
MU:7

FOOTBALL
NOVEMBER 19, 1960

quarterback, pulled a nifty jump pass from a tight formation and hit Sam Simpson in the end zone. Suder's kick failed.

END-OF-GAME MIX-UP

The game ended in a hassle. Kansas was guilty of a personal foul on the final play which placed the Jayhawks back on the Kansas 25. But a Mike Hunter-to-Don Wainwright pass failed as time ran out.

Coan was the big Kansas gainer with 67 yards on nine carries. Schick got 39 on 15, and Hugh Smith got 30 on six moves. Donnie Smith was Missouri's leading rusher with a meager 14 yards on seven attempts.

Hadl did himself proud, punting four times for an average of 41.3.

The game never really was much in doubt. Kansas was higher than the proverbial kite. The Jayhawks played it to win and that was just about it. But it was a terrific ball game that neither team deserved to lose.

FROM THE KANSAS CITY TIMES, 1960

Sporting Comment

BY ERNEST MEHL
(THE STAR'S SPORTS EDITOR)

Columbia, MO., Nov. 19

Anyone wanting an accurate definition of the word "gloom" should ask a Missourian.

The sun shone brightly over Memorial Stadium here late this afternoon but there was gloom. Deadly, dull, sickening gloom.

But in contrast there also was joy for rarely has there been a victory as cherished by the Kansans as this one by a 23-7 score over the Tigers.

The Kansans probably were in the minority in this record crowd of 43,000 but they could be distinguished by the smiles they wore.

For this not only was the sort of triumph they could have dreamed of. It was one which was won on merit.

Not even the most partisan Missouri fan could deny that the better team on the field in this classic came away with the heavy end of the score.

It was so completely convincing there was nothing to look back upon as a turning point. There wasn't any turning point. The Hawks, despite their early fumbles, were in command from the start.

One might argue that on another day there would not be this unmistakable superiority but he couldn't deny that it was there today – heavily outlined.

The facts and the statistics were all too overwhelming. For the first time this season the Tigers were outmatched and it was cruelly evident to the Missourians.

HAWKS HAD A CRYSTAL BALL

It was not until late in the third quarter that the Tigers could run off a first down; their second one came late in the fourth quarter.

Their favorite plays were being routed, the type of advances they had been making all season were being checked. The Jayhawks played as though they knew from the start every move the Tigers were likely to make and a number of them they seemed almost to anticipate.

Despite what must have been a rude shock to these Tigers they fought on even though the odds against them lengthened.

That the Orange Bowl invitation came while they were in the dressing room and still dazed by their experience was some consolation.

They deserved the bid, and there is no doubt but that they will represent the Big Eight conference well. But today the Jayhawkers were masters. Today the Kansans took the championship prize in the conference.

Since they couldn't go because of the N. C. A. A. ban imposed on them they won't mind the trip being enjoyed by the Tigers. What they have is the compensation of knowing they went into a game with the points against them and came out with a superb exhibition of line play.

Not before this season had the Missouri line been handled this way. Not before had so many punts been required.

On the first sequence of the game after the kickoff by the Hawks, the Tigers went nine yards in three plays and then kicked. Six of the yards were made by Norris Stevenson and they represented the most substantial gain until Ron Taylor ran for nine yards in the third period.

The next time Missouri had the ball

in the first quarter it failed to gain a single yard in three plays. In the third sequence it made two yards on three tries before punting. On the fourth sequence it was held to no gain in three attempts.

And if the Missourians construed all this as merely a feeling-out period after which the Tigers would pick up some momentum they didn't reckon with the plan which had been conceived for the Kansas defense.

Taking a chance on the Missouri passing attack, which has not been notable, the Jayhawks smothered the Tiger sweeps, forced the ball carriers to the outside and paid more attention to these threats than those up the middle.

It was a campaign which must have been worked out with great care and then carried out in a manner to delight the heart of Coach Jack Mitchell.

In some ways this was a game unique in this long series and we doubt whether anyone could have predicted the rout which developed.

TIGERS CARRIED A LARGE BURDEN

We have an idea that for the first time this season the Tigers reacted to the terrific pressure weighing on them.

Number 1 in the nation, opposing their traditional rival and thoughts of an Orange Bowl bid are difficult to forget while wanting to finish the schedule undefeated.

Psychologically the Tigers had a lot going against them. In contrast the Hawks, with a tougher schedule, had lost to Syracuse and Iowa, both of which had been ranked on top when the game was played. Then there was a tie with Oklahoma. The team also was called on the carpet by the NCAA and denied participation in the post-season classic.

The thoughts entertained by the Tigers were likely to enervate them to some extent and those held by the Hawks made them more fiercely determined to win this big one as a climax they could long enjoy.

The fact the Hawks fumbled three

times in the first quarter and the Tigers failed to take advantage must have made them aware that on this day at least, they were in control, that sooner or later they would break the scoring dearth.

The Tigers recovered the first Kansas fumble on the Missouri 48, in excellent position for a drive. They were stopped cold. They seized the next fumble on the Kansas 46 and once again they faced an inviting situation. Again they were stopped. And then even another fumble on the Kansas 43 and the Tigers were stymied for the third time.

A team given that many chances and failing to profit can't hope to win. Even though the Tigers made one magnificent goal-line stand, the Kansas victory became more and more inevitable.

A Missouri line, which has contributed a great deal to the team's success this season, had more than it could handle.

And a team which had the unusual experience of playing three No. 1 teams in one season wound up itself as a champion.

FROM THE KANSAS CITY TIMES, 1960

Battle Plan Mapped Out by George Bernhardt for K U.'s Forward Wall Throttles Missouri's Vaunted Power Sweeps.

LINE COACH DRAWS CREDIT

Object Was to Pressure Tiger Backs and Not Let Them Cut Back In

By Bill Sims
(A Member of The Star's Sports Staff)

Columbia, MO, Nov 19

Jack Mitchell, proud and beaming as he savored the greatest thrill of his coaching career, strode into the Kansas dressing room, walked straight to a blackboard as his happy Jayhawkers cheered and scrawled "Big Eight Champs."

Bill Burnison, a senior who played a great game as a linebacker, promptly picked up the chalk and added "No 1" as the deafening roar continued.

Obviously tired, but too exhilarated to notice it, the Jayhawkers to a man

RIVALS!

MU VS. KU

KU:23

MU:7

FOOTBALL

NOVEMBER 19, 1960

agreed that this was the one game they'd wanted to win more than any other, and all were in accord that the defense paved the way.

"There's no question our defense was the outstanding feature of the game," Mitchell concurred. "We were confident it was going to be good because the kids have been improving a little each week as the season progressed, but man, they were ready today.

"They really prepared themselves mentally. They've played the No. 1 team three times this year, and they were determined they were going to win this one.

"Actually, the boys never had gotten over last year's game with Missouri. They were awfully disappointed after having played so hard to barely miss it."

Mitchell explained the defensive strategy had been to force Missouri's vaunted sweeps into the sidelines and not let the Tiger ball carriers cut up field.

"All season, everyone has played them from the outside trying to turn them in," Mitchell said, "but George Bernhardt (defensive line coach) felt it would be more effective to keep the pressure on them from the inside out and not let them cut back in. Whenever they did, they ran right into our defenders and couldn't get any place. We just kept forcing them to the sidelines so they couldn't get up much momentum.

"Bernhardt did a tremendous job in working out the defense and showing the boys what he wanted them to do. Tom Triplett, our scout, and Bill Pace, our defensive backfield coach – well, just everyone did a great job.

"We felt Missouri's passing was effective and we had to be alert, but the big thing we had to do was stop those power sweeps and the kids did it."

Mitchell was asked if he thought the Jayhawks were the best team in the nation.

"Missouri has a fine bunch of boys," he said, "and the coaches have done a tremendous job in getting the maximum out of them."

Roger Hill, whose 47-yard field goal in the third quarter broke the scoreless deadlock, wouldn't say it was his biggest thrill but, "a pretty big one."

"That's the first one I ever kicked in college," he added, "and I knew it was good as soon as I looked up. There wasn't any doubt about it."

Doyle Schick, the fine blocking fullback and corner linebacker, perhaps was happier than most of the other Jayhawkers.

"This is the first time since I've been playing at K. U. we've ever won a big game and it's a great feeling," the senior who started his 30th straight game grinned.

Bert Coan, who caught the pass from John Hadl for K.U.'s first touchdown, revealed that Ed Mehrer, Missouri fullback, almost intercepted it.

"He barely missed it as he lunged in front of me," the game's leading ground gainer explained, "but Hadl threw it real hard and all I had to do was turn around and run."

Hadl, hailed by almost everyone who has seen him play as one of the finest backs in the nation, had praise for the middle of Missouri's line, especially the two guards, Paul Henly and Paul Garvis.

"Missouri was tougher up the middle than anyone else we've played," the classy quarterback said. "Those two guards are great but Missouri isn't as

> "(George) Bernhardt did a tremendous job in working out the defense and showing the boys what he wanted them to do. Tom Triplett, our scout, and Bill Pace, our defensive backfield coach – well, just everyone did a great job.
>
> "We felt Missouri's passing was effective and we had to be alert, but the big thing we had to do was stop those power sweeps and the kids did it."
>
> -Jack Mitchell

tough over-all as Iowa or Syracuse.

"We were readier for this game than any other since I've been at KU. It makes it a lot easier to forget last year now."

It was Hadl who caught a pass in the waning seconds last year in Lawrence and was downed just short of the touchdown which would have sent the Jayhawks out in front. But all thoughts of that game have vanished now as the Jayhawks revel in their new spot atop the Big Eight throne.

MISSOURI LINE PUTS CLAMPS ON K.U.

An undermanned and underappreciated Missouri team knocked Kansas out of a possible Orange Bowl bid with a clutch 10-7 victory over the Jayhawks. It was a payback for what the Jayhawks did to the Tigers the year before.

Like the Tigers the previous year, the Jayhawks still got a bowl bid. Unlike the Tigers, it wasn't the Orange Bowl.

"That was a heartbreaker," said Bill Mayer, long-time sports editor of the Lawrence Journal-World. "KU lost a game it should have won. We had John Hadl and Curtis McClinton. Jack Mitchell, the last KU coach with a winning record, still wanted the team to go to a bowl game. He took a vote and rigged it so it came out in favor of going. The team ended up in the Bluebonnet Bowl in Houston."

Kansas won that game against Rice, the first bowl victory in school history.

Kansas jumped out to an early 7-0 lead but the Tigers surged ahead in the fourth quarter. The Jayhawks got the ball back with a little more than two minutes left, but Hadl's pass went for a 16-yard completion on fourth and 17.

Here's how it appeared in the November 26, 1961, Star

Fired-Up Tigers Score in 4th Quarter Then Repel Late Bid for 10-7 Upset

By William E. Richardson
(A Member of The Star's Sports Staff.)

Lawrence, Kas., Nov. 25

Hard-charging Missouri crumpled up the form sheet in front of the Kansas Jayhawks today and pulled off a 10-7 upset before 40,500 fans.

A 2-touchdown underdog entering this annual football classic, M. U. wiped out a 7-3 lead in the fourth quarter with an 80-yard touchdown surge, then repelled a Kansas threat in the final minutes.

Bill Tobin who made the touchdown on a 3-yard sweep, added the extra point to account personally for all the Tiger scoring. Earlier, he booted a 27-yard field goal.

As has been the case all season, M. U. relied heavily on its finely-honed forwards. The Tiger linemen clamped a vise on John Hadl in the second half, almost minimizing the Kansas air game and most certainly limiting the Jayhawks' over-all offensive potential.

Ended by this upset was K. U.'s 6-game winning streak, and a possible Orange bowl bid. At the same time, the Tigers forced their way into the bowl picture and into a second place tie in the conference with Kansas. Both clubs finished with 5-2 league records.

In addition to the linemen, who gave forth with tremendous efforts, Missouri counted Ron Taylor, senior quarterback, and Paul Underhill, sophomore halfback, among its heroes.

Taylor steered the Tigers 80 yards in 13 plays to the clinching touchdown, with Underhill doing much of the running damage. Pass completions of 16 yards to Gene Oliver and 20 yards to Vince Turner featured the drive.

On the touchdown, Taylor faked the handoff to Underhill, making the motion for a dive play, then sent Tobin wide around left end on a pitch-out. Tobin crashed into the end zone to wipe out an advantage Kansas had enjoyed since the first quarter.

RIVALS!
MU VS. KU

MU:10
KU:7

FOOTBALL
NOVEMBER 25, 1961

The Jayhawks tallied first, punching out 15 yards in seven plays after Larry Lousch captured an errant pitchout. The yards came hard and it took a fourth-down slam by Ken Coleman, the fullback, to get the final one. Wallace Barnes converted with 6:54 remaining and while the Jayhawks had not scored in spectacular fashion, they had opened the gates for what many expected to be another impressive victory.

But that was about it for Kansas until the final fretful minutes. Once again a fumble, this one by Underhill, gave the Jayhawks a shot from the 25 with a little more than two minutes remaining.

Con Keating, reserve quarterback, killed the clock with an incomplete pass and Kansas sent Hadl into action.

On his first pass attempt, Hadl was forced to eat the ball for a 7-yard loss. He missed connections on a third-down aerial with 1:25 left, then set up a fourth down completion with an artistic maneuver.

Big John faked the draw play to Coleman, then threw in the left flat to Larry Allen, the left end. Allen, screened by blockers, threaded his way down the sideline, but had to change directions. He was nailed at the 16, one yard short of the first down needed to keep the K. U. hopes alive.

Missouri took over with 51 seconds left and Taylor, in no hurry, flopped on the ball twice as time ran out. Elated Tiger players rushed over to give Coach Dan Devine a ride off the field.

Missouri, which went into the battle with a casualty list numbering five starters, found it could move the ball, and well at that, when Devine's patched-up crew marched 49 yards following the K. U. touchdown.

A fumble by Turner ended the march with Kent Staab recovering for Kansas on the 34. The Jayhawks then mounted a small offensive but it fell a yard short and M. U. drew a reprieve on its 44.

Taylor entered the game on Missouri's first possession of the second quarter and led the Tigers on a march to the K. U. 9. Underhill was the workhorse this time too, rushing 28 yards in four carries. Jim Johnson, southpaw quarterback, relieved Taylor and fired two passes, the second one dropped in the end zone by John Sevcik.

With fourth-and-7, the Tigers went for a field goal. Taylor held at the 17 and Tobin's kick was on target – a 27-yard boot with 10:52 left in the second period.

Jack Mitchell (left) and John Hadl

Coleman. Johnson bumped the Kansas fullback out of bounds on the M. U. 16. Kansas saw its chances for a game-breaker expire two plays later when Curtis McClinton, the Jays' most consistent gainer, fumbled and Sevcik recovered on the 20.

Missouri's touchdown drive opened late in the third quarter. Andy Russell

After Staab and Kirshman handled Underhill for no gain, Taylor chose to fake to his halfback and send Tobin wide. It was a successful call and with it Mizzou owned its first lead of the game.

Picking up momentum, M. U. forced Kansas to punt after four plays and mounted another threat. Underhill, Tobin and Norm Beal, in for only a short time as the

As has been the case all season, M. U. relied heavily on its finely-honed forwards. The Tiger linemen clamped a vise on John Hadl in the second half, almost minimizing the Kansas air game and most certainly limiting the Jayhawks' over-all offensive potential.In addition to the linemen, who gave forth with tremendous efforts, Missouri counted Ron Taylor, senior quarterback, and Paul Underhill, sophomore halfback, among its heroes.

dented the line for short gains before Taylor spotted Jack Palmer open on a 9-yard pass to the M. U. 34.

Underhill picked up four before Taylor cranked up his arm again, spearing Oliver between two K. U. defenders on the Kansas 46. Tobin, showing some of his finest running form of the campaign, kept the drive alive with 7- and 5-yard gains on wide plays.

Underhill, used sparingly until mid-season, hit off the right side for 4 yards. Taylor went back to the pass on second down, connecting with Turner on a 20-yarder to the 8. Staab and Stan Kirshman halted Tobin for no gain and it looked as if the K. U. defenders were set for a stout defense of their goal.

However, the first inflicted penalty of the game occurred on the next play and K. U. was forced to dig in from its 3.

result of an injury, sliced out the key yardage in a 50-yard rush to the Kansas 8.

From here, Taylor, trying to set up a sweep, fumbled and Staab recovered for Kansas with 5:31 remaining. The Jayhawks worked out of the hole, recording a first down on the 20. But Missouri's line rose up to prevent a further advance as Bucky Wegener and Oliver nailed Hadl for an 8-yard loss to the 13 on third down.

Leiker boomed a 67-yard punt from a quick-kick formation on the fourth down and set the stage for the fumble and the thrilling wind-up.

Johnson and Paul Henley, a guard, led Missouri's tackling brigade with seven each. Staab, a center, had 10 and Ken Tiger, junior guard, was in on 8 for Kansas.

RIVALS!
MU VS. KU

MU:10
KU:7

FOOTBALL
NOVEMBER 25, 1961

Memorial Stadium in the 60's.

University of Kansas Archives

EARLY JAYHAWK BID KILLED BY TURNER'S 101-YARD RUN

It wouldn't be a stretch to say that the attention of Missouri and Kansas fans was not focused entirely on the game in 1963. Pushed back a week because of the assassination of President John F. Kennedy, the game was a tight affair that turned on a key defensive play.

The Jayhawks dominated play, not allowing the Tigers beyond midfield until the second half. But the key play in the first quarter gave Mizzou enough momentum to hold on for a 9-7 victory.

Kansas running back Ken Coleman was diving over the line on his way to a go-ahead touchdown when the ball popped loose. Vince Turner picked up the ball 1 yard deep in the end zone and raced 101 yards for the touchdown.

Legendary broadcaster Harry Caray, who was broadcasting the game for the Tigers, had this to say after the play: "I'll bet (Kansas coach) Jack Mitchell swallowed his cigar. I did too, and I don't smoke."

Here's how it appeared in the December 1, 1963, Star

BY JOE McGUFF
(ASSOCIATE SPORTS EDITOR OF *THE STAR*)

Lawrence, Kas.,

The football rivalry between Missouri and Kansas is steeped in improbability and yesterday's meeting between these ancient rivals was played with traditional fervor and perversity before a record crowd of 45,000 in Memorial stadium.

Missouri outplayed the favored Jayhawks only in the fourth quarter and crossed midfield only once under its own power but the resourceful Tigers gained a 9-7 decision.

Missouri accomplished its scoring on a 101-yard touchdown run by Vince Turner, who grabbed a fumble in the end zone, and a 22-yard field goal by Bill Leistritz in the fourth quarter.

The Jayhawks, who gained 128 yards rushing in the first half compared to 42 for Missouri, scored their lone touchdown midway in the second period on a drive of 44 yards.

Missouri did not move past its own 47 in the first half and was not able to advance past its 43 in the third period. Early in the fourth quarter Gus Otto intercepted a K. U. pass on his 32 and scored but the play was called back because of a clipping penalty.

This apparent bad break goaded the Tigers and they set off on their only long drive of the day, rolling 77 yards to the Kansas 5. With third and goal to go, a Tiger pass went incomplete. Leistritz was called in and booted the game-winning field goal from the 12.

There was 5:54 showing on the clock when Kansas received the ensuing kickoff but the Jayhawks, after picking up one first down, found themselves in a 4th-and-17 on their 30.

Tony Leiker went back to punt but instead attempted a screen pass. The Tigers alertly diagnosed the play and declined to rush. Lloyd Buzzi grabbed the pass but was hit immediately and that was the ball game, although the Jayhawks did get a chance to heave three desperation passes in the closing seconds.

This marked the seventh straight year in which the favorite has failed to win in this series and it was the sixth straight year in which neither team has been able to win on its home field. In 10 of the last 12 years, the margin of victory has been 12 points or less. The capacity crowd was given a clear indication in the first quarter that this was not going to be an ordinary football game.

On its second possession of the game, Kansas completely overpowered the Missouri line and drove 74 yards to the Missouri 2 in 16 plays. Coleman carried the ball 11 times and the longest gain was one of 15 yards by Gale Sayers.

So soundly were the Tigers being whipped at this stage that it seemed reasonable to question whether they could compete with the Jayhawks. Then, in as long as it takes a man in football gear to sprint 101 yards, the complexion of the game changed.

With second down coming up on the 2, Coleman challenged the M. U. line again. As he was hit at the line of scrimmage the ball flew out of his hands and straight into the arms of Turner, who was one step back in the end zone. Steve

RIVALS!
MU VS. KU

MU:9
KU:7

FOOTBALL
NOVEMBER 30, 1963

Renko was the only man close to Turner and he seemed too stunned to move. Turner raced past him and from that

to subdue the Jayhawks. Early in the second period they took over on the Missouri 44 following a punt and drove

extra point to give the Jayhawks a 7-6 lead with 6:51 left in the period. There were no other scoring threats before the half.

This marked the seventh straight year in which the favorite has failed to win in this series and it was the sixth straight year in which neither team has been able to win on its home field. In 10 of the last 12 years, the margin of victory has been 12 points or less.

point on the only obstacle in his path was the north end zone.

Leistritz attempted to kick the extra point but the ball was wide of the mark.

Even this jolting turn in events failed

to a touchdown in nine plays. Again the Jayhawks whipped the Missouri line from tackle to tackle. The longest gain in the drive was a 12-yard run by Renko.

Renko went the final yard on a quarterback sneak and Gary Duff kicked the

Missouri was able to run only 18 plays in the first half, exclusive of punts, and it seemed that the Tigers' only hope lay in improving their defense in the second half and hoping for a break.

The pattern of the game began to change ever so slightly in the third period. The Tigers were unable to organize anything resembling a sustained drive but they also managed to contain the Jayhawks, with the result that Kansas was not able to get past midfield until late in the period.

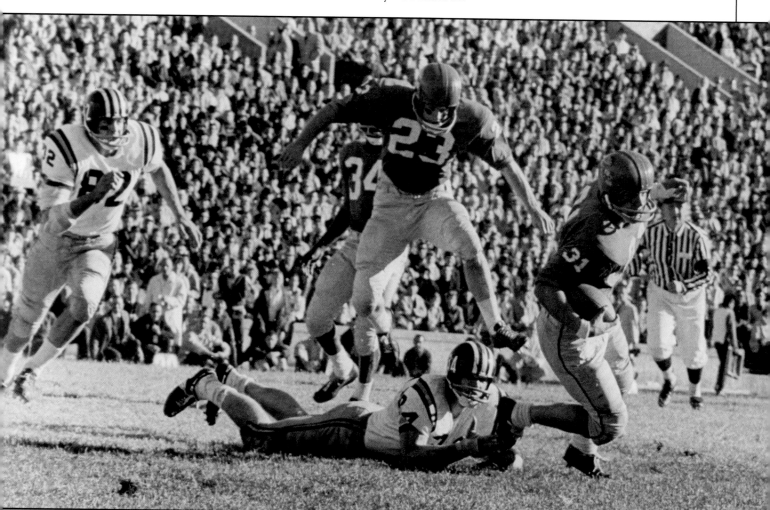

Ken Coleman (31) appeared headed in for the touchdown when he fumbled. MU's Vince Turner picked it up and raced 101 yards for the score.

As the fourth quarter opened, Kansas had a first down on the Missouri 35 and the Tiger partisans were squirming again. Renko threw an incomplete pass on first down and then tried another. Otto grabbed it and raced 68 yards to score but clipping was detected on the 33. Missouri retained possession but the ball was put down on the M. U. 18.

Now the Tigers had come to the moment of decision. If they hoped to win the game they had to put their disappointment aside and start moving. They proved equal to the challenge. For the first time they clearly began to outcharge the Kansas line.

Four running plays were good for 24 yards and a first down on the M. U. 42. Carl Reese and Carl Creekmore then carried the ball into Kansas territory for the first time during the afternoon.

GROUND GAME MOVES

The furious ground assault continued. The Jayhawks hurled themselves at the Tigers in an all-out effort to regain control of the situation but the Tigers had momentum on their side now. In eight running plays they moved from the K. U. 49 to a first down on the 10.

Reese picked up five yards in two carries and then Turner passed incomplete. In came Leistritz for the field goal attempt. The ball soared through the clear autumn air and the signal was given: the kick was good.

The Jayhawks still had almost six minutes in which to attempt a rally. They gained a first down on their 38. Two plays netted six yards and then Leiker was thrown for a 13-yard loss when a pitchout from Renko went astray.

On fourth down the Jayhawks attempted a screen pass off a fake punt but it produced only a 2-yard game and the Tigers were able to control the ball until the last 27 seconds.

Gary Lane, Missouri's ailing quarterback, played slightly more than half the game and was in throughout the Tigers' long fourth-quarter drive. Lane, who did not appear to be completely recovered from his recent attack of tonsillitis, alternated with Mike Jones.

Missouri did not complete a pass and the Jayhawks completed only two. They were good for only 11 yards. The total offense on both sides was among the lowest in the history of the series. Missouri gained 144 yards and Kansas 197.

Missouri's victory gave it undisputed possession of third place in the Big Eight and a 7-3 record for the season. The Tigers' conference record is 5-2. Kansas finished in a tie for fourth place with a 3-4 record. The Jayhawks had a 5-5 season record.

Gale Sayers, Kansas halfback, was the leading gainer of the afternoon with 68 yards to his credit. This pushed his season total to 917 yards and his career total to 2,042. He is the first junior in conference history to top the 2,000 mark.

FROM THE KANSAS CITY TIMES, 1963

SPORTING COMMENT

BY ERNEST MEHL
(THE STAR'S SPORTS EDITOR)

Lawrence, Kas..

The pressure was on Bill Leistritz as the ball was placed on the Kansas 12-yard line in the fourth quarter at a slight angle from the goal posts.

About six minutes remained in the fourth quarter, and the Jayhawks led 7-6. For the first time in this classic the Tigers, their line charging hard for the first time, had gone from their own 18 on 17 plays and six first downs where a pass by Vince Tobin was grounded in the end zone.

It was now fourth down and all Missouri's hopes rested on the right foot of this placekicker. Bill must have been conscious of the weight resting on this one effort he was about to make, but the crowd of 45,000 was not aware of it.

All it saw was the ball, the looming goal posts, the players poised. Then came the kick, a high one. The referee stared, then threw up both hands. The kick was good and, in a game in which they had to give ground repeatedly, the Tigers were in front. Now the Kansans had the ball, and there still remained enough time.

But the ease with which they had penetrated the Missouri defense in the first half was gone. Something unexpected had entered this game, not unusual in itself since the unexpected has become common whenever the Tigers and Hawks have met.

Yet probably not in the entire series dating deep back into the past has there been a struggle as surprising as this one. Never has one team been so poor at one

RIVALS!

MU VS. KU

MU:9

KU:7

FOOTBALL

NOVEMBER 30, 1963

state assumed command so completely at another.

Between halves with the Jayhawks leading, 7-6, and the Tigers having scored only as the result of an extraordinary incident which developed into a run of 101 yards by Turner, Vince, in the right spot at the right time, had the privilege of racing the length of the field. The Missouri cause had seemed dim to its supporters.

"Unless something happens," sighed one of these, "I don't see how we can make it. Kansas has too much power."

JAYHAWKS TAKE CHARGE IN A HURRY

In the first quarter there was no question of this superiority on attack. The first time the Hawks had the ball they were on the move until a pass was intercepted.

The second time found them starting from their 24. With Ken Coleman the spearhead and with Gale Sayers brilliant, the drive was maintained on five first downs and 16 plays to the Missouri 2-yard line when there happened something which startled everyone, including the Kansans.

As Coleman dove over the line the ball squirted out of his arms into the hands of Turner. One Jayhawk may have been close enough to dive for him, but it takes the mind some time to recover, and in this case Turner was on his way and out in the clear. By then it was too late.

It was Missouri with this 6-0 edge at the quarter. But in the second period, the Hawks asserted themselves. So at the half they were in front. Their line had outcharged the Tigers, their backs had been far more formidable.

But in many close games such as this one there is one point which, when

recalled, is accepted as having been the turning point.

The Tigers needed something to arouse them. The Jayhawks, with the barest of margins, needed at least one score to fortify their position.

This one point occurred at the start of the fourth period. Kansas had the ball in a drive which had started late in the third period from its 24-yard line. Ron Oelschlager had just churned eight yards to the Missouri 35 when the period ended and the team positions were reversed.

On the first play of the last quarter Steve Renko's pass was grounded. His second off to the right found Gus Otto, the Missouri halfback, charging on the scene to seize the ball.

Down the side lines Otto sped. After about 68 yards he had crossed the goal line. The cheers from the Missouri side faded quickly. There was a flag on the field. A penalty had been committed and there was no doubt that it was on Missouri.

Back trooped the players, the ball was handed to the referee, who spotted it on the Missouri 18-yard line. The Tigers had the ball, but they were hardly within striking distance and they had had no success in marching this distance before. But that penalty, harsh as it appeared at the time against the Missouri cause, could very well have been a spark to ignite the Missouri attack.

For the first time it began to move. For the first time the Missouri line made headway. For the first time plays began to click.

Ken Boston ran for seven, Carl Reese for nine, Carl Creekmore for 6, Saussele for seven. A first down on the 28, a second on the 42, a third on the Kansas 47 and that in itself was a new experience for the Tigers.

To be in Kansas territory with the ball.

The Kansas crowd looked on with unbelieving eyes. A Kansas defense so unshaken in the first three quarters was being forced to retreat. Saussele roared six to the 16, Reese six to the 10, again Reese four to the 5

Then a pass by Saussele went incomplete and the place kick by Leistritz was true. It was enough. In this case it was just as powerful as a touchdown would have been since this same kicker had missed the conversion after Turner's run and that failure had given the Jayhawks their slight lead.

It had to be the calling of Otto's run which had resulted in the mental stimulant the Tigers needed. The metamorphosis which was created brought about one of the most stunning finishes this series ever has witnessed.

And then, once astride the lead, the Tigers were zealous in protecting it. They had played this game with fewer yards in their pocket to spend than had the Jayhawks and they had to be careful how they spent them.

Almost numbed, it seemed, were the Hawks by this weird turn of events. A fumble but recovery cost the Hawks some ground and a pitch back to Tony Leiker missed the target. On fourth down and 17 yards to go and very little time remaining, Leiker, on punt formation, passed over center. The pass was complete, but not enough yards had been made.

It was now Missouri's ball, but once again in those closing seconds the Jayhawks got possession on their 24. Two passes were grounded, a third one knocked down. Then the fourth was intercepted by Vince Tobin and the game was over.

JAYHAWKS FIGHT OFF MIZZOU, 21-19

In 1967, new Kansas coach Pepper Rodgers did something that hadn't been done since 1960, lead the Jayhawks past Missouri. The next year, a victory over the Tigers, this time in Columbia, would mean a conference championship for the Jayhawks and a trip to the Orange Bowl on New Year's Day.

Kansas appeared to be the hungry team as the Hawks bolted to an early 14-0 lead, but the Tigers kept clawing back and cut the lead to 21-19 with just over 2 minutes remaining. But the Jayhawks got the necessary first down and were Orange Bowl bound. It was their first trip to the Orange Bowl since 1947.

Kansas safety Dave Morgan played a key role for the Kansas defense. He picked off two passes, including one returned for KU's first touchdown, and recovered a fumble. But less press went to Bobby Douglass, Kansas' quarterback.

"Bobby Douglass had a great game for them," said John Kadlec, then an assistant coach for the Tigers. "The way we came back, we always said that if the game had been five minutes longer, we would have won."

The game wasn't five minutes longer, and Missouri didn't win. Kansas finished 9-1 with the lone loss coming against Oklahoma.

Here's how it appeared in the November 24, 1968, Star:

Victory Nets at Least Share of Big Eight Title for Kansas

MORGAN HAS KEY ROLE

Safety's Defensive Work Plagues Tigers Before 62,200 Fans

BY JOE MCGUFF
(THE *STAR*'S SPORTS EDITOR)

Columbia, Mo.,

Quick-starting Kansas bolted to a 14-0 lead over Missouri yesterday in the first quarter, but then had to fight for survival in the closing stages of the game before emerging with a 21-19 victory. A record crowd of 62,200 in Memorial Stadium saw the 77th game in the series.

Kansas clinched at least a share of the Big Eight championship and will go into the Orange Bowl with a 9-1 record. The Jayhawks had not won as many as nine games in a season since 1905. Oklahoma, which defeated Nebraska yesterday, can tie for the conference title by winning its final game against Oklahoma State.

Missouri, which will play in the Gator Bowl, finished with a 7-3 record.

The thin margin of difference was supplied by a Kansas safetyman. His name is Dave Morgan, although the Tigers may have confused him with Henry Morgan of pirate fame.

Morgan intercepted a pass and returned it 35 yards for K. U.'s first touchdown. He recovered a fumble on the Missouri 19 to set up the final touchdown and broke up a Missouri drive in the third quarter when he intercepted a pass in the end zone after the Tigers had driven 66 yards to the 19.

RIVALS!
MU VS. KU

KU:21
MU:19

FOOTBALL
NOVEMBER-23-1968

M.U. REFUSES TO BUCKLE

Kansas had two opportunities to pull away from the Tigers, but Missouri, showing great discipline, refused to give in.

K. U. scored its first two touchdowns in eight minutes and five seconds. The second touchdown came on a 72-yard drive. One more touchdown and the game unquestionably would have turned into a rout.

Missouri hung on, finally drove 49 yards to score late in the second quarter and trailed only 14-6 at halftime.

Kansas scored its final touchdown early in the fourth quarter to take a 21-6 lead and again the spectre of a rout left Missouri fans and Gator bowl officials grim faced. The Tigers reacted aggressively.

They took the kick-off and drove 64 yards to a touchdown with eight minutes remaining. Two possessions later Missouri streaked 48 yards in three plays to slash the Jayhawks' lead to two points with 2:05 left.

JAYHAWKS HOLD BALL

Kansas needed at least one first down following the kick-off to maintain possession. The Jayhawks were able to get it and ran out the clock.

Missouri's defense played well in defeat. The Jayhawks were limited to 326 yards of total offense, well below their season average of 454.9. The Jayhawks had averaged 39.9 points a game prior to yesterday.

Kansas once again demonstrated its ability to move the ball quickly for big yardage. The Kansas defense gave up 398 yards of total offense, but the Jayhawks were ahead, 21-6, before the Tigers were able to start attacking them consistently for big yardage.

This is the first time ever that Missouri and Kansas both came into this game with bowl bids. They played in a manner that fully justified the selections of the Orange and Gator Bowl committees.

Outstanding individual performances were common. Bob Douglass, K. U.'s senior quarterback, had 188 yards of total offense. He finished with a career total of 3,832, breaking the K. U. record of 3,799 held by Ray Evans.

BIG DAY FOR MCMILLAN

Terry McMillan of Missouri had one of his finest days. He passed for 233 yards and ran for 34. John Riggins of K. U. led the rushers with 75 yards. Missouri's leader was Jon Staggers with 63.

K. U. came into the game with a reputation for starting quickly. The Jayhawks had scored 58 first-quarter points without giving up any. Missouri, in turn, has been a slow-starting team much of the season. This pattern held as the Jayhawks took command with deceptive ease.

Missouri, on its first possession, attempted a third-down pass from its 29. McMillan's intended receiver was Staggers, but Morgan picked the ball off at the 35 and there was no one between him and the goal. Bill Bell kicked the extra point, and it was 7-0 with 3:25 gone.

Kansas scored the next time it got the ball, zooming 72 yards in six plays. Kansas moved from its 28 to the Missouri 33 in three plays and a 15-yard personal foul penalty.

Douglass threw long to George McGowan. It appeared George Fountain might intercept, but he did not time his leap correctly and deflected the ball into McGowan's hands at the 2. McGowan went over and Bell added the extra point

to make it 14-0 with 6:55 remaining in the quarter.

KANSAS KEEPS MOVING

There was an unmistakable feeling at this point that the game could turn into a

---

Kansas had two opportunities to pull away from the Tigers, but Missouri, showing great discipline, refused to give in.

---

rout and it increased in the second quarter as K. U. moved the ball well on a strange drive that started on the Kansas 49 and ended 13 plays later on the Kansas 47. Kansas gained 42 yards but was assessed three penalties, two of them for 15 yards.

KU's 1968 Big 8 Championship Trophy

University of Kansas Archives

125

A record crowd of 62,200 saw the Jayhawks survive a late scare by the homestanding Tigers. The 21-19 win propelled KU to its first Orange Bowl berth in 21 years.

K. U. moved from its 49 to the Missouri 28, but then Douglass was thrown for a 10-yard loss. Next came two penalties, one for five yards and the other for 15. Donnie Shanklin broke loose on a 19-yard run, but on the next down K. U. was penalized 15 yards for holding. Bell finally punted from the 47.

Missouri showed no real ability to move the ball until it drove to a touchdown with two minutes remaining in the half.

Starting at the K. U. 49, McMillan passed to Greg Cook for 9 yards and then threw a fullback delay pass to Ron McBride for 20. McMillan ran a keeper around his left end to the 14 and Cook broke loose to the 5 on a trap.

McMillan faked a handoff to McBride, rolled around his left end and then pitched to Staggers who carried the ball over from the 3. Bill Sangster's kick for the extra point was blocked by Bill Hunt.

K. U. took the kickoff and put the ball in play on its 29 on third down. Douglass threw to McGowan on the Missouri 45. McGowan broke away from Fountain at the 40 and was finally pulled down from behind at the 6 on a great effort by Roger Wehrli.

Douglass was stopped for no gain on a rollout and then Wehrli made another great play, knocking down a running pass thrown in the end zone by Junior Riggins. Douglass was hit back on the 17, but escaped and ran to the 3 before being driven out of bounds.

Bell attempted a field goal from the 12. But it was wide and the Tigers went to the dressing room with a great psychological lift.

The third quarter was a standoff for the most part, although the Tigers did put together a drive that carried to the K. U. 19 before Morgan intercepted a halfback pass thrown in the end zone by Staggers. His intended receiver was Mel Gray.

Kansas made the score 21-6 with 10:50 remaining in the fourth quarter. With Missouri in possession on the 11, McMillan threw to Jim Juras, who made a good catch at the 19. He did not have firm possession, however, and fumbled when he was hit. Morgan recovered on the 19.

RIVALS!
MU VS. KU

KU:21
MU:19

FOOTBALL
NOVEMBER 23, 1968

Three running plays carried Kansas to a first down on the 8. Douglass swept his left end for 6. John Riggins gained a half yard. Shanklin ws stopped for no gain. On fourth down Douglass rolled around his right end and scored. Bell kicked the extra point.

Missouri took the kickoff and scored in eight plays. McMillan passed to Tyrone Walls for 12 and hit Tom Shryock for 15 to put the ball on the K. U. 37. He passed to Cook for four yards and then threw to Gray, who made a great leaping catch on the 3.

McMillan gained a yard. Staggers took a pitchout and ran around his right end to score. McMillan attempted a 2-point conversion. He wanted to pass, but was forced to run and was stopped short.

Missouri was unable to get beyond its 49 on its next possession, but a few minutes later the Tigers took over on the K. U. 48 following a punt and scored in three plays.

McMillan passed to Gray, who caught the ball at the 28 and ran to the 10 before being stopped. McMillan over-

threw Cook, but then threw to Cook again on a delay pattern and Cook went over. Sangster kicked the point and the score was 21-19 with 2:05 left. Kansas returned the kickoff to its 30. The Jayhawks gained only one yard on two plays, but they were able to keep possession when Douglass rolleed out and completed a pass to Mosier that was good for 19 yards. The game ended two plays later.

FROM THE KANSAS CITY STAR, 1968

K.U. COACHES GET SHOWER TREATMENT

By Bill Sims
(Assistant Sports Editor of The Star)

Columbia, Mo.

It was wet and wonderful in the Kansas dressing room yesterday after the Jayhawks held off determined Missouri for a 21-19 triumph and at least a share of the Big Eight conference championship.

All of the Jayhawk coaches were treated to fully-clothed showers by the shouting, jubilant players. Even Chancellor W. Clarke Wescoe's clothes were soggy as he congratulated Coach Pepper Rodgers, his assistants and players.

Sitting on a wooden folding chair while clad only in his undershorts, Rodgers tried valiantly to make himself heard as he answered the questions of newsmen who swarmed around him.

But when some of the members of the K. U. band burst into the dressing room and began playing the familiar "I'm a Jayhawk," Rodgers started the rhythmic clapping associated with it and then jumped onto the chair seat to lead it.

Earlier he had said, "The key play was that interception by Dave Morgan that gave us our first touchdown."

Someone pointed out that the senior roving safety had intercepted another pass and also had recovered a fumble to stop two other Missouri bids.

"I didn't realize he had done all that," the 37-year old head man said with a grin. Then, as his eyes twinkled, he added, "I'd like to say that Dave Morgan should be nominated for the back of something this week then.

"Another key play was that last pass from Bobby Douglass to John Mosier for a first down. We had a lot of key plays, but I remember those two.

"Sure I had some qualms about throwing that last pass. A lot of them, in fact. I was scared, but we needed to keep the ball to run out the clock (less than two minutes remaining in the game) and we had nine yards to go for the first down."

Morgan grinned as he said about his interception in the first period for the game's first touchdown, "I was thinking about spiking that ball (throwing it hard on the ground in the end zone) when I got to the 10-yard line. Whoomp. But you have to give a lot of credit to John Zook on that one. He put a tremendous rush on the passer.

I almost committed myself too soon on the one I intercepted in the end zone in the third quarter. I thought the halfback (Jon Staggers) was going to run with the ball, but I dropped back at the last minute and just got my hands on it."

There was nothing but praise for the Tigers from the K.U. coaches and players.

Rodgers commented, "This was a typical Missouri football team, always well-coached and well-prepared. They've got a tremendous team to be able to come back like that. It has to be a compliment to any team that can do that. There was a lot of great hitting out there.

"I have said before that when you look at Missouri on film, they don't look as good until you play them. They have excellent backs and speed."

ZOOK PRAISES M. U.

Zook, defensive end and captain of the Jayhawks, said, "We can't be disappointed with this win. Their backs have better speed as a whole than any team we've played.

"They didn't run anything we hadn't expected. They just executed real well. They're undoubtedly the hardest-hitting team we've played. Missouri's a physical team. Oklahoma's a finesse team."

Keith Christensen, offensive tackle, voiced much the same opinion. "That's the best football team we've played all year. They were tough. I'll tell you. They were clean blockers, clean players – real good boys."

One of the reporters commented to Rodgers that he got the feeling that the momentum had swung to Missouri late in the game. "Yeah, it looked like that to me, too," was the quick reply. Did the fact the scoreboard clock went on the blink in the second quarter and time had to be kept on the field by the officials make much difference? "Sure, not having the clock operating hurt our planning a little, but it was equal for them, too. I kept looking up there, especially late in the game, and sometimes I thought the game was over," Pepper answered.

AN OPPORTUNE BLOCK

Bill Hunt, who played an important role by blocking Missouri's first attempt for an extra point, said, "I was close to blocking one all last week (against Kansas State). I don't know how I was missing them. This one just happened to hit, but it couldn't have come at a better time."

George McGowan, who won a battle for the ball from Missouri's George Fountain that resulted in a touchdown pass to put the Jayhawks in front 14-0, in the opening period explained the play: "I think we both went up and tipped it. He was in a bad position and I was facing the end zone and the ball just bounded into my hands."

It appeared the junior split end from California might get another touchdown late in the second quarter when Douglass hit him with a pass down the middle that covered 65 yards, but McGowan was pulled down from behind at the M. U. 6 by

> *Zook, defensive end and captain of the Jayhawks, said, "We can't be disappointed with this win. Their backs have better speed as a whole than any team we've played.*
>
> *"They didn't run anything we hadn't expected. They just executed real well. They're undoubtedly the hardest-hitting team we've played. Missouri's a physical team. Oklahoma's a finesse team."*

Roger Wehrli and Butch Davis. What happened?

"Well, as Jimmy Ettinger (K. U. reserve quarterback) says, the bear jumped on my back. When you weave back and forth, it's harder for the defender to catch you. I think I just weaved the wrong way."

There was some concern on the part of the Jayhawk fans in the record throng when Douglass hobbled off the field on K. U.'s next-to-last possession. An injury to him could have been extremely costly as the Jayhawks prepare for their appearance against Penn State in the Orange Bowl New Year's night.

"Bobby's O. K.," trainer Dean Nesmith said. "He just got hit real hard when he was tackled out there, but there's nothing wrong with him."

Jayhawk fans all over the nation will echo that last statement. They don't think there's anything wrong with the entire team.

RIVALS!
MU VS. KU

MU:69
KU:21

FOOTBALL
NOVEMBER 22, 1969

1969
MIZZOU DROPS 69-21 BOMB ON K.U.

What a difference a year makes. In 1968, Kansas knocked off Missouri, 21-19, and went to the Orange Bowl. The Jayhawks were 9-2, counting the bowl loss to Penn State.

A year later, the Hawks were 1-9 and a humiliating loss to Missouri left Kansas coach Pepper Rodgers and his mates frustrated. Missouri pounded Kansas 69-21 in Lawrence. MU quarterback Terry McMillan passed for four touchdowns and ran for two more. He had 314 yards of total offense, and was hardly the only star. Mel Gray and Jon Staggers each scored three touchdowns for the Tigers.

John Kadlec, then an assistant with Mizzou, recalls that Missouri coach Dan Devine played Gray and Staggers, both starters, late into the game. Staggers' third touchdown came late in the fourth quarter, giving the Tigers a 63-21 lead.

Following the game, rather than meeting at midfield for the traditional handshake, Rodgers reportedly flashed the peace sign across the field to his counterpart, Devine. Reportedly, Devine only returned half of it.

It was Missouri's turn to go to the Orange Bowl and face Penn State. The Tigers finished the regular season 9-1 and tied with Nebraska for their first conference title since 1960.

Here's how it appeared in the November 23, 1969, Star

Lopsided Triumph Gives Tigers Big Eight Title Tie With Nebraska
M'MILLAN HURLS FOR 4
Mel Gray and Jon Staggers Each Score Three Times for M.U.

BY JOE MCGUFF
(THE *STAR'S* SPORTS EDITOR)

Lawrence, Kas.

From the standpoint of rejoicing Missouri fans, it was a game to remember. From the standpoint of grim-faced Kansas fans it was a game that will not be forgotten.

Missouri, in a climax to its greatest offensive season ever, scored a record-breaking 69-21 victory over the Jayhawks yesterday to gain a share of the Big Eight championship and finish its season with a 9-1 record. Nebraska defeated Oklahoma in its final game to become co-champions with the Tigers.

This is the first time since 1960 that Missouri has won or shared the Big Eight title. The Tigers were 9-0 coming into their final game in 1960. They lost to Kansas, but the game was later awarded to Missouri because Kansas used an ineligible player.

Records were strewn from goal post to goal post as the Tigers rocketed into a 21-0 lead in the first quarter and kept up a relentless attack. The score was 28-7 at the half and 56-14 at the end of the third quarter.

Quarterback Terry McMillan, playing his final regular season game for the Tigers, gave the Memorial stadium crowd of 51,000 a full-scale display of his talents.

He passed for four touchdowns, ran for two and amassed 314 yards of total offense. McMillan completed 13-of-24 passes for 295 yards and carried five times for 19 yards. His four touchdown passes are a Missouri record.

GRAY, STAGGERS LEAD WAY

Mel Gray and Jon Staggers each accounted for three touchdowns. Gray scored on passes of 63 and 26 yards and a run of 19, and Staggers had touchdown receptions of six and four yards. He also ran 18 for a score. McMillan's touchdown runs covered 16 yards and one yard.

Joe Moore and Mike Farmer also shared in the scoring, Moore going 53 yards and Farmer one.

Quarterback Phil Basler went over from the 1 for K.U.'s first touchdown, which came in the second quarter. He completed passes of 38 yards to Larry Brown and 79 yards to Ron Jessie for the other Jayhawk touchdowns.

The 69 points are the most ever scored against a Kansas team and the most Missouri has scored since 1913 when it defeated Drury, 69-0.

The all-time Missouri high is 76

KU's 1-9 record, a year after finishing 9-1, had Rodgers doing a lot of pacing.

yesterday. This is a record high against Kansas.

The most points ever scored before in a Missouri-Kansas game was 45 by the Tigers in both 1940 and 1941. Until yesterday the most one-sided game played between the two schools was the 1941 game that Missouri won, 45-6.

Missouri amassed 651 yards of total

and Kansas is an all-time high in a conference game. The previous record of 88 points was set in 1961 when Kansas defeated Iowa State, 55-33.

K.U.'s whopping loss completed one of the most amazing turnabouts in Big Eight history. A year ago the Jayhawks had a 9-1 season, shared the conference title and went to the Orange bowl. This year they finished with a 1-9 record.

BANNERS SPICE ACTIVITY

In the third quarter, after Missouri had taken a 42-7 lead, Kansas supporters walked around the track in front of the stands carrying two big banners that read: "Kansas will be back." They were followed by two Missouri students carrying a smaller banner that read: "M.U. Orange bowl, K.U. toilet bowl." The M.U. sign bearers were bombarded with debris and wound up fighting with a Kansas fan.

At the end of the day there was little

Records were strewn from goal post to goal post as the Tigers rocketed into a 21-0 lead in the first quarter and kept up a relentless attack. The score was 28-7 at the half and 56-14 at the end of the third quarter.

---

points scored against Missouri Valley in 1893. The highest total previously posted against Kansas came in 1954 when Oklahoma defeated the Jayhawks, 65-0. Oklahoma scored 10 touchdowns in that game, the same number Missouri scored

offense, 344 rushing and 307 passing. The Tigers fell only 14 yards short of the conference record, which they set against Kansas in 1949. Missouri's passing yardage represents a record high against K.U.

The 90 points scored by Missouri

DYNAMIC YEARS

RIVALS!
MU VS. KU

MU:69
KU:21

FOOTBALL
NOVEMBER 22, 1969

question but that bitter Kansas fans felt Missouri had run up the score.

The biggest winner of all may have been the Orange bowl committee which has been under attack in Miami for choosing Missouri as Penn State's opponent instead of Notre Dame. If the Orange bowl officials wanted a big victory to justify their selection, they got it and then some.

As one sided as the game was, Kansas showed surprising ability to move the football at times. Had the Jayhawks not made so many mechanical mistakes it might have been a more respectable game.

K. U. starting from its 20 following the opening kickoff, lined up in the I from an unbalanced line. It was the first time this season K. U. had used an imbalanced line and the Tigers were taken aback. The Jayhawks ran a trap and Jessie broke loose for 27 yards. On their next play they gave up the ball on a fumble.

Missouri drove to the 9, but Henry Brown missed a field goal attempt from the 16.

Kansas moved the ball out to the 46 in four plays. Jessie went 17 yards with a pitchout and John Riggins ran 10 yards around left end. Basler fumbled attempting to hand off to Jessie and Mark Kuhlman recovered for Missouri on the K. U. 44.

This time the Tigers made their break pay off. They reached the K. U. 19 in six plays. On second down, McMillan faked a handoff to Moore and gave the ball to Gray on an end around. Gray scored and Henry Brown kicked the first of his seven conversions. Ricci Stottler added two others.

GRAY HITS PAY DIRT

Missouri scored again on its next possession. With the ball on the M. U. 37, McMillan passed to Gray who caught the ball on the K. U. 14. Dick Hertel

lunged for Gray at the 5 and knocked him off balance, but Gray dove through the air for the final five yards.

Missouri drove 65 yards to score again with 1:06 left in the quarter. The big gainer came on a 27-yard run by Moore. McMillan passed to Staggers for the final four yards and the score was 21-0.

It was an amazing turn of events because even though Kansas was a 17-point underdog it seemed unlikely the game would turn into a rout so quickly.

Early in the second quarter, Kansas forced Missouri to punt for the first time, but the relief was short-lived. A short time later Sam Adams of Missouri blocked a punt and fell on the ball on the K. U. 16.

On first down McMillan passed to Gray who was wide open in the end zone and the score was 28-0.

Kansas took the kickoff and put together a 76-yard drive that consumed 10 players. A 34-yard pass from Basler to Larry Brown put the ball on the M. U. 26 and Basler later went over from the 1 on a sneak.

The half-time statistics were surprising. Missouri had 265 yards of total offense to 213 for Kansas and 14 first downs to K. U.'s 11.

If K. U. supporters felt they could take hope in these figures they were mistaken. The worst was yet to come.

MIZZOU KEEPS MARCHING

Missouri drove 72 yards to a touchdown on its first possession of the third quarter. The big gains came on a 38-yard pass to Moore and a 26-yard pass to Gray. McMillan passed six yards to Staggers for the touchdown and the score was 35-7.

As soon as the Tigers got the ball back the score became 42-7. Moore, on a first-down play following a Kansas punt,

took a handoff, veered outside his right end and raced 53 yards for the touchdown.

Kansas gave up the ball on a fumble following the kickoff with Dan Borgard recovering at the K. U. 18. Moore ran for two yards and then McMillan ran a keeper 16 yards to score.

Kansas took the kickoff and went 80 yards in five plays to score. The touchdown came on Basler's 38-yard pass to Brown who caught the ball at the 18 with no one near him.

Missouri took the kickoff and scored in five plays. A 43-yard sideline pass to Staggers put the Tigers in scoring position on the K. U. 17. McMillan went over from the 1 to make the score 56-14 with 38 seconds left in the third quarter.

Early in the fourth quarter, Basler and Jessie combined on a 79-yard pass play that reduced K. U.'s deficit to 56-21.

The Tigers, who had used Farmer at quarterback on a preceding series, brought McMillan back in and he led them on a 46-yard touchdown thrust. A 32-yard pass to Henry Brown put the ball on the K. U. 21. Staggers went over from the 18 two plays later on a draw and it was 63-21 with 9:30 left in the game.

Missouri drove 89 yards in 14 plays for its final touchdown. McMillan was at quarterback for the first three plays. Farmer took the Tigers the rest of the way and went over himself from the 1 with 1:52 left.

McMillan finished the season with 18 touchdown passes, a conference record. The previous high was 15 by Dick Mann of Iowa State set in 1951. McMillan has thrown 14 touchdown passes in the last five games.

The next stop for Missouri is the Orange bowl. As for K. U., Pepper Rodgers said earlier that next season would start right after the Missouri game.

QUESTIONS BRING IRE TO DEVINE

Devine had reason to smile after Missouri clinched its first league crown since 1960.

By Dick Wade
(Assistant Sports Editor of The Star)

Lawrence, Kas., -

Last Thursday Dan Devine made this observation on his Missouri team's upcoming game with Kansas: "We're walking into a hornets' nest over there." He was correct, painfully correct. But the Tiger coach wasn't stung on the playing field; it happened in his own locker room.

Thirty minutes after his Tigers had stormed past K. U. , 69-21, Devine still dripping wet from the traditional victory shower, was backed into a corner. About him gathered an assortment of newsmen – and some of them weren't friendly.

The mood of the session quickly developed. The first question was, "Why did you run up the score?"

Devine, obviously struggling to hold his temper, slowly said, "I resent that question. It is unnecessary; it is illogical. We came here to play a football game. What do you want us to do? Every time they got the ball, they moved it. Do you want us to let them score and not try to score ourselves?"

He looked about him, from reporter to reporter, not quite as calmly he said, "We brought 47 players over here. We used 47. And I want you all to know I've been on the other side of the fence – plenty of times. I've been beaten 49-0, and nobody said anything about it."

An attempt was made to cool things. A reporter asked if K. U. surprised him in any way – by using the unbalanced line, for instance. Devine said, "No, they've shown it before. But they use a lot of formations, conceal them well. That's a good team, a well-coached team."

Then came another barb. "Why did you leave McMillan in so long?"

Devine's eyes narrowed. Obviously, he considered this badgering. "What did you want me to do? Put in a rookie quarterback, let him fumble the ball away. Did you want us to let down, let them run over us?"

RIVALS!
MU VS. KU

MU:67
KU:66

FOOTBALL
JANUARY 16, 1968

Again Devine inspected those about him. Then he said, "When I was leaving the field, somebody came off the Kansas bench and yelled some things at me. The gist of it was that I ran it (the score) up. I don't mind that, that's emotion. But I don't think I have to defend my motives or reputation as a coach to the press – or anybody."

Then Devine clarified something: "I don't think they were members of the K. U. coaching staff. I didn't know them."

The conversation switched to M. U. play calling. It developed that McMillan called most of the early-game plays from the line of scrimmage and obviously did it well. And Devine had kind words for Phil Basler, the K. U. quarterback too, "He played well, real well. He ran especially well. But that doesn't surprise me. We tried to get him."

Then came the bomb – a bigger one than the 63-yarder McMillan threw to Mel Gray, bigger than the 79-yarder Basler threw to Ron Jessie.

It went this way: "What effect on the game did that choke-up story in *Sports Illustrated* have on the game?" This was a reference to a preseason item in the magazine that ran in this vein, "Several Big Eight coaches, including Pepper Rodgers of Kansas, believe Dan Devine of Missouri cannot win the big game."

Even though Rodgers had denied saying it, it has hung over this game, never discussed publicly but always present.

Devine almost flared. Then he braced up and said, "I don't know how that story came about. But however it happened, it was a cheap shot."

"It hurt our recruiting, it hurt our national image. I didn't use it in any way preparing our team for this game. And that's all I want to say about it."

That seemed to satisfy most of the interrogators. They drifted off. Only a handful remained to hear Devine say "this was a game I'm happy to win – by any score. This was our title game."

But McMillan, already dressed and headed out the door, heard. He looked at Devine, they exchanged smiles. Then the coach handed his quarterback a lapel emblem – a bright, symbolic orange. Missouri, of course, will play in the Orange bowl New Year's night.

That capped McMillan's big day. It reminded him that he was going home better than he left. He comes from Coral Gables, Fla., only a few miles from the Orange bowl. He wasn't even a regular in high school. He wasn't recruited by a Florida school. But the home folks will know he's there New Year's night.

That he set two more passing records yesterday – one for most T.D. passes by a Big Eight player, another for most T. D. passes by a Missouri player – he credited to his protection and his receivers.

But he did say this, "I didn't throw an interception today – and that has to be a record."

Then McMillan said the thing halfback Jon Staggers had brought up earlier: "Our seniors never had beaten Kansas, not even as freshmen.

"This was what we worked for; this was the day it all worked. We weren't running it up. We were playing football, real good football."

That McMillan, who had a 13-for-24 throwing day even though he missed his first six, was off early he attributed to Kansas' defense.

"They stayed in that 3-deep all the way, and they played it really well early. You had to lay it right in there. But I don't think anybody can cover a guy like Mel Gray (who caught three of McMillan's four T. D. passes) one-on-one long."

About that time, Sam Adams (the defensive captain), brought his father in to talk to Devine. Adams said this, "We wanted the championship (which the Tigers wound up sharing with Nebraska). We have a bowl bid. We didn't want to be embarrassed over here."

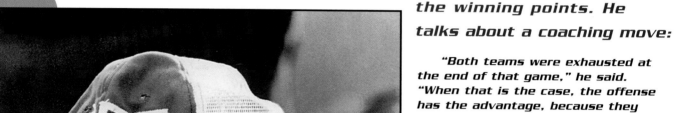

ONE BIG PLAY DOES IT FOR K. U.

Don Fambrough, the self-deprecating former head coach of the Kansas Jayhawks, can tell a story. When he looks back on the 1971 game between his KU squad and the hated Tigers of Missouri, Fambrough doesn't talk about the stifling defense both squads played. He doesn't talk about the big offensive play that gave KU the winning points. He talks about a coaching move:

"Both teams were exhausted at the end of that game," he said. "When that is the case, the offense has the advantage, because they know where they're going.

"We held a 7-0 lead late in the fourth quarter, but we were facing fourth down on our own 8-yard line. If we punted, our tired punter could have had it blocked for a touchdown. The best we could hope for was him getting off the punt—into the wind—and setting up Missouri with great field position.

"I called the punter over and told him to run around the end zone for as long as he could. I reminded him not to run out of the end zone. And above all else, I told him not to fumble. I said, 'Coach Fambrough is over on the sideline with a high-powered rifle. If you fumble, you'll never make it back to the sideline.'"

Punter Marc Harris managed to run around for 12 seconds before being tackled for a safety. Then, punting from his 20 with no rush, he punted it to the MU 32 and the Tigers could not mount a threat.

Here's how it appeared in the November 21, 1971, Star

RIVALS!
MU VS. KU

MU:7
KU:2

FOOTBALL
NOVEMBER 20, 1971

By Joe McGuff
The Star's Sports Editor

Lawrence, Kas.,

For a time yesterday it appeared that the 80th meeting of the Kansas-Missouri rivalry would produce the ultimate in futility, a 0-0 tie. It would have been an appropriate way for both teams to conclude the season, but in the end Kansas was resourceful enough to devise an outcome more satisfying to its followers.

In the third quarter the Jayhawks set off on what was to be their second and last long drive of the day. It ended with David Jaynes completing a 35-yard pass to Marvin Foster in the end zone. On the strength of that one big play the Jayhawks emerged a 7-2 victory.

Missouri's two points came on a safety that K. U. took intentionally with only a minute left to play.

For the most part this was a bumbling, uninspiring game but football purists could take some consolation in the fact that the lone touchdown play was brilliantly executed.

Foster ran a fly pattern and came racing down the sideline with Henry Stuckey, Missouri's defensive right halfback, matching him stride for stride. As they crossed the goal line Foster leaped for the ball and Stuckey leaped with him. Foster, a junior split end, came down with it and that was the ball game.

Bob Helmbacher kicked the extra point and Kansas led, 7-0, with 4:39 left in the third quarter.

Missouri had two scoring opportunities through the remainder of the game. The first one developed in the closing two minutes of the third quarter. Marc Harris punted to the M. U. 29 and Mike Fink returned the ball to the 49.

The Tigers drove to a first down at the K. U. 30. John Venturi passed to Chuck Link for five yards. Venturi was hit for a 2-yard loss on second down as the result of a broken play. It was one of the numerous mistakes the Tigers made and left them facing a third-and-7 situation. Venturi threw an incomplete pass and Greg Hill attempted a field goal from the 34 that was wide.

Missouri's last and biggest opportunity came in the closing minutes of the game. Kansas was pinned down on its 8 and had to punt. The ball hit on the K. U. 40 and bounced backwards five yards, where it was downed.

Venturi hit John Henley with a 15-yard sideline pass. Jack Bastable gained four yards to the 16. Venturi threw to Henley but the pass went incomplete. Don Johnson broke off tackle for two yards to the 14, bringing up a fourth-and-4.

A FOOT SHORT

Venturi passed over the middle to Link, who dived for the ball and was on the ground when he caught it. The ball was spotted a foot short of the 10 and that was the margin by which the Tigers missed their first down.

Kansas took over with two minutes left. After running three plays and drawing a delay of game penalty the Jayhawks found themselves on their 8.

Rather than risk a punt from their end zone and give the Tigers good field position the Jayhawks decided to take a safety. Harris took the snap from center and ran around in the end zone for 12 seconds before the Tigers could bring him down.

K. U. put the ball in play by punting from its 20 with one minute left. Harris punted to the M. U. 32 and Fink

returned the ball to the M. U. 48. On first down Venturi went back to pass. Eddie Sheats, K. U.'s defensive end, hit him and the ball popped out of his hand. Sheats recovered on the M. U. 37. Two plays later the game was over.

The Jayhawks' victory broke a 5-game losing streak and enabled them to finish the season with a 4-7 record in their first campaign under Don Fambrough. K. U. scored only two conference victories, the other one over Kansas State by a score of 39-13.

The season was almost a total disaster for the Tigers and their new head coach, Al Onofrio. Missouri won one game and lost 10, the lone victory coming against Southern Methodist in the third game of the season.

WORST SINCE '34 FOR M. U.

The 10 regular season losses are the most in Missouri's history. From a percentage standpoint this is the Tigers' worst season since 1934 when they posted an 0-8-1 record under Frank Carideo.

Although Missouri was unable to score on its own initiative yesterday the Tigers were in certain respects a more effective offensive team than the Jayhawks. Missouri had 322 yards of total offense to K. U.'s 211 and was much more active on the ground, accumulating 196 yards of rushing to the Jayhawks' 87.

But while the Tigers were able to move the ball with more consistency than Kansas they had a frightful time hanging on to it. They gave up the ball five times on fumbles, twice on interceptions and slowed themselves with repeated mistakes in execution.

Kansas penetrated Missouri territory only twice in the first half under its own momentum and aside from its touchdown drive did not get inside the Missouri 28 in the last half.

Missouri decisively outplayed Kansas in the first half, amassing 205 yards of total offense to the Jayhawks' 115. But all of the yards Missouri gained failed to produce any points, largely because of three fumbles and an interception.

Both teams missed good opportunities to kick field goals in the first half. Kansas drove from its 28 to the Missouri 4 in the first period. Helmbacher attempted

a field goal from the 11 but it was blocked by Otto Nichols.

Three plays later Kansas got the ball at the M. U. 28 as the result of a fumble but was driven back and had to punt.

In the second quarter Missouri drove from its 20 to the K. U. 12. Hill attempted a field goal from the 19 but it was wide. M. U. later reached the K. U. 28 only to fumble the ball away and later drove from its 17 to the K. U. 35 only to lose possession on an interception.

By half time it appeared that neither team was capable of scoring. That impression continued to grow until Jaynes and Foster combined on the one play that decided the game and enabled the Jayhawks to gain their 33rd victory in the series. Missouri has won 38 times and there have been nine ties.

RIVALS!
MU VS. KU

KU:14
MU:13

FOOTBALL
NOVEMBER 24, 1973

FROM THE KANSAS CITY TIMES, 1971

FAMBROUGH JUST HAPPY TO BE ALIVE

By Fritz Kreisler
A Member of the Star's Sports Staff

Lawrence, Kan. – "They probably thought I'd lost my mind," said Coach Don Fambrough, "but there was no way we were going to kick out of that end zone."

Thus the Kansas football coach explained the intentional safety with one minute to go that put the Jayhawks over the last big hurdle in their 7-2 victory over Missouri yesterday. With 1:12 left, Kansas faced a fourth-and-14 at its 7-yard line and rather than have punter Marc Harris punt into a 10-to-15 mile an hour wind, Fambrough ordered Harris to allow the charging Missouri line to tackle him in the end zone.

"About 10 of us decided it at the same time," Fambrough continued. "The big thing is that it worked, because they'd be stringing me to the post if it hadn't."

When Harris received the snap from center, he ran first to the left side of the field and then back to the right before being swarmed under by the Tigers. The object of that maneuver was to run off as much time as possible, thus giving the Tigers even fewer seconds to operate when they got the ball. Harris' scrambling took 12 seconds.

Fambrough was asked if he reminded Harris not to run out of the end zone. "I think about 25 times," the coach said. "That and hold on to the ball."

"I could still hear him as I ran onto the field," said Harris, a tall, wiry sopho-more from Lawrence. "I don't think it was so risky. I wasn't worried about drop-ping it. I thought it was a smart move. They just told me to stay in the end zone and hang onto the ball."

The play that made the intentional safety possible was a 35-yard touchdown pass from quarterback

> "The big thing is that it worked, because they'd be stringing me to the post if it hadn't."
> Don Fambrough

David Jaynes to wide receiver Marvin Foster in the third quarter. Foster, a swift junior from Central High School, said he got behind defender Henry Stuckey and took the pass at the goal.

"I just had maybe two or three steps on him, and David laid it right in there," explained Foster, his lean face still beaded with perspiration. "First it looked like it would be short, but it wasn't, and that's why I had to kind of jump for it. I think if he (Stuckey) realized the position of the ball, he might have tapped it, but it had a pretty good arch on it. He was watching me, and when I stopped he stopped. Then I saw the ball was going to be longer, and all I had to do was catch it."

STREAK PATTERN

Jaynes, who completed his sopho-more season with an 8-for-20 passing per-formance, called the touchdown a streak pattern, in which both wide receivers are on the same side of the field. The one on the inside heads for the goal posts, and the outside man (Foster) heads straight down field.

"I saw Marvin about even up and let go," Jaynes said. "Then I got knocked down and couldn't see any more, but I heard the crowd so I figured something good had happened."

The play was sent in from the bench. "We were trying everything on offense – long passes, short passes," said Fambrough when asked why that particular one. "Actually our protection was a little better considering we were playing Missouri. They're tough to hold out. The ball was thrown well and Marvin made a fine catch."

Fambrough also had words of praise for the K. U. defense. "Our defense was just tremendous," he said. "It was one that bends but doesn't break."

He also explained that the wind and desire for field position were the major factors in his decision to permit Missouri to receive the second-half kickoff, yet it was the lack of both in the final 1:12 that led to the decision on the clinching safety.

KANSAS AIR GAME CUTS DOWN TIGERS, 14-13

Don Fambrough, the two-tenured head coach of Kansas, says there was no such thing as an ordinary KU-MU game. The 1973 game certainly backs up his claim.

The two teams traded mistakes as they battled to a 0-0 halftime score. Missouri then scored two touchdowns in the third quarter, on a long run by quarterback Ray Smith and a long punt return by John Moseley. When the Tigers missed the second extra point, it hardly seemed like it would matter.

That seemed to inspire Kansas, who responded with a 76-yard drive for a touchdown. Then, a fourth-quarter drive, including a fourth-down conversion for a 14-yard touchdown in the final two minutes, tied the game. Kansas converted the extra point, then held on for the victory.

"That was the best memory of my coaching career, beating Missouri to clinch a berth in the Liberty Bowl," Fambrough said. "The way we won at the end was great. There's always something special in the games against Missouri. Everybody—even those who don't like football—go crazy when we beat Missouri.

"I started to say that I respect those people, but I don't."

Here's how it appeared in the November 25, 1973, Star:

By JOE McGUFF
SPORTS EDITOR

Lawrence, Kas.,

For most of three quarters yesterday's Kansas-Missouri game was bogged down in fumbles, interceptions and futility. Then, just when the crowd of 46,500 had resigned itself to a terminal case of boredom, the game erupted into a frenzied struggle that K.U. won 14-13, on a go-for-broke pass and a successful conversion kick.

Missouri ended the scoreless deadlock by striking for two touchdowns in a span of one minute and 41 seconds. The Tigers' first touchdown came on a 45-yard run by Ray Smith, who replaced John Cherry at quarterback and played the entire game. The Tigers scored again with 2:07 remaining in the third quarter on a brilliant 53-yard punt return by John Moseley.

Greg Hill, who had missed field goals from 44, 33 and 32 yards, boosted his extra-point attempt wide to the left. The miss was his first in 20 attempts. With Missouri seemingly in control of the game it did not seem too important at the time, but it proved to be the margin of defeat.

Kansas responded to the M.U. scoring burst by taking the kickoff and driving 76 yards in eight plays. Dave Jaynes, making his final appearance in Memorial Stadium, passed 14 yards to Bruce Adams with 13:56 left in the fourth quarter. Mike Love converted and the score was 13-7.

The Jayhawks' winning touchdown came on a 14-yard, 4th-down pass from Jaynes to his leading receiver, Emmett Edwards, with 1:37 left, but the sequence of events leading up to the score began with about six-and-a-half minutes remaining.

Kansas had been stopped at the Missouri 46 when Marc Harris got off a high punt that appeared headed for the end zone. Paul Bower caught up with the ball and batted it down at the 1 as his momentum carried him into the end zone. The Tigers tried desperately to get out of the hole, but they were able to gain only eight yards on three running plays before punting. Adams fielded the ball on the M.U. 47 and returned it to the 42.

The Jayhawks put the ball in play with 4:17 left. They moved to a first down at the 22 with 3:04 remaining. Jaynes, trying to pass, could not find a receiver and ran for two yards. Randy Ross dropped a pass in the flat. Robert Miller ran to the 16 but the Tigers were

RIVALS!
MU VS. KU

KU:14
MU:13

FOOTBALL
NOVEMBER 23, 1973

offside, giving K.U. an extra yard and an extra down.

With two minutes left Jaynes ran a keeper, but gained only one yard. Now it was 4th-and-2 and the game was on the line. The Jayhawks elected to try a short pass to Delvin Williams for the first down, but they also sent Edwards deep. Jaynes was to look at him first to see if he was open before he threw to Williams.

"It's a basic play we've worked on all season," McCullers said. "Emmett gave a super execution. In fact, it was super execution by 11 players. The players made it work, not me."

Edwards, the leading receiver in the Big Eight, lined up on the left side. He raced toward the goal line and cut in toward the goal post. Moseley, the fleet cornerback who is M.U.'s best pass defender, seemed uncertain as to which way Edwards would make his cut and lost a step on him. Jaynes saw that Edwards was open in the end zone and hit him with a perfectly-timed pass. Moseley lunged from behind the ball but could not reach it.

Love, a freshman playing his fourth game with the varsity, kicked the extra point and the Jayhawks led, 14-13, with 1:37 remaining.

Missouri, hoping to get into position for a final-field goal attempt, put the ball at its 36 following the kickoff. The Tigers moved quickly to their 45 and then Smith passed to John Kelsey. The play carried to the K.U. 49, but the Tigers were assessed a personal foul penalty that moved them back to their 36. It was a setback from which Missouri was unable to recover. Missouri had only one timeout

remaining and a minute showed on the clock. The Tigers ran four plays and turned the ball over to the Jayhawks with seven seconds left.

For Missouri the day was one of missed opportunities and mistakes. An indication of things to come developed just before the end of the first quarter when M.U. reached the K.U. 27 and Hill came in to attempt a field goal. He had the wind at his back but the Tigers let the clock run. The quarter ended before he could get his kick off. His attempt into the wind at the other end of the field was wide and short.

The Tigers, who won their first six games, ended the season by losing four of their last five. They dropped into fifth place in the Big Eight. Onofrio put Smith in at quarterback trying to inject some life into his sagging offense. The Tigers showed only minimal improvement, but in the end they lost because they could not hold a 13-point lead.

By winning Kansas jumped into a second-place tie with Nebraska in the Big Eight. The Jayhawks finished with a 7-3-1 record, their best since 1968, and are 4-2-1 in the conference. They won all six of their home games, the first time they have had a perfect record at home since 1951.

Jaynes, who has made several of the early All-American teams, enhanced his reputation with his two touchdown passes and strengthened his candidacy for the

Heisman trophy, given annually to the collegian selected as the No. 1 player in the nation.

Jaynes completed 17 of 36 passes for 173 yards. He finished the season with 2,131 yards and moved into second place on the all-time Big Eight list with a career total of 5,132. He passed Jerry Tagge, of Nebraska, who had 5,069 yards. Jaynes set a Big Eight record for career touchdown passes with 35.

Edwards, already the No. 1 receiver in K.U. history, finished the season with 802 yards. Edwards, a junior, has 2,008 career yards.

Like Missouri, K.U. was held down by its own mistakes through much of the game. The Jayhawks did not get beyond their own 37 in the first quarter. In the second quarter they reached the M.U. 22 but lost the ball on an interception. Just before halftime they recovered a fumble at the M.U. 25, but three plays later fumbled the ball back to Missouri.

The victory was the third straight for K.U. over Missouri. Don Fambrough has not lost to the Tigers since becoming head coach at Kansas and Al Onofrio has yet to defeat K.U. since taking over at Missouri.

KANSAS CURLS UP WITH EDWARDS

BY JACK LINDBERG
A MEMBER OF THE SPORTS STAFF

Lawrence, Kan.

Players, coaches and the Kansas faithful were all joyfully exhausted yesterday in the K.U. dressing room following the Jayhawks' 14-13 victory over Missouri.

Don Fambrough, the Kansas coach, sat on a bench with his arms on his knees, but he needed no questions from the semi-circle of writers around him. Fambrough told of the high points of the victory without being prompted.

There was, obviously, the winning touchdown pass – Dave Jaynes to Emmett Edwards; the vital point after kick, the booming punt by Marc Harris that sailed 45 yards high before being downed on the 1 by Paul Bower.

"We don't got this, and we don't got that," Fambrough said of his battle-scarred and injury-riddled Jayhawks. "All we got is an abundance of don't give-up-ness."

The game-winning play, a 14-yard Jaynes to Edwards completion, was called on the sidelines during a time out by Charlie McCullers, the offensive co-ordinator. The fourth-and-2 was a simple curl pattern with Edwards the secondary receiver. Delvin Williams, the tailback, was the primary receiver as the play was only designed to get the necessary first down.

"David was to take a look at Emmett," Fambrough said, "but we had to get the first down first. David was to hit the swing man."

Edwards said he raced toward the end-zone, faked to the outside and then curled back.

"No man can stay with me one-on-one," Edwards said. "He's good (John Moseley of M.U.). He's a tough little kid (5-9 and 160), but I gave him a good fake to the outside, he was playing me that way, and then I curled."

Mike Love, the freshman, then kicked the game-winning point and all Kansas had to do was sweat out the remaining 1:37.

"That kid will never kick a bigger one," Fambrough said of Love, the third kicker K.U. has used this season.

Fambrough said he was greatly concerned, but not discouraged after the Tigers erupted for a 13-0 lead.

"It would be easy to lay down after that," Fambrough said, "especially for the seniors. It had been a long season, they had won some big games and they had played hard up to there. That's the most courageous team I've ever seen.

"At 13-0 it was obvious we had to score on our next possession," the coach continued. So K.U. went 78 yards in eight plays with Jaynes hitting Bruce Adams on a 14-yard pass for the T.D. It was Adam's only reception of the day and his seventh T.D. catch of the season.

Then the teams traded possessions before M.U. was put into the deep hole by the Harris punt.

"Marc really kicked it," Fambrough said of the tremendously high punt. "And Paul must have run a hundred yards to get down there, to down the ball on the 1."

"We had to have something like that to win. You're damn right we had to make something happen."

The Kansas defense which "was out there at least four hours," according to the coach, forced a punt and K.U. had the ball 42 yards away with 4:17 left.

Jaynes got the team to the 14 in eight plays. Then came the time out and then the winning pass.

"It's a basic play we've worked on all season," McCullers said. "Emmett gave a super execution. In fact, it was super execution by 11 players. The players made it work, not me."

Edwards, the Kansas City Central High product, said he had been recruited by both Missouri and Kansas following his high-school graduation. He doesn't regret his choice, Kansas has beaten Missouri three consecutive times and Edwards has participated twice.

"Coach Fambrough was up and I was up," Edwards said. "I enjoyed it, I really enjoyed it."

James Bowman, another player from Central High, had a pass interception and a fumble recovery from his safety spot.

"I was just hoping that every game I got to play would be like this one," said Bowman, who suffered a fractured arm in

RIVALS!
MU VS. KU

KU:14
MU:13

FOOTBALL
NOVEMBER 23, 1973

the season opener against Washington State. He returned to playing status three games ago. "I felt I could help the team if I could get back." He got back too soon as far as the Tigers were concerned.

Dean Baird, the K.U. linebacker who was in on nine tackles, said: "I knew we'd come back. We just had to keep the faith. They (Missouri) have had trouble on offense, but I don't know why. They've got a fine offensive line and that (Ray) Bybee and (Tommy) Reamon are just great runners."

Mitch Sutton, the defensive tackle, made the final K.U. stop of the day when he sacked quarterback Ray Smith for an 8-yard loss. It was Sutton's ninth tackle of the day.

"We were in a prevent defense," Sutton said. "I had outside responsibility, but I was blocked at the line. I jumped over Reamon and then I hit him (Smith). I sure didn't want him to get away."

"No problem, no problem at all," said a smiling Jaynes who has quarter-

backed the three consecutive victories over the Tigers. "We played well, at least good enough to win."

"I was looking for the first down," he said of the winning pass. "Emmett made another super catch."

Fambrough said he was a little surprised that Missouri started Smith at quarterback but not Reamon at tailback. "We prepare for Missouri, not a quarterback," Fambrough said. It's about the same with Smith in there or the other one (John Cherry). Maybe Smith is a little better runner."

Kansas finished unbeaten at home. "How 'bout that?" Fambrough said. "We're picked to finish seventh or eighth. In some cases we were

even picked to finish off the page. It's sure a good feeling. Second (a tie with Nebraska) is sure a lot better than seventh or eighth."

K.U. now takes three or four days off prior to beginning getting ready for North Carolina State in the Dec. 17 Liberty Bowl in Memphis.

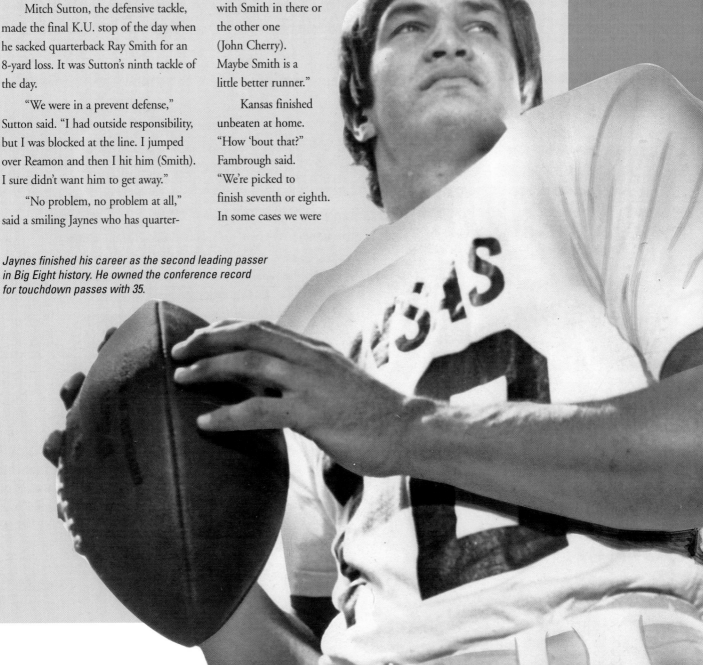

Jaynes finished his career as the second leading passer in Big Eight history. He owned the conference record for touchdown passes with 35.

M.U. Sweets Sour

By Rich Sambo
(A Member of the Sports Staff)

Lawrence, Kan.

In a nondescript kind of way the 14-13 loss to Kansas yesterday left the Missouri dressing room overtaken by a bittersweetness that can be the result only of a sometimes glowing, sometimes unsettling season.

Greg Hill, the man with the iron toe who has been winning games for two years, missed an extra point late in the third quarter. It proved to be the difference in the game.

John Moseley, a superb defensive back with a chance to receive All-American recognition, was sitting alone on a bench. His 53-yard punt return in the third quarter had staked the Tigers to their 13-0 lead. He had broken up three David Jaynes passes to Emmett Edwards, the leading receiver in the Big Eight Conference.

Yet for one lonely moment, on a fourth-and-2 situation at the Missouri 14-yard line, everything Moseley had contributed to the Missouri season was before him. Edwards streaked into the end zone on a curl pattern, clasped a perfectly thrown pass from Jaynes and scored the tying touchdown.

From Hill, who had converted 20-of-30 extra-point attempts this season: "It was a good snap and a good hold. I just didn't hit it right. I knew it as soon as I kicked it."

Said Moseley, who had returned a punt for 74 yards against Southern Methodist: "We were in man coverage. I was looking for an out pattern but I really didn't think they would throw the ball.

He just hooked into the middle. I wasn't in too bad a shape. I had a chance for the ball, went for it and didn't get it. Jaynes threw the ball right on the money."

Al Onofrio, the Missouri coach who has not beaten Kansas in his three seasons, saw the touchdown play much the same way. "It was a perfectly executed play," Onofrio said. "He (Edwards) was covered as closely as he could be covered. The ball was right on the spot.

"I wasn't surprised they went for the touchdown. Time was running out (2:37 left) and they figured they'd go for it then rather than try to make a first down. We knew we couldn't give up anything. It was just a perfectly executed pass.

"I was extremely sad that Greg missed the one extra point, which eventually was the difference in the game," Onofrio said. "Greg has helped us win so many games in the last two years. He has been a valuable part of our team. He had kicked 20 in a row so I guess the percentages finally caught up with him."

The game, which renewed the oldest rivalry west of the Mississippi, was not without its surprises. Ray Smith, a junior college transfer from Santa Maria, Calif., who has seen little action, started the game and went the distance.

"We decided Monday," said Onofrio, who gave no inkling of his decision prior to game time, "Cherry (John, No. 1 through the first 10 games) has had trouble with his ball handling the last three or four games – not that it was all his fault. I have been wanting to play Ray all along but I hate to put in a quarterback and then pull him out." Onofrio had no second thoughts about the move.

"Ray did a good job for his first game," the coach said. "He ran the option well (including a 45-yard touchdown) and passed well (6-of-13 for 61 yards)."

With time running out in the first quarter, Dean Zook, Kansas defensive end, nailed tailback Tommy Reamon for a 3-yard loss to the K.U. 27. Hill came out on the field and was setting up for a 44-yard field goal attempt when time ran out. So instead of having the benefit of kicking with a reported 8-mile an hour wind, Hill was forced to kick against the breeze after the teams changed sides.

"I didn't try to call time out," Onofrio said. "I could have called time out and it probably could have helped us."

So it seemed the best part of Missouri's day was wrapped around the 1 minute 44 seconds of the third quarter in which the Tigers scored both of their touchdowns.

"It was a very disappointing loss for us," Onofrio offered. "Both teams played extremely hard. We got the momentum and scored the two touchdowns and then they scored twice and took the momentum from us."

Had the speculation of a Sun Bowl appearance and the verification of acceptance to play Auburn before the loss to Iowa State last week taken anything away from this team?

"I can't say that it did," Onofrio answered. "But I think the bowls possibly could be picked at a later date than they are right now – Nov. 17 is a good date if that's the day the invitations are to be extended. I don't want this misinterpreted as an excuse for the outcome of the game."

CHAPTER 7

Being Good Stewarts

MIZZOU STUNS K.U., 67-66

Norm Stewart was in his first year as head coach of the Missouri Tigers, and things weren't going well. The Tigers were 4-7 in the non-conference season, and had started the Big Eight Conference season 1-2. They traveled to Lawrence to take on the Jayhawks, who were 8-3 in the non-conference and had won all three of their conference tilts.

So, holding to form, the Tigers won on the road.

The Jayhawks had assumed a 10-point lead inside of five minutes remaining. But the Tigers pulled back to a tie. When Rodger Bohnenstiehl hit one of two free throws with two seconds remaining, it looked like the rally was for naught. But then the improbable happened.

Tom Johnson was fouled just before the buzzer sounded. With no time left on the clock, he sank the first free throw to tie the score. Then, he drilled the second to give the Tigers the victory.

"We played a whale of a game," Stewart said, looking back on the game. "To me, there were two miracles. The first is that a foul was called on the last play of the game, in Lawrence. The second is that Tom Johnson made both free throws."

Here's how it appeared in the January 16, 1968, Times:

Tom Johnson Pops In Two Free Throws After Final Buzzer to Take Away an Apparent Kansas Triumph and Put It in Missouri's Victory Column

OWENS'S HOLD ENDS

Tigers Beat One of His Jayhawk Teams for First Time – Charity Toss by Bohnenstiehl Seems Clincher With 2 Seconds Left

By Bill Sims
(Assistant Sports Editor of The Star)

Lawrence, Kas.,

Missouri's Tom Johnson capped an amazing, almost unbelievable late-minute comeback by calmly firing in two free throws after the final buzzer had sounded to give the Tigers a 67-66

Big Eight basketball triumph over Kansas before a frenzied crowd of 11,000 here last night.

Johnson, the 6-foot-4 senior forward from St. Louis, may not have been as calm as he appeared to be as he toed the charity line for a 1-and-1 opportunity. With all of the other players standing at the side of the court watching anxiously,

he flipped in his first attempt to gain at least an overtime reprieve for the Tigers.

Then, taking a deep breath, he cradled the ball in his hand and sent it toward the hoop. The ball didn't touch the rim; it dropped through for Missouri's first victory ever over a Ted Owens-coached Jayhawk team.

134

BEING GOOD STEWARTS

RIVALS!
MU VS. KU

MU:67
KU:66

BASKETBALL
JANUARY 15, 1968

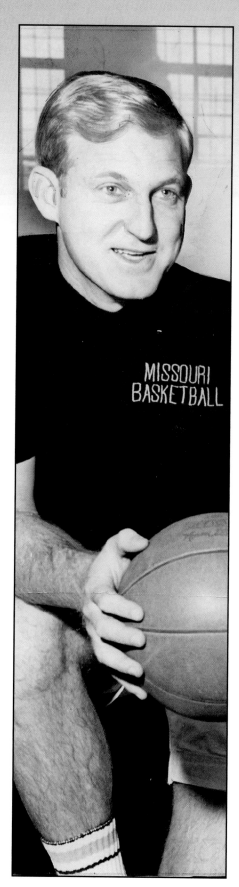

Only two seconds before the final buzzer, the partisan Kansas fans went into ecstasy as Rodger Bohnenstiehl was fouled with the score tied at 65-all. A hush fell over Allen field house as the 6-6 senior from Collinsville, Ill., went to the free-throw line and pumped the ball through to send the Jayhawks ahead.

Then Don Tomlinson took the ball out of bounds and fired a pass toward Johnson just over the mid-court line. K. U.'s Phil Harmon lunged in a desperate effort to deflect the ball or intercept, but he was called for fouling. That set up Johnson's winning shots that brought him a ride off the court on the shoulders of his happy teammates.

Missouri thus ended Owens' conference winning streak at home at 15 games. The Tiger victory also sent idle Oklahoma into undisputed possession of first place in the Big Eight with a 2-0 record. K. U. now is 2-1 and Missouri is 2-2 in league play.

Even if the game had gone into overtime, Kansas would have played with only six players available for duty. Chet Lawrence did not suit up because of a knee injury suffered Saturday night against Portland.

That left only 10 Jayhawks in uniform and four of them – Bruce Sloan, Jo-Jo White, Vernon Vanoy and Greg Douglas – already had fouled out.

Bohnenstiehl picked up his fourth with 18:30 to go in the second half and played the final 10 minutes after being rested. Only Dave Nash on the bench could have gone back into action.

This was not really as slam-bang an affair as one might imagine in looking at the foul statistics with 28 whistled against K. U. and 18 against Missouri. But there was plenty of contact and, at times, it did get a little rough.

MISSOURI WON'T QUIT

The Jayhawks seemed to have a lock on the victory when they forged ahead by 10 points, 64-54, with only 4:38 remaining. But, just as they had all evening when Kansas moved far in front, the Tigers battled back.

Johnson connected from the corner and Eugene Jones flipped in two free throws before Harmon countered with one charity at the 2:53 mark. That left Kansas in front, 65-58, and none of the fans was too concerned even then.

But in the next 40 seconds Tomlinson pumped one in from the right of the lane and Theo Franks converted two free throws to slice the Tiger deficit to three points.

With 1:39 showing on the clock, Tomlinson was fouled by Douglas and pushed his first attempt through. The second bounced away, but the Tigers recovered and 19 seconds later Gene Pinkney whistled home the tying basket from the left side.

Kansas took time out and deliberately tried to kill time. The delay game was successful and finally with 17 seconds left, the Jayhawks called time again.

FOUL RUNS OUT BUCKET

They worked the ball around for a few seconds before Bohnenstiehl shot and missed. Howard Arndt grabbed the rebound and fired, but he missed, too. Then Rich Bradshaw snared the ball and flipped it through, but the whistle had blown before he shot and the fifth foul was called on Pete Helmbock. That set up Bohnenstiehl's free throw and the climactic finish.

Kansas held a 33-29 lead at the half after being in front by as much as 10 points at one time. In the first three minutes of the second half, however, the Tigers solved the K. U. zone and gained a 38-37 advantage.

K. U.'s White and M. U.'s Johnson exchanged baskets before Jo-Jo sent the Jayhawks back in front, 41-40. Then he,

Douglas, Vanoy and Bohnenstiehl collaborated on a spree that enabled Kansas to pile up a 58-46 bulge with eight minutes left. But Johnson and Jones ignited a Missouri surge that brought about the pulsating climax.

Almost all of Missouri's scoring was concentrated among Johnson, Jones and Tomlinson; they scored 23, 22 and 12 points in that order. Each of them took 11 shots: Johnson and Jones hit on six and Tomlinson on four. For the game

the Tigers connected on 20-of-46 for 44 per cent.

The only Jayhawks in double figures were White with 22 and Bohnenstiehl with 15. Jo-Jo fired in 11-of-21 attempts. As a team, Kansas managed 25-of-65 for 38 per cent, but the Tigers were too sharp at the free-throw line.

K. U. had a whopping 39-26 margin in rebounding, with Bradshaw hauling in 12, Sloan nine and Bohnenstiehl eight.

Allen Fieldhouse has never been an easy place to play for visitors. When Norm Stewart won his first game there as a head coach, just like he had as a player in the first MU vs. KU game in 1956, it caught a few people by surprise.

RIVALS!
MU VS. KU

MU:67
KU:66

BASKETBALL
JANUARY 15, 1968

JOHNSON SHEDS ALSO-RAN ROLE

JO-JO WHITE FINALLY RANKS SECOND IN MATCH-UP

By Fritz Kreisler
(A Member of The Star's Sports Staff)

Lawrence, Kas.

Tom Johnson finally came out of Jo-Jo White's shadow last night.

Johnson's two free throws with no time remaining not only carried Missouri to a 67-66 victory over Kansas but also enabled him to steal the show from his old buddy from St. Louis. Even during their playing days at McKinley high school, Johnson had taken a back seat to White.

Then last year, when they finally met as college opponents for the first time, White led Kansas to two victories over the Tigers. It was the same story slightly more that two weeks ago when a dazzling second-half show by White carried the Jayhawks past Missouri in their Big Eight tournament meeting.

And the highly-partisan crowd of 11,000 in Allen field house last night expected much of the same. For more than 35 minutes, White repeatedly held the Tigers at bay with flashes of brilliance.

Then, with 4:56 remaining, White committed his fifth foul, and his influence on the game was ended irrevocably.

With Missouri down by one point, Johnson was fouled as he took a three-quarter court pass from Don Tomlinson just ahead of the final buzzer.

As he stepped to the foul line with a one-and-one bonus situation and the Kansas crowd yammering in his ears, Johnson remembered he had missed a free throw in the exact situation at the end of the first half.

"I was hoping I wouldn't miss," he said later after calming down in the Missouri dressing room. "Sure I was aware of the crowd. I was in the first half, too. But the coach just said to relax and play ball, and I tried to."

> "I was hoping I wouldn't miss," he said later after calming down in the Missouri dressing room. "Sure I was aware of the crowd. I was in the first half, too. But the coach just said to relax and play ball, and I tried to."
>
> — Tom Johnson

Coach Norm Stewart of Missouri didn't remember what he was thinking at the time. But Roy DeWitz, his assistant, said Stewart turned calmly to him and announced, "He's gonna make 'em."

Tomlinson said he didn't remember Johnson missing the free throws after time had run out at the intermission. "I know how he makes 'em in practice," Tomlinson said. "I was just praying to the Good Lord, and as soon as he made the first one, I just knew he had the second."

Strangely, Johnson had been on the Missouri bench until Pete Helmbock fouled out with seconds to go. "He just put 'em down, both of 'em," said Helmbock. "It's a great win. A great win. Our biggest, oh yeah."

The two free throws also enabled Johnson to finish as the game's high scorer with 23 points, one more than White.

"He's beaten me both years, and it's quite a thrill," said Johnson. He said he had taken on renewed hope when Jo-Jo had fouled out of the game. "Yes, I thought we had a chance. He (White) is quite a ball player," he said.

"But we never give up."

HAWKS SHAKE M. U. BID

Just like Missouri had done to Kansas in 1955, the Jayhawks came into Columbia and gave the home crowd a bad taste in the teams' final contest in a hallowed hall. The difference in this case was that Kansas had a chance after their loss to Missouri to close Hoch Auditorium with a victory.

When Kansas downed Missouri 71-69 to end the 1971 season, it was the last game played at Brewer Fieldhouse. Thirty-three years later, the Jayhawks did it again, ending the Tigers' run in the Hearnes Center, the successor to Brewer, with an 84-82 victory.

There was little surprise in this Kansas victory, other than the margin of victory. The Jayhawks came in with a 23-1 record, including a 12-0 league mark, and riding a 17-game winning streak. The Tigers, meanwhile, were 17-8, 9-4 in the league.

The Jayhawks took the game into overtime after trailing by nine at halftime and by four with just under three minutes remaining in the game. In the extra period, KU's Dave Robisch pulled down several key rebounds to secure the victory.

Here's how it appeared in the March 9, 1971, Times:

BY DICK WADE
ASSOCIATE SPORTS EDITOR OF *THE STAR*

COLUMBIA, MO.

That old Brewer field house magic, the additive that has sustained Missouri basketball for the last 42 seasons, failed in its dying-gasp effort last night when the Tigers dropped a 71-69 decision in overtime to Kansas in the last intercollegiate contest to be played in the old gray stone structure.

It was a tribute to the Jayhawks, the nation's No. 4-rated (24-1) team and the Big Eight's unbeaten (13-0) champion that they fought their way out of this one. They were down by nine, 37-28, at the half and trailed by four, 62-58, with 2:47 left in regulation.

And with a standing-room-only crowd of 6,000 howling and screaming for the Tigers – and the seats began to fill two hours before game time – the scene was set for the upset that would wrap up sole possession of second place in the Big Eight for M. U. and all but cinch a bid to the National Invitational tournament for the Tigers.

But not even that – plus the presence of 75 former M. U. lettermen who had played in Brewer – was enough to hold off the Hawks.

It was big Dave Robisch, the Hawks' 6-foot-10 all-league cornerman and a special target of the M. U. backers' razzing, who proved the difference. With the score 66-65 in Kansas' favor and 1:54 left, Big Dave went to work.

First he drove out of the left corner, forcing the M. U. defense to sink. He passed back out to Pierre Russell, wide open at 12 feet. Russell swished home the bucket that made it 68-65. Then, after Henry Smith hooked one home for M. U. to cut the margin to 68-67, Aubrey Nash drew an intentional (2-shot) foul with 46 seconds left.

ROBISCH KEY MAN

Nash missed both shots but Robisch pulled down the rebound on the second. He was fouled by Jeffries, and he made both opportunities off the one-and-one. That made it a 70-67 game with :44 to go.

Then came another big Robisch

rebound – after M. U. missed four straight shots – with 11 seconds to go. Again he was fouled as he pulled down the ball. He cashed the first of the one-and-one for a 71-67 lead. That nailed the lid on one of the most dramatic games played in the old arena.

Mike Griffin drove for an uncontested basket for M. U. with three seconds to go. But by that time the crowd was filing out – and the band was playing "Auld Lange Syne."

That same crowd was shaking the foundation when the teams came out to play the second half. Missouri held a 37-28 advantage, one built on sinking 17-of-22 free-shot chances and a brilliant effort by the five M. U. starters who played all the way.

But K. U.'s other big man, 6-foot-10 Roger Brown, staged a dramatic one-man show – in which he scored six points and passed off for two other goals – to shoot K. U. back on top, 40-38 with 16:13 to go.

But with 15:34 left, Brown lost a tip-in and also drew his fifth foul of the game. With him gone, K. U. met its first

KU:71
MU:69

BASKETBALL
MARCH 8, 1971

RIVALS!
MU VS. KU

key moment of challenge. Smith converted the foul shot to tie the score, 40-all.

With 12:48 to go, John Brown tied it for the Tigers again, 46-all with a tip. Then at the 10:32 mark, Greg Flaker fed Smith for a lay-up and Missouri had the lead back, 48-47. Kansas never held the advantage again until the overtime.

Mike Jeffries, Missouri's first relief man, came on with 13 minutes to go and scored eight points down the stretch. His lay-up with 5:16 left gave M. U. a 57-53 lead – and it seemed M. U. might do it.

That 4-point lead was still in place with 2:47 to go, after John Brown hit both ends of a one-and-one to run it to 62-58. But from there on in Missouri didn't score in the regulation portion of the game. K. U. pulled even on baskets by Nash and Greg Douglas, the tie-up coming with 55 seconds left.

M. U. called time with 45 seconds to go, then came back and worked for one shot. Flaker took it with five seconds left, driving out of the right corner – but the ball wouldn't go down.

FROM THE KANSAS CITY TIMES, 1971

BYE-BYE BREWER

PRIDE WINS IT FOR JAYHAWKS

BY FRITZ KREISLER
A MEMBER OF *THE STAR'S* SPORTS STAFF

COLUMBIA, MO.

The setting was perfect for an upset of major proportions. Brewer field house, home of Missouri's Tigers since 1930, reeked with nostalgia. Lettermen for the last 41 years were on hand for the farewell game with Kansas, the undisputed king of the Big Eight conference. The place bulged with a standing room crowd of 6,000 noisy fans and seemed to shudder with every ear-splitting roar.

Missouri, striving for a post-season invitation itself, carried the battle to the Jayhawks and succeeded in outplaying the Kansans much of the time. In the first half the Tigers built a 10-point lead, surrendered the advantage in the early minutes of the second half and matched the Jayhawks stride for stride down the stretch. Regulation time ended 62-all, but Kansas won it, 71-69 in overtime. It was a tense, rugged and fiercely-played game until Dave Robisch's three free throws in the last 44 seconds settled it.

Coach Ted Owens of Kansas said it was pride that fueled the Kansas comeback in the second half. "It would have been awfully easy for our players to say that because we've got the conference won we'll just go through the motions," he said. "But this is what has made this club. I don't know how many games we've won where the statistics and execution have made you feel like you shouldn't have won, but the element of pride has done it time after time."

More specifically, Owens acknowledged the tremendous work of 6-foot-10 Roger Brown, whose six points in the first 2:02 of the second half hauled the Jayhawks back into contention.

"Roger gave us a big lift," he said.

However, Brown played less than five minutes of the second half as he committed fouls No. 4 and 5 within a half-minute span and went to the bench with 15:34 remaining.

"I thought he had a beautiful tip-in," said Owens.

The tip-in was one of the sore points of the game for Kansas. Brown not only committed his fifth foul on the play, but the basket was also disallowed. Although Brown watched the rest of the game from the bench, he'd done the job of getting the Jayhawks moving.

Coach Norm Stewart of Missouri was deeply disappointed but still proud of the effort put out by the Tigers.

"We gave it a great shot," he said. "Our kids wanted to win real badly, had it won and didn't. I thought we had it won, but we made two crucial mistakes coughing up the ball with really no pressure."

BIG 8 CONFERENCE

1971
BASKETBALL
CHAMPIONS

University of Kansas Archives

STALLWORTH'S 50 RIPS M. U.

Gary Link was a sophomore forward for Missouri in 1972, so he was getting his first taste of big-time college basketball. When the Jayhawks and Tigers met in Lawrence, Link knew that the Tigers had their hands full.

Bud Stallworth, a consensus All-American, was playing his final game in Allen Fieldhouse for the Jayhawks, and Link knew he would be ready.

"Coach always instilled a great deal of pride in our team," Link said. "He had us ready to play anybody, even somebody like Stallworth."

Stallworth was more ready than the Tigers. He drained half his 38 shots from the field and 12 of 13 from the line for 50 points.

Missouri coach Norm Stewart takes much of the blame for Stallworth's big night. While the coach can't stop a player from scoring, a decision he made had an impact, at least if you ask Stewart.

"Al Eberhard could guard Bud Stallworth," Stewart says. "Now Bud was a great player and he still could have scored a lot of points, but Eberhard got two quick fouls and I took him off Stallworth. He finished with two fouls.

"Stallworth may still have scored a bunch of points, but I sat there on the bench like a yo-yo and did nothing to help our team stop him."

Link doesn't believe that anything could have stopped Stallworth on that night. "Coach Stewart told us that no one player can beat this team," he said. "On that night, one did."

Here's how it appeared in the February 27, 1972, Star:

By Fritz Kreisler
A Member of The Star's Sports Staff

Lawrence, Kas.,

Bud Stallworth of Kansas went out in a blaze of glory, and Missouri went down in flames here yesterday.

Playing his last game in Allen Field House, Stallworth unfurled the greatest scoring performance ever in a Big Eight Conference game with 50 points as he led the Jayhawks to a 93-80 victory over Missouri before a delirious crowd of 15,900 fans.

Although his sensational performance fell short by two of equaling the Kansas school record held by Wilt Chamberlain, it eclipsed the mark of 47 established last year by Cliff Meely of Colorado in a conference game against Oklahoma. Chamberlain's 52 came in a nonleague game against Northwestern. The most Chamberlain ever scored in a conference game was 46.

In beating Missouri, the Jayhawks knocked the Tigers out of first place in the hot Big Eight race. Now 8-3, Missouri dropped a game behind Kansas State, which defeated Oklahoma, 80-71, earlier in the afternoon. Both games were on regional television.

Kansas, 7-5 in Big Eight play is out of contention for the title, but the Jayhawks showed yesterday that they are not through with the basketball season. They accepted Missouri's challenge for a free-wheeling game, kept the Tigers off stride with a bothersome pressing defense and led with their ace – Stallworth.

> "I don't know if I've ever seen any better. No, I'm positive that's the best display I've ever seen."
> — Kansas coach Ted Owens

Stallworth was breath-taking from start to finish. Deadly with his pet jumper from 15 and 20 feet, the 6-foot-5 shotsmith was all over the floor, rebounding, fast-breaking, going for loose balls and dishing it out on the

RIVALS!
MU VS. KU

KU:93
MU:80

BASKETBALL
FEBRUARY 26, 1972

Ted Owens was quick to point out that Bud Stallworth's performance was one of the best he's ever seen.

rugged inside game. He rifled in 19 of 38 shots from the field and 12 of 13 free throws.

He was unstoppable. Missouri tried nearly every conceivable defensive maneuver, but never came close to handling him. The Tiger defenders stayed with him every inch of the way and kept a hand in his face. None of his points came cheaply, but he seemingly couldn't miss.

Mike Griffin, the Tigers' quickest player, started out on him, but Griffin gave away five inches in height, and Stallworth answered by scoring 13 of the Jayhawks' first 19 points, earning a 19-all tie. Then the Tigers switched to

bulky Mike Jeffries, 6-4, who is deceptively quick for his 210 pounds. Stallworth answered that by scoring 11 straight points in a 3-minute span to spark the Jayhawks to a 30-27 lead.

Jeffries guarded Stallworth most of the rest of the game, although Gary Link took over for awhile and the Tigers even used a zone and chaser briefly in the second half.

By half time Stallworth had 27 points, but Missouri was astride a 43-41 lead. The Tigers had done a reasonably good job of keeping their cool in the face of Stallworth's individual brilliance. Led by Jeffries, John Brown and Al Eberhard, the Tigers had taken advan-

tage of a brief spell in which Stallworth scarcely touched the ball to forge leads of 39-34 and 43-37.

But Stallworth and Dave Taynor brought the Jayhawks to within two in the last 1:30 of the first half, and Stallworth's outside jumper at the outset of the second half caught the Tigers at 43-all.

The score was tied three more times at 45-all, 47-all and 51-all before Aubrey Nash, Neal Mask and Stallworth shot in three straight baskets to open a 57-51 lead.

That was the beginning of Missouri's downhill slide. The Tigers never again pulled even, although they managed to keep on the heat until the waning minutes. The big breakthrough

came with about four minutes left when a 3-point play by Stallworth and a rebound basket by Mask in a 26-second span pushed the Jayhawks to a commanding 78-66 lead.

With Brown out of the game on fouls, Missouri managed to come back within 83-80 with 1:04 left; but heavy fouling took its toll in the final minute. The Jayhawks cashed 10 of 12 chances in the last 64 seconds. Appropriately it was Stallworth's two with four seconds remaining that wrapped things up.

The game was fiercely competitive, and the fans made the most of it. Twice play was halted briefly because of debris on the floor. In the first half Coach Norm Stewart of Missouri was socked with a technical foul when he jumped up in protest of a foul. In the second half Brown and Stallworth exchanged sharp words at midcourt after Brown had fouled the Jayhawk ace. Brown fouled out with 3:12 remaining, and the Kansas fans serenaded him with the Wheaties song. Jeffries and Greg Flaker also fouled out in the last minute.

Brown finished as Missouri's high scorer with 23, but Jeffries was right behind with 22 and Eberhard with 19.

All of the ingredients for an unusual game were present yesterday. Watching from the stands was Mrs. Isaac Stallworth of Hartselle, Ala. Also present were members of the 1952 Kansas team that won the national championship. They were introduced at half time, and the biggest ovation was given to big Clyde Lovellette, the scoring star of that team. But the decibel count on that one could in no way compare with the one awarded Stallworth at the end of the game.

"It's easy to diagnose. We just played terrible defense – as poor as we've played all year.

"Another factor involved was that we just don't have anyone who can match up with him (Stallworth). We don't have a size and quickness man who can go with Stallworth.

"We go with Griffin for quickness but give up size. We go with Jeffries (6-4) and gain a little size, but give away quickness. Link (6-5 reserve) at times didn't do too badly. We changed defenses once or twice on him but didn't get back out on him (Stallworth) and he got some easy shots."

— Missouri coach Norm Stewart

RIVALS!
MU VS.KU

KU:93
MU:80

BASKETBALL
FEBRUARY 26, 1972

JAYHAWKS' SIGN SAYS IT ALL ABOUT BUD

BY DEL BLACK
A MEMBER OF THE *STAR'S* SPORTS STAFF

LAWRENCE, KAN.

A sign unfurled before the game best describes yesterday's 93-80 basketball victory by Kansas over Missouri.

"When you say Bud Stallworth, you've said it all." And the band blared the appropriate beer commercial as the partisan Allen Field House crowd of 15,600 stomped its feet and sang the lyrics.

Stallworth made several things clear as the 50-point culprit in knocking Missouri out of a share of the Big Eight Conference lead.

"No, I wasn't tired," the K. U. ace smiled. "You don't get tired when you're winning.

"Yeah, I was up for this one. When you're a senior and you've got a string (21 straight league victories at home) going like we have, you give it the best you can."

Coach Ted Owens of Kansas needed little coaxing in calling Stallworth's performance the greatest he has seen.

"I don't know if I've ever seen any better," Owens said. "No, I'm positive that's the best display I've ever seen," he quickly added.

Norm Stewart, Missouri coach, summed up the defeat and Stallworth's gunnery solemnly and concisely:

"It's easy to diagnose. We just played terrible defense – as poor as we've played all year.

"Another factor involved was that we just don't have anyone who can match up with him (Stallworth). We don't have a size and quickness man who can go with Stallworth.

"We go with Griffin for quickness but give up size," Stewart said, explaining the game-opening defensive assignment pitting Mike Griffin (6-feet) against the 6-5 Stallworth. "We go with Jeffries (6-4) and gain a little size, but give away quickness. Link (6-5 reserve) at times didn't do too badly. We changed defenses once or twice on him but didn't get back out on him (Stallworth) and he got some easy shots."

Stallworth indicated he was delighted to be defensed by Griffin.

"When you're guarded by a shorter guy," Stallworth said, "you can get the shot off easier and when you get the first few down, everything starts to fall."

About the tactics employed by the hefty (210) Jeffries, Stallworth countered:

"He body checks a lot. The best thing I can do is try to get around him. If you push and shove him he'll wear you out. I tried a lot of cutting and tried to get back to him and get set up."

Stallworth, who missed his first shot of the game connected on 10 of his 23 first-half field-goal attempts and went 7-for-8 from the free-throw line.

He came back to hit his first two shots of the second half on the way to a sizzling 9-for-15 show. He went 5-for-5 from the stripe in the windup 20 minutes.

Agreeing he was pressing late in the first half when missing a half dozen shots in a row, Stallworth said: "Yeah, I was, but I thought I'd get fouled on a couple of them, too."

Technically, Stallworth didn't miss a free throw. He was deprived of a charity shot that went in during the first half when Wilson Barrow stepped into the lane too soon.

Stallworth, whose mother traveled from Hartselle, Ala., to watch her first game in Allen Field House, said knowing that Kansas State had won earlier that day supplied no incentive to spoil things for Mizzou.

"I don't care who wins the championship," he snapped. "We just came out to beat Missouri."

The postgame Jayhawk dressing-room scene was complete with the old grads in the persons of members of K.U.'s 1952 N.C.A.A. championship team.

Asked if he had any craving to play in Allen Field House, Clyde Lovellette, onetime Jayhawk great, answered, "If I could shoot like Bud Stallworth."

And yesterday Stallworth was shooting.

JAYHAWKS PUNCH OUT MISSOURI, 77-72

It wasn't the first time and it wasn't the last time. Kansas and Missouri tangled and scrapped during their basketball game, as tensions rose. On this occasion, Mizzou lost its all-conference forward, Jim Kennedy, while the Jayhawks lost back-up center Donnie Von Moore.

No one was quite sure what caused the fight between the two players, but it quickly escalated into a bench-clearing brawl.

"Donnie Von Moore chased Kennedy out into the hall of Allen Fieldhouse," KU broadcaster Max Falkenstein said. "They were gone for a few minutes."

Actually, they were gone from the game, because when action resumed, both players had been ejected. A physical game followed, and the two coaches had heated words.

"Coach (Ted) Owens and I had to meet the commissioner after that game," former Missouri coach Norm Stewart remembered. "He told us to stop acting like children."

Here's how it appeared in the January 9, 1977, Star:

By Rich Sambol
A Member of the Sports Staff

LAWRENCE, KAN.

When Kansas and Missouri meet in anything you can expect a lot of emotion. But things got a little out of hand yesterday on the floor of Allen Field House.

The game was supposed to be basketball. But it turned out to be more of a boxing match.

Neither team won the fight that erupted in the first half – Donnie Von Moore of Kansas and Jim Kennedy of Missouri were dismissed from the game – but Kansas came out on top on the scoreboard, 77-72.

"It was a hard loss, but the loss was incidental," said Norm Stewart, the Missouri coach.

Stewart was shoved by a fan while he was still on the court after the game and he said he and the team were verbally accosted on the way to the dressing room.

"There is no place in basketball for conduct of coaches, players and fans like there was today…and I am talking about Kansas University. We were intimidated out of the game," Stewart said.

With 13:38 left in the first half Missouri lost Kennedy, its all-conference forward, and Kansas lost Von Moore, its substitute center, when the two traded punches under the Missouri goal.

Both benches emptied and the fight continued in the northeast corner of the arena. When the officials established control both Kennedy and Von Moore were ejected.

The score was tied at 12-12 at the time and when play finally resumed after the delay the game proceeded without further altercations, although it was rough the rest of the way. Kansas lost two players – Ken Koenigs and Herb Nobles – on fouls and Missouri one – Kim Anderson.

"All we talked about at half time was going out and playing hard in the second half and not worry about what happened," said Ted Owens, the Kansas coach. "I think the fact that we shot 50 per cent in the second half showed that we played with a lot more poise."

In the first five minutes of the second half Kansas turned Missouri's 41-35 halftime advantage into a 49-45 Jayhawk lead and held a 4-point margin two other times before Missouri came back to deadlock the score at 53-all on a follow dunk by Clay Johnson.

Missouri went back ahead, 63-57, at the 9-minute mark, but that's when John Douglas, K. U.'s junior college transfer from Leighton, Ala., went to work. He scored 13 of K. U.'s final 18 points, including a couple on the likes of a shot you don't see everyday.

As the clock dipped under the 5-minute mark Douglas rang up a basket that wasn't even a shot. As he drove the lane the ball slipped out of his grasp and alley-ooped toward the backboard. It hit high off the glass and bounded in.

The live audience of 9,650 took delight in that one. Then, less than 30 seconds later, Douglas had a rebound follow shot that turned the game around. The 6-2 forward spun underneath the

RIVALS!
MU VS. KU

KU: 77
MU: 72

BASKETBALL
JANUARY 8, 1977

glass and twisted in a reverse lay-up that knotted the score at 71-all with 4:20 to go.

Missouri, the defending conference champion and victor over Kansas in the final of the Big Eight Holiday tournament in Kansas City 11 days ago, held the lead only one more time.

Kim Anderson accomplished that when he put down the front end free throw on 1-and-1 with 3:04 left. Eleven seconds later Douglas came up with another rebound and follow shot and Kansas had a 73-72 lead.

Missouri controlled the ball until Anderson put a move on Douglas, attempting to drive the baseline. Both players hit the floor and Douglas thought he had fouled out of the game. Instead, the foul was called on Anderson who had fouled out.

Kansas slowed the tempo, too, but lost the ball when Clint Johnson and Scott Sims of Missouri collided and hit the floor. No foul was called, but the referees ruled the ball went out of bounds off Johnson's leg.

With 1:03 to play Sims missed from the field and Kansas ripped down court on a fast break. Brad Saunders would up with a lay-up, but missed the shot while being fouled by Larry Drew.

Saunders put down the first free throw for a 74-72 Kansas lead, but missed the second.

Missouri, which scored only one point in the final five minutes and 50 seconds of the game, grabbed the rebound and then cooled its heels until calling time out with 22 seconds left.

With 16 seconds to go Sims lofted a 20-footer toward the goal and Douglas, who seemed ever-present down the stretch, went up for the rebound. He was fouled and made the first attempt from the line in the 1-and-1 situation.

Milt Gibson gave Kansas another free throw at :02 and after Missouri threw away the in-bounds pass, Douglas put up a 40-footer that counted as the result of a goal-tending call.

And that's the way it ended. But, somehow, a super individual effort was lost in the shuffle.

Norm Stewart and Ted Owens had heated words for each other and the officials during the physical contest at Allen Fieldhouse.

FROM THE STAR, 1977

STEWART'S EARS BURNED

BY RICH SAMBOL
A MEMBER OF THE SPORTS STAFF

LAWRENCE, KAN.

Shortly after the fight between Missouri and Kansas players yesterday both head coaches got into the act as they exchanged heated words.

"I was disappointed at the words spoken to me by Coach (Ted) Owens," said Norm Stewart, Missouri's head coach, who met Owens at mid-court to talk about the incident. "It was something to the effect, 'That's how you coach basketball.'"

The fight erupted in the first half and two players, Donnie Von Moore of Kansas and Jim Kennedy of Missouri, were ejected.

"The individual that struck the first blow wasn't thrown out of the game," Stewart said. "And that player has a history of that type of conduct."

Although the player's name was never mentioned by Stewart the reference was to Herb Nobles, a K. U. forward. Nobles threw an elbow at Kennedy, who retaliated and the fight was on.

"I'm sorry it (the fight) had to be part of the game," said Owens.

"I'm sorry we had to be a part of it. I only know our side of the story. Maybe when I look at the films I can make a better judgment about it."

But Stewart was more emphatic.

"I don't care what side you're for," he said. "People saw it on television. It could have been very serious – it was serious. It could have been very serious.

"If the fans had gotten into it, it would have been ridiculous."

MU POUNCES ON KANSAS

The high school graduating class of 1979 was very good to Missouri basketball. Steve Stipanovich, from the St. Louis area, and Jon Sundvold, from Blue Springs, Mo., anchored a class that earned four straight Big 8 championships for Norm Stewart's Tigers.

Stipanovich had his coming-out party against Kansas, as the 6-11 freshman scored 29 points and missed only two shots all night, one from the field and one from the line. He was helped by Kansas City native Larry Drew, who poured in 17 points and added seven assists.

Sundvold did not play a key role in his first home game against the Jayhawks, but his leadership would be felt by the Tigers

over his career and would be the source of many ill feelings for the Jayhawks.

"They killed us," said Tom Hedrick, then the Voice of the Jayhawks. "We couldn't do anything. We left there feeling terrible."

It was a feeling that would last for the next four years

Here's how it appeared in the February 10, 1980, Star:

By Rich Sambol
A Member of the Sports Staff

Columbia, Mo.,

Larry Drew didn't have to be asked how he felt. "Lovely, lovely, lovely," rolled off his lips, as if he had rehearsed all afternoon.

He had the opportunity. Drew and his Missouri teammates jumped in front of Kansas so fast Saturday in a Big Eight Conference basketball game that the Tigers spent most of their time looking back. Missouri led by 20 points with 5 minutes to go in the first half, then coasted past the Jayhawks 88-65.

Missouri's victory – the 18th in 22 games this season for the 15th-ranked Tigers – was accomplished before a record home crowd of 12,704. The turnout surpassed the 12,600 that attended the first basketball game played at Hearnes Center in November, 1972.

The crowd saw Steve Stipanovich, Missouri's heralded freshman center, enjoy the finest scoring game of his collegiate career as the Tigers, 7-3 in Big Eight Conference play, stayed in title contention.

Stipanovich was almost flawless, making 10 of 11 field-goal attempts and nine of 10 free

Steve Stipanovich

RIVALS!
MU VS. KU

MU:88
KU:65

BASKETBALL
FEBRUARY 9, 1980

throws for 29 points. The total was the best for a freshman in MU history.

"Stip is a great inside player," said Drew, Missouri point guard from Wyandotte High School in Kansas City, Kansas. "You get that ball inside to him and he can turn it on."

Stipanovich, who had only nine points in the first half, previously had scored 25 against Arkansas State. His best Big Eight game had been 20 against Nebraska nine games ago, and he had not made 20 since.

"Oh, sure, it's satisfying, especially in a game against Kansas," said the 6-foot-11 Stipanovich. "We lost to Kansas the first time we played them, and reading the newspaper articles…you just want to go out there and kill them."

That the Tigers did…and Ted Owens, Kansas coach, knew it.

"We just got too far behind," he said, "We were at their mercy."

The fans loved every minute of it. The crowd gave each Tiger a standing ovation as he left the game in the closing moments. The loudest outbursts were for Stipanovich and Drew.

Drew, who scored 17 points, was nine of nine at the free-throw line. He also had seven assists – most of them going to Stipanovich, who befuddled Kansas defenders by taking a lob pass and going up to the basket. Stipanovich also displayed his accuracy near the free-throw line, which made him doubly tough to cover.

"We wanted to get an early jump on them and make them play defense," said Stipanovich. "Anytime you can get an early lead, the other team gets down. We knew KU would."

Kansas was called for 29 fouls. The Jayhawks lost Tony Guy and John Crawford on fouls within 3 minutes of each other

midway through the second half, preventing the Jayhawks from making any kind of real run.

"They were getting called for fouls because they were fouling a lot," said Stipanovich. "They were physical inside, and they were trying to intimidate. You can't let that bother you.

"You can't fight back. If you do, it's all over."

Missouri was sensational in the first 7 1/2 minutes of the game. In that span the Tigers hit nine of 13 field-goal tries (two of the misses were blocks). Drew went two for two from the free-throw line and the team turned the ball over only once.

That spree shot the Tigers into a 20-6 lead, a deficit from which Kansas could not rebound. The closest KU came after Mizzou's initial burst was nine points, 20-11 and 64-55.

Before Kansas closed the gap to nine on a free throw by Darnell Valentine with 6 1/2 minutes left in the game, the Jayhawks pulled within 10 five times. Each time Missouri answered with two free throws or a basket.

With the Tiger's lead cut to nine, Drew and Stipanovich each sank two free throws to get Missouri ahead by 13. And, just inside the 4-minute mark, the Tigers went on an 8-1 spurt that left the shell-shocked Jayhawks trailing 78-59 — and on the way to their 12th loss against 10 victories.

The frustrated Jayhawks, in fact, dropped their third game of the week. Kansas lost to Nebraska Tuesday night and Iona Thursday night. KU is in sixth place in the Big Eight with a 4-6 record.

Missouri protected its statistical ranking as the best field-goal shooting

Ted Owens didn't have much to smile about after watching his Jayhawks get dominated by Mizzou.

team in the country. The Tigers were making 57.5 percent of their floor shots coming into the game, and MU made 28 of 46 against Kansas (60.8 percent), the ninth time this season the Tigers have exceeded 60 percent. Missouri has been under .500 only twice.

While offense was a forte, the defense was not a handicap. Missouri forced the Jayhawks into 19 turnovers, and Drew did an exceptional job on Valentine, Kansas point guard who had been smoking in his last six games. Through those six, Valentine had averaged 18.7 points a game.

Valentine had only five points by halftime and finished with 10.

1982

MU SQUEAKS PAST KU 42-41

The Missouri basketball class of 1983 had proved that it could win in a number of styles. They had scored 80 points or more in 36 of 84 games played in their first 2¹/₂ years in Columbia. They also knew how to play a low-scoring game. They had won 11 games in which they scored 65 points or fewer in that same span.

So it was no surprise that the Tigers prevailed in one of the lowest-scoring games in series history against Kansas.

"We could play however we wanted to," former coach Norm Stewart said. "We could run or we could slow it down. The longer we held the lead, the farther back in the lane we got."

Missouri had defeated the Jayhawks 41-35 in Columbia earlier in the 1982 season, and the return match was just as low scoring. Missouri took a 42-38 lead with 8:39 left in the second half, and didn't score again. But their defense stifled the Jayhawks, only allowing them to score three points.

"It was like a game in the 40s," Stewart said, referring to the decade, not the score.

After Missouri missed the third of three free throw attempts in the final minute, KU got control of the ball down just one. They not only couldn't score, they didn't get off a shot.

"I was so mad I couldn't interview (Coach) Ted Owens," said Tom Hedrick, who was calling the game as Voice of the Jayhawks. "I told my color guy that he had to do it."

Here's how it appeared in the February 10, 1982, Times:

STEPHEN SAMUEL STIPANOVICH
Basketball
1980-83

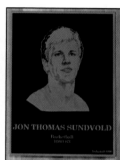

JON THOMAS SUNDVOLD
Basketball
1980-83

By STEVE RICHARDSON
A MEMBER OF THE SPORTS STAFF

LAWRENCE, KAN.

A basketball bounced on a path to nowhere amid a maze of bodies. If the right Kansas player had picked it up, the Jayhawks might have upset fourth-ranked Missouri.

But nary a Kansas player could come up with it, let alone get off a last-second shot, and Missouri preserved a pulsating 42-41 victory over Kansas Tuesday night before a crowd of 14,000 at Allen Field House.

Kansas forward David Magley drove the lane with less than 10 seconds left. However, Missouri guard Jon Sundvold poked the ball away. Like a pinball in some giant machine, the ball bounced back and forth.

"I got my hand on the ball," Sundvold said. "I had it; then it was gone. I tried to find it, but it kept rolling backward and went through some people's legs."

It wound up in the hands of Missouri center Steve Stipanovich, who clutched it with 2 seconds left. He still had it when the game ended.

"It makes you sick inside, not to get a shot off," said Kansas Coach Ted Owens.

"I had the ball with 4 seconds left," Magley said. "I was going for my shot,

and I am usually pretty defensive about my shot."

But it was Missouri's defense and ball control in the last 8 minutes that won this game. It was the Tigers' 20th victory of the season against one loss,

> **"I got my hand on the ball. I had it; then it was gone. I tried to find it, but it kept rolling backward and went through some people's legs."**
> **—Missouri guard Jon Sundvold**

which came last Saturday in Columbia, Mo., against Nebraska, 67-51. The victory moved Missouri to 9-1 in the Big Eight Conference and caused Kansas to tumble to 12-9 overall and 3-6 in the Big Eight. It was Kansas' third straight loss.

The Tigers didn't score in the last 8

RIVALS!
MU VS. KU

MU:42
KU:41

BASKETBALL
FEBRUARY 9, 1982

With the talent on his 1981-1982 team, the third of four straight conference champions, Stewart could point to an up-tempo game or a slow-down game.

minutes, 39 seconds of the game after forward Ricky Frazier put them ahead 42-38 with two free throws. But during the same period, Kansas could manage only three points. The Tigers held the ball the greater part of that stretch – a maneuver they employed in a 41-35 victory over the Jayhawks earlier this season in Columbia. Missouri wanted Kansas out of its 2-3 zone.

"If they stay back in the zone, it's a folly," said Coach Norm Stewart of Missouri. "They want you to stick up an 18- or 20-footer, then they have five guys on the boards. We've got to get a good shot, within 12 or 15 feet of the hole."

Owens wasn't unhappy about the stall, because Kansas forward Tony Guy and Kansas center Brian Martin had four fouls. But as has been the case often this season, Kansas didn't have the ball handlers to make Missouri pay.

After Frazier's free throws, Magley made an 8-footer, slicing the lead to 42-40. Missouri, which held the ball nearly

3 minutes before Frazier's free throws, hung onto it for 3 more minutes before Magley picked up a steal.

Seconds later Kansas threw the ball away without getting a shot.

From that point, Missouri held the ball for 1^{1}/2 minutes. With 3:45 to play Marvin McCrary drove for a layup but missed, and Kansas grabbed the rebound.

Kansas scored the game's final point when Magley, fouled by Stipanovich on a rebound of a shot by Tony Guy hit a free throw. Magley, however, missed the other foul shot and Missouri still led 42-41 with 3:27 remaining.

The Tigers kept possession until Michael Walker made a bad pass with 1:12 left. Magley missed a long shot with 50 seconds left. But Missouri seemed willing to give the game away. The Tigers missed three free throws in the final minute.

Magley fouled Walker, and it was ruled a two-shot intentional foul. But

Walker missed them both.

On the rebound of Walker's second miss, Magley fouled McCrary. But McCrary missed, setting up Kansas' last-gasp effort.

"I thought we found a way to win," Stewart said.

Frazier found a way. He celebrated his 24th victory in high style, leading all scorers with 20 points, and he was automatic from the field and line. He made all eight field-goal attempts and all four free throws.

Meanwhile, Kansas got 14 points from Guy, who was held to only two points in the second half by McCrary. Kansas forward Jeff Dishman scored 10 points.

But it came down to a bouncing ball.

"On the final play, Tony was supposed to go underneath," Owens said. "However, McCrary went above the screen and we were unable to get Tony the basketball."

CHAPTER SEVEN •

149

JAYHAWKS ESCAPE FROM TIGER'S JAWS

It's not always the stars. Sometimes the least-expected play decides a big game.

Such was the case in 1985 when Tad Boyle's steal sealed a victory for the Jayhawks at home against Missouri.

The Tigers had led 41-30 inside 17 minutes to play, but the Jayhawks were the ones who showed their claws. KU went on a 27-16 run in a span of less than 10 minutes, and the score was tied at 57-all with just over seven minutes left.

The lead see-sawed back and forth until Kansas took the lead for good at 69-68 with just over a minute remaining when Greg Dreiling hit two free throws. After both teams missed shots, Dreiling missed the front end of a one-and-one and Missouri came down court with a chance to win.

That's when Boyle stepped in front of a pass intended for Jeff Strong. When Dreiling hit one of two free throws, the only thing eft for Missouri was to try a desperation 30-footer at the buzzer.

Here's how it appeared in the January 23, 1985, Times:

BOYLE'S THEFT HELPS KANSAS SEAL VICTORY

By Steve Richardson
A Member of the Sports Staff

Lawrence, Kan.

Tad Boyle, a 6-foot-5 senior guard who normally rides the bench, made the play of his career Tuesday night at Allen Field House. Boyle's simple steal with 7 seconds remaining put the finishing touches on a Kansas rally that turned an 11-point deficit in the second half into a 70-68 victory over Missouri.

"If you would have asked someone before the game if I would make that play, they would have told you you were crazy," Boyle said. "But crazy things happen, I have learned, in this game. Things can change awfully quickly."

Kansas, ranked 15th in the country, led 69-68 after center Greg Dreiling

missed the first free throw of a one-and-one situation with 12 seconds remaining. Then Boyle, who has played only about 10 minutes a game this season, stepped up and made the play. Missouri guard Bill Roundtree was attempting to get the ball to Jeff Strong, another Tigers guard.

Boyle stepped into the passing lane, snared the ball and dribbled around the court. In the meantime, Dreiling was fouled by Missouri's Derrick Chievous

with 4 seconds remaining. Dreiling was awarded two shots because Chievous grabbed him and was called for an intentional foul.

> "If you would have asked someone before the game if I would make that play, they would have told you you were crazy. But crazy things happen, I have learned, in this game. Things can change awfully quickly."
>
> —Kansas hero Tad Boyle

Dreiling again missed the first free throw. But he made the second one, and Kansas led 70-68.

Missouri's Malcolm Thomas threw up a 30-footer as time elapsed. The ball hit the rim and bounced away, leaving Missouri with a 10-8 record overall and 0-3 mark in the Big Eight. The confer-

RIVALS!
MU VS.KU

KU:70
MU:68

BASKETBALL
JANUARY 22, 1985

ence start is the worst for a Norm Stewart team at Missouri since he arrived in 1967.

"I'm not going to take credit for Greg's free-throw shooting," Kansas Coach Larry Brown said. But Brown hugged Dreiling as the two charged off the court, taking a 14-3 overall record and a 2-1 conference mark into a game against Colorado on Saturday in Boulder, Colo. "I put in Tad at the end because they went to a smaller lineup. And I have a lot of confidence in Tad. We played man to man at the end; we don't play it a lot, but we practice it every day. I think Roundtree was trying to avoid Cedric (Hunter)."

Hunter, who scored a career-most 16 points, was hounding Roundtree, and Boyle expected the ball would go to Strong.

"I have always had confidence in myself," Boyle said. "That may have surprised some people. I was anticipating they would want to get the ball in Strong's hands."

And why not? Strong, who had 22 points, had taken the potential go-ahead shot with 15 seconds remaining, but it was off target. Dreiling grabbed the rebound.

"We had our players on the right spot (on Strong's last shot), but we just didn't do it," Stewart said. "Strong got fouled. But you never get that foul."

Kansas trailed 41-30 with 16 minutes, 53 seconds remaining, but the Jayhawks, who have won 12 straight games at Allen, went to work. Danny Manning, Kansas' 6-foot-11 freshman star, scored 15 of his game-most 23 points in the second half.

Kansas finally caught Missouri at 57-57 when Manning made a three-point play on a resounding dunk shot and free throw with 7:13 left. Manning had 13 points in a little less than 8 minutes, bringing Kansas back into the game.

"I never thought we had the game won," Missouri's Thomas said. "Kansas is the type of team that you can't just shut out. They have great inside players, and they have great outside players. There was just no way we could hold them down.

"We tried our best to defense Danny Manning, but he's just too good to hold down an entire game."

Manning scored a crucial basket with 1:41 left when he tipped in a miss by Kansas' Ron Kellogg. Chievous then missed a Missouri shot with just more than a minute left. Dreiling grabbed the rebound and was fouled by Blake Wortham. Dreiling made two free throws for a 69-68 Kansas lead.

The Tigers held the ball until 29 seconds remained and 15 seconds on the 45-second shot clock. They called a timeout then and set up the last shot, which went to Strong.

It was off, and Kansas had survived an evening on which Manning, Kellogg and Dreiling all finished with four fouls and Calvin Thompson, battling a hamstring injury, fouled out of the game.

"This team has a long ways to go," Boyle said. "We were struggling early, and we were struggling tonight. We are still not a great team, but we have the players to be someday."

Kansas fell behind 35-30 at half-time, trailing 30-21 in the final 5 minutes of the first half. The Tigers dominated the boards 35-22 for the game, and many of Kansas' fouls were from trying to protect their inside defense. Missouri had a 12-rebound edge at halftime.

Missouri's 6-9 Dan Bingenheimer hounded Dreiling much of the game. Dreiling finished with seven points and

Tad Boyle

five rebounds.

"He did a good job," Dreiling said of Bingenheimer. "I had never seen him play before. He really came at me, and he kept me away from the ball."

SEVEN

THREE-POINTER BY MU FRESHMAN BEATS KANSAS

It was a preview of things to come.

Lee Coward hit a three-pointer in the final seconds to give Missouri a 63-60 victory over Kansas. Three weeks later, he hit a 15-footer with four seconds left as Missouri defeated Kansas 67-65 to win the Big 8 Tournament in Kansas City. It allowed the Tigers to sweep the regular and post-season Big 8 titles.

In the contest in Columbia, Coward's shot was the second big play in the final minute for the Tigers freshman. With the score tied, Coward stole the ball from Danny Manning, setting up Missouri's final possession.

Coward played a key role in the second half. He had 11 points, four assists and three steals, and his steal and jump shot gave Missouri a nine-point lead with just over 14 minutes remaining. Kansas stormed back, but Coward was brave enough to take the key shot, and he delivered.

"Lee beat them twice in a span of just a few days," former coach Norm Stewart recalled gleefully.

Here's how it appeared in the February 12, 1987, Times:

COWARD'S SHOT WITH 3 SECONDS LEFT WINS IT 63-60

BY STEVE RICHARDSON
OF THE SPORTS STAFF

COLUMBIA, MO.

Missouri freshman guard Lee Coward thought nothing of it. He glided to the deep corner of the court and took a look at the desperate situation developing.

Then stop, pop. His 22-foot shot with 3 seconds remaining downed Kansas 63-60 Wednesday night at the Hearnes Center.

It was the Lee Coward show the entire final minute. He also caused a steal from Kansas' Danny Manning with 50 seconds remaining that set up Missouri's winning possession and ended 17th-ranked Kansas' nine-game winning streak. The Jayhawks failed to get a shot off in the final 3 seconds.

"I love it," Coward said. "I'm the pressure player. When I got the ball, I set and I pumped and then I waved at the basket. It wasn't hard. I have done that in high school all the time.

"I thought my steal was the play that won the game. Earlier I threw the ball away, and I told Derrick (Chievous) I would make up for it. Danny tried to take the ball behind his back. A big man can't do that. I mean a 6-11 player was not going to come down the court

and do that to us."

Kansas, 7-2 in the league and 18-6 overall, was in a position to take the Big Eight Conference lead when Coward, again, threw the ball out of bounds when he was trying to hit Missouri's Greg Church on the baseline with a minute remaining. The score was tied 60-60, but Kansas never got a shot off attempting to take the lead.

Coward redeemed himself when he caused the steal.

"I was trying to get away from Church," Manning said. "And when you do that, there's usually a blind spot. Coward knocked it loose, and Church

BEING GOOD STEWARTS

RIVALS!
MU VS. KU

MU:63
KU:60

BASKETBALL
FEBRUARY 11, 1987

dived for it. If I had it to do over, I would have just backed them down and not tried to go past them."

That set the stage for the dramatic ending and allowed Missouri, 6-3 and 16-9, to move within one game of leaders Oklahoma and Kansas in the Big Eight standings.

The Tigers worked the ball down to less than 15 seconds when Chievous, who led all scorers with 26 points, drove the lane and was covered. In midair he passed the ball to Mike Sandbothe, who was under the basket. Sandbothe was fouled by KU's Keith Harris and tumbled to the floor and clutched at his leg. He had cramps in the leg and had to leave the game with 12 seconds remaining.

So Missouri Coach Norm Stewart looked down his bench for a replacement to shoot the one-and-one free throw. It turned out to be Devon Rolf, a junior walk-on, who hadn't played yet.

"He came over to the sideline and said, "Who wants to shoot?" Rolf said. "I wanted to. I felt good. The shot felt good, and I thought it was in, but thank God for Greg Church."

Church came down with the missed free throw by Rolf. He then passed it out to Lynn Hardy, who eventually got it to Coward for the winning shot.

"He was open," Kansas' Jeff Gueldner said, "(Mark) Turgeon came over to help me on Lynn Hardy, and that left him wide open."

Coward was a spunky player throughout the second half. He finished with 11 points, four assists and three steals. He sparked Missouri in the second half when the Tigers went ahead by nine. His steal and jump shot gave Missouri a 45-36 lead with 14:11 remaining.

"I thought my steal was the play that won the game. Earlier I threw the ball away, and I told Derrick (Chievous) I would make up for it. Danny tried to take the ball behind his back. A big man can't do that. I mean a 6-11 player was not going to come down the court and do that to us."
—Missouri guard Lee Coward

Kansas, however, came back behind Manning, who finished with 21 points. The Jayhawks eventually tied the score 60-60 when Manning made two free throws after he was fouled by Sandbothe. Manning played only 26 minutes because he had to sit out nearly 14 minutes in the first half with two fouls.

KU had a 15-2 lead when Manning left. But the Jayhawks trailed 32-30 at halftime. Manning re-entered the game at the beginning of the second

half, but the Jayhawks could never regain the lead. Sandbothe scored two baskets at the beginning of the second half, and away the Tigers went.

"I was surprised he didn't put me back in," Manning said of Coach Larry Brown. "But he kept saying we were OK."

Brown said that if the game had gotten out of hand, he would have put Manning back in during the first half. But Missouri's only first-half lead was at halftime, and Brown wanted to save Manning for the stretch.

Manning looked as if he was off to a great game, similar to his 40- point career high against Notre Dame on Sunday. He scored six straight points and a Hearnes crowd of 12,767 was moaning. Then he was called for foul No. 1 with 17:56 remaining in the first half. About 4 minutes later, here came No. 2 when he fouled Sandbothe on the baseline.

"I thought it was going to be a good game," Manning said. "Then came that ridiculous second foul."

While Manning was cooking early, Missouri missed nine of its first 10 shots and Kansas was sailing with a 15-2 lead.

But when Manning went out, the game changed in favor of the Tigers, who slowly came back behind Chievous. The Tigers outscored Kansas 30-15 in the final 14 minutes of the first half.

"They took Manning out, and we lost our composure," Kansas forward Chris Piper said.

The Jayhawks, at that point, switched to what looked like a match-up zone and a 1-3-1 zone. And that's when Chievous went to work. Chievous scored the last six points of the first half.

MANNING'S 37 POWERS KU PAST MISSOURI

Danny Manning proved he was one of the best players ever in the series with a 37-point effort that helped Kansas take a one-game lead over Missouri in a hotly contested Big 8 race. Manning later that year would lead the Jayhawks to the national title, but his focus on this night was Missouri.

"That was one of the best nights he ever had," said Max Falkenstein, a KU broadcaster for more than 50 years. "He scored 15 of the last 18 points for Kansas. MU had won 21 straight games and Danny stopped them."

Manning certainly had help, but he was the key. He scored 23 points in the first half, as they Jayhawks led 38-29 at intermission. He had nine of those points during a 20-0 run that took an 8-6 deficit and gave the Jayhawks the lead for good. He also had eight rebounds, three blocked shots, two steals and an assist.

Here's how it appeared in the February 28, 1988, Star:

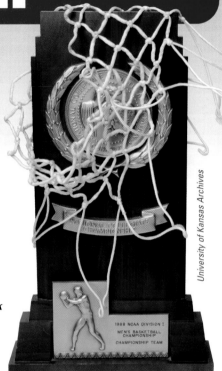

University of Kansas Archives

TIGERS DISAPPOINT RECORD HOME CROWD

BY BOB GRETZ
SPORTSWRITER

COLUMBIA

Two weeks ago, Missouri was basking in the national spotlight after an upset victory at Nevada-Las Vegas pushed them back into the Top 20 rankings by the Associated Press.

On Saturday, Danny Manning and Kansas turned that light off. With Manning scoring 37 points, the Jayhawks handed Missouri an 82-77 defeat in front of a Hearnes Center record crowd of 13,610.

It was the first home loss in 22 games for Norm Stewart's team, and the Tigers are 1-3 since that victory in Las Vegas. The loss left them 6-6 in the Big Eight Conference and 17-8 for the season. An NCAA tournament bid that

once seemed assured, now appears uncertain. The Tigers have two games remaining – at home against Oklahoma and at Kansas State – and the Big Eight Conference tournament in two weeks at Kemper Arena.

"I don't think about the NCAA," Stewart said. "I'm thinking about Oklahoma. If a team plays hard all year, and does the best it can, it will be selected.

"Kansas had a tremendous game. They had the answers today. You've got to give them credit."

The victory provided a tremendous boost to the chances of the Jayhawks of making the NCAA tournament field. They are 7-5 in the Big Eight and 18-10 overall. The game ended the Jayhawks' four-game "Death March" that Coach

Larry Brown dubbed the last two weeks with games against Kansas State, Duke, Oklahoma and Missouri.

"We've been fighting and playing great teams close, and we had nothing to show for it," Brown said. The Jayhawks finished that stretch 2-2.

"This game reminded me of the Duke game. We came out and played great defense and they were only down nine points at halftime. I was concerned."

But whenever Brown becomes concerned, he just looks to Manning for help. And as he has for the last four

Manning may have scored 37 points in his last effort against the Tigers, but his defense was as important to his game as his offense.

BEING GOOD STEWARTS

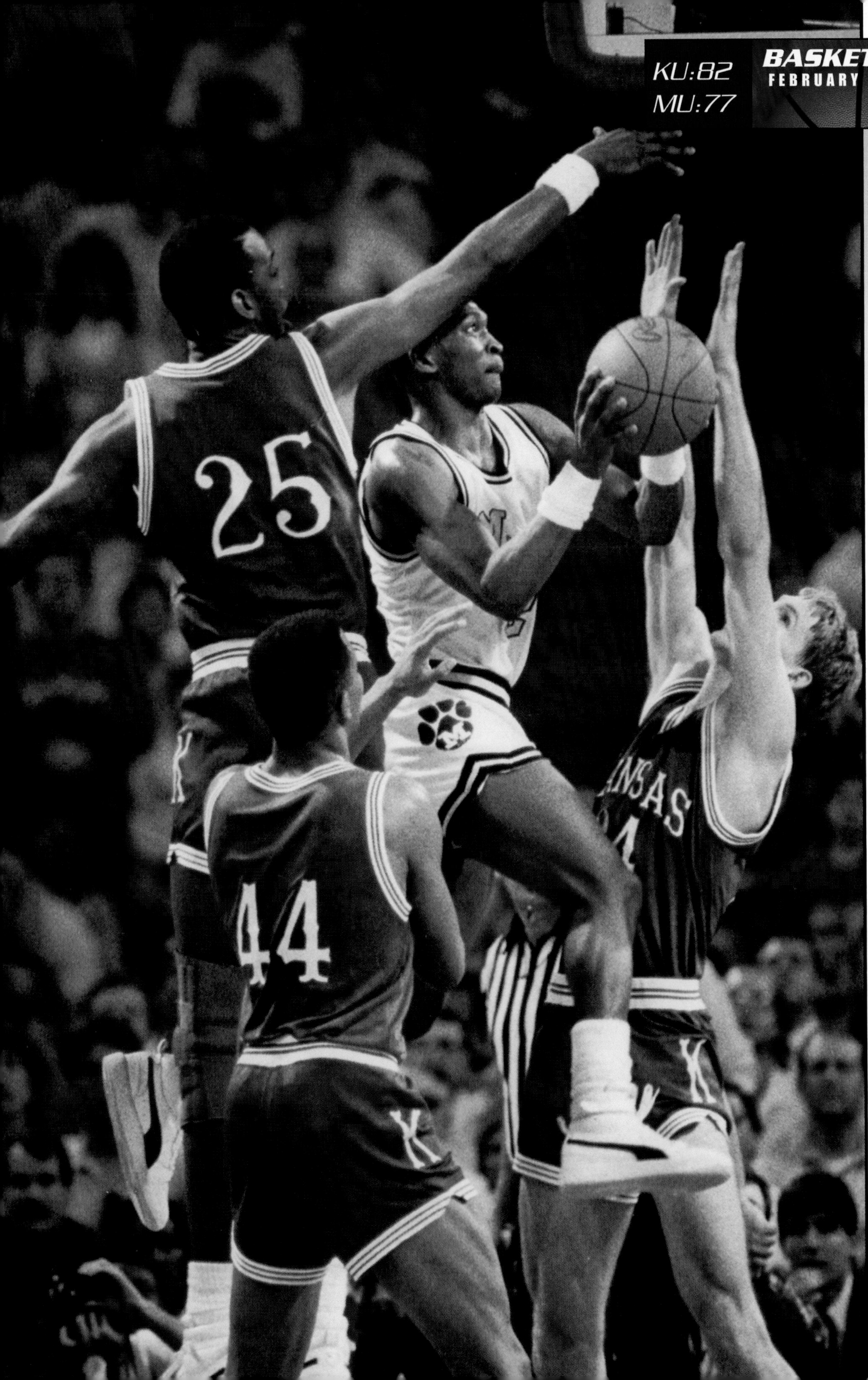
25
44

several times in the second half, but they could not get closer.

"They never did quit," Brown said. "We did all kinds of things at the end of the game to give them a shot. They were trading two shots (on free throws) for three-point shots. We don't normally hit our free throws."

The stretch that ultimately won the game for the Jayhawks began with Missouri leading 8-6. Kevin Pritchard's basket tied the score with 16 minutes, 32 seconds to play in the half. It would be another 7:42 before the Tigers scored, and by then Kansas had a 26-8 lead.

The key play in the run was a three-point play by Manning, who scored inside and was fouled by 6-8 Greg Church. A pushing match started among 6-10 Doug Smith of Missouri and Manning and Milt Newton of the Jayhawks, but officials quickly broke it up and brought both teams together to warn them against fighting.

For Missouri, the rest of the half was spent trying to fight its way back into the game. The Tigers trailed 28-13 after two free throws by Manning. By intermission, though, they had cut the margin to nine points, thanks to three points down the stretch from both Chievous and Leonard. Chievous made two free throws near the end to make it 38-29.

"Except for that first 10 minutes, I thought our team did a heck of a job," Stewart said. "We made a tremendous comeback, with a lot of different combinations. We got a combination out there that broke out and wanted to play."

In the first half, Kansas was outhustling Missouri for loose balls and rebounds, and an unhappy Stewart tried many different people to break the spell. He finally settled on the group of Leonard, Smith, Buntin, Lee Coward and John McIntyre with Chievous coming off the bench later

in the second half.

Chievous, who according to Stewart was ill before the game, had 20 points, and Leonard contributed 17 points and played tough defense on the inside against Manning in the second half.

Two three-pointers from Coward, a tap in by Smith and a driving basket by Chievous cut the Kansas lead to 52-50 with 12:04 to play.

> **"People have been talking about Danny having an off year, but this is his best year ever. All you've got to do is look out there and see.**
>
> **"We couldn't take Danny out for long, or (Derrick) Chievous and (Nathan) Buntin would have gone wild."**
> **—Kansas coach Larry Brown**

From that point on, every time the Tigers got close, Kansas answered. Missouri pulled to within two points on three occasions, the last coming at 58-56 on a dunk by Leonard.

But two free throws from Keith Harris and a three-point basket by Newton gave the Jayhawks a seven-point lead with 7:20 to play. Missouri could not cut the margin any closer than five points the rest of the way.

"This was a great win for us," Manning said. "It's tough when you are playing top teams every night and you work hard and don't get the win.

"This one was very nice."

years, the 6-10 senior provided it. Manning scored 23 points in the first half, when the Tigers tried several different people on him defensively with little success. Manning also contributed eight rebounds, three blocked shots, two steals and an assist while playing 36 minutes. He came out only because he got into foul trouble late in the first half.

"People have been talking about Danny having an off year, but this is his best year ever," Brown said. "All you've got to do is look out there and see.

"We couldn't take Danny out for long, or (Derrick) Chievous and (Nathan) Buntin would have gone wild."

Missouri was unable to stop Manning in the first half as he hit nine of 11 shots. He displayed a wide assortment of shots against 6-8 Mike Sandbothe and 7-1 Gary Leonard. He made his first six shots and had 13 of Kansas' first 19 points.

And he keyed a 20-0 Kansas run in the first half with nine points. It was a blow that Missouri could not overcome. The Tigers pulled to within two points

BEING GOOD STEWARTS

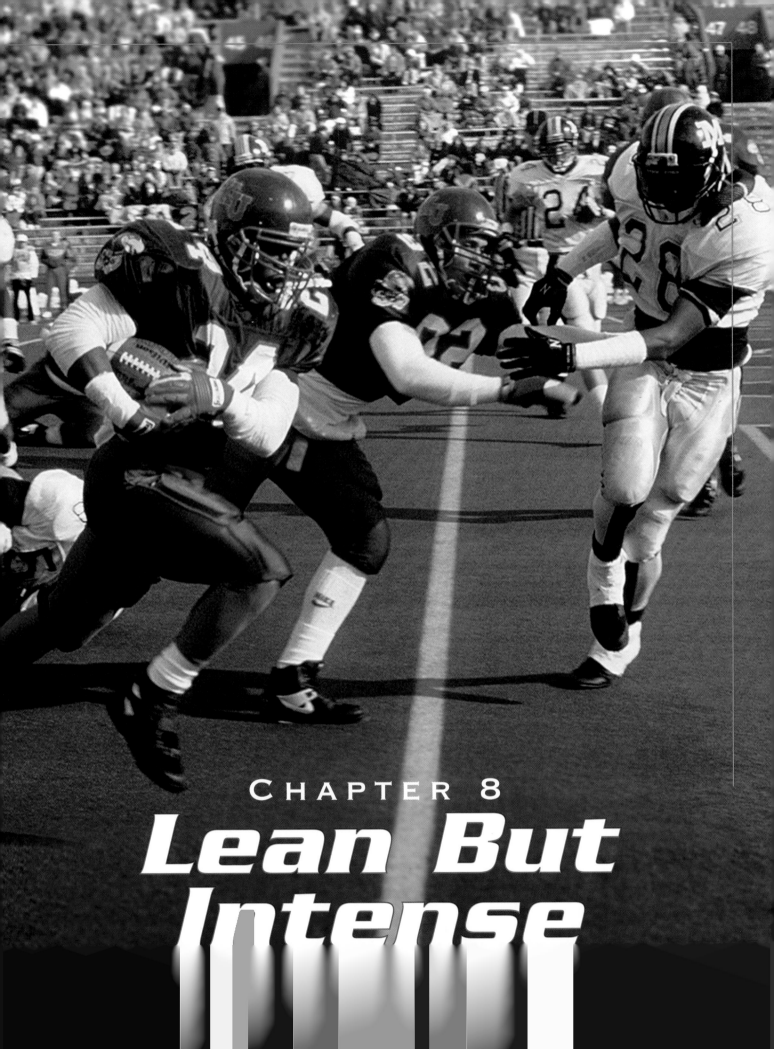

CHAPTER 8
Lean But Intense

Win or Else

It doestn't pay to lose to your biggest rival. Don't agree? Ask Pepper Rodgers, Don Fambrough, Al Onofrio or any of the other football coaches at either Kansas or Missouri since 1970. Kansas has had eight, counting the two tenures of Fambrough and not counting current mentor Mark Mangino. Missouri has had six, not counting current head man Gary Pinkel.

Of Kansas' eight coaches who have left since 1970, six were fired. Mike Gotfried (1983-85) left to go into broadcasting and Glen Mason (1988-96) left to take the head position at the University of Minnesota. Only Dan Devine has left Missouri on his own accord. He left after the 1970 season to take over at Notre Dame.

That makes 11 coaches who have been fired from one of the two schools in the last 34 years. How many of them lost their last game to their arch rival? Try 10. The lone exception was Woody Widenhofer, who was fired after the

1988 season despite defeating Kansas 55-17. Of course, that gave the Tigers a 3-7-1 record and gave Widenhofer a three-year mark of 13-31-1, the second lowest winning percentage in Missouri history.

HERE'S A RUN-DOWN OF EACH COACH'S SWAN SONG

• **In 1970,** MU won 28-17 at Columbia. Kansas coach Pepper Rodgers, despite leading the Jayhawks to the Big 8 Conference title and an

Orange Bowl berth two years earlier, was fired after completing a four-year run at 20-22. It is the closest to .500 that any Kansas coach has achieved since.

• **In 1974,** the Tigers won in Columbia again, this time by the score of 27-3. Don Fambrough finished his first four-year run at 19-25-1. He stayed on campus as Bud Moore's assistant, and he got another chance—to be fired—after Moore's turn.

FROM LEFT TO RIGHT:

Onofrio
Powers
Valesente
Widenhofer
Stull
Smith
Allen

• **In 1977,** KU edged the Tigers 24-22. Al Onofrio, who owned a 3-4 record against Nebraska, with the lowest ranking of any of those seven Cornhuskers teams being No. 12, finished his career against Kansas at 1-6. His overall record was 38-41-0.

• **In 1978,** Warren Powers took over at Mizzou and the Tigers shut out the Jayhawks, 48-0. Bud Moore's overall record had deteriorated in each of his four years, culminating with a 1-10 in his last campaign.

• **In 1982,** MU took the game in Columbia, 16-10. Fambrough was fired for the second time. His overall record was 36-49-5, including 4-4 against Missouri. He lost four of his last five against the Tigers. Fambrough claims to be the only coach fired twice by the same Division I team. Now that's something to brag about.

• **In 1984,** Kansas handed Powers and the Tigers a 35-21 loss in Columbia. Powers is the only coach on this list with a career mark better than .500 (46-33-3, .580), and was 4-3 against the Jayhawks. But three in losses in his last four tries against KU earned Powers the ax.

• **In 1987,** MU defeated Kansas 19-7, ending the two-year coaching career of Bob Valesente. Valesente managed only three victories in his first year, with one of the losses being a 48-0 whitewash at Missouri. That was his good year. His team was 1-9-1 the next year and he was sent packing.

• **In 1988,** MU humbled Kansas 55-17, but even this couldn't save Widenhofer's job. "Woody" had showed improvement in each of his first three years, going from 1-10 to 3-8 to 5-6. But his final season saw the Tigers slip back to 3-7-1, including a five-game losing streak heading into the final game against Kansas. The victory was not enough.

• **In 1993,** Kansas had improved to be one of the better programs in the country. The Jayhawks trounced the Tigers, 28-0, and it was good-bye Bob Stull. Stull's five-year career record was not much better than Widenhofer's, 15-38-2 (.291). He never managed more than four wins in any season.

• **In 2000,** KU and MU squared off in the "Survival Bowl," with the losing coach almost certainly facing extinction. Kansas won, 38-17, and Tigers coach Larry Smith's seven-year run was over. Kansas coach Terry Allen went 4-7 to survive another year. But the next year…

• **In 2001,** Missouri won 38-34 in Lawrence. Even though it was only midway through the conference season, the handwriting was on the wall. Allen lasted just two more games and was fired with three games to go.

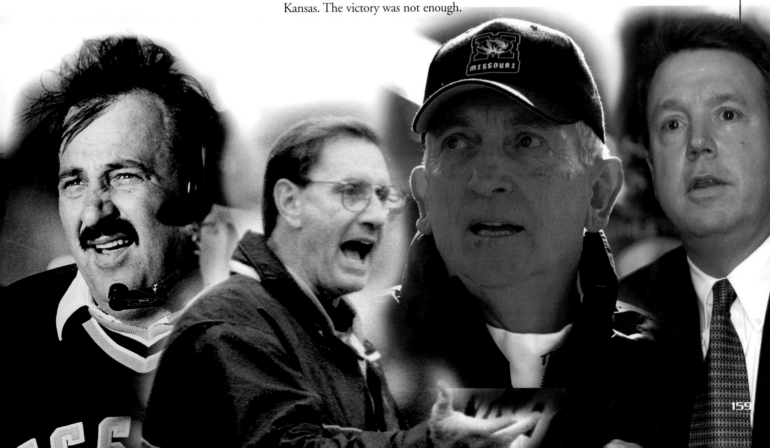

HERE COMES THE SUN — KU, 42-24

Kansas came into the season-ending contest against Missouri needing a win to clinch a berth in the Sun Bowl. It took the Jayhawks a while to get rolling, but once they did, "roll" is the best way to describe the result.

Kansas rushed for 556 yards, the most ever against Missouri at that time. In the third quarter alone, Kansas accumulated 301 yards of total offense and turned a 10-7 deficit into a 28-17 lead.

Three running backs went over 100 yards for Kansas, led by Laverne Smith, who tallied 236 yards on 15 carries. Norris Banks and Dennis Wright also eclipsed the century mark. Nolan Cromwell, Kansas' quarterback, added 70 yards of passing on 5-of-7 passing, as the Jayhawks netted 628 yards of total offense.

Cromwell was the key to the Jayhawks' bowl season in 1975, at least according to John Kadlec, current color analyst on the Missouri football network and then an assistant coach for the Tigers under Al Onofrio.

"Nolan could do anything he wanted," Kadlec said. "That was evidenced by the fact that he played defensive back in the NFL. Of all the KU football players I coached against, Nolan was the greatest."

The only thing that kept Missouri in the game was the seven fumbles by the Jayhawks, four of which were recovered by the Tigers.

Here's how it appeared in the November 23, 1975, Star:

By Jack Lindberg
A Member of the Sports Staff

Lawrence, Kan.

Overcoming what had been a near-fatal case of fumbleitis, the Kansas Jayhawks gulped massive doses of Missouri yardage and earned a holiday in the Sun Bowl with a 42-24 football victory yesterday.

Laverne Smith, Norris Banks and Dennis Wright churned up the heavy yardage as Kansas notched the most points it has ever scored against Mizzou in 84 attempts. At the same time the Jayhawks nudged into the Missouri record book for the most yardage rushing by an opponent – a whopping 556.

The impressive triumph before a

In the third quarter Kansas made the current superlatives "awesome" and "super" seem mild. On the way to scoring three touchdowns and in setting up a fourth only two plays into the final period, the Jayhawks rolled up an astounding 304 yards of total offense in 15 minutes on the clock.

crowd of 52,450 in Memorial Stadium set up the Jayhawks for a Dec. 26 Sun Bowl battle in El Paso, Tex., with Pittsburgh.

Smith, Banks and Wright had their greatest days ever wearing the Kansas Blue. Smith, a halfback, had touchdown runs of 67 and 56 yards on the way to 236 yards in 15 carries. He had 182 yards against Colorado last year. Fullbacks Banks and Wright (from

Mound City, Mo.), each went over the 100-yard barrier. Banks picked up 120 yards in 17 carries and Wright added 113 on only nine attempts. Twice Wright bolted up the middle for 20-yard T. D. blasts.

Billy Campfield, K. U.'s other halfback – the blocking one – located the end zone twice from two yards out on pitches to the left.

And for the complete get-well tonic, Nolan Cromwell, the K. U. wishbone doctor, hit 5 of 7 passes for 70 yards as Kansas had 628 yards of total offense against the third best defensive team in the Big Eight.

But the Missouri offense cannot be overlooked, either. The Tigers, who led, 7-0 and 10-0, rushed for 296 yards with tailback Tony Galbreath getting 175 of them plus a touchdown, and Steve Pisarkiewicz passing for another 105 yards and two touchdowns to Henry Marshall, the premier split end in the Big Eight.

Missouri also recovered 3 of 5 K. U. first-half fumbles and 4 of 7 in the game to keep the contest close until the fourth quarter.

In the third quarter Kansas made the current superlatives "awesome" and "super" seem mild. On the way to scoring three touchdowns and in setting up a fourth only two plays into the final period, the Jayhawks rolled up an astounding 304 yards of total offense in 15 minutes on the clock. Missouri had 101 of its 401 total yards in the same period.

It was the third quarter in which Kansas came from a 10-7 deficit to a 28-17 lead and then got healthy in the final period with the T.D. flow ending as Campfield pranced in with seven seconds left.

In first tearing up the Missouri middle with Banks and then Wright, and turning to Smith on draws and a pitchout to the right, Kansas outdid the 498 yards Oklahoma rushed against the Tigers last year.

"We made a little adjustment to our game plan," said Bud Moore, the Kansas coach, who was picked to finish seventh in the conference but came on for a 7-4 season and 4-3 in the Big Eight.

"We planned to do what the defense gave up. But this time we blocked the tackle and 'read' the end where usually you just 'read' the tackle. That's the way they played it all year."

And that's exactly the way Coach Al Onofrio of Missouri saw it, too.

"We knew what they were doing," Onofrio said. "They had a good scheme and we didn't react to it." When asked about the K.U. passing, Onofrio replied, "We felt all along they could pass, but it wasn't their passing that beat us – it was Laverne and that quick fullback draw."

K.U.'s fumble problem caused pain twice in the first half. Cromwell fumbled the first time with Kenny Downing of M.U. recovering on the Kansas 40. The Tigers went that 40 in eight plays with Pisarkiewicz passing five yards to Marshall for the T.D. Marshall's two scoring catches gave him nine for the season and a share of the M.U. record book with Mel Gray, who had the same number in 1969. Galbreath carried five times in the drive.

Kansas, in three plays after the kickoff, went to the M.U. 8 where Banks coughed it up and Steve Meyer got it for the Tigers. Banks had carried from the Kansas 46 for 19 and Wright came in and blasted over right guard for 42 to the 12. Banks went four and bobbled. The Jayhawks, however, held and Tim Gibbons was on target with a field goal from the 19. That came on the first play of the second quarter.

Finally getting field position with 5:18 left in the half on a Jim Goble punt that went out-of-bounds on the Missouri 48, the Jayhawks chewed up 52 yards in six plays with Wright blasting over left guard for the 20-yard scoring run.

Each team fumbled twice in the final minutes of the half.

Smith had only 40 yards rushing at the half, but from then on he inhaled real estate like he was an addict to artificial turf.

On the third play after intermission the Wichita junior, who is now the No. 3 all-time rusher at K.U. with 2,096 yards (jumping over Charlie Hoag who had 1,914 from 1950-52), took a hand-off on the draw from Cromwell, shot up the middle, got a great block from Skip Sharp

> "Kansas deserved to win because they outplayed us... they just outplayed us, outhit us and outkicked us."
> —Bob McRoberts, Missouri's leading tackler

about the M.U. 30 and went 67 yards.

Only 44 seconds of the second half had slipped away. Kansas then forced another Goble punt, a 35-yarder for field position on the Kansas 41 and the Jayhawks ran three plays for a 10-yard first down to the M.U. 49 and lost seven back to the 44 on a poor Cromwell pitch to Campfield.

On the draw Smith was hit near midfield, spun on one hand, turned left, shook off another tackler, and outraced everyone for 56 yards. That came slightly more than three minutes after the other, but it took its toll on the Tigers.

Mizzou was hungry for yards and marched 74 yards with Galbreath shredding the middle for the last nine. That made it 21-17 with 8:52 left in the quarter.

It was here that Missouri lost it. Eric Franklin of Kansas dropped the ball on the kickoff and Mark Kirkpatrick of M.U. recovered on the 17.

Galbreath got two the hard way over tackle. Then Rich Dansdill, freshman fullback subbing for injured John Blakeman, roared to the 2. Dansdill, however, was in motion and it was second-

and-13 from the 20. Dansdill got two of them back, Pisarkiewicz threw incomplete and Gibbons was wide to the right on a field goal attempt from the 25.

Kansas answered with a 5-play, 80-yard march right out of the wishbone playbook. Smith had the big gainer, a 41-yard advance in which he reversed his field twice. Wright had a twin 20-yard T.D.

Campfield went in from the 2 by giving cornerback Bruce Carter a neat hip for a K.U. touchdown on the second play of the fourth quarter to cap a 95-yard march that took 11 plays.

Missouri, back on offense, went 79 yards with Marshall catching a 3-yard toss from Pisarkiewicz. Kansas ended

the scoring with a 69-yrd drive and Campfield's second T.D.

Gibbons equaled Mizzou's field goal record for a season with his 13th. Greg Hill had a baker's dozen twice – 1972 and 1973. Kansas rushed for the most team yards ever for a K.U. season with 3,488 to wipe out the 3,116 total posted in 1950. And Cromwell had 218 carries for the season to pass the K.U. standard of 209 set by John Riggins in 1970.

"Nolan Cromwell is the best wishbone quarterback I've ever seen," said Moore. "There's no doubt about it. I wouldn't trade him for any quarterback in America."

And after his statement following

the opening season loss to Washington State that his team wouldn't win a game, Moore said, "It's the same group of youngsters, but now they know what they are capable of doing.

"Our offense controlled the football and took the pressure off the defense. Our pass defense was good and we had some big plays (two interceptions), but penalties hurt us – that and first-half fumbles. I was hoping we could stop them and that we could keep moving the football."

Missouri finished with a season 6-5 season and 3-4 in the conference. M.U. leads in the series 39-36-9. And with 42 points the '75 Jayhawks outdid the 1951 team's 41-28 victory.

FROM THE KANSAS CITY STAR, 1975

KU WISHBONE FINDS A WAY

BY STEVE SCHOENFIELD
K.U. SPORTS CORRESPONDENT

Lawrence, Kan.

Oklahoma coaches take note. The Alabama staff just might want to listen, too.

Kansas has found the well-kept secret of how to move a wishbone offense against the Missouri Tigers' 8-man defensive line.

The Jayhawks' discovery worked well. K.U. piled up 556 yards rushing in its 42-24 victory over Missouri yesterday. And they earned a Sun Bowl berth to boot.

The secret weapon begins by sending the running back who's on the same side of the field as Kenny Downing, Missouri's All-Big Eight cornerback, in motion. That takes Downing, the Tigers' leading tackler, out of the play.

"Downing's such a good player and makes so many tackles," said John Levra, the K.U. offensive coordinator, "that we tried to keep him as far away from the action as possible."

That's only the beginning. John Morgan, a senior center, explains the rest.

"They put those eight guys on the line," Morgan said. "The noseguard plays in one of the gaps between me and the guard and their ends come straight at the quarterback. We double team the nose – he wasn't strong enough to stop both of us – and then there's a cushion up the middle."

So how come none of the other teams that played the Tigers discovered that?

"I don't know," smiled Vince Semary, the K.U. offensive line coach. "We knew that would work. I guess it's

...," he said, giving the thinking man's symbol by pointing his forefinger to his temple.

It obviously all worked. The Kansas offense steamrolled its way past the Tigers. Three backs rushed for personal bests. Laverne Smith, a junior halfback, was the biggest gainer rushing for 236 yards on only 15 carries, including scoring jaunts of 67 and 56 yards.

"The line was just blowing them out," he said. "When they do that I can run anywhere I want. Once they let me get into the secondary, I had a straight view of the end zone. I saw it all the way."

Fullback Dennis Wright saw clear daylight, too. He had two 20-yard touchdown runs on the way to scampering for 113 yards on nine carries.

RIVALS!
MU VS. KU

MU:42
KU:24

FOOTBALL
NOVEMBER 23, 1975

THEY DESERVED THE DEFEAT

BY RICH SAMBOL
A MEMBER OF THE SPORTS STAFF

Lawrence, Kan.

Four seconds into the second quarter yesterday Missouri's football team looked like it had just bought a ticket to the Sun Bowl.

Tim Gibbons split the uprights with a 29-yard field goal and the Tigers pulled ahead of Kansas, 10-0. But from then on the show belonged to Laverne Smith, Dennis Wright, Norris Banks and Nolan Cromwell.

The Kansas offense turned on a prolific ground game, an assault that riddled the Missouri defense for 556 yards, the most the Tigers have ever given up on the ground.

"This is the first time I believe we deserved to lose," said Bob McRoberts, M.U.'s leading tackler among linemen and linebackers. "All the others were flukes as far as I was concerned, and that goes back as far as Michigan.

"Kansas deserved to win because they outplayed us…they just outplayed us, outhit us and outkicked us."

Smith, who became the third leading rusher on K.U.'s all-time charts with his 236-yard performance, broke Missouri's back with touchdown runs of 67 and 56 yards at the start of the second half.

"He had a great afternoon," said Al Onofrio, the Missouri coach. "He took that draw and ran anywhere he wanted with it.

"Those two runs were what took our momentum away."

Missouri's offense took its lumps, too, despite the fact Tony Galbreath gained 175 yards in 26 carries. Steve Pisarkiewicz, the Tiger quarterback who entered the game with the best passing credentials in the Big Eight, received his share.

Pisarkiewiez was sacked only once, a 9-yard loss by tackle Mike Butler, but the K.U. defense made its presence felt in terms of dropping greeting cards all afternoon.

"They played basic football and controlled the line of scrimmage," said Pisarkiewicz, who completed 10-of-24 passes for only 105 yards and threw two interceptions. "They overpowered us man-for-man.

"Their pass rush was their best defense. People had their hands up all afternoon knocking the ball down. The pass rush was their pass defense."

So what started out to be a pretty good offensive afternoon turned out to be one of the longest afternoons of the season.

"We were beatin' them pretty good," said Mike Owens, a starting guard. "But they started stunting their linebackers after we took that 10-0 lead and we became a little rattled. We held them out some of the time but they beat us enough to make a difference."

Despite the game-breaking effect of the touchdown runs by Smith early in the third quarter Missouri wasn't ready to give up. The Tigers scored on a 9-yard run by Galbreath, and then Eric Franklin fumbled the ensuing kickoff with M.U. recovering on the Kansas 17.

On the second play after Mark Kirkpatrick's recovery Rich Dansdill, a freshman fullback who was inserted into the line-up because of a knee injury to John Blakeman, powered his way to the 2-yard line. The play was called back when Dansdill was penalized for illegal motion.

"We moved the ball well but we couldn't seem to sustain it," Owens said.

"It seemed like there was always a fumble (two lost by Curtis Brown in the first half), a penalty or an interception would always get in the way.

"But I still don't think you'll find a better team that is 6-5."

The loss dropped Missouri into a tie for fifth place in the conference with Oklahoma State, which seems like a far cry from a national rating the Tigers gained with their 20-7 victory over Alabama in the season opener.

"It's very difficult to compare teams when you play them at a different time of the year," Onofrio said. "But I've said all along I think there are stronger teams than Alabama in the Big Eight."

Did the Tigers feel extra pressure because a bowl game in the balance?

"We might have talked about going to the bowl before the game," Pisarkiewicz said, "But you forget all of that when you get on the field. When game time rolls around it boils down to the game itself.

"People were just teeing off on us."

KANSAS BLOTS OUT MIZZOU'S SUN

During Al Onofrio's seven-year career as head coach of the Missouri Tigers (1971-77), he went 3-4 against Nebraska. All seven years the Huskers came into the Missouri game ranked in the top 12 teams in the nation. In their four losses, they fell to the teams ranked Nos. 1, 6, 3 and 11. In their three victories, they defeated the second-, twelfth- and third-ranked Cornhuskers.

So why was Onofrio fired after seven seasons in Columbia? Because he could not beat the rival Jayhawks. At least that's the theory of John Kadlec, who was an assistant on Onofrio's staff.

"Those were games where you put your life on the line," Kadlec said. "We lost most of them, and we got fired."

Onofrio was 1-6 against Kansas, with the only win coming in 1974.

As the teams prepared for their 1976 encounter, the Tigers had a bid to the Sun Bowl in their hands, as long as they won the home game. Kansas would have nothing to do with that scenario, as they raced to a 24-0 halftime lead and cruised to a 41-14 victory.

Just as he had the year before, Laverne Smith carried the load for the Jayhawks. He rushed for 150 yards, after stinging the Tigers with 236 the year before. The other key for Kansas was the play of backup quarterback Mark Vicendese. "Nolan Cromwell had gotten injured against Oklahoma in the sixth week of the season, which derailed the season for us," said then Voice of the Jayhawks Tom Hedrick. "Mark ran the option to perfection and the Jayhawks rolled."

Here's how it appeared in the November 21, 1976, Star:

BY JOE MCGUFF
SPORTS EDITOR

Columbia

A Sun Bowl bid was shining in Missouri's future when it lined up for the opening kick-off yesterday in Memorial Stadium, but the invitation disappeared in the gloom of a 41-14 loss to an inspired Kansas team that held its errors to a minimum and slashed the M. U. defense for 421 yards rushing.

Missouri trailed, 24-0 at half time and was down, 34-0, before scoring its first touchdown with 5:28 remaining in the fourth quarter. K. U. has won five of its last six meetings with the Tigers and the Jayhawks' wishbone offense has produced 83 points in the last two games.

Laverne Smith completed his college career by rushing 20 times for 150 yards and moved up from fifth to third on the all-time conference rushing list with 3,192 yards. It was the fourth game of the season in which he had rushed for more than 100 yards.

For Missouri this has been a season of astonishing victories and bewildering losses, but even though the Tigers have built a national reputation for unpredictability, K. U.'s ability to totally dominate the game came as a shock.

Turnovers and the Tigers' inability to stop the K. U. wishbone attack were the key elements in the decisive events of the first half.

A fumble ended Missouri's first drive after the Tigers reached the K. U. 15. Kansas' first score came on a field goal that was set up by a 59-yard drive and the Jayhawks went in front, 10-0, when Skip Sharp intercepted a pass thrown by Steve Pisarkiewicz and returned it 46 yards.

K. U. drove 62 yards in five plays to increase its lead to 17-0 and then went 30 yards for a touchdown just

> "I truly believe the execution of Vicendese was the difference. Our quarterback execution was superb. The big problem since we lost Nolan (Cromwell) was the mistakes we were making. I felt if we could eliminate the mistakes we could win."
>
> —Kansas coach Bud Moore

LEAN BUT INTENSE

RIVALS!
MU VS. KU

KU:41
MU:14

FOOTBALL
NOVEMBER 21, 1976

before half time after gaining possession on an interception. A fumble at the M. U. 18 by Pete Woods set up the Jayhawks' fourth touchdown.

Mark Vicendese, a sophomore quarterback starting his second game, operated the Kansas wishbone brilliantly and gained 111 yards rushing. The Jayhawks had 10 turnovers a week ago against Colorado, but yesterday they had only three.

Bud Moore, the K. U. coach, said he came into the game convinced his team could move the ball against Missouri if it did not stop itself.

"I truly believe the execution of Vicendese was the difference," Moore said. "Our quarterback execution was superb. The big problem since we lost Nolan (Cromwell) was the mistakes we were making. I felt if we could eliminate the mistakes we could win.

"Our defense played extremely well against one of the best offensive teams in the nation. We all made some mistakes this year, including myself, but I'm just thankful we finished a winner.

"Because of the circumstances this is probably our best victory since I've been here." We've had a great deal of adversity."

Coach Al Onofrio said he did not know whether the Tigers were distracted by the bowl talk, but he added that for some reason they lacked intensity in the first half.

"It seemed like they were ready to play football," Onofrio said. "We had good practices. The bowl thing? Well, I don't think you ever know. I don't think you can ever tell how it affects a squad. It's very obvious we did not play our best. We missed Leo (Lewis) very much.

"They didn't play as well as we hoped they would, but for what reason you don't know. For years after the Oklahoma game we have not come back and played the football we are capable of playing."

In the last two weeks Missouri has given up 857 yards rushing to two wishbone teams, Oklahoma gaining 436 a week ago.

"When you play against one thing all year and then go against the wishbone it's tough," Onofrio said. "Against O. U. we thought we played well except for five or six plays. It's not so much alignments, it's intensity. There's just a small difference, but we didn't play defense with intensity in the first half."

There was no indication at the outset that the game would develop into a Kansas rout. K. U. suffered a net loss of five yards on its first possession and then M. U. drove from its 42 to the Kansas 15. At that point the turnover problem began. Earl Gant fumbled and Caleb Rowe recovered for K. U. at the 11.

The Kansas offense did not begin to assert itself until late in the first period. With 4:50 remaining, the Jayhawks drove from their 29 to the Missouri 12 where they were stopped. Mike Hubach kicked a 29-yard field goal.

On their next possession the Jayhawks drove from their 10 to the M.U. 9 before giving up the ball on a fumble. Six plays later Sharp picked off a pass intended for Lamont Downer and ran 46 yards to make the score 10-0.

This play was one of the turning points in the game, but it would not have been overly important if the Tigers had been able to hold Kansas. The Jayhawks, however, were gaining confidence and momentum.

They next took over at their 38 following a punt and scored in five plays. Vicendese ran 29 yards on a third-and-8 play and Bill Campfield produced the touchdown on a 28-yard burst over his left tackle.

Missouri was now at a point where it could not afford to give up another touchdown, but with 26 seconds

remaining before half time K. U. gained possession at the M. U. 30 after an interception by Rowe.

On second down, Smith took a pitch and ran 15 yards to the 13. He gained eight on a pitch around the right side and with seven seconds left

Onofrio

Vicendese tried to throw a quick pass to Jim Michaels, a tight end, in the end zone. The pass was incomplete, but Missouri was penalized for having too many men on the field.

Vicendese threw to Michaels again on the same play and completed the pass for a touchdown with two seconds remaining.

Moore explained that the Jayhawks felt they could run the play and still have time for a field-goal attempt if they failed.

The K. U. victory was its most one sided in the series since 1930 when it was 32-0. The Jayhawks finished with a 6-5 record, the first time they have had back-to-back winning seasons since the period of 1960-61-62. Missouri also finished with a 6-5 record.

MU ROLLS BY KANSAS

This one cost Bud Moore his job.

Moore, the fourth-year coach at Kansas, had defeated the Missouri Tigers three straight years. But a 48-0 loss to the Tigers in the penultimate game of the 1978 season gave the Jayhawks a 1-9 record. After they lost to their other rival, 36-20 to the lowly Kansas State Wildcats, Moore was given his pink slip.

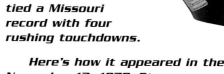

It's hard to say that this one loss to Missouri was the only blemish. The Jayhawks were outscored 345-124 for the season. Coming off a 3-7-1 season, saved maybe by the fact that two of those three wins were against Missouri and Kansas State, and the KU brass felt it was time for a change.

The Jayhawks were never in this game. They gave up 465 yards on the ground, and 552 overall, which paled in comparison to the 799 they surrendered the week before *against Nebraska. James Wilder led the Tigers with 160 total yards, while Earl Gant added 130 and tied a Missouri record with four rushing touchdowns.*

Here's how it appeared in the November 12, 1978, Star:

By Joe McGuff
Sports Editor

Columbia

In the view of Missouri football fans, no season is an unqualified success unless it includes a victory over Kansas, preferably by a one-sided margin. Saturday Missouri defeated Kansas 48-0, but for once even the most passionate of alums may have had too much of a good thing.

A week ago in Lawrence, Kas., many of the Jayhawk fans left early as Kansas was routed by Nebraska 63-21. Saturday even the Missouri fans in the crowd of 64,263 at Faurot Field began to leave in the opening stages of the fourth quarter.

Missouri broke the game open by scoring four touchdowns in a span of 8 minutes, 44 seconds beginning late in the first quarter. Kansas had several scoring opportunities before halftime but could not capitalize on them and

Missouri scored again on its first play from scrimmage in the second half.

From that point on the game moved tediously to a conclusion, although Earl Gant did his best to enliven the proceedings by scoring four touchdowns to set a single-game record for a Missouri player.

Gant's first two touchdowns came on runs of 11 and 27 yards in the second quarter. He went 16 yards to score in the third quarter and ran 30 yards for a touchdown in the fourth. He finished the day with 130 yards of total offense, but he was second in that department to teammate James Wilder, who had 160.

The Tigers executed the option play with great success and amassed 465 yards rushing. They had 552 yards of total offense against the injury-wracked Jayhawks, who gave up 799 total yards to Nebraska last week.

Missouri's victory followed losses to Colorado and Oklahoma State and in the view of Coach Warren Powers

revived the Tigers' bowl hopes.

"I think we're still in it," Powers said. "A lot hinges on next week. We can control our own destiny. If we beat Nebraska we'll go to a bowl even if I have to pay our way there."

The Tigers have a 6-4 record, but have played one of the most difficult schedules in the nation.

Missouri's margin of victory equals the largest in the 87-year history of the series. The record was first set in 1969 when Missouri ran up a record point total in defeating Kansas 69-21.

The 48 points represents the second highest total scored by either team, and the shutout victory is the first since 1966 when the Tigers won 7-0.

While the decisive victory revived Missouri's season, the crushing defeat heightened the crisis atmosphere developing around the Jayhawks, who have lost nine of their 10 starts.

"We haven't made any improve-

RIVALS!
MU VS. KU

MU:48
KU:0

FOOTBALL
NOVEMBER 12, 1978

ments in a while," said Bud Moore, whose job as head coach of the Jayhawks is in jeopardy. "That's obvious by the score."

"I think our players gave an honest effort. There were a number of reasons we were beaten today, but I won't go into that."

Pressed to expand on that point, Moore said, "I'm talking about injuries, about everything we've been talking about all year long. The last two games have been extremely frustrating."

Commenting on the position in which the Jayhawks find themselves, Moore said, "It's not hopeless. We have another game to play. It's ridiculous to even think that."

Powers termed Missouri's victory satisfying and added, "The last two weeks have been very trying for this football team…this is something we needed to bring us out of a big slump."

Although the game was hopelessly one-sided, Kansas did have some scoring opportunities in the first half. The Jayhawks connected on a 39-yard pass play to the MU 42 on the first play from scrimmage following the opening kickoff and later recovered a fumble at the MU 32. The first threat was stopped at the MU 34 and the second ended in a missed field goal attempt.

Missouri's first touchdown came with 4:06 remaining in the first quarter. The Tigers drove 73 yards in nine plays and Wilder ran 21 yards to score after taking a pitch from Phil Bradley.

Missouri regained the ball four plays after the kickoff on a pass interception by Russ Calabrese. A pass interference call moved the ball to the KU 31, and the Tigers scored in five plays, with Bradley going over from the 4 on a keeper.

Missouri drove 75 yards in six plays for its third touchdown with Gant taking a pitch and getting the final 11 yards around his left end. Missouri

drove 56 yards following an interception to score its fourth touchdown. Gant taking a pitch around left end and going 27 yards to score with 10:22 left in the second period.

Kansas reached the MU 8, 13 and 17 before halftime, but came away with no points.

On Missouri's fist play from scrimmage in the second half, Wilder broke off left tackle, pushed and dodged through a cluster of players and ran 40 yards to score.

Missouri went 83 yards in 12 plays for its sixth touchdown, and then Gant completed the scoring with his 30-yard run up the middle with 6:35 remaining in the fourth period.

Moore, asked if Wilder and Gant had been left in the game overly long,

replied, "That's their business, not mine."

"We played hard," Powers commented. "We played a complete game. I was really happy to see the way our running game went. I said last week I didn't give our team a chance to run the ball. We came out determined to run.

"We have big, strong running backs in Gant and Wilder. They take their toll of a football team."

One of the most lively incidents of the gray afternoon took place at halftime when a fan came out of the stands, ran through the KU band and knocked over one or two members. He was tackled by a tuba player and later subdued by police.

For the Jayhawks, it was their best open-field tackle of the day.

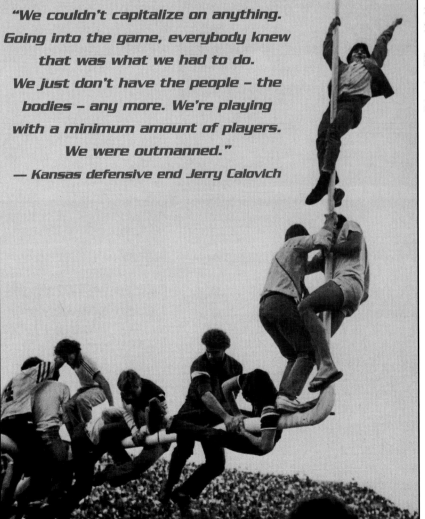

"We couldn't capitalize on anything. Going into the game, everybody knew that was what we had to do. We just don't have the people – the bodies – any more. We're playing with a minimum amount of players. We were outmanned."
— Kansas defensive end Jerry Calovich

University of Missouri Archives

MU'S GANT FINDS KEY TO SUCCESS

BY DON KAUSLER JR.
MU SPORTS CORRESPONDENT

Columbia –

Two weeks ago, Earl Gant was a football player to be pitied.

Missouri's senior running back dropped a long pass in the open field that would have gone for a game-winning touchdown against Colorado. The Tigers lost the crucial game, and Gant shouldered much of the blame himself.

Needless to say, Gant didn't make many fans that day.

Saturday, however, things were different. Much different.

Gant rushed for 134 yards on 15 carries and scored four touchdowns, a school record, to help Missouri crush Kansas 48-0.

He was smiling as he walked off the field. Strangers came up to him to shake his hand or pat him on the back. Others shouted congratulatory messages from the stands.

Yesterday's goat was today's hero.

"It feels good," the soft-spoken running back said afterward. "It feels real good."

Gant, though doesn't feel his performance is worthy of forgiveness for his sin against Colorado.

"This doesn't really make up for it," he said, "but it'll cover up for it."

Five, 10, 15 years from now, Gant said he probably would remember the game against Colorado more than this one.

"I think that dropped pass lost us the game," he said. "Besides, people tend to remember bad things more than they do good things."

But don't think the victory over KU was just another game for Gant.

"I'll remember this one, too," he said with a broad smile.

Gant did a favor for the person responsible for upkeeping the Missouri record book. When he scored on a 16-yard run late in the third quarter to give the Tigers a 41-0 lead, he became the 20th player in Missouri history to score three touchdowns – in a single game. Most recently, Curtis Brown came up with the hat trick, as he scored three times against USC in 1976.

When Gant took a handoff and plowed 30 yards up the middle for MU's last touchdown of the dark afternoon, 19 players had their names erased from the record book.

Gant said the last touchdown was his most satisfying.

"I remember No 39 (actually No. 62, Barnest Hogwood) got a good hit on me right before that one," said the 6-2, 207 pound native of Peoria, Ill. "I think I gave him a straight arm to the face (on the TD run).

"I wanted that one. I wanted them all."

Oddly enough, Gant didn't start the game. He was ineffective last week against Oklahoma State as the Tigers rushed for only 23 yards in 29 attempts, and Coach Warren Powers decided to go with a backfield of James Wilder and Gerry Ellis to start Saturday's game.

Gant said Powers' decision didn't upset him.

"I know it was the best thing for the team," he said. "I'm not going to argue with that. But I was determined to do what I could while I was in there."

What Gant did was win back a lot of fans.

ONLY TH

BY KEN DAVIS
KU SPORTS CORRESPONDENT

Columbia, Mo.

After one play Saturday, Kevin Murphy, Kansas split end, thought it was all over.

Murphy was on the receiving end of a 39-yard pass play for the Jayhawks on their first play of the game. And he was sure KU was on its way to another victory over Missouri.

The only problem with Murphy's logic was the fact that Missouri went on to defeat KU 48-0 before a crowd of 64,263 at Faurot Field.

It was all over, all right. But not for the Tigers.

"We've tried to throw on first down before," Murphy said in the KU locker room. "But we've never completed one before. I thought we had the momentum, and I thought everything was going right."

Things didn't go right for the Jayhawks much longer. KU could get no farther than the Tigers' 34-yard line after that pass and was forced to punt. From that point, it was all up hill for the Jayhawks, who are 1-9 overall and 0-6 in Big Eight Conference play.

KU found itself down by 21 points early in the second quarter as Missouri's backs ripped through the Kansas defense play after play.

RIVALS!
MU VS. KU

MU:48
KU:0

FOOTBALL
NOVEMBER 12, 1978

FROM THE KANSAS CITY STAR, 1978

FIRST PLAY WAS RIGHT FOR KU

"Their backs were so big that they just came through the line real clean," said Leroy Irvin, KU free safely.

Indeed, the Tiger backs were immaculate. James Wilder and Earl Gant swept for 160 and 137 yards, respectively.

Kansas found the task of coming back insurmountable. But that's not to say the Jayhawks didn't have chances to get back into the game.

Before MU scored, Jerry Calovich, defensive end, recovered a fumble by Phil Bradley at the Missouri 37. Four plays later, Mike Hubach missed on a 44-yard field-goal attempt.

In the second quarter, KU found itself inside the MU 20-yard line on two consecutive drives, but failed to score. A pass interception that Leroy Irvin returned 26 yards and a 35-yard punt return, also by Irvin, seemed to be breaks for the Jayhawks.

But KU couldn't capitalize on any of them.

"We couldn't capitalize on anything," Calovich said. "Going into the game, everybody knew that was what we had to do.

"We just don't have the people – the bodies – any more. We're playing with a minimum amount of players. We were outmanned."

MU's defense didn't help matters for the Jayhawks. The Tigers' defense relentlessly blitzed the KU offense, resulting in 53 yards in lost yardage and four interceptions.

"They were blitzing a lot," said Harry Sydney, KU's starting quarterback. "We didn't pick it up because they were showing it late. Every time we made a big play, they

would blitz and set us back. We just couldn't get it in. It's hard to explain."

Sydney was replaced by freshman Kevin Clinton in the second quarter. Clinton didn't have any better luck than Sydney, completing 9-of-22 passes with two interceptions and rushing for minus 21 yards. Sydney came back into the game for KU when Clinton injured his wrist while being tackled.

"It was poor," Clinton said of his performance. "I didn't feel good about it. I missed a lot of blitzes. Their blitzes were perfectly timed."

Twice in the second quarter KU was faced with fourth-down situations inside the Missouri 15-yard line. Both times KU elected to go for first downs instead of settling for field goals.

Some of the Jayhawks were not happy with the choices to go for first downs and touchdowns instead of going for three points.

"The first couple of times we were down 21-0." Clinton said. "I think it would give us a boost to get some points on the board. But that's Coach Moore's decision."

Charles Casey, defensive tackle, said he thought it would have been a big help just to have three points at halftime. "I think it would have given us some momentum," Casey said. "But I don't make the decisions."

For Calovich, losing to MU was something he had never experienced. And for the senior from Kansas City it was a worse feeling than the 63-21 defeat to Nebraska last week.

"The only thing that consoles me is that I beat them three times," Calovich said. "Right now, it hurts. It's embarrassing.

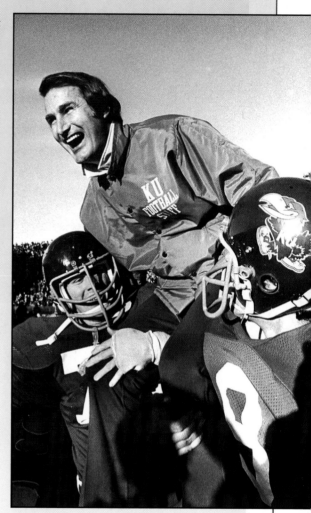

Bud Moore had many uplifting times at Kansas, but a 48-0 loss at Mizzou in 1978 was not among them.

There's nothing that can be said about it. It hurts a little bit worse than Nebraska because this is a bigger rivalry."

PUNTING GAME HELPS KU PIN MIZZOU WITH 19-11 LOSS

Defense wins championships. And although no championship was riding on the line for either the Jayhawks or the Tigers in 1981, one defense outdid the other for the victory.

FOOTBALL
NOVEMBER 21 1981

KU:19
MU:11

RIVALS!
MU VS. KU

Kansas, with starting quarterback Frank Seurer on the sideline with a dislocated throwing elbow in the first quarter, and back-up Steve Smith ineffective, used great defense and superb punting from Bucky Scribner to defeat the Tigers 19-11 and clinch a berth in the Hall of Fame Bowl. The Tigers went to the Tangerine Bowl despite the loss.

"That's the best defensive effort I saw in my 17 years of broadcasting KU football," Tom Hedrick said. "After Seurer got hurt, the defense had to win the game and they did. Linebacker Kyle McNorton played like a son of a gun."

The Jayhawks trailed 3-0 at half-time, partly because the Tigers had turned the ball over four times. Two big defensive plays in the second half helped KU establish the lead. A safety on a punt snap that went through the end zone, and an interception that led to a field goal gave the Jayhawks a 5-3 lead. Another interception, this one by Roger Foote, was returned for a touchdown and the Jayhawks led 12-3.

Scribner punted 11 times for the Jayhawks, with seven ending up inside the 20-yard line. The other four attempts saw two efforts of 50 yards or more. Missouri constantly was fighting an uphill battle against a ferocious Kansas defense.

Kansas extended the lead to 19-3 before Missouri scored a late touchdown and a two-point conversion to make it a one-possession game. But the Tigers could not recover the onside kick, and the Jayhawks held on.

Here's how it appeared in the November 22, 1981, Star:

BY JOE MCGUFF
THE KANSAS CITY STAR

Lawrence, Kas.,

Kansas has built a reputation as a football team that responds well to adversity, but at halftime of its game with Missouri, Coach Don Fambrough was concerned that his team had suffered an overdose Saturday.

Quarterback Frank Seurer suffered a dislocated right elbow with the game only 8 minutes and 56 seconds old. Kansas had 60 yards of total offense in the first half and zero yards rushing. Despite four Missouri turnovers, the Jayhawks trailed 3-0 and Fambrough was thinking he might have to replace Seurer's backup, Steve Smith.

Slowly – and with some help from

Missouri – Kansas turned the game around in the last half and scored a 19-11 upset before 47,500 spectators at Memorial Stadium. The victory was fashioned on defense, a strong kicking game, field position and two key interceptions.

Bucky Scribner, the Kansas punter, kicked inside the Missouri 20 on 7 of 11 attempts and two of his four other kicks carried 50 yards or more. All five of his second half punts left Missouri starting inside its 20.

In the first half Missouri started from its 20, 13, 35, 10, 20, 10 and the KU 39. On the Tigers' first five possessions of the last half they started from the 13, 13, 9, 13 and 16.

"Both teams have good defenses and right off the bat the short corner kicks set the tone," Scribner said. "I've had

better days, but I was super cautious about not kicking the ball in the end zone. I felt if they were going to beat us they were going to have to drive 80 or 90 yards."

Kansas scored its first two points on a safety that resulted from a bad snap that went into the Missouri end zone. A field goal that followed an interception made the score 5-3 at the end of the third quarter. Safety Roger Foote supplied the decisive play of the game when he intercepted a pass and returned it 27 yards for a touchdown that gave Kansas a 12-3 lead with 9:42 left in the fourth quarter.

The Jayhawks drove 48 yards in six plays for their final touchdown and then Missouri went 60 yards to score with the help of two 15-yard penalties assessed against the Kansas fans who ran on the field and tore down the goal

CHAPTER EIGHT •

posts with 43 seconds left. An on-side kick was unsuccessful.

The victory enabled the Jayhawks to finish the season with an 8-3 record and ended a three-game losing streak against Missouri, which finished 7-4, and accepted a Tangerine Bowl invitation.

"We've been called lucky and we've been called an ordinary football team," Fambrough said, "but we're a pretty good ordinary football team that's overcome a lot of adversity. We came back from losing our quarterback and looking kind of helpless. I've never been associated with a football team that has more determination.

"I feel this team deserves a bowl bid. We won't pout if we don't get a bid, but it will be a big mistake if we don't go."

Kansas' record is its best since 1968, the last season the Jayhawks went to the Orange Bowl.

Missouri's Warren Powers, who lost to Kansas for the first time in his four years as Tiger coach, praised the Jayhawks' tenacity and complained about the Tigers' mistakes.

"Kansas overcame some obstacles with losing Seurer," Powers said. "They came back and played a fine game, Our kicking game broke down, our offense broke down with turnovers. I thought our defense played great most of the day."

Missouri lost the ball three times on interceptions and three times on fumbles.

The defensive nature of the game was apparent from the outset, but Kansas was just starting to move the ball at the time Seurer was injured. The Jayhawks had picked up one first down and Seurer threw a 13-yard completion on the play in which he was injured.

"I got knocked back and my arm was behind me," Seurer said. "I tried to break my fall and someone fell on me. That's when I was hurt."

Although Seurer suffered a muscle tear in addition to the dislocation, he might be able to play if Kansas gets a bowl bid.

Kansas put together a long drive in the second quarter, but the Tigers held at the 26 and Bruce Kallmeyer was short on a field goal attempt from the 33.

Three fumbles and one interception kept the Missouri offense malfunctioning, but the Tigers took advantage of Scribner's only poor punt of the day and drove from

their 39 to the KU 9. Bob Lucchesi kicked a 26-yard field goal as the half ended.

Smith saved his quarterbacking job when the Jayhawks opened the second half with a drive that produced three first downs and 36 net yards rushing.

The Jayhawks' first points came when Missouri's Eric Schmidt went back to punt and the snap carried over his head into the end zone. Two Kansas players pursued the ball, but Missouri's Craig White fell on it for a safety.

On Missouri's next possession, Mike Hyde, who played the last half after Brad Perry suffered bruised ribs, threw a pass that was intercepted by Chris Toburen. The Tigers drew a spearing penalty on the play, moving the ball to the Missouri 19. Kansas could not get a first down, but Kallmeyer kicked a 28-yard field goal.

Missouri mounted its first long drive of the day and moved from its 9 to the

Kansas 8 early in the fourth quarter. The Jayhawks held and Lucchesi's field-goal attempt was wide to the left from the 15.

"That gave us a new life," Fambrough said. "Sometimes you feel like you can't play another down. I'm sure our defense felt that way. But that was a little spark that caused some players to rise to the top."

Missouri began its next possession on the 13 after Scribner punted to the 20 and James Caver lost 7 yards trying

to outrun his pursuers. On third down Foote intercepted a pass intended for Caver and returned it for a touchdown.

Kansas began its final touchdown drive after Missouri gave up the ball on downs at its 18. After E. J. Jones ran for one yard, Garfield Taylor carried five straight times for 47 yards. His touchdown came from 15 yards out.

The game took an ugly turn during Missouri's touchdown drive. The game was delayed several times when fans swarmed onto the field and the goal posts already had been carried away. There was little security in the stadium and if Missouri had recovered the on-side kick, the situation might have gotten out of hand.

"It was something you hate to see happen," Fambrough said. "There's no place for that in college football. I apologize personally for what happened. It takes away from a fine football game. It hurts the University of Kansas."

> "We've been called lucky and we've been called an ordinary football team, but we're a pretty good ordinary football team that's overcome a lot of adversity. We came back from losing our quarterback and looking kind of helpless. I've never been associated with a football team that has more determination."
> —Missouri coach Don Fambrough

RIVALS!
MU VS. KU

KU:19
MU:11

FOOTBALL
NOVEMBER 21 1981

FROM THE KANSAS CITY STAR, 1981

ONLY ONE BOWL BID WAS LEFT — AND KANSAS GOT IT

BY RICH SAMBOL
SPORTSWRITER

Kansas had one shot at getting a bowl bid, and the Jayhawks got it.

They will play Mississippi State in the Hall of Fame Bowl on Dec. 31 in Birmingham, Ala. The bid officially will be extended today after a 4 p.m. meeting of the Hall of Fame's executive committee.

Kansas played itself into the post-season football game with a 19-11 victory Saturday over Missouri, which was witnessed by selection committee member Albert Mills. Before leaving the press box in Lawrence, Kan., Mills said Kansas had his vote.

"Kansas is our top choice," Bob Lochamy, executive director of the Hall of Fame Bowl, said Saturday night by telephone from Birmingham. "No one else is in our picture."

Lochamy said the committee agreed last week that all members would meet today before making an official announcement.

"Our scouting committee has scouted throughout this country and they are in the process of either coming home tonight or in the morning," Lochamy said. "It appears to be nothing more than a matter of formality.

"We are very impressed with Kansas' victory not only over Missouri but also its last three games. I don't think Kansas' three losses are anything to be concerned about."

Unlike most of the other teams that received bids Saturday, Kansas was assured of nothing going into the regular-season finale. But the pieces fell into place as the day wore on.

Notre Dame, which the Hall of Fame had interest in as a long shot, lost to Penn State. South Carolina, the bowl's next choice, lost to Clemson. Brigham Young, another possibility, won the Western Athletic Conference's automatic bid in the Holiday Bowl by beating Utah.

Thus, Kansas became the obvious choice. But that doesn't mean the Jayhawks were undeserving. They will play Mississippi State, a 7-4 team that lost to Mississippi 21-17 on Saturday.

Kansas, 8-3, finished its regular season by winning four of its last five games, including the last three in a row. Their three losses were to Nebraska, Oklahoma and Oklahoma State, all three bound for bowl games.

Nebraska, 9-2, as the Big Eight Conference's champion, will play Clemson, 11-0 in the Orange Bowl on New Year's night in Miami, Fla. Nebraska finished its season with a 37-14 victory over Oklahoma, and Clemson wrapped up its first unbeaten season since 1948 by defeating South Carolina 29-13.

Despite its loss to Nebraska, Oklahoma, 5-4-1 with a game left next weekend against Oklahoma State, accepted a bid to play Houston, 6-3-1, in the Sun Bowl on Dec 26 in El Paso, Texas. Oklahoma State, 7-3, defeated Iowa State 27-7 and accepted a bid to play Texas A&M, 6-4, in the Independence Bowl on Dec. 12 in Shreveport, La.

Missouri, 7-4, also received a bowl bid, its fourth in as many seasons under Warren Powers. The Tigers never have played in four consecutive bowl games. Missouri will play Southern Mississippi, 8-1-1, in the Tangerine Bowl on Dec 19 in Orlando, Fla. Southern Mississippi also lost Saturday, falling to Louisville 13-10.

The double defeat did not bother the Tangerine Bowl selection committee. Vernon Hinely, the bowl's president-elect watched the game in Lawrence, and afterward said:

"You don't like to see your teams lose, but our selections were made on the season, not one game. Several other bowl teams were beaten today.

"We have been close to Missouri the last three or four years, and Missouri is the kind of team that fills our bill. We're a secondary bowl trying to get higher up on the ladder. We have the kinds of teams that will give us what we wanted."

Kansas will have a bigger payday than Missouri. The Tangerine Bowl, Hinely said, would be worth about $300,000 to each team. Mills said the Hall of Fame would pay about $400,000, a record. Missouri and South Carolina shared in the previous Hall of Fame best, each getting $262,000 for the 1979 game.

"This is really fantastic," said Steve Hatchell, assistant commissioner of the Big Eight Conference. "The exciting thing is that we have a lot of young teams going to bowl games. Actually, this is more exciting for the future than it is for the present. It's really great."

KU TRIPS MIZZOU IN SEASON FINALE

In a game that would make baseball philosopher Yogi Berra proud, the 1989 contest between Kansas and Missouri wasn't over until it was over. And then, it just barely was.

"That was one of the most exciting finishes I can remember," said Max Falkenstein, who in more than 50 years of broadcasting KU athletics has seen his share of fantastic finishes. "Missouri scored in the final minute in near darkness to come within two, but the two-point conversion failed."

The two teams combined for 90 points, 56 in the second half, and 923 yards of total offense. The lead changed hands only three times, but no lead appeared safe. Kansas trailed 21-13 at the half, but returned the second-half kickoff deep into Missouri territory. Tony Sands scored two plays later and the race was on.

By the time the Jayhawks took the lead for good, at 39-35 with just over 10 minutes remaining in the game, there was little doubt that it would go down to the finish.

Kansas punted with a one-point lead with just under three minutes left. Ron Pointer fumbled the punt for Missouri on his own 13-yard line and the Jayhawks recovered. After three running plays, KU had first-and-goal on the 1. There was some discussion on the Kansas sideline about trying to run out the clock, but instead quarterback Kelly Donohoe punched it over with 2:03 left.

Missouri then charged 70 yards down the field and scored a touchdown with 29 seconds left. A pass to Byron Chamberlain for the two-point conversion was just beyond the end line, and Kansas prevailed.

Here's how it appeared in the November 19, 1989, Star:

TIGERS MISS TIE WHEN 2-POINT TRY FAILS

By Jeffrey Flanagan
Sportswriter

Columbia

It was a game neither team appeared to know when to say when.

But in the end, it was the Missouri Tigers who couldn't bring themselves to take one more gulp from this scoring binge as the Kansas Jayhawks prevailed, 46-44 Saturday afternoon at Faurot Field.

Missouri's last minute effort to tie the score failed when quarterback Ken Keifer's two-point conversion pass to Byron Chamberlain was ruled out of the back of the end zone.

"Standing on the sideline, we just knew there was no way they were going to get that conversion and tie it," Kansas quarterback Kelly Donohoe said. "We just knew."

Donohoe might have been the only one with that firm conviction on a day when deficits seemed merely an inconvenience.

"Not exactly a pitcher's duel, huh?" Jayhawks Coach Glenn Mason said. "I'm just happy we did what we had to do. We had to stop them one time and somehow we did."

Kansas (4-7, 2-5 Big Eight) ended a three-game losing streak to Missouri (2-9, 1-6), which was of great importance to some in this, the oldest collegiate football rivalry west of the Mississippi River.

"I can't tell you how great it is to beat those guys," said Donohoe, a senior. "You couldn't have asked for a better script to end my career."

Donohoe and the Jayhawks appeared to have written the final page when he scored on a 1-yard sneak with 2 minutes, 3 seconds left. That put Kansas

RIVALS!
MU VS. KU

KU:46
MU:44

FOOTBALL
NOVEMBER 18, 1989

up 46-38. The touchdown was set up when Jay Litteken pounced on a fumbled punt by the Tigers' Ron Pointer at the Missouri 13 with 2:31 left.

"Who would have thought that I'd be standing here saying we might have scored too quickly," Mason said with a smile.

> "Not exactly a pitcher's duel, huh? I'm just happy we did what we had to do. We had to stop them one time and somehow we did."
> —Kansas coach Glenn Mason

After three runs by Maurice Douglass set the ball first-and-goal at the 1, Kansas took a timeout.

"We discussed the possibility of running some time off the clock by going to one knee a couple of times," Donohoe said, "but in the huddle everyone shouted to go for it, sneak it in, so we did."

Not without help from the Tigers.

"We told our defense to let them score," Missouri Coach Bob Stull said. "That was our only chance to win the game.

"We told our defense, 'This is going to sound weird, but let them score.' At first, they looked at me, 'What the heck are you talking about?' That's the first time I've ever done that."

The strategy left Keifer with plenty of time to retaliate, as he had all afternoon. Keifer completed 29 of 48 passes for 444 yards and four touchdowns. He also set single-game school marks with the 29 completions and 444 yards, and tied the mark of four touchdowns.

Keifer drove the Tigers 70 yards in nine plays and Tommie Stowers (103 yards in 22 carries) bulled in for the score from the 1, bringing the Tigers to

within 46-44 with 29 seconds left. On the conversion, Keifer dropped back and lofted a pass over the linebackers to Chamberlain just beyond the end line.

"I couldn't see it," Stull said. "He must have stepped out. It was close, but I had no idea from where I was standing."

"It's a tough way to lose."

The play capped a dramatic second half as both teams moved effortlessly down the field.

Missouri finished with 498 total

yards, while Kansas had 425.

"We just came out in the second half and felt they couldn't stop us," Donohoe said. "We were able to run the ball and we spread the offense out, using a lot of quick routes that kept them off-balance. It was a terrific feeling."

It was also a long climb for Kansas, which spotted Missouri leads of 14-0, 21-13 and 28-19.

Missouri, which led Iowa State 21-0 last week in the first quarter only to lose 35-21, tried in vain to prevent a reoccurrence.

"The difference between this week and last week was we kept coming back and kept competing," Stull said. "It was a shootout."

But the beginning of the end may have come when KU's Charley Bowen took the second-half kickoff and returned it 47 yards to the Missouri 37.

Seven plays later, Tony Sands, who rushed for 215 yards in 29 carries, bolted around left end for 7 yards and a touchdown, making the score 21-19. Sands' two-point conversion run failed.

The touchdown triggered a scoring outburst that kept the 33,981 fans out of their seats. Two plays after Sands' touchdown, Missouri answered with a 79-yard touchdown strike from Keifer to Linzy Collins (nine catches, 193 yards). Collins ran a simple out pattern, made

the catch around the 30, then sprinted past the cornerback down the sideline.

Missouri hardly had a chance to enjoy its 28-19 lead. On the next play from scrimmage, Sands bolted around left end for 66 yards and a touchdown. This time Kansas kicked the conversion, pulling to within 28-26 with 11:26 left in the third.

On their next possession, the Jayhawks drove 69 yards in 14 plays with Sands scoring again, this time on a 9-yard run with 3:47 left in the quarter. Once again, Sands tried to run for a

CHAPTER EIGHT

two-point conversion and failed, but Kansas led for the first time 32-28.

Right back came Keifer and the Tigers on a 59-yard, eight-play drive. Keifer capped the march with a 29-yard scoring strike to Skip Leach (five receptions, 88 yards), which made it 35-32.

The play, an inside screen, was the same one run on the Tigers' final scoring drive of the first half, when Keifer and Damon Mays hooked up on a 28-yard touchdown. Mays also caught a 5-yard score from Keifer in the first quarter.

Kansas took the lead for good at 39-35 when Donohoe capped a 32-

It was a major step forward for Mason and his program. Not only did he win the unofficial "Triangle Trophy" – in honor of the Bermuda Triangle, that mythical place into which victories and, sometimes coaches, disappear – by beating both of his major recruiting rivals – Kansas State and Missouri. It was the way the Jayhawks did it that gave him the most joy.

yard, five-play drive with a 1-yard run with 10:09 left in the game. The drive was set up when Hassan Bailey intercepted Keifer at the Kansas 47 and returned it 21 yards.

Dan Baker's 39-yard field goal with 6:48 left pulled Missouri to within 39-38.

FROM THE KANSAS CITY STAR, 1989

QUICK TD BY KU GAVE MU A SHOT

By Gib Twyman

Columbia

How nutty was it out there Saturday as Kansas claimed the undisputed Bermuda Triangle title with a 46-44 victory over Missouri?

This nutty.

Missouri figured its only chance of winning was to give up another touchdown to Kansas.

Now, anyone who has seen Mizzou play this year knows that if there is one thing the Tigers are adept at, it is giving up touchdowns.

So this was a snap. But both coaches agreed this was just about the only way MU could rally. And, as the Faurot Field scoreboard whirred up to warp speed and approached a Three Mile Island meltdown, that is nearly what the Tigers did.

"We gave them the last touch-

down. We figured it was the only way we could get a tie," said Missouri Coach Bob Stull.

Kansas Coach Glen Mason, with a smile so wide it could have filled a Jayhawk beak, said that, in fact, his team almost scored too early in making the score 46-38 on quarterback Kelly Donohoe's 1-yard sneak with 2 minutes, 3 seconds left.

"I tell you, fellas, I really almost made a critical error in coaching today," Mason said. "First of all, I said, 'Let's just not score. Let's kill the clock, maybe down to the fourth down, then run it in.' Then I said, 'Let's at least kill it on the first down.' But we got it in on the first down. We scored too fast.

"Can you imagine me saying that – 'We scored too fast?'"

The reason one could imagine a coach, not just Mason, but any coach – saying a thing like that is because this

was a game in which nobody could stop anybody.

As Mason said, "Everybody went up and down the field like there was no tomorrow."

It threw the coaching instincts off kilter. Stull, also, said you wouldn't immediately know what was the right thing, with teams zooming up and down the field at will.

"That's the first time I've ever let a team score," said Stull.

What would he have done if he were in Mason's shoes? "I probably would have scored, but thinking about it, maybe the next game I'd be thinking about it a little differently," he said. "If you thought the situation out long enough, you'd probably down it twice on the 1-inch line and score on the next play. You'd almost have to be moving backwards. It's kind of hard to do."

That both coaches were discussing

such a thing gives you an idea of what kind of a game it was as the teams combined for 923 total yards. Kansas had 425, keyed by Tuxedo Tony Sands, who ran nearly at will for 215 yards on 29 carries through a Tiger defense that rarely looked even a mild threat to stop him.

"From the films, we thought we could run up and down the field all day on them, and that is what we did," said Donohoe, who contributed just enough passing – 163 yards on 11 of 25, to keep MU off balance. "We mixed it up pretty good and they just never seemed to get onto us."

Actually, there appeared to be nothing more complicated needed than a pitch to Sands left, a pitch to Sands right, and just let the slo-o-ow reacting Tiger linebackers wave at him.

Quite an irony for a school that once prided itself on the old student body left, student body right pitches in MU's glory days, hard as they are getting to remember them.

Yet is was a shame for MU to lose a game in which its own offense performed so splendidly. As opposed to the Iowa State game a week ago when it blew a 21-point lead and then went straight into the dumper, the Tigers responded with a great amount of pluck Saturday.

Mizzou racked up 485 yards of total offense as quarterback Ken Keifer passed for a school-record 444 yards on 29 completions and tied the MU record with four touchdowns. His 2,314 yards for the season erased Terry McMillan's 20-year-old Mizzou record of 1,963 yards.

Linzy Collins, Keifer's favorite target, had 193 yards on nine catches, Damon Mays had two nifty touchdown catches and, lo and behold, the Tigers even had a running game with 103 yards from Tommie Stowers.

"Against Iowa State, when they came back, we lost our confidence and didn't play," said Stull. "But today when KU came back, we came back at them with a fine effort."

For Stull, it was a familiar WAC-ky game – one from his old Western Athletic Conference days at Texas-El Paso, where 49-48 scores are nearly mandated by league bylaws.

"You just need to keep responding. They score, you must score. The second half, that's the way both teams did. You couldn't do anything but admire the way both offenses rose to the occasion," said Stull.

This was the first time Mizzou had been involved in a game in which both teams scored more than 40 points. It was the most points in an MU-KU game since MU Coach Dan Devine ran it up against KU Coach Pepper Rodgers 69-21 in 1969.

More to the point for KU, it was sweet revenge for some one-sided lashings at the recent hands of the Tigers – 55-17 last year and 48-0 in 1986.

And it was a major step forward for Mason and his program. Not only did he win the unofficial "Triangle Trophy" – in honor of the Bermuda Triangle, that mythical place into which victories and, sometimes coaches, disappear – by beating both of his major recruiting rivals – Kansas State and Missouri.

It was the way the Jayhawks did it that gave him the most joy.

"Last year, I thought we came out ready to play, but we got down to them quickly and it was over," he said. "This year, they got up quickly, but the kids refused to quit. It was a heck of a game from a spectator standpoint."

Donohoe said one big reason the Jayhawks kept their heads up after MU's early 14-0 lead was the Iowa State game.

"They've been known to let some leads get away. We told ourselves on the sideline that we could come back on them."

Mason said, "It was one of the few games since I've been here that we found a way to win. It came down to a two-point play, and we finally stopped somebody."

Fittingly, it seemed the two-pointer was not exactly stopped by the defense. Keifer's pass to wide receiver Byron Chamberlain was complete, but officials ruled his feet came down out of the end zone.

> Last year, I thought we came ready to play, but we got down to them quickly, and it was over. This year, they got up quickly, but the kids refused to quit. It was a heck of a game from a spectator standpoint.

"You run out of room down there," said Mason. "Our defensive back sets up back there and the only place the guy can catch it is out of the end zone, so we did a good job on the play."

As nail-in-the-coffin decisive as that play was, though, Mason singled out another one as extremely big in the victory. That was the recovery by reserve senior fullback Jay Litteken of Ron Pointer's bobbled punt reception at the MU 13 with 4:17 to play. With KU up 39-38 and time for seemingly a million more touchdowns still possibly to be scored, that recovery kept MU from returning fire momentarily in the shootout. That is the one play that seemed to seal MU's doom.

SANDS RUSHES TO NCAA RECORD

Tony Sands turned in a record-setting day, rushing for 396 yards on 58 carries in a 53-29 victory for Kansas over Missouri. The carries and the yardage were not just Kansas records. They were not just conference records. Both were NCAA Division I-A records at the time. LaDainian Tomlinson of Texas Christian rushed for 409 yards in 1999. The 58 carries is still a record.

The 5-6 senior had 156 yards at halftime and 297 at the end of the third quarter. He could have had 400, but the Kansas linemen picked him up and carried him off the field on their shoulders. The Jayhawks had the ball on the Missouri 4-yard line with 20 seconds left.

Sands' effort was just one of many stellar offensive performances in the game, for both sides. Kansas quarterback Chip Hilleary rushed for three touchdowns and 80 yards. Missouri back-up quarterback Jeff Handy replaced starter Phil Johnson, who separated his right shoulder on the second play of the game. He completed 17 of 28 passes for 245 yards and two touchdowns.

But the story was all Sands. Kansas coach Glen Mason joked about taking him out before he reached the NCAA record total. He said the players would have had a mutiny. Apparently, even a coach's decision couldn't have stopped Sands on this day.

Here's how it appeared in the November 24, 1991, Star:

KU RIPS MU 53-29. BACK'S 396 YARDS AND 58 CARRIES BOTH SET MARKS

BY BLAIR KERKHOFF
STAFF WRITER

Lawrence

Kansas tailback Tony Sands ran Saturday where no one in NCAA history had run before.

In Kansas' 53-29 victory over Missouri, Sands established Division 1-A records for rushing with 396 yards and carries with 58. If the Kansas offensive linemen hadn't carried the 5-foot-6 dynamo off the field on their shoulders with 20 seconds remaining, Sands might have entered a college football twilight zone.

Sands departed when Kansas had the ball on the Tigers' 4. One more snap could have netted Sands an even 400.

As it was, the Jayhawks were more than satisfied – with the records, the victory and, at least in the afterglow of Sands' performance, a 6-5 record that represents the team's first winning mark since 1981.

"I'm on an emotional high," Sands said. "I feel I can go out and play another game."

The record 386 yards of San Diego State freshman Marshall Faulk stood for 10 weeks. The record for attempts, 57 by Kent Kitzmann of Minnesota, had

stood since 1977.

When Kansas got its final possession with 4 minutes, 40 seconds remaining, Sands had tucked away the Big Eight record of 342 set by Colorado's Charlie Davis in 1971. No NCAA record was certain, but Kansas Coach Glen Mason made sure Sands would get a shot.

"He deserved a shot," Mason said. "The only thing I was worried about was him getting hurt."

The final drive and record chase started on the Missouri 23. Sands lost 4 on first down, but a long pass took the Jayhawks across midfield. Sands' 19-yard run gave him 382. On second and

● LEAN BUT INTENSE

RIVALS!
MU VS. KU

KU:53
MU:29

FOOTBALL
JANUARY 16, 1968

10 from the Kansas 19, Sands went around the left side and out of bounds, a 7-yard gain that gave him the record with about 56 seconds left.

But coaches in the press box communicating to those on the sidelines weren't sure. Sands got one last call for another 7-yard gain. The record assured, Kansas called a timeout, and Sands got a shoulder ride to the bench.

"I wanted to make sure we didn't screw it up and leave him 1 yard short," Mason said.

Through three quarters, Kansas needed every one of Sands' yards. Although Missouri, a 14-point underdog, never led, the Tigers, behind reserve quarterback Jeff Handy, nipped at the Jayhawks' heels most of the afternoon.

Handy replaced starter Phil

Johnson, who left the game on the second play after separating his right shoulder. Handy completed 17 of 28 passes for 245 yards and two touchdowns. Victor Bailey caught both plus a school-record third thrown by receiver Skip Leach on a gadget play.

Kansas answered with Sands and quarterback Chip Hilleary, who rushed for three touchdowns and 80 yards.

FROM THE KANSAS CITY STAR, 1991

KU LINE GETS SANDS UP HIGH

BY GIB TWYMAN

LAWRENCE — The Kansas Jayhawks spent Saturday kicking Sands in the face of Missouri's 98-pound-weakling defense.

The result: Tony Sands had a game that will not be soon forgotten.

Sands, KU's pint-size running back with the 10-gallon heart, blazed to 396 yards in 58 carries, both NCAA records.

While Sands fueled a highly satis-fying 53-29 victory and a 6-5 finish for KU, the emotional focus fittingly was on Tony, the Real Tiger on the field.

"I hope no one resents the fact that I left Tony in the game. I felt he had every right to go for the record," Kansas Coach Glen Mason said.

It was almost exactly the opposite reaction. After Sands hit 396 with 20 seconds left, an entire stadium seemed to ache for 400. Why not let him go for it?

"Man, I can't do anything right,

can I?" said Mason with a laugh.

Sands had his record and his health, the main things to Mason. The symmetry and magic of 400 didn't occur to him.

But Mason added, "If I'd tried to take Tony out earlier, you'd have seen a coach mugged by his players. I was not in control down there. They were.

"And at one point, Pat Ruel (assistant head coach) called a play that wasn't Tony Sands. I about fired him on the spot."

RIVALRY THRIVES ON DEEP ROOTS

Corby Jones

For recent fans of either Kansas or Missouri, the rivalry is all about basketball. The two schools have had outstanding basketball teams for decades, while the football fortunes have been down more than they have been up.

But the rivalry got started—at least on the athletic field—in football. The games were played in Kansas City for years, until threats of violence against the fans (from one side's to the other) caused too much concern. That, and the lost revenue for local merchants, convinced the athletic departments to move the games back to campus permanently in 1946.

The two schools tasted some success in the 1950s and the Tigers even reached No. 1 status in 1960, before they got beat by Kansas. Back-to-back Orange Bowls, first by Kansas in 1968 then by Missouri a year later, were the highlight of the rivalry in the 60s.

Losing to the other team quite often caused head coaches to lose their jobs—it's that important. Long-time Tigers and Jayhawks still care passionately about the football game. Maybe it's because there's only one each year. Whatever the reason, for some it's all about who wins on that Saturday.

As they prepared for the 1995 showdown, Missouri freshman Corby Jones, who would end his career 2-2 against the Jayhawks, looked forward to facing the team he had hated since his youth.

Here's how it appeared in the November 4, 1995, Star:

QB LEARNED ABOUT MU-KU LONG AGO

LEAN BUT INTENSE

180

RIVALS!
MU VS. KU

Corby
Jones

FOOTBALL
NOVEMBER 4, 1995

BY MIKE DEARMOND

Lawrence

Corby Jones will line up behind center at the University of Kansas this afternoon on the only side of the ball he ever could. The Missouri side.

Jones, a freshman quarterback for the Tigers, wasn't even a gleam in poppa Curtis' eye back when the two schools initiated the Border War 104 years ago. Curtis, Missouri's running-backs coach, wasn't a gleam in his father's eye either.

But young Corby - by the chance of Curtis having played a bit of ball at Ol' Mizzou back in the glory days of the '60s - was indoctrinated early.

something called a Kansas Jayhawk. When these strange birds beat his beloved Tigers, the tension between his dad and the Prices seemed palpable.

"Joe's mom and dad would be having a great time about it, and my dad would just snub them," Corby recalled.

But not until Curtis returned to Missouri to coach in 1993 - and Corby followed a Friday night of quarterbacking Hickman High with a Saturday afternoon of watching Missouri football - did Corby really tap into what today can be all about.

"When I got here it was all about Kansas Week," Corby said. "I go, 'What is Kansas Week?' And I'd go to the stadium and see Jayhawks hanging with

only three games ago against Nebraska, has provided Missouri with the stretch its offense so desperately needed.

He's learning as he goes. He knows his speed seems to help more in the field's first 80 yards than in the last 20.

"My checks are cut down inside the 20," Jones said. "In that way it's easier. But executing the plays is more difficult. There's less room. Speed is not as much of a factor there."

Coach Larry Smith has been selling the rivalry to his players all week. Kiddingly, the man from Van Wert, Ohio, and Bowling Green has put it this way:

"To me this is comparable to the Van Wert-Salina football game, to the Bowling Green-Miami (Ohio) rivalry, the Ohio State-Michigan, the Tulane-LSU, the Arizona-Arizona State, the USC-UCLA and Notre Dame," Smith said. "It's the same kind of thing.

"It's what you go after. It's up there. You point to that."

Corby Jones makes his own comparison, based on personal experience of a triple-overtime grudge match in a driving rain between Columbia high school rivals.

"Hickman vs. Rock Bridge last year," he said. "That was the biggest one. Everybody you knew was talking about it. We wanted that game.

"We won 43-42.

"Two-point conversion.

"I ran it, bootleg left.

"I've never wanted anything as badly as I wanted that game."

Except maybe today's.

> *"When I got here it was all about Kansas Week. I go, 'What is Kansas Week?' And I'd go to the stadium and see Jayhawks hanging with nooses around them. Who-o-o-a!"*
> *—Corby Jones, MU freshman quarterback who spent his last two years of high school in Columbia*

"It was kindergarten, first or second grade," he said, trying to trace his first memory of black and gold. "We had these mugs. And I used to always drink my hot chocolate out of a black Tiger mug with a Tiger on it and Missouri Tigers written on it in yellow. Every Saturday morning before hockey practice.

"I had a black Missouri Tiger suitcase. I had dozens of sweatshirts. We had quite a few glasses. But I wasn't allowed to drink out of those because I would break them.

"We had Faurot Field on a little plate-type deal."

He first came in contact with Missouri's alter ego about the sixth grade, when his family was living in Dallas and he noticed the parents and older brother of his best friend, Joe Price, had this strange need on fall Saturdays and winter nights to cheer for

nooses around them.

"Who-o-o-a!"

Perhaps because he has been in harm's way for parts of three games, Corby Jones isn't waving anything like a black-and-gold flag in the face of the men he'll be lining up against today.

He's aware of the current status. Kansas, ranked No. 11 in the nation, is 7-1 and headed to a bowl game. Missouri, at 2-6, can finish no better than 5-6 if it wins its final three at Kansas, at Colorado and against Iowa State.

So he pays homage to the possible and the more probable.

"Yeah, I think we can win our last three games," he said, "and beating KU is the first step in doing that. If nothing else, that satisfies our revenge factor."

Jones, who took off his redshirt

RUN CONTINUES FOR KU

Sixth-ranked Kansas had seen its dream of an undefeated season crash and burn the week before their 1995 showdown with Missouri, with a 41-7 loss at Kansas State. But just like falling off a bike, the Jayhawks got back on and rode a familiar ride to victory over the Tigers.

L.T. Levine rushed for 100 yards, marking the seventh straight year that Kansas had a 100-yard rusher against the Tigers. The Jayhawks had 296 yards on the ground and won for the third straight time over Mizzou.

The Jayhawks threw a touchdown pass in the final two minutes, which did not seem to please Missouri coach Larry Smith. Kansas coach Glen Mason thought maybe it was a throwback to the old days when the rivalry between the two schools was more about football than basketball.

The victory raised KU's record to 8-1 and helped the Jayhawks get back into the top 10 before the next week's game against Nebraska. They lost that game but finished the season with a 10-2 record, including a Hula Bowl victory over UCLA. The 10 wins tied a school record accomplished only twice and last in 1905.

Here's how it appeared in the November 5, 1995, Star:

JAYHAWKS ONCE AGAIN TOP TIGERS

BY BLAIR KERKHOFF
STAFF WRITER

Lawrence

Familiar refrains resonated from Kansas' 42-23 triumph over Missouri in Saturday's 104th Border War.

The Jayhawks won for the third straight season, and their average victory margin in those games is 21 points.

Kansas pounded out 296 rushing yards, including 100 by L.T. Levine, which means a KU running back has gained at least 100 yards on the Tigers in seven straight seasons.

Missouri coach Larry Smith, peeved that Kansas threw for a touchdown with 1 minute, 28 seconds to play, offered a one-armed gesture to the Jayhawks across the field, reminiscent of the 1969 incident in which Kansas Coach Pepper Rodgers claimed to have flashed a peace sign at Missouri's Dan Devine and got half of if it in return.

Kansas Coach Glen Mason said he didn't see the message but broke into a smile when he heard about it.

"Hey, maybe this is getting to be a real heated rivalry," Mason said. "I know you guys would love that. It would make your day if we had rolled around on the field or something."

"That's their choice" was all Smith had to say about the Jayhawks' passing for a touchdown. He and Mason shook hands after the game.

Smiles came easily for Mason. No. 11 Kansas, 8-1 overall and 4-1 in the Big Eight, broke open a close game by outscoring the Tigers 28-6 in the second half.

The victory set up the biggest game of Mason's tenure, a home meeting next Saturday against top-ranked Nebraska for a piece of the conference lead.

It has been nearly three decades since the stakes have been this high for the Jayhawks. Kansas is off to its best start since 1968, when it last owned a share of the league title.

Missouri, 2-7 and 0-5, threw a fright into the Jayhawks early. The Tigers controlled the lines in the first half, and scrambles and option keepers by freshman quarterback Corby Jones kept Kansas off-balance.

Short touchdown runs by Jones and Brock Olivo helped stake Missouri to a 17-14 halftime lead.

"We played a heck of a game for 2 1/2 quarters," Smith said. "Then we lost control."

The game swung on the Tigers' first series of the third quarter. Jones was looking for Rahsetnu Jenkins on a flanker screen, but Kansas linebacker Chris Jones picked it off and angled 35 yards for a touchdown.

"The interception didn't finish us off, but it got the ball rolling," Smith said.

The clincher came later in the

RIVALS!
MU VS. KU

KU:42
MU:23

FOOTBALL
NOVEMBER 4, 1995

quarter. A short punt set up Kansas at its 49. Wide receiver Isaac Byrd ran a post pattern and caught a bomb from Mark Williams for the score, completing a demoralizing quarter for Missouri. The Tigers had run 23 plays to the Jayhawks' nine but trailed by 11 entering the fourth quarter.

The Jayhawks made it 35-17 on Eric Vann's 2-yard run with 9 minutes left, and Corby Jones was pulled for the better passing Kent Skornia. He directed the Tigers' last scoring drive, finishing it on an 18-yard pass to Frank Jones.

"We knew to beat them we had to stop the option, and we didn't stop them very well in the first half," Kansas defensive end Kevin Kopp said. "But no one was yelling or anything at halftime. We know what kind of team we are, we know we're better

than Missouri, and we had to come out and prove it in the second half."

Kansas had something else to prove. Its perfect season crashed a week earlier in a 41-7 loss at Kansas State.

"A lot of people who had supported us with our No. 6 ranking had started showing some doubt," said tight end

Jim Moore, whose two touchdown receptions included the final score. "And maybe we kind of doubted ourselves a little after a 41-7 loss.

"But this was a great job by our guys getting focused and not overlooking Missouri."

Kansas coach Glen Mason was not worried that there was too much of a spread against the Tigers.

FROM THE STAR, 1995

LAST TD INTENSIFIES OLD GRUDGE

BY JONATHAN RAND

LAWRENCE — I asked a Missouri alumnus who manages a Kansas bank whether he would be going to the Missouri-Kansas game. He said he didn't need the humiliation of sitting near Jayhawks fans yukking it up over pounding the Tigers.

I thought he'd shown too little faith when Missouri took a 17-14 halftime lead and Kansas couldn't handle the Tigers' running attack. Then Missouri coughed up a gift touchdown, the universal shot in the foot practiced by perennial losing teams, and Kansas

was on its way to a 42-23 victory.

It was a good decision for the Missouri alum to stay home, especially when Mark Williams threw a touchdown pass to Jim Moore with Kansas ahead by 12 and just 1:28 left. My friend might have shared the arm-jerk reaction Missouri Coach Larry Smith made toward the Kansas bench.

Trying to score wasn't rubbing it in. Throwing on first and goal from the 6 was.

There have been stranger doings than a team blowing a lead of under two touchdowns in the last 90 seconds. Missouri was out of timeouts,

though, and Kansas could have tried pounding into the end zone and milking the clock.

That would have been the high-percentage way to ice the game. An incomplete pass would have stopped the clock. An interception returned all the way would have put Missouri just an onside kick away from possible victory.

The touchdown pass gave Missouri cause for intensifying its grudge next year in Columbia. Now it will take some focus off Kansas' victory and 8-1 record.

MU AT LOSS FOR WORDS

Rumors were circulating that the losing coach in the 2000 version of the Border War would lose more than a game. Larry Smith of Missouri and Terry Allen of Kansas both had their jobs on the line as they squared off in Columbia.

Missouri fans felt like their coach stood the better chance to keep his title, or at least quiet the critics for one week. Despite identical 2-3 records, the Tigers entered the game coming off a win, while the Jayhawks had been hammered in their last two games. All three of Missouri's losses were to ranked teams.

But it was Allen and the Jayhawks who dominated the game, almost assuring Smith that this would be his last time on the sidelines against Kansas. Kansas dominated in total offense (453 to 247) and time of possession (37:51 to 22:09). The Tigers also committed five turnovers.

Smith was done at the end of the season, and when first-year coach Gary Pinkel led the Tigers to a 38-34 victory on the Jayhawks home turf in 2001, it marked the end of the Terry Allen regime.

In this game, Missouri managed to cut the KU lead to 17-14 midway through the second quarter, but the Jayhawks responded with 14 unanswered points. The Tigers managed only a field goal the rest of the game.

Here's how it appeared in the October 15, 2000, Star:

TIGERS CAN'T EXPLAIN LOPSIDED LOSS TO KANSAS

By Howard Richman
The Kansas City *Star*

Columbia, Mo.,

As Kansas players struck up a celebration with their fans after the Jayhawks stuck it to Missouri for the second straight year, Tigers' junior wide receiver Eric Spencer couldn't help but notice the jubilation.

"I thought to myself as I watched them celebrate while I was walking off our field, 'How did we let that happen?'" Spencer said after KU's 38-17 victory at Memorial Stadium. "I know we're better than that."

Spencer was one of few bright spots for MU. He caught a 60-yard touchdown pass from Darius Outlaw that cut KU's lead to 17-14 with 5 minutes, 17 seconds remaining in the first half. But the Jayhawks responded, and in winning dealt a serious blow to what postseason hopes the Tigers might have had.

MU, a team that was whispering that it had bowl aspirations, got bowled over by a KU team that dominated.

So what went wrong?

"We got our (rear ends) kicked. They beat us every way possible," said MU coach Larry Smith, whose Tigers dropped to 2-4 overall and 1-2 in the Big 12.

KU, 3-3 and 1-2, rolled up 453 total yards on offense compared with 247 for MU. The Jayhawks owned the clock, possessing the ball for 37 minutes

and 51 seconds. MU aided KU's cause by committing five turnovers, four of them on Outlaw interceptions.

The Jayhawks' defensive front had even more success than their secondary. KU stuffed MU's running game to the tune of 10 net yards on 26 carries.

Junior tailback Zain Gilmore, who had 169 yards last week in a 24-10 win over Oklahoma State, was held to 29 Saturday, while Outlaw and Justin Gage combined for minus-19.

"We thought we'd be able to establish the running game," Gilmore said, "but they came real hard off our guards, and I really couldn't find any holes to get up field."

Smith had said last week his offen-

LEAN BUT INTENSE

RIVALS!
MU VS. KU

KU:38
MU:17

FOOTBALL
OCTOBER 14, 2000

sive line didn't play well the previous game, and it was just as bad against KU.

"I don't have a clue as to why we didn't perform," MU left tackle Joe Glauberman said. "The guys were pumped. We were ready. Now, I just don't know what to say. It was horrible. It's embarrassing to lose to KU like this, and on homecoming. It doesn't make sense."

Smith said the final straw was the 62-yard punt return for a touchdown by KU's Roger Ross, which extended the Jayhawks' lead to 31-14 late in the third quarter.

MU had an opportunity to get the touchdown back when strong safety Marcus Caldwell intercepted a tipped pass at KU's 13. But the Tigers instead got a 31-yard field goal from Brad Hammerich and never threatened again. The Tigers' defense wore down in the

second half. It particularly showed during a KU drive in the fourth quarter when the Jayhawks converted three consecutive third-down plays, including a 12-yard run for a touchdown by tailback David Winbush on third and 7.

Smith, in an effort to address this setback promptly, has decided to practice today. Usually, the team only comes in on Sundays for treatment of injuries. Today, though, won't be a day of rest for MU, which seeks answers as to what went so wrong.

"Never in the world did I think something like this would happen," MU senior nose tackle Pat Mingucci said. "But it did. And we've got to bounce back. I have total confidence in this team. We shot ourselves in the foot, but we've got to find a way to get over it."

Larry Smith

FROM THE KANSAS CITY STAR, 2000

JAYHAWKS DOMINATE AT MISSOURI

By Jason King
The Kansas City Star

Columbia

Kansas football coach Terry Allen was walking toward the Jayhawks' locker room Saturday – smiling and rock-chalking all the way – when he realized there was something left to do on Missouri's Faurot Field.

So he called all the players back – some were high-fiving Kansas fans, some were gloating in front of television cameras, some were headed toward the showers – and gathered them into a circle. They knelt, then bowed and gave thanks.

Outside of divine intervention, which is unlikely, what was the reason

for Kansas' 38-17 victory over Missouri?

Did the Tigers see KU's 2-3 record and get complacent? Or could it be that the Jayhawks aren't nearly as bad as the reputation they toted into Columbia?

Heck, could it be that KU is actually pretty good?

"It's a special day, I guess," said Allen, beaming brighter than he has all season.

KU, now 3-3 overall and 1-2 in the Big 12, entered Saturday's Border War reeling from two straight losses – albeit to powers Kansas State and Oklahoma – and searching for the confidence and swagger that had permeated throughout August two-a-days.

But after a three-hour stretch in

which they dominated Missouri, 2-4 and 1-2, the Jayhawks paraded around their locker room touting revitalized bowl hopes and their first conference road victory after 14 straight losses.

"We're 3-3 right now but, in the minds of the players, we're 1-0," said Allen, who won for just the second time in 18 chances on the road in his career at Kansas. "We started a new season on Monday, and we're 1-0 in that season."

Allen responded to last week's 52-13 loss to K-State by making the Jayhawks practice on Monday, normally an off day. KU also went through more contact drills than normal, and Allen trimmed his team's travel roster from 80 to 64 to rid the sidelines, he said, of players who lacked focus.

The affects of Allen's iron fist showed Saturday.

The Jayhawks' defense held MU, which racked up 492 yards against top-ranked Nebraska two weeks ago, to just 247 yards of total offense. The Tigers gained just 10 rushing yards on 26 attempts, and MU ball carriers were stopped seven times behind the line of scrimmage.

"We couldn't sustain a drive all day," said MU coach Larry Smith, whose team was just three of 13 on third-down conversions. "Our defense was on the field way too much."

That's because KU's offense, which had 10 turnovers in its previous two games, showed poise for the first time this season. KU had 453 yards of total offense while limiting Missouri star defensive end Justin Smith to just one assisted tackle.

The Jayhawks set the tone early, going 57 yards on their opening drive before settling for a 38-yard field goal from Joe Garcia. Neither team scored again until the second quarter, when the Jayhawks appeared they might have slipped back into the troubles that have plagued them previously.

KU quarterback Dylen Smith lost a fumble on his own 3-yard line when he was hit by Pat Duffy. But the Tigers gave KU the ball back on their first play from scrimmage, as running back Zain Gilmore fumbled on the Jayhawks' 2.

KU's Moran Norris then committed the game's third turnover in 19 seconds when he lost a fumble in his own end zone. MU's Duke Revard recovered the ball for the touchdown and a 7-3 lead.

"It'd be easier to be a bickerer and a fighter when that transpires," Allen said. "But the defense didn't let it bother

them, and the offense took it to heart and made some plays of their own."

KU receiver Roger Ross put the Jayhawks up 10-7 by catching an 8-yard slant pass from Dylen Smith midway through the second quarter.

On his team's ensuing possession, MU quarterback Darius Outlaw – making his second career start – was intercepted by Tim Bowers, who returned it for a touchdown and a 17-7 lead.

Eric Spencer scored on a 60-yard pass from Outlaw on the Tigers' next possession, but that was about it for MU's offense. The only other thing it mustered was a 31-yard field goal by Brad Hammerich near the end of the third quarter.

KU, meanwhile, opened the second half with a 58-yard drive that resulted in a 3-yard scoring run by Smith, who finished with 77 rushing yards and 234 passing.

And when Ross returned a punt 62 yards for a touchdown with 4:31 left in the third quarter, it was obvious the Tigers had lost their gusto.

"They were kind of cocky at the beginning," Ross said. "But when we started driving, they were shocked. They knew after our first couple of drives that they weren't going to be able to play with us."

Offensive lineman Marc Owen, the leader of a unit that yielded just one sack after allowing 12 combined the last two weeks, said: "In our last two games, you could tell when our heads dropped. So we looked over at Mizzou and saw their heads drop and knew what they were feeling. We'd been there. But that's over now."

BY JOE POSNANSKI

Columbia

They both knew what this game meant. Larry Smith has been through these kinds of games a million times in his million-year career. Terry Allen, well, all this was kind of new to him. But they both knew exactly what this game was all about.

This was one of those survival games.

Winner gets the Cadillac.

Loser gets fired.

"Terry! Terry!" the few Kansas fans who showed up chanted after the Jayhawks beat Missouri 38-17 on Saturday afternoon.

From the few Missouri fans who stuck around, there was nothing but dead silence.

Sure, both coaches knew long before this game even began. This is the mud and blood and guts of college football. Oklahoma and Kansas State were busy playing the latest game of the century, but that's not real life. That's Hollywood and glitz and ESPN "Game Day."

Here in Columbia, you had two coaches fighting for their lives.

They both knew exactly what was going on. Heck, this was one of the toughest weeks of Terry Allen's life. His team was embarrassed against K-State last week, humiliated, and the furious e-mails poured in to athletic director Bob Frederick. These days, death threats come in e-mails. Nobody writes letters anymore.

"If e-mails were bullets," Frederick says, "I'd be dead already."

Meanwhile, Larry Smith has known all year that his job teeters. It's been a long while since people thought of him as the savior who took Missouri to

LEAN BUT INTENSE

RIVALS!
MU VS. KU

KU:38
MU:17

FOOTBALL
OCTOBER 14, 2000

FROM THE KANSAS CITY STAR, 2000

ALLEN WINS SURVIVAL CONTEST FOR KU

back-to-back bowl games. No, now people remember how Smith's team quit against K-State at the end of last season, and how Smith refused to risk it all and go for it on fourth down against Michigan State early this season.

So, this game was to save the season, and it was to save jobs, and it was all Kansas. The Jayhawks played with passion.

You know, there was a desperation to Terry Allen this week. He changed things around. He turned up the fury in practice. He challenged his players hearts. He made them crash into each other over and over until they understood just how tough they had to play in order to win.

This kind of coaching doesn't come easily for Allen – he's a good man with a good heart. He treats his players like young men. He has them over for dinner. He trusts them; some would say he trusts them too much. He has never wanted to be one of those coaches who grab facemasks and kick garbage cans and scream until their faces glow red.

But, like Allen said when the week began: "Desperate times call for desperate measures." And even though Thomas Paine probably said it first, well, Thomas Paine never had people rip him on his own radio show. Allen raised the intensity. He got a little angrier too. "It's time," he told his players, "to start playing football right."

"We were putting ourselves on the line," Allen said. "When things start going bad, everyone questions everyone. The offense questions the defense, the players question the coaches, the coaches

question the players, it all goes bad. So we said, "That's it. No more. We're going to change things. It was a risk. But we had to do it."

Allen had been in on his share of losing efforts, so he had empathy for the defeated Tigers.

And it worked. KU's players' played their guts out Saturday. The score doesn't begin to tell the story. Missouri needed a fumble, a long pass, and an interception just to get their points. They had 10 yards rushing. Their offense seemed bewildered. Their defense tired. The Kansas players – led by the gutsy running of David Winbush and the heart of quarterback Dylen Smith – simply overwhelmed. They were tougher. They showed more will. They won easily.

"We played hard," Missouri quarter-

back Darius Outlaw said. "But we didn't play really hard. There was heart. But we all didn't play with a lot of heart."

In these survival games, you have a big winner and a big loser. Larry Smith is the big loser. He certainly lost his job Saturday. If you know Missouri athletic director Mike Alden at all, you know he demands success, won't accept anything less, and getting pounded by Kansas at home on homecoming would not qualify as "success." The Internet already overflows with all the candidates to replace Smith.

Meanwhile, Allen was the big winner. The Jayhawks are 3-3, a bowl game is possible now, and the poisonous e-mails should die down for a little while.

KU PICTURE-PERFECT IN RIPPING TIGERS

It didn't seem right, Kansas and Missouri playing each other with-out the air being crisp. Many times the elements had been a factor in the outcome of this series. But as the teams lined up for the 2003 version of their rivalry, the warm September sun beat down on the field. September 27 was too early on the calendar for the teams to face each other. And it didn't sit right with the old guard.

RIVALS!
MU VS. KU

KU:35
MU:14

FOOTBALL
SEPTEMBER 27 2003

"The game still means so much of the season for the winner," said John Kadlec, who played and coached in the series more than 20 times as a Missouri Tiger.

"It's supposed to be the last game of the year," said Don Fambrough, who also played and coached in the series, but as a Jayhawk. "There's two football seasons at Kansas. The game against Missouri and the rest of the games."

Even the broadcasters get into the discussion. "The Kansas-Missouri game was the biggest event in the area," said Tom Hedrick, who had a front-row seat for the series for 17 years as the Voice of the Jayhawks. "People planned what they were going to do around the KU-MU game. It was that big of a deal. It absolutely should end the season."

The current versions of the Tigers and the Jayhawks probably cared little about the tradition of closing the season against each other. Many of the players were in grade school the last time that happened. Instead, this was the conference opener for both teams. Kansas came in a surprising 3-1 with—gasp—bowl aspirations. Missouri was 4-0 and ranked 23rd. They were dreaming of a Big XII North Division championship.

Missouri led 7-0 at the end of the first quarter and led 14-13 at the end of the third quarter. But the Jayhawks dominated the fourth quarter, outscoring the Tigers 22-0. It was the Jayhawks' first win over a ranked opponent in 13 tries and helped them win four straight games for the first time since 1995.

Senior quarterback Bill Whittemore led the Kansas offense. He passed for 111 yards and rushed for 76 more. But his leadership in the fourth quarter proved to be the difference for the Jayhawks.

Here's how it appeared in the September 28, 2003, Star:

By Jason King
The Kansas City Star

Lawrence, Kas.

When the time finally came to take off his headset – when he knew his team's 35-14 victory over Missouri was all but complete – Kansas coach Mark Mangino high-fived a few coaches, hugged a few players…ant then searched the sidelines for a camera.

Wasn't long before Mangino found KU photographer Jeff Jacobsen.

"Be ready," Mangino told him. "I want a picture of the whole team with the scoreboard in the background."

Moments later – after a brief post-game pep talk – KU's players re-emerged from their locker room for the celebratory snapshot. The only things missing from the photo were the Memorial Stadium goal posts.

Fans had torn them down a few minutes earlier after one of the most monumental victories in recent KU memory.

Bill Whittemore passed for 111 yards and rushed for 76 more in leading Kansas to an upset of previously unbeaten Missouri in the 112th annual Border War. One season after finishing 2-10, Mangino and the Jayhawks are suddenly the surprise of the Big 12 with a 4-1 record.

They also appear to have regained the fan support that was so glaringly missing during the Terry Allen era. A sellout crowd of 50,071 turned out for Saturday's game, marking the first time since 1975 that Kansas has drawn a capacity crowd for an opponent other than Nebraska, which traditionally carries a large fan base.

Kansas' victory over No. 23 Missouri increases the Jayhawks' chances of earning a postseason bowl berth for the first time since 1995. Kansas needs two more victories to reach the six needed to qualify for a bowl. Included among KU's seven remaining games are winnable home matchups with Baylor and Iowa State.

Whatever the case, the Jayhawks weren't looking that far ahead Saturday. They were too busy rejoicing in a victory that – with or without the post-game photo – will be hard to soon forget.

Kansas trailed 14-13 at the end of the third quarter before outscoring Missouri 22-0 in the fourth.

A 6-yard run by KU tailback Clark Green – and a two-point conversion pass from Whttemore to Denver Latimore – put KU ahead 21-14. KU held Missouri on its next possession then extended the lead to 28-14 when Whittemore scored on a 4-yard run with 7:35 left.

Missouri never threatened again.

Kansas tacked on another score when John Randle found the end zone on a 3-yard run with 3:21 remaining. The goal post "ceremony" followed soon after.

Mark Mangino led the Jayhawks to a stunning 35-14 victory over the Tigers and firmly into bowl contention.

As students prepared to rush the field, KU athletic director Lew Perkins was reminded that his department would be responsible for purchasing new uprights.

"No problem," a giddy Perkins said.

A few feet away stood legendary KU player John Hadl, who offered these words: "This goes to show that everything we thought about Mark Mangino was right. We've been waiting for something like this for a long time."

The Jayhawks, meanwhile, stood back and watched as their fans hoisted the fallen posts and carted them off to nearby Porter Lake.

"Hey," safety Tony Stubbs said, "they did it to us last year."

Yes, it was only one year ago when Missouri fans – and a few players, too - tore down the Faurot Field goal posts after a 36-12 victory over KU.

And the Tigers, 4-1, had every reason to think they'd walk away with a Border War victory again this season, too. Especially since KU entered the game ranked 88th in the country in total defense.

But Kansas – which features eight new defensive starters – found a way to stop Missouri and Heisman candidate Brad Smith.

A sophomore, Smith entered the game averaging 249 yards of total offense. But he had just 95 yards Saturday. Heck, Missouri's entire team only mustered 196 yards. Even Division I-AA Jacksonville State (234 yards) was more successful against the Jayhawks.

"Obviously," MU coach Gary Pinkel said, "I got outcoached today."

Lopsided as Saturday's score was, things could've been a lot worse for Missouri. Kansas receiver Moderick Johnson dropped a touchdown pass in the end zone, and a 48-yard field-goal attempt by Johnny Beck was thwarted when Curtis Ansel mishandled the snap.

Even so, the Jayhawks had no problems moving the ball.

Kansas got on the scoreboard first when Charles Gordon's 61-yard punt return led to a 1-yard scoring run by Whittemore. The Jayhawks led 6-0 after missing the extra point.

Missouri responded with a 4-yard touchdown scamper by Smith. But KU led 13-7 at halftime after Green's 4-yard run in the second quarter.

Kansas outrushed MU 207-134. Whittemore threw just 22 passes.

A 9-yard pass from Smith to

RIVALS!
MU VS. KU

KU:35
MU:14

FOOTBALL
SEPTEMBER 27 2003

Darius Outlaw catapulted Mizzou back on top 14-13 midway through the third quarter. Neither team would score again until Kansas' fourth quarter onslaught.

The drive that put Kansas ahead 21-14 was a 72-yard march that saw Whittemore carry five times for 32 yards. He also completed a 15-yard pass to Brandon

Rideau on a crucial third down play.

"We felt like, if we got in a shootout, we had the trigger man to win the shootout," Mangino said of Whittemore.

As always, Whittemore refused to shoulder the credit for Saturday's victory. He said he was just happy to see everyone's hard work finally paying off.

"Last year everyone talked about wanting to make a turnaround, but nobody knew how," Whittemore said. "This year we're just going out and doing it."

FROM THE KANSAS CITY STAR, 2003

WHITTEMORE WAS FIRMLY IN CONTROL

By Jason King
The Kansas City Star

Lawrence, Kans.,

There were two great scenes Saturday afternoon. The first happened just a few seconds before the game ended, just a few seconds before Kansas finished off a 35-14 demolition of Missouri and set off the biggest football celebration in Lawrence since disco was young

What happened was several hundred fans assembled along the sidelines. They prepared to stampede the field and tear down a goal post. And this little guy in a blue Kansas shirt – a security guard, apparently – rushed over and screamed "No, no, no! You can't be on the field!"

The clock ran out. The game was over. The fans rushed the field. And this brave little guy stood in the middle of the mayhem with his hands up in the air and shouted, "No! No! No!" while all these Kansas fans rushed by like it was a Beatles movie or something. Somebody should give that kid a raise.

The second great scene was of Kansas quarterback Bill Whittemore

watching a goal post go down. He just watched quietly, without any emotion on his face, as those kids on the goal post swayed and tugged and jumped. After a while, the goal post went down. Whittemore watched it fall.

Then he jogged easily off the field.

His work was done.

Somebody should give that kid a raise, too.

"Bill didn't say a word all week about this being a big game," Kansas coach Mark Mangino said. "But before the game, I looked in his eyes. And his eyes told me he came to play."

Nobody talks much about Bill Whittemore. Saturday, eyes were supposed to follow Missouri's Brad Smith., the Heisman candidate, the All-America candidate, the superstar. Whittemore was better. A lot better. In part, that's because Missouri decided to dust off some archaic game plan, first chiseled, I believe, by Aborigines on the walls of Australian caves thousands of years ago. By the end of the game, in which he piled up a grand total of 95 yards of

offense, Smith looked even more frustrated than the security kid trying to single-handedly stop a herd of Kansas fans from running on the field.

"Bill didn't say a word all week about this being a big game," Kansas coach Mark Mangino said. "But before the game, I looked in his eyes. And his eyes told me he came to play."

Whittemore, meanwhile, was fabulous. He did everything right. When he had a chance to run, he ran for 76 yards, and two touchdowns. When asked to throw, he completed 14 of 22 passes (and he had three or four passes dropped on him, including a sure TD pass).

More than anything though, Whittemore controlled the game. Some players can just do that. When Kansas needed a play, Whittemore delivered a play. He bounced off a tackle to get a first down. He lofted a soft pass over a

WHITTEMORE WAS FIRMLY IN CONTROL

CONTINUED

linebacker on third down. He eluded a defender and drilled a pass into a receiver's chest when the game was on the line.

"Bill is the man," Kansas receiver Mark Simmons said. "In case you did not know."

Few know. Whittemore does not get much hype. He's just the kind of guy you can't hype. He's not particularly fast. He does not do flashy things like leap over defenders or zing the ball 65 yards down the field. He does not put up monster numbers.

He even talks quietly. Saturday was Kansas' biggest home win since, well, who knows when. Missouri was ranked. There was a sellout crowd. Kansas has had just five sellout crowds since 1975 – all against Nebraska. The combined score of those five games? Nebraska 261, Kansas 35.

So, there was a hungry crowd to entertain, and there was also revenge to consider. Whittemore ended his season last year while trying to slide against Missouri. Whittemore is a head-down kind of player; he never really learned how to slide. He wrecked his knee. He did not blame Missouri for that.

He was not too thrilled, however, when after that game some Missouri players helped the fans tear down the goal posts.

"Oh, we talked about that," Whittemore said. "We definitely talked about their players on the goal posts."

That was about as emotional as he got. The rest of the time, he talked about his offensive line and he credited just about everybody else in America except himself.

"We've got to take them one game at a time," Whittemore said for the record 348th consecutive week, dating back to his Pee Wee football days.

That's how it is with Whittemore. He's an old-time college quarterback. You cannot know him by watching a few highlights or listening to him talk. No, he's a player you have to see play again and again to appreciate. He takes the hits. He makes good decisions. He wants to win more than anyone on the field.

"Bill does not talk about himself," Simmons said. "But he's one of the best quarterbacks in the country."

Saturday, after the game, the entire Kansas team went back on the field to have a photo taken in front of the scoreboard. That's a nice touch. But I hope someone got the photo of Bill Whittemore looking up as those goal posts came down. I could not see his face through the crowd. But when the goal posts fell, I thought I saw him nod just a little bit.

"Were you thinking about last year's Missouri game?" someone asked him.

"No," he said. "I did not finish that game. I finished this one, though."

Roy's Impact

TIGERS TOPPLE KU IN BATTLE OF GIANTS

There's nothing quite like beating the No. 1 team in the country. Missouri did that twice to Kansas in 1990.

The first contest was in Columbia, and the Tigers knocked off the Jayhawks with a strong second-half performance. The fourth-ranked Tigers won, 95-87, as four players tallied at least 20 points. Kansas led 46-43 at halftime, but the Tigers quickly grabbed the lead behind four points from Doug Smith and never looked back.

Missouri was the only one of the top eight teams in the rankings that week not to lose, so they assumed the top spot when the new poll came out. They held that spot until losing at Kansas State a couple weeks later. So when the return engagement happened in Lawrence on February 13, the Jayhawks once again owned the No. 1 ranking. This time, the Tigers were No. 2.

Second verse, same as the first.

The Tigers outscored the Jayhawks 13-7 in the final five minutes, including 6-of-6 from the line, to hand them a 77-71 loss in Allen Fieldhouse. After Missouri led by 10 at the halfway point of the second half, the Jayhawks answered with six straight points, coming off three steals. They eventually tied the score at 64-64, but never could take the lead.

RIVALS!
MU VS. KU

KU:95
MU: 87

BASKETBALL
JANUARY 20, 1990

Defense proved important in this battle, as the Tigers held Kansas to just 44 percent shooting from the field. The Jayhawks had led the nation in field-goal shooting (53.6 percent) coming in.

"We always felt that every game was important, but nationally these games were the most important," long-time Missouri coach Norm Stewart said. "The reason I remember them so well is we won them both.

"Before the second game, Dick Vitale said that Missouri was going down. Our kids wanted to tell him what they thought of his prediction, but I didn't want any part of that."

Here's how it appeared in the January 21, 1990 Star and the February 14, 1990, Star:

GEORGETOWN LOSS GIVES MU CHANCE TO BE NEXT NO. 1

BY JEFFREY FLANAGAN
STAFF WRITER

Columbia

Who could have expected more? All the talk, all the hype and all the buildup matched the event Saturday as No. 4 Missouri handed Kansas its first loss and likely toppled the Jayhawks from the No. 1 ranking with a gritty 95-87 victory before 13,300 jubilant fans at the Hearnes Center.

As things turned out, it might be the Tigers who replace the Jayhawks on top the national polls. Second-ranked Georgetown lost 70-65 to Connecticut, leaving no unbeaten major-college teams. In fact, Missouri was the only one of the top seven teams which won Saturday, and No. 8 Duke lost earlier in the week.

The Tigers, 17-1 overall and 4-0 in the Big Eight Conference, beat Kansas almost the way they mapped it out – with power inside and quickness around the perimeter. Four Tigers reached the 20-point mark, led by Anthony Peeler's 24.

"Just a tremendous victory," said a smiling Tigers Coach Norm Stewart, who celebrated his 55th birthday.

"I'm really happy for the ballclub.

"I know Kansas is deserving of their ranking, and they're an excellent team."

But the Jayhawks fell for the first time after 19 victories and likely coughed up their top spot in the Associated Press poll, although both teams seemed uncomfortable discussing the rankings.

"Everybody thinks I'm lying," Kansas Coach Roy Williams said, "but (the ranking) doesn't affect me."

Ditto the Tigers, who didn't appear anxious to clutch the No. 1 baton from the Jayhawks.

"I don't want to be No. 1," said Tigers guard Lee Coward, who now may not have much choice. "You're just setting yourself up when you're No. 1. I'd much rather be No. 3 or No. 4 or wherever. It's a better spot to be in."

Added Tigers forward Doug Smith, "I don't care about No. 1. It's not important right now. The important thing is we got the victory today."

And Smith had much to do with that. A 6-foot-10 junior, he scored 19 of his 23 points during the second half. With Missouri trailing 46-43, Smith scored the first two baskets of the second half and the Tigers never trailed again.

Smith hit 10 of 15 shots overall, eight of 11 after halftime when the Tigers engaged in a determined effort to unleash him inside.

That plan had gone haywire in the first half when Smith picked up two quick fouls and spent a majority of the time on the bench. Enter Smith's partner underneath, Nathan Buntin, who came off a season-low of two points against Oklahoma State last Tuesday and hit his first seven shots in the first half.

Buntin finished with 22 points on 11-of-14 shooting. He also grabbed 10 rebounds.

> *"I thought Lee may have forced a few shots. But he's a scorer, and he has to take his shots. I don't have a problem with that."*
> *— Missouri coach Norm Stewart on guard Lee Coward*

"I think the guys were trying to get me involved early," Buntin said. "I just responded."

Williams was more emphatic. "Nathan was just unbelievable," he said.

And when Buntin and Smith weren't muscling inside against the rotating Jayhawks' front line, Peeler and Coward tried slashing through the perimeter.

baseline, was fouled and completed the three-point play. That capped a 6-2 spurt that put the Tigers up 57-51 with 15 minutes, 55 seconds left.

"I thought Lee may have forced a few shots," Stewart said. "But he's a scorer, and he has to take his shots. I don't have a problem with that."

Stewart did have a problem with

Pritchard had seven of his 16.

The result was a 46-43 halftime lead for the Jayhawks.

"We kept trying to go for the knockout punch," Peeler said. "You don't do that to a team like Kansas."

And was that the lesson from Stewart at halftime?

"He just said to be patient," Peeler said, "and work the ball around. He said to relax."

"You can't concentrate on stopping one of them because the other two can hurt you just as bad. And most of the time, all three get the job done."

— Kansas forward Freeman West on the trio of Anthony Peeler, Doug Smith and Nathan Buntin

---

Peeler, who hit only five of 15 shots, nonetheless was a menace to the Jayhawks. Forcing his way through double-teams, he drew a bundle of fouls and nailed all 14 free-throw attempts.

Coward wasn't bashful either. He scored 20 points, six during a crucial stage early in the second half. With Missouri up 51-49, Coward drained a three-pointer, then scored along the

his team's play in the first half.

The Tigers struggled with the Jayhawks' backdoor plays and alley-oops. Mark Randall, a 6-9 junior who had 18 points, scored 10 for Kansas in the first half on five-of-six shooting.

When the Tigers collapsed inside, seniors Jeff Gueldner and Kevin Pritchard fired over the top. Gueldner scored 10 of his 14 in the first half and

The victory was especially sweet for Peeler, who is from Kansas City.

"All the Detroit guys on the team were saying this would mean more to me, beating Kansas," Peeler said. "People back home were getting on my friends and family, saying we couldn't beat Kansas. This feels good."

But Peeler and the Tigers were careful not to fan any fires for the rematch, Feb 13.

"They're a very good basketball team," he said. "We have a lot of respect for them."

Said Williams, "They beat us. But I hope there is another day."

Roy Williams and Norm Stewart had intense competition on the court, but they had great appreciation and respect for each other off the court.

RIVALS!
MU VS. KU

KU:77
MU:71

BASKETBALL
FEBRUARY 13, 1990

FROM THE KANSAS CITY STAR, 1990

TIGERS BEAT NO. 1 JAYHAWKS AGAIN

NO. 2 MU SURGES LATE, PULLS OUT 77-71 DECISION

BY BLAIR KERKHOFF
OF THE SPORTS STAFF

Lawrence

As the battle for the nation's No. 1 ranking boils down to a border war between Missouri and Kansas, the Jayhawks must be relieved to know the regular-season series with the Tigers is over.

Missouri beat Kansas 77-71 on Tuesday, completing an unusual sweep — both of the Tigers' victories came after the Jayhawks had ascended to the top spot in The Associated Press poll.

The victory Tuesday for No. 2 Missouri was just as gratifying as the first, a 95-87 decision on Jan. 20.

"It's a great win because it was in the conference, it was against Kansas and it was at their place," Missouri center Doug Smith said.

In maintaining their lead in the Big Eight, the Tigers, 23-2 overall and 9-1 in the league, concocted a formula to ground the Jayhawks: aggressive man defense, field-goal efficiency and accurate free-throw shooting.

All were key in Missouri's final run after Kansas, 24-2 and 7-2, tied the score 64-64 with 5:31 remaining.

The Tigers broke from the deadlock when Anthony Peeler followed Smith's missed shot. Another follow, this one by forward Nathan Buntin off a missed free throw with 3:02 left, extended the Tigers' advantage to 71-66.

Missouri then made its final six free throws and sealed the victory.

It appeared the Tigers would need all of them after a three-pointer by Kansas guard Kevin Pritchard pulled the Jayhawks to 73-71 with 1:07 remaining. Pritchard had made one of his last nine shots before that basket.

"Even with 2 minutes left I thought it was Kansas' game," Jayhawks reserve guard Adonis Jordan said.

But the Jayhawks then fouled the wrong Missouri player twice. Freshman Travis Ford, who leads the Big Eight with 89.3 percent, hit four straight in one-and-one situations around a missed three-pointer by Kansas' Rick Calloway.

rowed the gap. Reserve center Mike Maddox hit shots on consecutive possessions, making it 63-59.

"That's when we went into our prevent offense," Stewart said.

Kansas lost a chance to get it closer when forwards Mark Randall and Alonzo Jamison made just one of five free throws on the next three Jayhawks possessions.

Kansas eventually caught the Tigers, but the Jayhawks couldn't top them. Although it hurt the nation's top floor-shooting team (53.6 percent before Tuesday) to make just 44 percent from the field Tuesday, Kansas' free-

> "It was a tough, gutty win," Missouri Coach Norm Stewart said. "I can appreciate this being one vs. two, but it comes down to us playing better and handling situations."

"It was a tough, gutty win," Missouri Coach Norm Stewart said. "I can appreciate this being one vs. two, but it comes down to us playing better and handling situations."

That's something the Tigers failed to do midway in the second half when they lost a 10-point lead. A Buntin slam pushed the Missouri cushion to 63-53 with 10:14 remaining.

But the Tigers got sloppy with the ball. The Jayhawks came up with three steals over the next 3 minutes and nar-

throw woes in that stretch crippled its comeback and allowed the Tigers to catch their breath.

"In the big games you've got to hit those shots," Maddox said. "Basically, they hit theirs when they needed them, and we didn't hit ours."

Kansas was eight of 16 from the line. Missouri finished 19 of 24 and shot 55.1 percent from the field. The Tigers own the top two shooting percentages against Kansas this season

Randall's misses spoiled an other-

wise exceptional game. Randall, the Jayhawks' leading scorer, was seven of nine from the field and matched his season average of 15 points.

Although Kansas succeeded in slowing the Tigers' inside attack – a thorn in the first meeting – the Jayhawks had trouble containing Peeler.

Peeler finished with 22 points, six assists and six rebounds. He made all six of his free throws, making him 20 for

20 against Kansas this season.

As solid as his performance was, Peeler said a period early in the second half, one in which he didn't score, was the game's turning point.

Kansas had made up a two-point halftime deficit and tied the score 41-41 a minute into the second half. But Missouri got two important transition baskets, three-pointers from guard John McIntyre, who lost himself twice in the

corner on the break, and extended the lead to 47-41.

"We came up with a couple of steals, and John made those shots to quiet down the crowd," Peeler said.

The Jayhawks, on the other hand, struggled. Calloway made just four of 12 shots and missed all five of his first-half shots. Pritchard was four for 15. Also, guard Jeff Gueldner scored just five points, less than half of his average.

FROM THE KANSAS CITY STAR, 1990

BIG THREE ONCE MORE MAKE MU A WINNER

BY BART HUBBUCH
KU SPORTS CORRESPONDENT

LAWRENCE, – Kansas learned the hard way Tuesday night that it doesn't matter how much work and preparation the Jayhawks put into stopping Anthony Peeler, Doug Smith and Nathan Buntin.

Missouri's dangerous threesome always seems to beat them anyway. And a lot of other teams, too.

"You can't concentrate on stopping one of them because the other two can hurt you just as bad," Kansas forward Freeman West said after the Jayhawks' 77-71 loss to the Tigers at Allen Field House.

"And most of the time, all three get the job done."

They certainly did Tuesday, combining for 49 points and 18 rebounds and helping No. 2 Missouri beat No. 1 Kansas for the fourth straight time dating to last season.

Peeler, however, drew most of the Jayhawks' attention and promptly threw it back in their face, scoring a game-high

22 points on eight-of-14 shooting and six-of-six shooting from the free-throw line.

"All we wanted to do this time was keep him in front of us, but he still ended up hurting us," said swingman Rick Calloway, who was one of several Jayhawks who guarded Peeler.

"He's not a great shooter, but he knows how to score. He has that kind of knack for scoring that's so tough to stop."

Kansas, which saw Smith and Buntin combine for 45 points in its loss last month at Columbia, considered defense in the lane against Missouri's two bruising inside players to be the key Tuesday.

Smith and Buntin didn't do as much damage offensively this time (11 points and 16 points, respectively), but the two combined for 12 rebounds, including a crucial offensive rebound by Smith off a missed free throw with 28 seconds left.

"We did the best job we could on their two post players, but they're never going to shut them down completely." Jayhawks forward Mike Maddox said.

> "He's not a great shooter, but he knows how to score. He has that kind of knack for scoring that's so tough to stop."
>
> —KU's Rick Calloway about Anthony Peder

"We did a better job on them this time, but they came out on top."

Buntin didn't seem to notice any extra defensive work by Kansas inside, playing nearly a flawless game. He hit six of eight shots and four of six free throws and grabbed seven rebounds.

Smith, the Tigers; 6-foot-10 center, scored 23 points in the game in Columbia but wasn't nearly as effective Tuesday. He was hit with two first-half fouls and scored only 11 points on three-of-seven shooting.

It was the rebounding of Buntin and Smith, however, that troubled the Jayhawks the most.

RIVALS!
MU VS. KU

KU:74
MU: 70

BASKETBALL
FEBRUARY 12, 1991

WILLIAMS BENCHES STARTERS LATE IN FIRST HALF. JAYHAWKS RESPOND

Some people wonder how much of a difference a coach makes once the game starts. Some will say that his or her role is to recruit the players, prepare the team and then make only minor adjustments. The players make the difference.

Roy Williams proved that theory wrong with one of his most famous coaching moves, as Kansas defeated Missouri, 74-70. The Jayhawks came into the game leading the nation in field-goal shooting at 55 percent. After 13 minutes of play, they had hit just 3-of-14 shots (21 percent) and they trailed 31-22 at the half, their lowest halftime point total in five seasons.

Williams took his five starters out of the game as a group and sat them on the bench for the final 6:55 of the half. The reserves only lost a point the rest of the way and shot 33 percent (4-of-12). Kansas was able to stay within reach because Missouri was equally dreadful from the line, connecting on just 11 of 24.

Williams said very little to the starters as they sat on the bench. Instead, he let them sit and think about how poorly they had played. He went ahead and lashed them in the locker room at halftime. One of the two tactics worked, because the Jayhawks scored the first six points of the second half. Missouri then reeled off six straight, but an 11-2 run by KU tied the score at 39-all just 5:15 into the second half.

Kansas eventually pulled away to an 8-point lead with just under four minutes remaining, and the Tigers were done. Neither coach was happy with his team's effort for the game, but Williams at least had the consolation of a victory.

Here's how it appeared in the February 13, 1991, Star:

By BLAIR KERKHOFF
STAFF WRITER

Columbia

Silence was golden for Kansas in its 74-70 victory over Missouri on Tuesday night.

At halftime, Jayhawks Coach Roy Williams chewed out the team, specifically the starters, for lethargic play in the first half.

But in Williams' estimation, those words may have had the same effect as his coaching tactic with 6 minutes, 55 seconds to play in the first half.

That's when Williams, disgusted with the play of his starters, yanked them all. When they came off the floor hardly a word was spoken.

"Maybe I was afraid of what I would say," Williams said. "I also think silence sometimes is as strong as anything you could say."

Kansas' problems were plenty. Start with shooting, something the Jayhawks usually do well.

Kansas, which entered the game leading the nation in field-goal percentage at 55.0, went seven of 26 for the half (26.9 percent). It got field goals on consecutive possessions only once, and the 22 points were their lowest for a half in five seasons.

The starters were three of 14 for the half. Leading scorer Terry Brown was zip for six.

There were more problems. Kansas wasn't forcing the issue on defense, and Missouri was. The Tigers came up with eight first-half steals.

"There was no concentration," Williams said. "We weren't running the plays or executing. It was a myriad of problems.

"I've taken them out five at a time before, but I don't know if I've ever left them out for that long. But then I don't know if I've ever been as discouraged with them as much as I was at that point."

> **"They just seemed more excited that we were in the first half. We just weren't ready to play."**
> —Terry Brown

The reserves, which included the team's three freshmen, lost a point. The Tigers led 21-13 when the substitutions were made, and it was 31-22 at halftime thanks to Patrick Richey's buzzer-beating three-point play.

The players were at a loss to explain their poor start.

"They just seemed more excited that we were in the first half," Brown said. "We just weren't ready to play."

So they sat and watched as Richey, Richard Scott and Steve Woodberry - three freshmen - and juniors David Johanning and Sean Tunstall finished the first half.

"I was very embarrassed," Kansas center Mark Randall said. "I'm glad he did it (pulled the starters) because it sure got everybody thinking."

The message got through as the Jayhawks responded immediately in the second half. Brown rolled in a running 12-footer and moments later a three-pointer. Adonis Jordan's free throw with 18:14 remaining closed the gap to 31-28.

The Kansas defense also took charge. Missouri opened the second half with three straight turnovers.

"I thought a big key was turning up the defense in the second half," Randall said. "We finally got some pressure on them."

Williams vented to his team at halftime, but the silent treatment may have had the most effect.

RIVALS!
MU VS. KU

KU: 74
MU: 70

BASKETBALL
FEBRUARY 12, 1991

FROM THE KANSAS CITY STAR, 1991

JAYHAWKS TOP MISSOURI 74-70 AFTER TRAILING BY NINE AT HALFTIME

BY JEFFREY FLANAGAN
STAFF WRITER

COLUMBIA – Try and catch Kansas now.

The Jayhawks, overcoming a dreadful first half, powered back from a 13-point deficit and toppled the fading Missouri Tigers 74-70 on Tuesday night at the Hearnes Center.

The Jayhawks, ranked No. 11, moved to 18-4 overall and 7-2 in the Big Eight. First-place Kansas now has 11/2-game lead over Oklahoma State and Nebraska.

"It's not over, but (Kansas) is in an awfully good position," Tigers Coach Norm Stewart acknowledged.

Missouri, which led 31-22 at half-time, fell to 13-8 overall and 5-4 in the league.

The Tigers' first-half lead could

"It was a team effort. Everyone who stepped up to the line contributed. If we just make the normal level we shoot, we have a little more comfort level."

Instead, the Jayhawks, who made only seven of 26 shots from the field in the first half, were handed an opportunity to creep back into contention.

"We didn't give up," Kansas Coach Roy Williams said. "Our kids were not ready to play in the first half. I can't believe that could happen against a team like Missouri, but that's college basketball.

"Missouri's missed free throws gave us a chance to come back."

Kansas' comeback came quickly. In the first 2 minutes after halftime, Missouri committed three straight turnovers and Kansas responded with

> "We didn't give up. Our kids were not ready to play in the first half. I can't believe that could happen against a team like Missouri, but that's college basketball."
> - Kansas Coach Roy Williams

jump shot that restored order for Missouri at 37-28, the Jayhawks went on an 11-2 run and tied it 39-39 with 14:45 left.

"We just started having a lot of breakdowns and stopped moving," Stewart said. "All the things we did well in the first half – cutting to the back door, sliding through screens for a jumper, moving to the ball – we stopped."

Eventually the Jayhawks went up 61-53 with 3:36 left as Richard Scott worked free inside for a basket.

Missouri whittled the margin to two, 69-67, with 45 seconds left. After Brown hit a free throw that made it 70-67, the Tigers had two chances to tie it. But freshmen Melvin Booker and Jed Frost each missed three-pointers on the next possession.

> "I thought the ballgame for us was lost in the first half," Stewart said. "It was a team effort. Everyone who stepped up to the line contributed. If we just make the normal level we shoot, we have a little more comfort level."
> - Missouri Coach Norm Stewart

have been substantially more, but Missouri made only 11 of 24 free throws.

"I thought the ballgame for us was lost in the first half," Stewart said.

two jump shots by Terry Brown, one a three-pointer, and a free throw by Adonis Jordan, pulling within 31-28.

After Doug Smith, who scored 23 points and grabbed 14 rebounds, hit a

JAYHAWKS QUELL TIGERS' CHARGE

Team beat superstar in the season-ender in 1992.

Anthony Peeler poured in a career-high 43 points, including 19 points in the final 7 1/2 minutes, but Kansas still won, 97-89. Peeler's final bucket, the third of three straight treys, cut the Kansas lead to 91-89, but nobody else scored for the Tigers and the Jayhawks prevailed.

The Kansas side was more impressed with Peeler's efforts than his teammates and coaches. Jayhawk player and coach alike praised Peeler's effort. But Kansas had the victory in their back pocket so they could afford to be effusive.

Peeler and the Tigers had lost two straight, and they came out firing, taking a 31-23 lead midway through the first half. But Kansas went on a 12-0 run to erase an eight-point deficit and take the lead for good. By halftime, it was the Jayhawks up by eight.

Peeler scored 26 of his 43 in the second half, and his scoring barrage kept the Kansas faithful on the edge of their seats. But it was not enough as the Jayhawks won the Big 8 Conference by a full three games.

Here's how it appeared in the March 9, 1992, Star:

By Blair Kerkhoff
Staff Writer

Lawrence

Anthony Peeler's superlative effort did not spoil Kansas' celebration.

The Jayhawks toasted their Big Eight championship after Sunday's 97-89 victory over Missouri, then saluted Peeler, who scored 19 of his career-high 43 points in the final 71/2 minutes. His shooting clinic kept the Jayhawks from breathing easily until the final few seconds.

"I can't think of the right word," Kansas Coach Roy Williams said. "I can say fantastic, unbelievable and all that garbage, but that doesn't give you the right image of what I thought (Peeler) did today."

But it wasn't enough. The Jayhawks outmuscled the Tigers inside, turned on the pressure defense in strategic

moments and defied a trend by making free throws.

Third-ranked Kansas, 23-4 overall and 11-3 in the Big Eight, won the title by three games. The 11th-ranked Tigers, 20-7 and 8-6, have lost three straight but left with a small measure of satisfaction.

"When you play them to the buzzer on their floor, you've got to feel pretty good," Missouri Coach Norm Stewart said. "At least that's what they say."

The Jayhawks hit their last 10 from the stripe and completed an 86-percent effort (31 for 36), their best in 75 games. The biggest shots belonged to

Rex Walters, who knocked down two with 25.7 seconds remaining and gave Kansas a 93-89 lead.

Twenty seconds earlier, Peeler completed Missouri's scoring with his third straight three-pointer, a shot from the deepest right corner.

"I can say fantastic, unbelievable and all that garbage, but that doesn't give you the right image of what I thought (Peeler) did today."

— Roy Williams

The Tigers who trailed, 78-64 with 7 minutes, 56 seconds remaining, had closed to 91-89.

"He was unconscious," said Alonzo Jamison, Kansas' defensive specialist, who was one of several Jayhawks Peeler scorched. "He had the glare in his eye."

RIVALS!
MU VS. KU

KU: 97
MU: 89

BASKETBALL
MARCH 8, 1992

It was evident from the start. Missouri, coming off two losses, including a 14-point loss to Oklahoma in Peeler's final home game, was eager to make amends. The Tigers controlled things early and bolted to a 31-23 lead.

But Kansas, a loss at Iowa State fresh in its minds, also had something to prove. It already had clinched the conference title, but a second straight loss would have canceled Kansas' net-cutting ceremony and sent the Jayhawks into the league tournament riding a two-game skid.

"We had to get back on track," KU guard Adonis Jordan said. "And we definitely turned it around."

The process started when the Jayhawks wiped out that early eight-point deficit with a 12-0 run, sparked by defense. Four of Missouri's seven turnovers in the first half came during that run.

The Jayhawks didn't trail after that. Steve Woodberry's three-pointer beat the buzzer and gave Kansas a 53-45 halftime lead.

Several times in the second half, the Jayhawks seemed poised to run away. But Peeler made certain the Tigers remained prominent in Kansas' rear-view mirror.

Anthony Peeler's 43 points was not enough to lift Missouri past conference champion Kansas.

PEELER, KU BEST IN BIG EIGHT

BY GIB TWYMAN

LAWRENCE – Don't even bother sending out the ballots. In these economically tight times, save the 29 cents a pop.

Anthony Peeler is the Big Eight player of the year. The 43-point performance against Kansas Sunday was the exclamation.

Or, as Jayhawk Coach Roy Williams put it, after his team's 97-89 victory, "I told Anthony I've worked with Michael Jordan and James Worthy and Sam Perkins and Brad Daugherty and 14 first-round draft choices, and I've never seen any of them put on a better exhibition than his today."

A.P. on ABC.

But that was the player of the year.

For the team of the year, we must go to the other side of the floor, to Kansas.

The third-ranked Jayhawks put on another magnificent display of tough, deep team play that underscored the Big Eight title they'd already clinched.

"I told our kids this is the best league in the country, and you are the champions of it," Williams said. "To win by three full games is just mind-boggling."

So, really, is the Royball that made it possible. This means lots of minutes for lots of players, a shock-troop effect that just erodes the other guy's will.

Eye-catching stat Sunday: KU's bench outscored MU's 65-3.

And despite Peeler's outrageous show, KU's Everyman numbers leaped out as this game developed.

By halftime, before Peeler just left the planet and went into orbit, he had 17 points. He'd shot 13 times. Jevon Crudup shot eight. Next highest total: Melvin Booker's two.

KU, meantime, had five guys

"I told our kids this is the best league in the country, and you are the champions of it. To win by three full games is just mind-boggling."

— Roy Williams

---

between four and six shots each: Alonzo Jamison, Rex Walters, Adonis Jordan, Eric Pauley and Richard Scott. They'd scored from six to 11 points.

While Mizzou spent much time turning down makable shots, going strictly with a Triple-A offense – Anthony, Anthony and Anthony – KU was getting production from nearly everyone.

"We do have better numbers than they do," Williams said, pointing out Jamal Coleman's absence. "Our goal was to pound it inside to get down to their eighth and ninth men. Our guys did a pretty good job of it."

Yet, occasionally, you'll hear something to the effect that KU ought to win with all that depth.

That's only backward. Williams recruits depth. He coaches it. He uses it.

Give him the credit for making it happen.

And yet, Sunday, the numbers game almost wasn't enough. Peeler nearly beat a 23-4 team, which just doesn't lose at home, single-handedly.

Asked what worked best on Peeler, Williams laughed and said, "Better just go get a book on defense and try everything in there.

"We threw Jamison, Jordan and (Steve) Woodberry at him, three pretty good defensive players. We tried a box-and-one and half-court trap. He still knocked them down."

As Peeler buried one more three-pointer from somewhere in the stands, making it 91-89 with 45 seconds left, Williams considered the ultimate compliment.

"I was actually going to foul him in the backcourt," Williams said. "We were getting one and two at the line while he was hitting threes.

"We'd have been better off making him shoot free throws."

Peeler's assault tied Oscar Robertson as the second-best effort ever against KU. And, as MU Coach Norm Stewart, said, "Anthony was truly outstanding, like another lefty who had a pretty good game for us once."

He meant Willie Smith, who hit 43 against Michigan in the 1976 NCAAs.

Every sixteen years or so, you'll see a game like A. P.'s. And a player like him.

RIVALS!
MU VS. KU

MU: 81
KU: 74

BASKETBALL
FEBRUARY 20, 1994

MISSOURI DELIVERS, NOW AWAITS DUE

Melvin Booker cleared the Phog.

Missouri trailed by eight points late in the second half of their game in Allen Fieldhouse, but Melvin Booker loaded the Tigers on his back and carried them to victory. The victory raised the Tigers' record to 11-0 in the conference and kept alive their hopes of an undefeated conference season.

"The game was tough. We played a terrific game," former Missouri coach Norm Stewart said. "Melvin came to me before the game and asked me about the sign at one end of the fieldhouse. He said, 'I'm a senior, and I always wondered what it means,' referring to the 'Beware of the Phog' sign.

"I told him about Phog Allen and the influence he had on college basketball. Then I told him that the KU fans think that influence still exists and casts a fog over opponents in that building.

"After the game, Melvin came up to me and said, 'Coach, do you think I cleared the Phog?' I said, 'Yeah, Melvin, but please don't say that to the newspapers."

Here's how it appeared in the February 21, 1994, Star

University of Missouri Archives

SECOND-HALF SURGE ROCKS JAYHAWKS, CLINCHES TIE FOR BIG EIGHT CROWN

BY BOB DUTTON
STAFF WRITER

Lawrence

Missouri solidified its claim as the Big Eight's best and established itself as a national contender Sunday with a stirring 81-74 victory over Kansas at Allen Field House.

Trailing by eight with 8¹/₂ minutes remaining, the Tigers turned to senior guard Melvin Booker to save their unbeaten conference season.

He responded with 10 points in a 94-second span that forged a 63-63 tie.

Booker was marvelous after missing his first four shots. He made eight of his next 11 in producing a career-high 32 points, helping the Tigers clinch a tie for the Big Eight title.

After Kansas took its last lead at 66-63 on a three-pointer by Jacque Vaughn, the Tigers got two baskets from

Melvin Booker (left) and Lamont Frazier celebrated keeping alive their hopes of an unbeaten conference season with an 81-74 victory.

"Unless it's the last 10 seconds, we don't worry about it," Tigers guard Lamont Frazier said. "We've proved that we can come back, over and over again."

This time, Missouri tightened its defense and allowed Booker to handle the point production.

"I felt it was somebody's job to step up," Booker said. "I'm a senior, so that's what I wanted to do."

He made two free throws, then a 21-footer from the top of the circle that pulled the Tigers to within 61-58. After Steve Woodberry answered with a basket before Booker fired in another three, then a long two-pointer from the corner.

The one-man lightning burst tied the game 63-63. And although nearly 7 minutes still remained, the feeling permeated the big barn that, on this day, Missouri just wouldn't be denied.

"This one was special," Tigers Coach Norm Stewart said. "We dug ourselves a hole, and everyone had a part in getting us out. The determination was tremendous."

"I felt it was somebody's job to step up. I'm a senior, so that's what I wanted to do."
— Melvin Booker

Determination, grit, moxie – choose any appropriate intangible – allowed Kansas to hang with the Tigers until the final minute. Not at full strength because of injuries, the Jayhawks mustered an answering salvo after falling into a 37-28 hole late in the first half.

KU just didn't have enough to trade punches for 40 minutes against an opponent on pace to become the Big Eight's first undefeated regular-season champion in 23 years.

Kelly Thames before Booker put the Tigers ahead to stay at 72-69 with a 22-footer from the left side with 2:20 remaining.

"He's a great player who proved himself (Sunday)," said Vaughn, who had a career-high 21 points in a losing effort. "In the crucial part of the game, when they needed buckets, he hit three shots in a row. And I was right there in his face."

Missouri, ranked No. 12 at the beginning of last week, should crack The Associated Press' top 10 today. The Tigers are 20-2 overall and 11-0 in the Big Eight Conference. The Tigers can clinch sole possession of the regular-season title with one more victory, or if Oklahoma

State loses one of its last four games.

The Jayhawks, ranked fourth, fell to 21-5 and 6-4.

"Maybe we'll get a little more respect now," Booker said. "We came to Allen Field House and won. But we really don't like much of the national attention. We want to lie low and let everyone wonder about this Missouri team."

That might be hard to do now. The Tigers exhibited a cool-hand approach in handling the usual packed throng of 15,800 at Allen Field House. Even while trailing 61-53 after Sean Pearson rammed home a long three-pointer with 8:53 left, Missouri never blinked.

RIVALS!
MU VS. KU

MU: 81
KU: 74

BASKETBALL
FEBRUARY 20, 1994

FROM THE KANSAS CITY STAR, 1994

BARRAGE PIERCES KANSAS' ARMOR

BOOKER'S HOT HAND HANGS LOSS ON JAYHAWKS

BY BLAIR KERKHOFF
STAFF WRITER

LAWRENCE — When an opponent lights up the Jayhawks for at least 30 points, it often means a Kansas victory. Of the last 15 opponents before Sunday that featured a 30-point scorer, 13 lost.

Melvin Booker and Missouri bucked the trend Sunday. The Jayhawks were powerless to stop Booker, the Tigers' senior point guard, in the final $8^1/_2$ minutes of Missouri's 81-74 victory at Allen Field House.

"Melvin Booker was sensational," Kansas Coach Roy Williams said. "All those recruiting experts, it shows how much those guys know. Out of high school he wasn't highly recruited, but he's passed up just about every guard in college basketball right now."

Booker, who finished with 32 points – 24 in the second half and 17 in the final 81/2 minutes – became the first player since Colorado's Stevie Wise in 1991 to score at least 30 on the Jayhawks in a winning effort.

"The toughest thing about Melvin is he can shoot and he can drive," Kansas point guard Calvin Rayford said. "When a player has two weapons like that you have to respect them both, and that makes it tough."

When it mattered most, Booker bombed away. Kansas appeared to catch a huge break when a three-point try by Missouri's Paul O'Liney went in and came out, and the Jayhawks' Sean Pearson connected for three at the other end. That gave Kansas a 61-53 lead with 8:53 remaining.

> "The toughest thing about Melvin is he can shoot and he can drive. When a player has two weapons like that you have to respect them both, and that makes it tough."
>
> – Kansas point guard Calvin Rayford

Booker assumed control innocently enough, with two free throws at the 8:26 mark. But in a 65-second stretch, he knocked in two three-pointers and an 18-footer that tied the game 63-63.

With the score tied 69-69, Booker struck again, this time with a three-pointer against the Jayhawks' 1-3-1 zone defense. Booker slipped in, stroked it home with 2 minutes to play and Missouri never lost the lead.

"We were trying to throw him out of rhythm because he had hit the three-pointers and the shot in front of our bench," Williams said. "But we had played that zone two or three

times in a row and he had found a little more comfortable feel against it.

"But if we run the defense properly he shouldn't be able to take the shot from there. That was a big-time hoop."

Even a Booker mistake turned into gold for Missouri. With the Tigers clinging to a 72-71 lead inside a minute, Booker drove and found himself in the air with his back to the basket. He tossed up a wild shot that was blocked by Kansas' Scot Pollard.

The ball caromed into the hands of Jevon Crudup, who laid it in and was fouled by Pollard. The three-point play gave the Tigers a four-point lead, and the Jayhawks never had the ball with a chance to tie.

"We converged on Melvin, then Jevon made a heck of a play," Williams said. "Seniors have a way of doing that."

THE ANTLERS

Every school has fans. Every school has its own brand of unique fans. In the Kansas-Missouri rivalry, the best-known fans are "the Antlers," the group of students at Missouri who heckle the visiting teams.

Kansas players, coaches and fans all have their opinions of the Antlers. Tom Hedrick, who broadcasted KU games for 17 years found a great way to get them off his back.

"One time I went to the game and the Antlers were already in their seats," Hedrick said. "They decided that I would be their target that night. So they called out to me, 'Hey, Tom Heartache.' I knew that it would be a long night, so I had to act quickly.

"I launched into my best Harry Caray imitation and said, 'Holy Cow, I haven't seen Tom Hedrick. I don't think he's going to be here tonight. I'm Harry Caray and I'm filling in for him on KU radio tonight.' Apparently they believed me, because they didn't harass me again that night."

The Antlers sometimes got carried away with their taunts and actions. The language often was colorful, and no one was safe from their attacks. Their behavior got so bad in 1995, it caused then-Mizzou athletics director Joe Castiglione to ban them from their seats right behind the visitors' bench. Finally, he relented and they were able to return to the arena, just in a "less-threatening" location.

Here's how the story appeared in the December 10, 1995, Star:

Larry Brown, who coached Kansas from 1983 through 1988, sported a gift he received from the Antlers.

208

ANTLERS ARE BACK

By MIKE DEARMOND
STAFF WRITER
AND JOANNA STAMMAN
MU CORRESPONDENT

The Antlers were back Saturday night for Missouri's game against Jackson State.

Missouri's vociferous jeer group lost its preferred seating and official recognition from the school for the current school year because of previous antics, but its members found good seats anyway.

"They are just like any other students," Missouri Athletic Director Joe Castiglione said. "They bought those tickets."

They weren't at courtside, as they used to be. But they were about 20 rows off it (one group of about 20) and 10 rows off it (another group of five).

Black shirts, gold Antler emblems, sarcasm and all.

"The ref is a doorknob," they screamed as another whistle blew with 16 minutes, 13 seconds left in the first half.

Best Antler cheer? "Brock Olivo, Brock Olivo," they called when the game got particularly physical.

Olivo, seated on the front row, just off where The Antlers used to sit, declined to acknowledge the recognition.

The basketball players were happy to see the Antlers back.

"My boys were in town," Julian Winfield said. "I like that. I was happy to see them back. That's one thing I think about on a road trip when they heckle us. In the back of my mind, I think that they have to come back and deal with the Antlers."

So you're disappointed they don't have their usual seats?

"No," Winfield said. "I'm glad that they are back. You're not getting me in trouble with Big Joe (Castiglione)."

GRRRREAT GAME!

Missouri had one more answer than question and prevailed in two overtimes over top-ranked Kansas. Corey Tate hit a bucket with 5.6 seconds left to give Missouri the lead in the second overtime. This lead finally stood up, as Kansas' final attempt was no good.

Raef LaFrentz had a big play at the end of regulation, and Tate and Jason Sutherland came up big in both overtimes.

With Missouri up three with a little more than 10 seconds left, the Tigers chose to foul Jacque Vaughn before he could get to the front court and put up a shot. Vaughn made the first free throw, then intentionally missed the second. LaFrentz grabbed the rebound and put the follow shot in to tie the score.

"Raef pushed (Derek) Grimm in the back and got the rebound," former Missouri coach Norm Stewart said. "After the game, he told me that he got away with one."

LaFrentz didn't admit that to the official and his basket counted. In the first overtime, Tate hit two free throws with 10 seconds left to send it to the second OT. Sutherland had a big three in the first overtime, and then did the same with the Tigers down three in the second extra session.

As the Tigers prepared for the game-winning shot, Vaughn knocked the ball away from Tyron Lee. Tate picked it up and made a 16-footer for the win.

Here's how it appeared in the February 5, 1997, Star:

TIGERS TRIUMPH, END KU'S SHOT AT PERFECT SEASON

BY BLAIR KERKHOFF

Columbia, Mo.,

The new Kansas streak is one. Loss.

Missouri forward Corey Tate ended a classic game in one of college basketball's most-storied rivalries by rattling in a 16-footer with 5.6 seconds left, giving the Tigers a 96-94 two-overtime victory over the top-ranked Jayhawks on Tuesday night.

Opportunity set up the winning shot. Kansas appeared to have come up with a steal when Jacque Vaughn knocked the ball away from Tyron Lee. The ball dribbled to Tate, who snatched it up and made the jumper.

Kansas had time left to salvage the game, but it didn't get off a shot. The Tigers forced Jerod Haase up the right sideline. Instead of attempting an off-balance shot, Haase fed it to Raef LaFrentz, whose jumper from inside the three-point line would not have counted had it gone in.

Kansas, 22-1, was the last of the unbeatens. Now it faces a journey to sixth-ranked Iowa State on Sunday to avoid successive losses for the first time in four years.

"22-1, that's not bad," LaFrentz said. "A loss had to happen sometime."

That it came at Columbia should come as no shock. Upset? The records and rankings may suggest it, but the Tigers, 12-10, have developed a habit of knocking off high-flying Jayhawks. Kansas fell here as a third-ranked team a year ago, and Missouri twice defeated a No. 1-ranked KU team in 1990.

No 39-0 for Kansas.

"I knew it was unrealistic, and it wasn't going to happen," KU coach Roy Williams said.

RIVALS!
MU VS. KU

MU: 96
KU: 94

BASKETBALL
FEBRUARY 4, 1997

After blowing a golden opportunity to win in regulation, Missouri coach Norm Stewart was just looking for more time.

"After the first (overtime), I just said, 'Get it to the second one and you'll win,'" Stewart said.

Now the Tigers - get this - have a chance to derail the nation's second-ranked team. Wake Forest comes calling Sunday. The Tigers in the polls? NCAA Tournament consideration?

Let them savor this one first. Both sides had their heroes and opportunities to win. For the Tigers, it was Tate and Jason Sutherland. Tate's two free throws with 10 seconds left in the first overtime ensured a second.

Sutherland, who didn't start for the second straight game, came up with huge three-pointers in each overtime. With Kansas leading 89-86 with 2:42 remaining in the second overtime, Sutherland was trapped in the right corner. Double-teamed. Nowhere to pass. But his off-balance three-pointer swished through, and the game's momentum changed.

"We had a hand in his face," Haase said. "When you hit a shot like that you're destined to win the game."

Sutherland's three-pointer in the first overtime also erased a three-point lead. No team led by more than three in the final 10 minutes of regulation and in either extra period.

For the second straight game, LaFrentz was a monster in the overtimes, scoring 12 of his 26 points. Saturday against Nebraska, LaFrentz scored 11 of the Jayhawks' 22 in overtime. And it was LaFrentz who came up big at the end of regulation, when the Tigers failed to put it away.

With Missouri leading 70-68 with 13.5 seconds left, Derek Grimm, an 85-percent shooter from the line, missed the first of two. He dropped in the second, and guard Dibi Ray did the right thing by fouling Vaughn.

MU led by three. Vaughn was shooting two. He made one. Vaughn then intentionally missed the second. LaFrentz was there to grab the rebound for the stick-back and a 71-71 score with 7 seconds left.

The Tigers pushed it up court and got a decent look, but Ray's jumper from just inside the three-point arc banged off the back of the rim and Kansas had made it to overtime.

"I thought after regulation, that was the toughest hill we had to climb because we had the game won," Stewart said. "It could have been curtains."

Kansas and Missouri scored on every possession of the first overtime except for the Tigers' first and the Jayhawks' last.

Missouri made all 12 free throws in the first extra period, the final two dropped in by Tate with 10 seconds left, making it 86-86.

Vaughn then took his time working the ball up court. The play was his to make. He pulled up for a contested 17-footer and it banged off the side, sending the game into the second extra period.

The Tigers won because they played to their strengths and even to one of the Jayhawks'. MU made 30 of 34 free throws and outrebounded the Big 12's top board team 43-37.

Paul Pierce, who entered the game with a 15.2-point average, fouled out in regulation with four points. That left the Jayhawks without two starters as Pierce joined injured starting center Scot Pollard on the bench.

FROM THE KANSAS CITY STAR, 1997

MISSOURI LOVES
ESPECIALLY IF THE

BY JASON WHITLOCK

COLUMBIA- So much for college basketball's greatest border war opening the Big 12 era with a whimper.

Missouri's Tigers, a team in apparent disarray, took America's only undefeated Division I team, Kansas, into two overtimes Tuesday night and won 96-94, adding yet another thrilling chapter to Kansas vs. Missouri and engineering perhaps the greatest upset in this series.

Missouri's Corey Tate decided the outcome with a basket with 5 seconds to play. Tate's bucket ended a game that Missouri should have won in regulation, but Derek Grimm, an 85 percent free-throw shooter, misfired on two of four free throws at the end of regulation.

That allowed Kansas to tie the game with a Jacque Vaughn free throw and a Raef LaFrentz rebound basket in the final seconds of regulation.

It appeared that Kansas had dodged yet another upset bid. The Jayhawks had to go overtime to subdue Nebraska on Saturday. This time they didn't have the answers.

The Tigers entered with an abysmal 11-10 record compared with Kansas' perfect 22-0.

Nothing seems to bring out the best in Missouri and its legendary coach, Norm Stewart, more than coach Roy Williams' Jayhawks. Last year the Jayhawks visited the Hearnes Center with a nearly spotless record, 19-1, only to fall to the Tigers 77-73.

A boisterous, sellout crowd and solid play from its three best players - Grimm, Kelly Thames and Jason Sutherland - keyed Missouri's upset.

Grimm, Thames and Sutherland weren't big factors in Missouri's Saturday victory over Kansas State. Stewart had no idea whether they would be ready to handle the challenge of playing No. 1 Kansas.

But Grimm scored Missouri's first eight points, hitting two three-pointers

three-pointers. He finished the game with 18 points. His fallaway, baseline three-pointer that tied the score at 89-89 in the second overtime should become a part of Missouri lore.

Call Sutherland dirty all you want, but at crunch time, call him the coolest, most fearless player in college basketball.

The Tigers still have no chance of being selected for the NCAA Tournament. But it was nice for a night to see them play up to their potential. It makes you wonder, however, why over the last two seasons that Stewart has inspired the Tigers to play this well only against Kansas.

Missouri fans celebrated wildly Tuesday night. If I were them, I'd be mad. Why do they only get to see the

Nothing seems to bring out the best in Missouri and its legendary coach, Norm Stewart, more than coach Roy Williams' Jayhawks. Last year the Jayhawks visited the Hearnes Center with a nearly spotless record, 19-1, only to fall to the Tigers 77-73.

and a layup. Thames scored 24 points and marvelously defended Kansas' Raef LaFrentz, who scored 12 of his 26 points in the overtime sessions.

Sutherland, who has been in Stewart's doghouse, carried the Tigers in overtime, nailing a couple of crucial

Tigers play hard and smart once a year, when Kansas visits Columbia?

That's the question Norm Stewart should be asked during March when the Jayhawks are in the NCAA Tournament and the Tigers are sitting at home.

RIVALS!
MU VS. KU

MU: 96
KU:94

BASKETBALL
FEBRUARY 4, 1997

COMPANY, VISITOR IS KU

As for Kansas?

The burden of perfection may have been too great.

The Associated Press' No. 1 team for 10 consecutive weeks, the team with more depth and more talent than any other in college basketball, might be crumbling under the weight of perfection.

Kansas' poor play lately can't all be attributed to senior center Scot Pollard's injury.

The Jayhawks are out of sync, and it doesn't have to do with Jacque Vaughn's play. Vaughn was terrific during the second half of Tuesday's game. He hit important shots and found teammates open for good looks.

Williams might need to consider going to his three-guard lineup full time. B.J. Williams, Pollard's replacement, is struggling as a starter. The Jayhawks are a better team when Vaughn, Jerod Haase and Billy Thomas or Ryan Robertson are on the court together. The Jayhawks get more easy, fast-break baskets with that lineup, and Vaughn is effective at finding Haase, Thomas and Robertson for open three-point shots.

Roy Williams once again felt heartbreak at the hands of the Tigers.

SUTHERLAND WINDS DOWN MU CAREER

When it comes right down to it, there was nothing that different about Jason Sutherland. He was a hard-nosed player, not afraid to dive for a loose ball or make the hard foul to prevent an easy layup.

But if you ask Kansas fans, the dirtiest player in college basketball history is one Jason Sutherland. They talk about hard fouls on Jerod Haase. They talk about the things they like in their own players.

Sutherland was part of Norm Stewart's Tigers from 1993-97. He was in the top 30 in career scoring for the Tigers, including third all-time in three-point field goals made and fourth in three-point field-goal percentage. He's second in career free-throw percentage, trailing only Jon Sundvold. But the stats don't tell the story of Sutherland. He would do anything—anything—to help his team win. Including toeing the line on being too aggressive.

The story chosen could have been about any number of players. Both sides had players fans loved to love or hate, depending on the name on the front of his jersey. But Sutherland seems to be the poster child for antagonism. As his career was drawing to a close in 1997, Mike DeArmond painted the picture of the oft-misunderstood Missouri star.

Here's how it appeared in the March 5, 1997, Star:

TIGERS GUARD HAS COME UNDER FIRE FOR HIS STYLE OF PLAY

BY MIKE DEARMOND
STAFF WRITER

Norm Stewart has called it bizarre and biased. Now he's calling the perception of the Last Days of Jason Sutherland "mishandled."

Stewart blames many for making Sutherland's style of play one of the most cussed and discussed matters of the Big 12 season. Sutherland, he said, has been mishandled.

"By officials," said Stewart, who today will bring his Missouri Tigers to Kansas City for the start of all the hoopla surrounding the first Big 12 tournament.

"By some of the coaches. I think the press has had their share of it, too. And certainly we haven't done a good job."

If Marc Antony noted in his last goodbye that he came not to praise Caesar, it's probably not the proper place or time to either praise or bury a mere college basketball player. Even one who is one of the prime entries in the annals of Big Eight and Big 12 controversy.

Sutherland is skittering from the limelight these days. But catch him if you can, and the words tumbling out of his mouth are both what you might expect and a surprise.

"I don't really care what people think," said Sutherland, chin thrust out. "If they don't like me for how I am? I don't care. Honestly."

Only there is a part of the Ultimate Tiger that would like to explain - to Jayhawks, to Cowboys, to Cornhuskers, to Cyclones, to referees - just what it has been like these last four seasons.

"I kind of would," he admitted. "But it doesn't matter. It's kind of too late now."

On the best of days, Jason Sutherland is everything a coach could want, and not just a coach like Stewart.

Missouri was dead against Colorado when Sutherland threw in seven unanswered points, pulling the Tigers into a contention they had no right to enjoy and from which they ultimately fell.

Sutherland is one of three current Tigers to score 1,000 career points. He has tied Melvin Booker's career mark for three-pointers at Missouri. In all games this season, he leads all Big 12 players in free-throw percentage at .862.

And yet last Saturday's game at Kansas State turned on a technical called against Sutherland, an occurrence that Stewart and Jason's father, Jim, contend has become all too common.

"They've become vindictive toward Jason," Jim Sutherland charged of game officials.

In Missouri's game against Texas Tech last week, Jim Sutherland alleged, one referee shoved a basketball into Jason's stomach as he took the line to shoot a free throw. When Jason asked about the hard handoff, Jim Sutherland said, the official allegedly said: "Shut up and shoot your free throws."

nical foul regardless of the circumstances.

And that, for a while, threatened to put Jason between the rock of his father and the hard place of his basketball coach. "As far as criticism, if the reader thinks it's criticism, so be it," Jim Sutherland said at one point several weeks ago. "I'm his father. I have a right to feel the way I feel."

For his part, Stewart has attempted to treat Jason Sutherland no differently from the way he does his other players.

Sutherland was always in the middle of the battles with the Jayhawks.

Stewart's loyalty to Sutherland does not prevent him from taking the view from the other side of the fence.

"There are some things about the game and some other things that I would like him to complete and understand before his senior year is over," Stewart said recently. "It's been a mystery to me why we haven't been able to get it done."

Jim Sutherland has been upset by Stewart's propensity to pull Jason after a hard foul or an intentional foul or a tech-

"My feeling is," Stewart said, "if the ballplayer is performing or is playing, then I'm going to play him. All that other doesn't bother me."

Soon, it will be over. Missouri's next loss is the last time Jason Sutherland will wear a Tigers uniform. It will be the last time, in a collegiate arena, he will hear the boos of his detractors. Or the roar of those who are behind him.

BLACK AND GOLD SUNDAY

There were rumors, for sure. But no one knew for sure whether the Tigers' trip to Lawrence in January 1999 would be Coach Norm Stewart's last game against Kansas.

The two teams had played 13 days earlier in Columbia and the Jayhawks won 73-61. Amid the swirling controversy over Stewart's status, the Tigers had to face the 19th ranked Jayhawks at Allen Fieldhouse, where they hadn't lost a conference game since the Missouri game five years earlier. In fact, the Jayhawks had lost a total of four conference games—other than to Missouri—since that game in February 1994.

So what's the problem?

Freshman Keyon Dooling scored 15 points to lead the Tigers to a 71-63 victory. Scrappy guard Brian Grawer led the Tigers with 18 points. Albert White also had 15 and Jeff Hafer had 11.

The Tigers opened up a big lead in the first half and led by 14 points three times before Kansas cut the lead to 39-30 at halftime. The Jayhawks kept chipping and got to within one point at the 2:01 mark, but they never could tie it or take the lead.

Stewart left Allen Fieldhouse a winner, just like he had been in his first trip, an 85-78 victory in the first MU-KU game at Allen when Stewart was a player in 1956.

"I certainly had my detractors by then," Stewart said looking back. "But my guys played extremely well and we won. It's a good final memory from there."

Here's how it appeared in the January 25, 1999, Star:

TIGERS SHOW THEY HAVEN'T LOST KNACK AGAINST KU

By MIKE DEARMOND
THE KANSAS CITY *STAR*

Lawrence, Kas.,

Keyon Dooling and Missouri, seemingly poised like Humpty Dumpty on that storied wall, gathered themselves out of chaos Sunday and beat No. 19 Kansas 71-63.

They did what no other team had ever done in the Big 12, what no other team in the Big Eight had done since Missouri last did it in the Tigers' season of league perfection on Feb. 20, 1994.

Beat Kansas. At Allen Fieldhouse. Ended the Jayhawks' 35-0 home run against all conference comers.

"The last couple of years," said a beaming Missouri coach Norm Stewart, "we're the only ballclub that's been able to beat 'em."

Both times that came in Columbia, where Kansas just two weeks ago throttled the Tigers 73-61, putting an improbable cast on Missouri's ability to return the favor at a place where the Jayhawks had won 66 of 67 games since Missouri's '94 triumph.

"I thought coming over here today," Stewart said, "if we can't beat 'em, who's going to beat 'em?"

Missouri had larger concerns, of course, than KU's inhospitable home.

The Tigers, just a week ago Saturday, collapsed at Colorado, where freshman sensation Dooling finished the game in tears at the end of the bench during a 19-point loss.

The Tigers' concern was real enough that MU's Albert White said Sunday's nationally televised game was nothing less than an opportunity "to see whether we're going to crack or not."

The Tigers didn't. And certainly Dooling didn't, turning in a 30-minute, 15-point, three-block testimony to toughness. He didn't start. But he finished. He wasn't allowed to talk to reporters. But if his game didn't say it all, then the reaction of others did.

"Keyon is extremely gifted," KU coach Roy Williams said, "He's as talented as any freshman guard who's come into this league in a long time."

ROY'S IMPACT

Keyon Dooling extended himself for 30 minutes, with 15 points and three blocks in Norm Stewart's final game in Lawrence.

Teammate Jeff Hafer said: "Keyon is a spectacular player. He does things most people are in awe of. So when you're a competitor and you have his ability, you're going to come back.

"Keyon can step up at big times. You all saw the baseline shot he hit late in the game. That's one of the best shots I've ever seen, over (KU center Eric) Chenowith. It's just purely something you can't teach and you can't practice."

The shot in question was, without question, a huge one for Missouri, which was led by Brian Grawer's 18 points. Dooling and White's 15 each and Hafer's 11.

The Tigers led by 14 points three times in the first half. Kansas began to

rally near the end of that half, which ended with MU up 39-30. Chenowith's two free throws pulled the Jayhawks to 59-57 with 4:11 to play.

Dooling beat fellow freshman Jeff Boschee off the dribble left and then floated a baseline jump shot high over Chenowith, giving the Tigers a 61-57 edge with 3:45 to play.

KU's Ryan Robertson, who missed his first nine shots, came up big with a rebound and follow for his only basket of the night, pulling KU within 61-59.

When Nick Bradford drove the right side for a basket, KU pulled within 62-61 with only 2:01 to play.

A give-and-go – with Hafer giving and going and then scoring on a pass

from White – put Missouri up 64-61 with 93 seconds left.

White slammed home a basket with 54 seconds left.

Dooling hit a free throw with 32.4 seconds left. Grawer canned two more with 16.8 to play and Hafer the final two free throws with 1.1 seconds to go in an emptying field house as MU dropped the first Big 12 defeat of the year on now 13-5 (overall) and 5-1 (in the league) Kansas.

Missouri improved to 13-4 and, more important, recovered to 4-2 in the league, only one game behind Kansas.

"Probably some teams thought they could beat us because we'd lost a couple," said White, who added seven

CHAPTER NINE

rebounds and three assists despite playing just 21 minutes because of foul trouble.

"This definitely says a lot. Because not even the best teams in the country can come in here and win very often."

Missouri's defense, AWOL two games running, was back with a vengeance.

"We felt we needed to pick the ball up in transition," Hafer said, noting the emphasis on stopping Robertson and Boschee before the KU guards could get much of anything going.

"We didn't want them to get a lot of easy buckets, which is notorious for KU basketball. Regardless of whether you score or not, they're going to push it right back down your throat. What

we wanted to do was stop their transition, about a stride and a half outside the three-line."

"It's all about coming back and regrouping. Tonight he showed his toughness."

— Albert White about Keyon Dooling

That opened up things for T. J. Pugh, who came off the KU bench and scored 13 points.

But Boschee and Robertson finished a combined five of 21 for 13 points. And Chenowith, despite 13

rebounds to key a 46-32 KU edge in that department, made just five of 16 shots on the way to 13 points.

Ultimately, Missouri won for the same reasons KU won two weeks ago. Guard play, intensity, poise under pressure.

The shoe fit a lot of Tigers on Sunday, but none any better than Dooling.

"It's all about coming back and regrouping," White said about Dooling. "Tonight he showed his toughness."

Williams said: "I don't think Norm will be getting any calls on his call-in show about Keyon Dooling this week, except praise for him."

FROM THE KANSAS CITY STAR, 1999

WHAT NEVER CHANGES? DEATH, TAXES... NORM

JOE POSNANSKI

LAWRENCE — People pop up all over the place these days and say Norm Stewart is behind the times, to which you have to respond: Well, of course he's behind the times. Geez, the man has been behind the times for 38 years, ever since he started coaching at Northern Iowa, back in the Kennedy/Camelot days.

Norm Stewart is 64, but really he dates to biblical times, you know, floods, plagues, miracles, that sort of thing. He was never in style. But he keeps on going, doesn't he, keeps on going, keeps on laughing, keeps on beating Roy Williams and Kansas once a year.

Take this Keyon Dooling thing. Dooling, a freshman, is the hottest high school recruit to come to Missouri in a decade.

He's a bright Parade All-America kid from Florida who

has this grace about him, an easy flow to his game. He's one of those guys you watch warm up and say "Now, that's a superstar." He's also one of these modern kids, the kind that Stewart can't relate to anymore.

Well, a week ago, Stewart yanked Dooling from the game against Colorado, screamed at him, ripped him, the whole shebang. Apparently, Dooling was very upset, maybe he cried, maybe he didn't, and supposedly he yelled something at Stewart which sounded like "I want to win, too, but I can't play for you."

Oh, boy. Everybody flipped out. You know what everybody said about Stewart. He can't communicate with the players anymore. He's too mean and tough for the kids of today. He's a dinosaur. Rumors swirled that Dooling would transfer. Missouri tried to patch up things with a news-release statement from Dooling ("Everything is fine!" the release/Dooling said), but nobody was convinced. People

MU: 71
KU:63

BASKETBALL
JANUARY 24, 1999

RIVALS!
MU VS. KU

worried that Missouri would lose Dooling, this incredible young player, all because Norm had lost touch. The talk-radio lines burned.

So, what happened Sunday? Keyon Dooling played brilliantly. Missouri beat Kansas 71-63, and there was Norm Stewart afterward, deadpanning away when someone asked him whether this was a crucial victory.

"Oh, yeah," he said, with that straight-man look. "I was really worried about my job before this."

Dooling was fabulous. Sure, he scored 15 points, handed out a couple of assists, blocked three shots, all those things, but more he controlled the game with his slashing, his patience, his presence. One play, he moved the ball from one hand to the other while he dangled in the air. On another, he stripped the ball away from Kansas' Ryan Robertson and dunked.

On another, he drove the baseline, started to shoot, saw Kansas' Eric Chenowith closing in and instead lofted this high, arching shot that hopped over Chenowith's hand and plopped into the basket.

Most of all, though, in the middle of the Allen Fieldhouse mayhem Sunday, as the boos hissed, as the Kansas players flurried around him, Dooling held up his hand and motioned to his teammates, as if to say "Hey, relax. It's all under control, baby. It's all under control.

"He's a great point guard," said Kansas' own freshman point guard, Jeff Boschee. "They look a lot more fluid when he's out there controlling

things."

Yes, he's a brilliant talent, but he also decided to play at Missouri. That means he decided to play for Norm Stewart. It's not as if Stewart just showed up in Columbia. You would think, after 31 years of Show-Me Rants, players would understand that Stewart is not just going through some phase.

coached a heck of a ballgame, his kids played a heck of a ballgame, and when it all ended and he was asked about Dooling, he said, as Norm always says, "I thought all of our guys played well, including Keyon."

Then, Dooling had his say also. There are still rumors that he's unhappy, but then freshmen often are unhappy. He can do incredible things at

---

Stewart is what he has always been: He's angry and intense and sarcastic and funny and a little bit crazy and bigger than life. He hasn't changed one bit. What he did to Keyon Dooling he had done 10 billion times before to 10 billion different players, and as long as he's coaching, he will keep on benching kids and screaming at them. Some times, you don't like it. I don't like it, players don't like it, but none of that matters.

No, Stewart is what he has always been: He's angry and intense and sarcastic and funny and a little bit crazy and bigger than life. He hasn't changed one bit. What he did to Keyon Dooling he had done 10 billion times before to 10 billion different players, and as long as he's coaching, he will keep on benching kids and screaming at them. Some times, you don't like it. I don't like it, players don't like it, but none of that matters. Do we complain about erosion? Forget about it. The world changes. Norm Stewart does not.

Stewart had his say on Sunday. He did not start Dooling at the beginning of the game or the start of the second half. He did not let Dooling speak to reporters after the game. He

Missouri if he wants. He played 30 minutes Sunday, and he played wonderfully, patiently – when he's playing well. Missouri might be the best team in the Big 12 – and, heck, he might even have made an impression on Stewart. Apparently, after the Colorado fiasco, the players returned to practice Tuesday, and Stewart started them off with a dunk contest. A dunk contest!

"Yeah, I think it reminded all of us to have a little fun," Missouri's Jeff Hafer said. See? Norm's fun. He's playful. He's the modern-day Norm.

"Of course," Hafer continued, "he worked us like dogs the rest of the week."

The Mighty Quin

NO NORMAL GAME

It didn't seem possible that Norm Stewart would not be stalking the sideline, especially for a game against the hated Jayhawks—"that team to the west"—according to Stewart.

But Stewart's "retirement" after 32 years meant that Quin Snyder would lead the Tigers against the Jayhawks. Snyder certainly understood the concept of intense rivalries, having played and coached for Duke in their twice-yearly confrontations with North Carolina—ironically Kansas coach Roy Williams' alma mater.

But for fans in these two states, there is no better or more intense rivalry than Kansas vs. Missouri. As the teams prepared to face off January 22, 2000, for the first time in Snyder's coaching career, The Star's Mike DeArmond took a look at what awaited the dapper Mr. Snyder.

Here's how it appeared in the January 22, 2000, Star:

MISSOURI'S SNYDER GETS HIS SHOT AT BORDER WAR

BY MIKE DEARMOND

Columbia

Kansas coach Roy Williams understands that at noon today at the Hearnes Center, it will be different from his previous 23 games on the sideline against Missouri.

For the first time in Williams' coaching career, Norm Stewart won't be taking that let's-get-it-on crouch along the MU bench as the Tigers prepare to face Kansas.

Thirty-two seasons of Stormin' Norman have given way to the first season of 33-year-old Quin Snyder.

"It's a different program now, and Quin is putting his identity all over it," said Williams, who battled to a 13-10 edge in his often-legendary meetings with Stewart. "With each and every passing year, we'll still remember what Norm did and his accomplishments, but with each time that you play them that goes in the background more and more."

Still, it will seem strange without Stewart, won't it? Williams says the MU-KU affair didn't clutch his heart until his third season at Kansas, when the Jayhawks finally beat the Tigers after four straight losses.

"I don't think any coach appreciates

it or understands it early," he said. "I think Norm did because he had been involved with it as a player. I don't think that I did initially, and I don't think Quin will."

There is the first point of contention between Williams and Snyder, the kind of "don't-tell-me-how-I'll-feel" that Stewart used to build into the cause for holy war.

"I sense that everyone wants to believe that I don't get it," Snyder said.

"I get it."

Indeed, Snyder's players don't notice a drop-off in intensity on the sideline this season. The Stewart crouch

Quin Snyder had no idea of the intensity between the basketball programs at Kansas and Missouri until he experienced it.

has simply given way to the Snyder prowl.

"Coach Snyder is one of the most competitive people I've ever been around my whole life," MU senior Jeff Hafer said. "One of the most fiery people.

"You can almost tap into him. We're going to feed off of him, and he's going to feed off of us in this game. We're going to be ready to play."

We know how this all got started. Missouri and Kansas go by the nicknames hung upon them during the Civil War. Jayhawker was an epithet to Missourians, a source of pride for folks around Lawrence after the town rebuilt follow-

ing the raid led by William C. Quantrill as the head of Missouri border ruffians.

The Tiger was selected as the University of Missouri mascot in 1890, in honor of an armed guard of Columbia irregulars who protected the town against Kansas-based marauders during the Civil War.

And there's always been something to fight about. This year, it's the battle over whether MU's Kareem Rush - who is still on suspension - was punished fairly by the NCAA compared with KU's Lester Earl, who escaped NCAA sanction because he essentially turned state's evidence against his old school, LSU.

THEN THERE WAS LAST YEAR

On Jan. 11, then-No. 15 Kansas swarmed over a 12-2 Missouri team like so many killer bees in Columbia. MU hit 16 percent of its shots in the first half, was down 17 points at halftime and scratched back within six with 4:37 to play.

But KU, behind Ryan Robertson's 17 points and Eric Chenowith's 13 rebounds, won 73-61. Then, as far as MU fans are concerned, the Jayhawks rubbed it in.

Robertson, the St. Charles, Mo., kid who spurned MU for KU, jived along the sideline in payback for every boo Tigers fans had rained down upon him. Chenowith joined in, holding the "Kansas" emblazoned on his jersey out for every Tiger fan to see.

"I remember that," Hafer said. "They were at midcourt, yelling up at our fans. They were excited that they had won here; they finally got one."

This week, Chenowith attempted to downplay that bit of in-your-face.

"I think that got exaggerated," Chenowith said. "I was just going to go hug Ryan and run off the court. That was it. Before I knew it, the whole team was over there, and coach Williams was showing off his 20-foot sprint in getting over there, breaking it up. It just got out of hand."

Then 13 days later, on Jan. 24, Hafer and the Tigers reacted in completely opposite fashion after a 71-63 upset of No. 19 Kansas, the first league loss at home for the Jayhawks in 35 games.

"We remembered that when we went down there," Hafer said. "We won down there and did our celebrating in the locker room. We've won games before. We had just won another one."

Incidentally, Hafer said the private celebration wasn't done on the instruction of Stewart.

"If anybody had wanted to stick it to 'em," he said, "it would have been coach Stewart."

MU was 33-41 vs. KU in Stewart's tenure as coach - he missed a Feb. 11, 1989, Tigers victory over the Jayhawks when he was battling colon cancer.

Stewart – a Missouri native and former Tigers player who was so deeply steeped in the tradition of the Border War that he often couldn't bring himself to refer to KU as more than "that team to the west" - personally stoked the flames of the rivalry.

Owens wasn't the only KU coach whose skin Stewart could get under.

In one of the nicer things he ever said about Stewart, Williams once offered: "He doesn't care what anybody else thinks." Mutual admiration

Williams and Snyder, meanwhile, have begun their coaching relationship civilly.

"You've got to be yourself, and Quin has already shown that he's doing that," Williams said. "He looks very confident in what he's doing. ... He's going to do very well."

Neither coach makes much of a popular sidebar to this Midwestern transformation of an old North Carolina-Duke rivalry. Williams was an assistant coach for the Tar Heels and Snyder a player and assistant for the Blue Devils.

Snyder said of North Carolina-Duke: "It's like the Missouri-KU rivalry. It's big."

Lee Rashman, who's 24 and came with Snyder from Duke to be his director of basketball operations, is one of the newcomers to the MU-KU rivalry who seems to have the best handle on what this really means.

"I've already heard," Rashman said. "It's nastier than Duke-Carolina."

Always has been. And even without Norm Stewart, maybe it always will be.

KU WANTS TO BEAT MU BECAUSE...

1. It will keep the Jayhawks in first place.
2. ABC-TV is here, and the nation is watching.
3. Coach Floppy Locks needs to know who's boss in this rivalry.
4. Former Jayhawk Ryan Robertson wants to give all of his kind supporters in Columbia a belated Christmas gift.
5. It will silence the Antlers the way a pop quiz does.
6. The Jayhawks want to follow up on that 21-0 victory in football.
7. That Quantrill guy. Still owe him.
8. Norm. Still.
9. Border War bragging rights. Nothing better for fans.
10. The Jayhawks are ranked No. 7. They should win.

- Bob Dutton

GAME FOR ANYTHING

FOR THE SAKE OF THEIR TEAM, BIG 12 FANS RESORT TO ALL KINDS OF INTERESTING STRATEGIES WORTH SCREAMING ABOUT

As the Big XII Conference prepared for its post-season basketball tournament in 2001, Ivan Carter took a whimsical look at some of the more notorious fans of Big XII schools.

Here's how it appeared in the March 8, 2001, Star:

BY IVAN CARTER

When teams roll into Kemper Arena for this week's Big 12 men's basketball tournament, their players will be sporting game faces.

And so will their fans.

With bragging rights, a conference title and possibly spots in the NCAA Tournament on the line, hometown fans will be the difference in making Kemper sound and feel like Iowa State's Hilton Coliseum, Oklahoma State's Gallagher-Iba Arena, Kansas' Allen Fieldhouse and Missouri's Hearnes Center.

Inside these and other Big 12 arenas this winter, otherwise-hospitable Midwesterners made sure their visitors felt anything but welcome.

They held up crude or comical signs. They waved their arms violently, hoping to catch the opponent's attention if even for just a second. They screamed until their voices went hoarse, turning the simple act of shooting free throws into a near-deaf experience.

And the players noticed.

"Everywhere you go, it's crazy," said Iowa State senior guard Kantrail Horton. "Kansas has Allen Fieldhouse, where they're waving all kinds of things and yelling everything in the world at you. Missouri is always rowdy. At Oklahoma State, it's small, so they can mess with you up close. Our fans are obviously great. At Nebraska, they were really messing with me, chanting my name and stuff like that.

"Every Big 12 crowd is tough in its own way."

Whether it's Missouri's infamous Antlers greeting Kansas State point guard Larry Reid with chants of "Little Bow Wow" in reference to the pre-teen rap artist or Iowa State fans serenading Kansas center Eric Chenowith with cheers

---

"It's our job to get people going, to get into the heads of the other team if we can. A good player will always get a little extra attention, and if they've said or done something stupid, you know we're going to find out about it and use it. Sometimes you can tell when you're inside a player's head and it's affecting him. That has to help our team. Plus, it's fun."

—Jeremy Krueger, also known as "The Grand Poobah" of the Antlers

---

of "Chenoworthless," Big 12 basketball fanatics are sometimes obscure, often funny and every now and then, downright mean.

But, as Kansas Citians will discover this week, they are never boring.

"Most games, I want to go down and check the pulse of some of our fans," said Missouri senior Jeremy Krueger, also known as "The Grand Poobah" of the Antlers. "That's why it's our job to get people going, to get into the heads of the other team if we can. A good player will always get a little extra attention, and if they've said or done something stupid, you know we're going to find out about it and use it.

"Sometimes you can tell when you're inside a player's head and it's affecting him. That has to help our team. Plus, it's fun."

Perhaps no player has a better perspective on Big 12 fans than Chenowith, who probably could write a senior thesis on heckling. But that hasn't caused him to lose his sense of humor about it.

"I've just about heard it all," Chenowith said. "Probably the best thing I ever saw was at (Oklahoma State) one time when this guy held up a sign that said 'Chenowith is the next Will Perdue.' That was pretty funny.

"The thing about it is, I've never seen a crowd block a shot or grab a

rebound for the other team. It still comes down to who plays better on the court."

But don't tell that to Big 12 fans, who will be on their "best" behavior at Kemper.

Undoubtedly, at some point during the tournament, a player will step to the free-throw line in a close game and feel his powers of concentration severely tested. Not by the shot, but by the commotion behind the basket.

During Texas' Feb. 3 visit to Allen, Longhorns guard Darren Kelly found himself in just such a position after Kansas coach Roy Williams was called for a technical foul after tossing his jacket into the stands.

As Kelly calmly dribbled and set himself to shoot, the crowd behind the

basket included eight shirtless guys with "Roy's Boys" painted across their chests, hundreds of others waving long foam clappers and an entire section of wild-eyed people screaming.

Keeping his focus despite the frenzy, Kelly sank the free throw.

"Oh, it definitely makes a difference," said Kansas sophomore Chris Schaller, better known as the apostrophe-S in "Roy's Boys." "Except for the time last year when we painted 'LUKE' on our backs for Luke Axtell and he bricked two free throws. That probably wasn't such a good idea.

"Most of the time, though, it works in our favor."

Not that hostile crowds always throw players off their games. In fact, Iowa State's Horton says he feeds off the junk that comes his way.

"I love playing in front of our fans and seeing them get jacked up after a big shot or dunk or something," Horton said. "But I've got to admit that there is nothing like hitting a big three-pointer and hearing their fans go totally silent.

"When you do that, even the craziest people have nothing to say."

QUIN'S QUANDARY

SNYDER CAUGHT UP IN RIVALRY BUT CAN'T SEEM TO CATCH KU

Quin Snyder said he understood the rivalry when he approached his first game against Kansas in 2000. But he wasn't prepared for how hostile it could be and how important it was.

A former Duke player and assistant coach, he felt like the North Carolina-Duke rivalry had prepared him for the Border War. He quickly found out that it was a different animal altogether.

Even though he still stood in the shadow of Norm Stewart, his predecessor of 32 years at the Missouri helm, he was the man in charge for the Tigers. Seven previous contests against the Jayhawks (Snyder stood 2-5, including an 81-59 victory in that first match-up) made him much more prepared for what was ahead as he prepared for the season-ender in 2003.

Here's how it appeared in the March 9, 2003, Star:

BY MIKE DEARMOND

Norm Stewart faked left.

"The top of the intense fans maybe get a little carried away," said Stewart, the legendary former Missouri basketball coach, of Sunday's meeting between archrivals Kansas and Missouri on the basketball court that is named for him.

Stewart faked right.

"They don't understand that competitors compete during the game. And then, it's over."

And then, Stormin' Norman delivered the punch line.

"Unless you lose."

Once upon a time, Quin Snyder - four seasons into replacing Stewart at the MU helm - might not have fully understood. Perhaps it was too easy the first time out. On Jan. 22, 2000, Snyder's first Missouri team ripped Kansas 81-59 in Columbia.

After losing 83-82 on March 5 in Lawrence that season, Snyder sensed a bit more history. More often than not, 156 times to 90, the Jayhawks have won. Snyder is 2-5 against the Jayhawks.

But with each mounting loss in Snyder' MU tenure - Kansas has beaten Snyder's Tigers four straight times, including 76-70 in Lawrence on Feb. 3 - Snyder has been less and less surprised by the ferocity of the Border War.

Of the fans, of the players, of the news media, of himself.

"You're not a part of it before," confessed Snyder, weaned on the Duke-North Carolina rivalry as a guard, then an assistant coach, at Duke.

"At this point, I'm more than knee-deep in it," Snyder said.

"And I love it."

So does Kansas coach Roy Williams, except perhaps for the telephone calls he received in the wee hours Friday morning from an anonymous source that Williams suspects is a member of the infamous MU fan group, The Antlers.

"The first one was at 2:27 this morning," Williams said, adding his telephone rang again at 2:45 a.m. and 3:05 a.m.

"Someone told me I needed to check with the phone people to see if I could get call transfer and transfer them to Quin's number.

"I thought it was a heck of an idea."

Snyder has had his own version of early-morning telephone distractions. Every time an MU-KU game rolls around, Snyder is faced with the comparisons.

Snyder to Stewart. Snyder to Williams. Snyder's MU players to Williams' KU players. The MU program to the KU program.

Kansas brings a No. 6 national ranking into Sunday's 1 p.m. tipoff before CBS' television eye (Channels 5, 13). The Jayhawks are 23-6 overall, 13-2 in the Big 12 and already at least co-champions of the conference.

Missouri is unranked at 18-8, and at 9-6 is destined to finish either fourth or fifth in the Big 12. That's a slight improvement from three straight years of finishing sixth under Snyder.

"I don't care what you say, you start looking at that stuff and you see some of the stuff that is written or said, it's going to affect you," Snyder said. "You end up being Don Quixote. You're out there fighting the windmills."

Missouri will be fighting more than windmills on Sunday. The Jayhawks can lay sole claim to a second straight Big 12 Conference regular-season title by beating Missouri. KU players have been talking all week about making sure their championship rings are exclusive.

"We want the rings," KU senior guard Kirk Hinrich said, "and we don't want to share them with anybody."

Proving perhaps that the more things change, the more they simply swap perspective, Williams seems to have stepped into Stewart's shoes. Now in his 15th season of the Border War,

Williams delivered a pre-game comment with a humorous barb on Friday.

"I wonder," Williams said of his anonymous caller, "if the guy is ever going to graduate. I think it's the same guy. It didn't sound like Norm."

Snyder and the Tigers had hoped to come surging into the Kansas game. But on Wednesday night at Iowa State, Missouri fell flat on its face, losing 71-55.

Instead of having fourth place to themselves, with a victory over Kansas nailing down a first-round bye in the Big 12 tournament, Missouri needs some help.

Even if Missouri beats Kansas on Sunday, Oklahoma State also has to lose at home to Texas A&M on Saturday.

"Let this game hurt," Snyder said after the Iowa State pratfall, "but learn from it."

And the Tigers would like that lesson to come at the expense of the Jayhawks. Moving to 15-0 at home at KU's expense might boost Missouri ahead of a dreaded 8-9 NCAA Tournament seed, regardless of what the Tigers do in the Big 12 tournament.

"I look forward to Sunday," Snyder said, "and the impact it can have.

"Our season's not going to be over after that game. But, it can give you a lot of momentum, regardless of the result, because it tests you.

"The thing for us, anytime you have a rivalry like that, it has the opportunity to make you better. That competition can really raise your level as a team."

The same thought was on the mind of MU's Rickey Paulding.

"Guys will have a little more urgency," Paulding said, "it just being Kansas."

THE SHOT HEARD 'ROUND THE BORDER

There's n old saying that's perfect in sports: "I'd rather be lucky than good."

For years, the Kansas Jayhawks and the Missouri Tigers have had good basketball programs, often trading places at the top of the conference standings. When both teams are good, the contests reflect that.

But just as often, when one of the teams has a clear advantage in talent, the game still turns out to be a thriller. Such was the case in 2003, when the sixth-ranked Jayhawks came into Columbia to face the struggling Tigers. The

After Aaron Miles' three-point shot led to a stunning, come-from-behind victory for Kansas, he had a little fun with the silent Missouri crowd.

Tigers had a solid team, as evidenced by their appearance in the NCAA Tournament. But the Jayhawks had the clear advantage with two future NBA Draft Lottery picks in the starting lineup.

The game went back and forth, and with less than two minutes remained, the Tigers led by three. Point guard Aaron Miles, a 24-percent three-point shooter, launched an off-balance three that tied the score and deflated the Hearnes Center crowd.

The game was still tied, but Kirk Hinrich's three just moments later gave KU the lead for good.

Here's how it appeared in the March 10, 2003, Star:

KU FORTUNES TURN ON MILES' UNLIKELY THREE

BY JASON KING
THE KANSAS CITY STAR

Columbia

Maybe Aaron Miles had a rabbit's foot tucked into his shorts. Perhaps he picked a penny off the ground as he walked into the Hearnes Center.

Whatever the case, there has to be some explanation for the way No.6 Kansas came from behind and beat

Missouri in Sunday's 79-74 thriller at the Hearnes Center. The win gave the sixth-ranked Jayhawks sole possession of their second straight Big 12 title.

Kirk Hinrich's 25-foot three-pointer with 22 seconds remaining broke a 74-74 tie. But it was Miles' shot less

RIVALS!

MU VS. KU

KU:79
MU:74

BASKETBALL
MARCH 9, 2003

than a minute earlier that will be forever fixed in the minds of both Border War participants.

"Somebody up above must have wanted us to win," said Miles, KU's point guard. "I'm not going to lie. I know it was luck."

Here's how it all went down:

Trailing 74-71, Kansas had possession as the game approached its final minute. Miles dribbled the ball on the left wing, but he couldn't escape the defensive pressure of MU guard Ricky Clemons. Still, as the shot clock wound down, Miles had no option but to shoot.

"(Clemons) was right on me," said Miles, who came in shooting 24 percent from three–point range. "I could see the rim, so I just aimed at it."

Somehow, Miles' 23-foot, two-handed, line-drive desperation heave from the hip swished through the bottom of the net. Just like that, the game was tied 74-74 with 1 minute, 21 seconds left.

"It was a horrible shot," MU forward Travon Bryant said. "(Miles) is a better shooter shooting it like that than actually having his feet set.

"He can't shoot the ball a lick, and he throws that up. It's…lucky."

Missouri never regained its composure after Miles' three-pointer. Tigers' swingman Rickey Paulding bricked a shot on the other end. KU rebounded the miss and then scored the game-winner on Hinrich's long three-pointer – again, with the shot clock winding down – with 22.1 seconds remaining.

Loud as the Hearnes Center had been, it suddenly became quiet as the final horn sounded. Jayhawks players taunted Missouri's fans as they ran off

the court. Hinrich pointed to the "Kansas" on his jersey. Miles and Keith Langford cupped their hands around their ears to mock the suddenly hushed crowd.

Langford, who last week received a few nasty e-mails and phone calls that he thought were from the Antlers – Missouri's notorious student group - said he couldn't resist bragging as he left the court.

"They can take their Antlers and put them…" said Langford, sparing reporters a more vivid description of the image he was picturing. "I'd just like to have seen the look on their face at the end of the game.

"All of that mess they do – calling our house and everything – it was all a waste. Now they have to sit there and be sick for another year."

> "It was a horrible shot. (Miles) is a better shooter shooting it like that than actually having his feet set. He can't shoot the ball a lick, and he throws that up. It's… lucky."
> - MU forward Travon Bryant

Indeed, Kansas' victory marked the fifth straight time the Jayhawks have toppled the Tigers. The win couldn't have been more meaningful to Hinrich and forward Nick Collison, the All-America candidates who won in their final trip to the Hearnes Center.

Hinrich and Collison each scored 20 points.

"We couldn't be happier right now," Hinrich said. "We're the No. 1 team in the Big 12, and we've got a shot at getting a No. 1 seed in the NCAA Tournament. I'm just elated."

Although not as flukish, Hinrich's game-winning three-pointer was equally as dramatic as the one Miles had made seconds earlier.

With about 50 seconds remaining, Hinrich passed to Collison on the baseline, but Collison air-balled a 12-foot jump shot. Luckily for the Jayhawks, reserve guard Michael Lee was able to snare the offensive rebound over Clemons.

"I thought they were going to call over-the-back," Lee said. "I was lucky to get away with it."

Lee gained his footing and then fired a pass to Hinrich, who was about 6 feet behind the top of the key. Hinrich made his game-winning three-pointer as the shot clock expired.

Paulding, who finished with 21 points, then missed a three-pointer on the other end that would have tied the game. Kansas rebounded, and Langford made two free-throws that secured the victory with 1.1 seconds remaining.

"As soon as I caught it, I saw I had room," said Hinrich, recalling his winning shot. "I knew it was going in."

MU's Bryant said he wasn't surprised that Hinrich made the long-range shot under pressure.

"You expect Hinrich to make those shots," Bryant said. "He brings a lot of daggers. At least he was squared up."

LUCKY? YES, BUT JAYHAWKS ARE STILL BEST

By Jason Whitlock

Columbia

Call it luck. Call it an injustice. Call it an answered prayer.

But whatever you do this morning, make sure when you see a member of the Kansas basketball team, you call him an outright Big 12 champion.

Don't let Kansas' fortuitous 79-74 victory over the Missouri Tigers, which came courtesy of two hail Mary three-pointers in the final 90 seconds, cause you to lose sight of the big (12) picture.

The Jayhawks, 24-6 overall and 14-2 in conference, proved that they are indeed the Big 12's best, worthy of a No. 1 NCAA Tournament seed and a serious threat to reach the Final Four.

We've wasted the season yakking and moaning about what the Jayhawks don't have – depth, a Jeff Boschee-type shooter, solid role players, Drew Gooden and a healthy Wayne Simien.

What about what the Jayhawks do have: poise, senior leadership, good chemistry, toughness, two All Americans, Roy Williams and as of late, a spark from swingman Michael Lee?

Those ingredients were good enough to win the Big 12 Conference. And if that's good enough to outdistance Texas, Oklahoma, Oklahoma State, Colorado, Texas Tech and sweep the Missouri Tigers, then it should be enough for the Jayhawks to make a run in the Big Dance.

If Kansas can win here, at the Hearnes Center, with the Antlers yelling and the Tigers desperately trying to beat a rival, making the Sweet 16 should be easy.

If Kansas can win here, at the Hearnes Center, with the Antlers yelling and the Tigers desperately trying to beat a rival, making the Sweet 16 should be easy.

Again, you can call the Jayhawks lucky because of the back-to-back wild three-pointers. But a couple of Clemons' threes were nearly as lucky.

No. Missouri fans shouldn't focus in on Kansas' good fortune. They should spend Monday wondering why the Tigers jacked up 25 three-pointers on an afternoon when Travon Bryant and Arthur Johnson could have fouled out KU's entire front court.

Bryant and Johnson shot a combined 10 of 21 from the field and scored 24 total points. Rickey Paulding and Jimmy McKinney shot a combined zero of 10 from three-point land. Given Graves' constant foul trouble and the absence of Simien, the Tigers' reluctance to feed the post was an inexcusable strategy error.

It's those types of small mistakes that have contributed to Kansas' five-game winning streak in the Border War. The Jayhawks are so experienced and so expertly led by Williams that they rarely pass up an opportunity to exploit an obvious weakness.

Don't sleep on these Jayhawks. They may not be done surprising us.

THE GRAY BOX FADES TO BLACK

MU BASKETBALL ENJOYED DEAFENING CROWDS, 400-PLUS WINS IN 32 YEARS AT HEARNES CENTER

The last game in the Hearnes Center, the home of Missouri basketball for 32 years, was here. Memories of championships and disappointments, heroes and goats, danced in the heads of the 13,000-plus spectators who would fill the arena one last time.

Nearly 500 games had been played, and Missouri had won 85 percent of them. The Tigers had won eight conference championships and had finished with 28 winning records and only four losing marks.

Kansas, the hated rivals to the west, would be the last opponent. It was an appropriate way to close out the facility. Missouri needed the win more than Kansas. The Tigers' slim NCAA hopes would be dashed with a loss.

But somehow, even a post-season berth paled in comparison to winning the last game in Hearnes.

The day of the last game, Mike DeArmond strolled down Memory Lane with one last look at the Old Gray Box.

Here's how it appeared in the March 7, 2004, Star:

BY MIKE DEARMOND
THE KANSAS CITY STAR

Columbia

The Hearnes Center, home to Missouri basketball for nearly 32 years, has been called a lot of things. Some of them have been complimentary.

Where the Tigers Roar. Hell on the Hinkson (or close to it). The House That Norm Built.

And if you have to ask "Norm who?" to be told Stewart is the last name of the curmedgeon of a coach who spent all but five of his 32 season prowling the sidelines at the Hearnes, well then you haven't been paying attention for much of those three-plus decades.

You may not care that Missouri and archrival Kansas, fittingly, are retiring the Hearnes Center at 1 p.m. this afternoon with the 477th Mizzou men's hoops happening in the old

shoebox on the hill.

But you'll be in the minority. Really, you will. Because the Hearnes Center has helped make Missouri basketball.

Since the Hearnes Multi-Purpose Building – its official name – opened Nov. 25, 1972, the Hearnes has been one of the 15 toughest places for a visiting team to win a basketball game in the nation.

A Missouri men's basketball team

has won 405 times in the previous 476 games played here. That's an 85 percent winning percentage. Or, for the visitors, that's a 15 percent winning percentage.

Believe it or not, Kansas stands only 13-18 against Missouri in the Hearnes, by far the best record among any current member of the Big 12 Conference with the exception of Texas, which has won three of a mere five games it has played at the Hearnes.

"The tradition that has been built there is unique," said current MU coach Quin Snyder, himself steeped on the Duke-North Carolina rivalry of his college playing days. "I feel fortunate to have had a chance to be the coach here for five years in that building."

On Oct. 1, 2004, Snyder, and both men's and women's basketball, will move into the new $75 million basketball palace now taking shape on the south side of Hearnes.

But…

"I'm sure we'll wander in the fieldhouse every now and then and pay our respects to the old lady," Snyder said.

They'll make a grand show of doing that today.

An anticipated 41 former MU players – including John Brown, Lynn Hardy, Jevon Crudup, Jim Kennedy, Clay Cooper and Kansas City native twins Beau and Cliff Minx – are expected back today, to say goodbye. There will be a special video presentation at halftime. Posters, special programs. There will be keepsakes galore.

Stormin' Norman Stewart will be there, with special guests former Missouri Gov. Warren Hearnes and Hearnes' wife, Betty. It is for Gov. Hearnes that the place is named.

It was Hearnes who persuaded the Missouri General Assembly into appropriating $7.65 million on Jan. 5, 1967, to build the facility that has been home to basketball, gymnastics, volleyball, track, graduation and commencement ceremonies, and countless concerts from Bob Hope to Nelly.

Betty Hearnes said she was stunned when the facility was named after her husband.

"They usually," she said in a recent interview, "name buildings after people who are dead."

Stewart had another take, telling the tale of how he got in trouble for not telling folks the governor was coming to a game one time, and the fallout from the surprise.

"You're going to get me fired," Stewart told Hearnes.

"He said, 'Not as long as I'm governor.'"

"I said," Stewart added, 'Well, you might not be governor as long as I'm coach.'"

Truthfully, though, there are those who will wave goodbye to the Hearnes Center with but a tip of the hat to the nostalgia.

Hearnes, in the dingy fourth-floor practice gym, was where the college careers of Kelly Thames and Jeff Hafer almost came to an end because of injuries. For all intents, Thames' did. He was never the same player after blowing out his knee there.

Even Jon Sundvold – MU great, NBA player and now a national television commentator who makes his home in Columbia – recognizes the warts the Hearnes always had.

"It was never designed to be a basketball arena," Sundvold said. "It was a multipurpose building. There are a lot

of seats in there that just are a long way away. They aren't good seats."

Hearnes for many years suffered because of what some younger fans called "the blue hairs," older fans who bought season tickets early and held on to them long after the will to rise and roar had passed. Not until recent years were more than a few students – and the infamous private cheering group known as The Antlers – seated low enough to be really heard when the urge to yell overcame them.

There was never any luxury seating, like the 25 top-dollar luxury suites planned and nearly all already sold for the new arena. Bathrooms were too far and too few. So were concession stands.

The only person truly pleased from start to finish by the Hearnes Center was probably the concrete concessionaire. Or perhaps the manufacturer of the original sound-deadening Tartan Turf playing surface, or the company that built the several generations of wood basketball floors needed to replace it.

"It was kind of sterile," former MU great Steve Stipanovich once said of the Hearnes before the latest round of renovations that splashed the school colors of black and gold around what was originally a grey interior.

Gray Lady Downer, the Hearnes was once called. The Shoebox. The Concrete Box.

Never, Sundvold noted, was the Hearnes, as a facility, compared to Oklahoma State's Gallagher-Iba Arena, or KU's storied Allen Fieldhouse or even Kansas State's old barn-burner of a basketball hot-house, Ahearn Field House.

But tough on the visitors? Sure, Hearnes was always that. From the time Norm Stewart's sixth Tiger basketball team in its debut season in Hearnes went 21-6 overall and 12-1 at the Hearnes, on through today.

"The teams that we had there made it a tough place to play," said Sundvold, himself a member of four straight Big Eight championship teams at Mizzou. "And the fans that cheered for those teams make it a tough place to play."

Did Hearnes ever have the decibel level, the claustrophobia, of Oklahoma State's old or newly remodeled Gallagher-Iba Arena? No. Except when Kansas came to town.

Did it ever have the tradition of Allen Fieldhouse. No. Not really. Never.

But today it will, contended MU athletic director Mike Alden, who never tires of telling the story of how his uncle was in charge of the wiring and plumbing when the Hearnes Center was built.

"The place is going to be really rocking," Alden said. "It is going to be packed to the brim. There is going to be a fever pitch over what's going on in here.

"And then there is also going to be a sense of nostalgia. It's our senior day."

Arthur Johnson, Rickey Paulding, Travon Bryant and Josh Kroenke – who together have played in more NCAA Tournament games (eight) than any other class in school history – will be saying goodbye.

Asked to measure his own anticipated emotions for today, Paulding said, "I don't know yet. I know it's a big game for us. My last home game of my career. But I can't anticipate what feelings I'm going to have."

But you know what? This isn't the end of Missouri basketball, but a continuation. There will be no more

Hearnes Center. But there will be more Rickey Pauldings and Arthur Johnsons, more Larry Drews, and Steve Stipanovichs. Perhaps another Doug Smith, another Jon Sundvold, another Anthony Peeler, another Kareem Rush.

Yes, all those Missouri greats began and ended their careers in the Hearnes.

It is just that those future greats will seek their memories, build their legends, just beside the old lady, which will remain home to intramurals, meetings, and conventions, become the highlight home of volleyball and gymnastics.

"Maybe," Snyder said, "we'll have to have a séance and move all the ghosts into the new arena."

For basketball, only the echoes will remain. And perhaps, that is enough.

FINISHED!

ON PADGETT'S LATE SHOT, KU WINS A WILD ONE

There was so much emotion in the building as the Missouri Tigers closed the Hearnes Center, their home of 32 years. As Gary Link, a member of the Tigers basketball teams from 1971-74 and the color analyst on Missouri's basketball radio network for the past six seasons said, it ended the way it was supposed to end.

"It was only appropriate that the final game was against Kansas," Link said. "There's always more pressure on the home team, because nobody expects the visiting team to win.

"But you want the rivalry to be strong. You'd never go eight or nine years without beating them—or losing to them. It's always a good battle."

The game was like so many others—it came down to the final play. It was a bitter ending for Mizzou, with no sweet to go with it. David Padgett hit a baseline jumper with two seconds left to give Kansas an 84-82 victory. The Old Gray Box would see no more basketball.

Here's how it appeared in the March 8, 2004, Star:

By Jason King

Columbia

As David Padgett sprinted off the Hearnes Center court Sunday, an elderly man wadded up a piece of paper and hurled it at his head. A different fan shot him the finger, and another sprawled out – deflated – in his path.

But Padgett never slowed down.

Trotting toward the Kansas locker room, all Padgett could think about was the unplanned, baseline jump shot he'd just swished that helped the Jayhawks beat Missouri 84-82.

"That," Padgett said later, "was the last thing I expected to happen."

Along with being the final shot ever at the Hearnes Center, Padgett's game-winner with 2 seconds remaining also will go down as one of the most painful fieldgoals in the 32-year history of the building.

Padgett's jumper came after receiving a dish from KU guard Keith Langford, whose path had been blocked as he tried to snake toward the basket. With no time to pass, Padgett's only choice was to fire off a straight, "line drive" shot over his defender.

"It's the last thing I ever expected to go in," Padgett said. "When I caught it, I didn't think there was enough time to make a move toward the basket or anything. So I just turned around and kind of heaved it up there."

Missouri's crowd went silent after Padgett's jumper ripped through the net, marking the second unlikely dagger KU has delivered at the Hearnes Center in two seasons. It was only a year ago, you may remember, when Aaron Miles sparked the Jayhawks to victory with a desperation three-point heave in the final minute.

"I guess the rims are a little bigger here," said KU forward Wayne Simien, smiling.

At least it seems that way for the No. 21 Jayhawks, who won despite squandering a 10-point lead late in the second half. Valiant as its comeback attempt was, Missouri didn't help its cause by going just 19 of 32 from the free-throw line. The Tigers missed on the front end of five one-and-one opportunities.

The victory, which came in the Big 12 regular-season finale, gives Kansas a 20-7 record overall and a 12-4 mark in conference play. The Jayhawks finished in a tie with Texas for second place in the league standings.

RIVALS!
MU VS. KU

KU:84
MU: 82

BASKETBALL
MARCH 7, 2004

Bill Self's squad will receive a first-round bye in this week's Big 12 tournament in Dallas. Kansas, the No.3 seed, on Friday will take on the winner of a first-round game between No. 11 seed Texas A&M – and, you guessed it – No. 6 seed Missouri.

"There's obviously a great chance we could play (Missouri) again," said Self, who has a 5-0 career record against the Tigers. "If that's the case, then we certainly could have picked an easier (first) opponent."

Indeed, Sunday's game marked one of the most vicious battles in the history of the Border War. Kansas, which has won seven of its last eight meetings with Missouri, led 77-67 after Miles' three-pointer with 4:54 remaining.

Missouri, though, kept its poise and whittled away at KU's lead. Center Arthur Johnson scored eight points during a 9-0 run that pulled the Tigers within 77-76 with 1:43 remaining. Johnson scored a game-high 37 points Sunday.

"We didn't have any offense in the last 4 minutes at all," Self said. "We played not to lose, and they made some great plays."

Kansas led 79-76 when things almost got out of hand. A layup by Missouri's Jason Conley shaved the Jayhawks' lead to 79-78. Kansas then advanced the ball to half-court before calling timeout with 47 seconds remaining.

On the inbounds pass, KU freshman J.R. Giddens accidentally bounced the ball off Conley's leg. Conley came up with a steal and a thunderous dunk that gave Missouri an 80-79 advantage. Only 47 seconds remained.

"When we're down by one point in the huddle, I told everyone that we're going to win," Miles said.

"I just said, 'Calm down, we're

David Padgett's baseline jumper over Arthur Johnson was not only the game-winner. It was also the last shot taken in the 32-year history of the Hearnes Center.

TEN

235

going to win. We've just got to be poised.'"

Miles followed his own advice. A 27.8 percent shooter from three-point range, Miles took a feed from Langford and swished a shot from beyond the arc that put Kansas ahead 82-80 with 21 seconds remaining.

Conley tied it back up with two free throws on the other end before Padgett made his game-winner.

Self said that, on the last possession, the plan was for Langford – the best player on the team when it comes to creating a shot – to either come up with his own shot or dish off to a teammate.

"Keith is our go-to man," said Miles, who had 15 points and eight assists. "I believe in him a lot. I know he's going to make good decisions. He's one of the best scorers in America. He creates for everyone."

Langford scored 19 points, and Giddens added 14 for a KU squad that made 10 of its 18 three-pointers. The Jayhawks shot 57.1 percent from the field – including 64 percent in the decisive second half.

Kansas' performance was somewhat stunning, considering KU had lost its last four road games by an average of 15.3 points.

"Not many people expected us to come in here and win," Langford said. "We've been playing with the burden of Nick (Collison) and Kirk (Hinrich) on our shoulders. It seems like everything is coming together at just the right time."

EMOTIONS RUN FAR TOO LOW IN HEARNES FINALE

By Jason Whitlock

COLUMBIA – It felt like a funeral inside the Hearnes Center on Sunday afternoon.

A standing-room-only crowd supposedly came to celebrate the retirement of a historic basketball arena, but, as the Missouri Tigers and Kansas Jayhawks renewed one of college hoops' fiercest rivalries, most of the 13,611 spectators and all of Quin Snyder's players behaved as though Sunday was about burying the 2003-04 season.

Mission accomplished. The Jayhawks made just enough clutch plays down the stretch to survive Missouri's frantic, late-game rally, handing the Tigers a crushing 84-82 defeat that might just eliminate Mizzou, 15-12, from NCAA Tournament consideration.

"It's as difficult a loss as I've ever been associated with," a sullen Quin Snyder said. "The urgency of the situation was not lost on our team."

Missouri had many reasons to play hard and smart and courageous Sunday afternoon. It was Senior Day for Rickey Paulding, MU's ninth all-time leading scorer; Arthur Johnson, MU's all-time leading rebounder, Travon Bryant, and Josh Kroenke. Norm Stewart was in the house, and Mizzou's chancellor announced at halftime that the floor in the new gym would be named Norm Stewart Court, just like at the Hearnes Center. Plus, the Tigers felt as if they absolutely had to have Sunday's victory to nail down an NCAA Tournament bid.

Why the funeral? Why was the Hearnes Center so quiet? Why didn't the Tigers overwhelm the Jayhawks with emotion?

"Early on we had a hard time finding some emotion," Snyder pointed out.

What? No emotion. How could that be? The tumult of this season finally drowned the Tigers. The double-

THE MIGHTY QUIN

RIVALS!
MU VS. KU

KU:84
MU: 82

BASKETBALL
MARCH 7, 2004

overtime victory over Oklahoma State was a fluke, a final gasp. The Tigers and their fans entered the final Border War at the Hearnes Center on a stretcher. Kansas coach Bill Self, 5-0 against Snyder, fittingly performed the eulogy.

The Tigers hung with Kansas for most of the day. But you never had the feeling until the end – when Missouri erased a 10-point deficit - that the Tigers were really into it. Favorable officiating (26 Kansas fouls to 15 MU fouls and a 32-14 advantage in free-throw attempts) kept Missouri in Sunday's game.

With Kansas center Jeff Graves limited to 15 minutes because of foul trouble, the Tigers should have dominated the backboards. They didn't. Kansas won the battle 38-33. And given the direness of the situation, a Norm Stewart-like defensive effort was expected. That didn't happen either. In the second half, Kansas sank an amazing 64 percent (16 of 25) from the field. The Jayhawks drilled their open looks.

And in the game's final 30 seconds, Aaron Miles unspooled a backbreaking three-pointer – one prettier but reminiscent of his 2003 MU backbreaker – and David Padgett added an unforgettable highlight – the game-winning 8-footer from the baseline – to an otherwise disappointing freshman season.

You could mistakenly call Sunday's outcome a stunner, a surprising, tragic end to a historic building. But the Tigers and their faithful weren't lying to themselves. The Hearnes Center isn't all that historic. It was poorly constructed and hasn't been home to all that many great moments.

Seriously, Corey Tate's game-winner over then-No.1 Kansas in 1997 was selected as the Hearnes Center's greatest moment. When your all-time greatest moment is in the middle of a 16-17 season it's easier to understand why Sunday felt like a funeral. Mizzou is about two decades late burying the Hearnes Center.

FROM THE KANSAS CITY STAR, 2004

NARROW LOSS FUELS MISERY AT MISSOURI

BY MIKE DEARMOND

COLUMBIA – There was the suffering inflicted in the final 4.8 seconds of the NCAA Tournament by Tyus Edney and UCLA. And Colorado's Fifth Down gridiron goring. And, of course, Nebraska's impossible victory on the Kick 'n' Catch.

Well, Missouri should have expected this bloody Sunday.

Of course Kansas freshman David Padgett would drop in an 8-foot shot from the right baseline with 2 seconds left, giving Missouri's biggest of rivals an 84-82 victory.

Of course it would come in the last regular-season basketball game in a Hearnes Center swimming in emotion even before the Tigers' four seniors took the home court for the last time.

Of course Tigers' senior center Arthur Johnson would score a career-high 37 points that just wouldn't be enough, leaving an entire state unsure of the greater tragedy.

That the Tigers lost. That Johnson was so magnificent in that loss. That it all hurt so very much.

"There were so many things about this game that made me think we have to win," said a spent Missouri coach Quin Snyder.

Of course, Missouri could have won. It wouldn't have been such a gut-wrencher had it not been that way.

The Tigers rallied – improbably – from a 77-67 deficit with less than 5 minutes to play.

Jason Conley's steal and stuff gave Missouri an 80-79 lead with 49.4 seconds remaining. And Conley tied the game 82-82 with 15.4 seconds left on two free throws after Tiger-tamer Aaron Miles – who tied Missouri here last year with an improbable hip shot – put the Jayhawks ahead 82-80 with a pure three from the left wing with 20.1 seconds to play.

But KU's Keith Langford calmly brought the ball up court.

And suddenly, Padgett, frustrated all day trying to cover Johnson, had the ball. He got the basket, only his third of a six-point day.

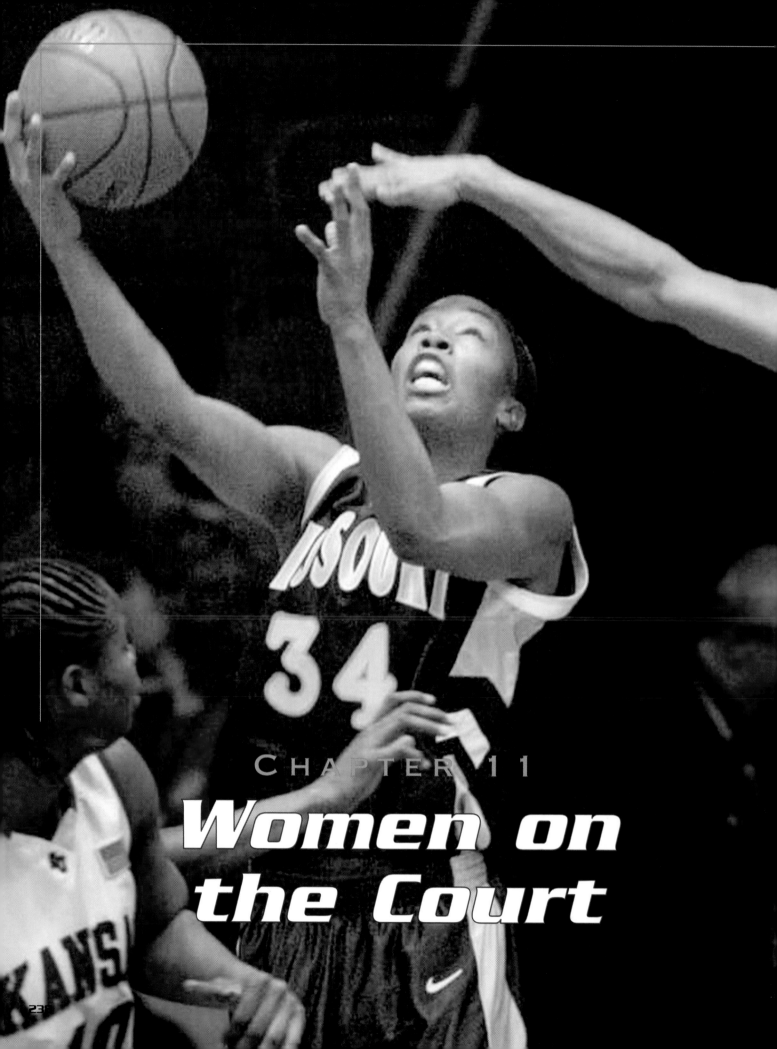

CHAPTER 11

Women on the Court

FANNING THE FLAMES

The Border War rivalry in women's basketball has never attracted the attention and focus that the men's has. There are various reasons – and The Star's Mechelle Voepel zoomed in on some in this report, preceding the matchup between the two teams in the women's 2005 Big 12. MU would go on to beat the Jayhawks in a close one – revenge for two prior losses against Kansas.

This chapter also includes a profile by Voepel of women's basketball coach and pioneer Marian Washington, whose KU career parallels closely the changes brought on by Title IX. Plus we reprint a Kansas City Star opinion piece on the notorious fight that occurred between the Missouri and KU women's teams in 2004 – a surefire sign that, while muted, the KU-MU rivalry among women is more than just a spark.

KANSAS, MISSOURI REALIZE BETTER PLAY WILL BRING MORE INTEREST TO RIVALRY

By Mechelle Voepel

Columbia

Sure, the "Border War" or "Border Showdown" or whatever you want to call it is a big deal in every sport. But its "temperature" in women's basketball can sometimes be lukewarm.

It's not because the players for either Missouri or Kansas don't feel it. But fan interest on both sides has never been overwhelming. That may be, in part, because MU and KU haven't been simultaneously successful for a long enough period to really develop a passion among a significant portion of Tiger and Jayhawk fans.

No one expects it to be anything like the legendary animosity and excitement that's generated by the men's basketball rivalry. But even by the standards of potential women's hoops interest in Columbia and Lawrence, you can't help

but think it could be a lot better.

Today, though, the No. 8 seed Jayhawks meet the No. 9 Tigers in a game that tends not to draw as well simply because of the time: noon on a Tuesday. These two get things under way in the Big 12 women's tournament, though not so much thinking about who will be watching but what both can accomplish.

"It's a matter of us staying focused and confident for 40 minutes. It's one of those things we kind of go day-to-day with," MU coach Cindy Stein said. "With a young team, sometimes they look for somebody else to get the fire going. We've got to get them confident in their own abilities, and that's been a process."

KU coach Bonnie Henrickson is experiencing her first Big 12 tournament, and her Jayhawks had their first regular-season sweep of Missouri this year since

1999. KU won 63-61 in Lawrence on Jan. 22 and 60-42 in Columbia on Feb. 5.

Henrickson isn't about to listen to any of that hokum about how tough it is to beat a team three times in a season.

"We've heard that a lot," Henrickson said. "But I told our team that I'm a firm believer that you can't possibly turn beating someone twice into a negative. The most important thing for us is to focus on what we did well."

"This group is very mature and realistic. We talked after that game in Columbia about how they had a game like we did when we lost big at home to Iowa State, where nothing went right. We recognize how much better Missouri will be this time."

The KU-MU rivalry did boil over in an unwanted way last year, when the teams got into a brief postgame skirmish after the Jayhawks won in Columbia.

Missouri's Tiffany Brooks scored over KU's Aquanita Burras (right) and Crystal Kemp in the Tigers' victory Tuesday at Municipal Auditorium.

Most of the instigators and "eager" participants in that shovefest, though, are no longer with either team.

KU junior Crystal Kemp, who acted as a peacemaker then, thinks that situation was just a rare combination of events.

"I think there was frustration and a lot of emotion for both teams," she said. "A lot of people's emotions just got the best of them. There's no place for all that."

Kemp does, though, enjoy the positive aspects of the rivalry. She grew up and went to high school in Topeka, but she was born in Dallas and lived there until she was 6. So her childhood and adolescent sports interest was about all things Texas.

"It wasn't until my sophomore year in high school that I really got into Kansas more," she said. "It meant a lot to beat Missouri twice this season, especially because people were not expecting us to do anything in the Big 12."

But back to why the "rivalry" isn't all it could be ... Kansas and Missouri have both gone to the NCAA Tournament in the same year only once: in 1994. And

Henrickson, even though she's still new to all this Jayhawk-Tiger stuff, knows that is part of why the women's hoops Border matchup has not gotten a fraction of the attention that it has on the men's side.

"With the men, even in a year where one might be down and one is up, the rivalry doesn't lose intensity because of the history and tradition of both teams," she said. "I think both Cindy and I can help our programs move in the right direction. They have a new facility, we've made a lot of commitments to our program. We're both working to compete in an elite level in this conference."

And, ultimately, Stein said, that's the thing both teams should zone in on.

"I think definitely the KU-MU rivalry is taken extremely seriously by our team," she said. "I never downplay that at all, because it's something that's emphasized – not so much by us coaches as by the players.

"Both our teams have had the talent and can play the types of games to make for a great rivalry. We shouldn't worry so much about the number of fans, but the quality of the games. That's what will bring fans."

FROM THE KANSAS CITY STAR, 2005

TIGERS CLAW BACK
WITH A DETERMINED EFFORT, MISSOURI AVENGES TWO LOSSES TO KANSAS

By Mechelle Voepel

With just under 4 minutes left and Missouri's women trailing by two, LaToya Bond lost the ball out of bounds. A definite unforced error. A little more than a minute later, though, Bond drove to the basket and scored.

That "just keep moving forward" attitude was a big part of what propelled

the No. 9 seed Tigers to a 62-57 victory over No. 8 Kansas in the opening game of the Big 12 women's tournament Tuesday at Municipal Auditorium.

Asked about the drive that tied the game, though, Bond didn't really remember it.

"It was a heck of a play, wasn't it?" MU coach Cindy Stein interjected.

"What you just saw with LaToya, that's just her. She just plays. She's very unselfish. We've really focused on the next play, whether you just made a great play or they made a great play. We're focused on what we've got to do next."

That's good advice for any basketball player or team, but it's been an absolute necessity for MU. The Tigers,

11-17, fell in both their regular-season meetings with KU and at one point in the Big 12 schedule lost eight in a row. They were without Stein for two games in February while she was with her critically ill father, who passed away.

And, of course, all season long they have missed the consistent production of last year's seniors Evan Unrau and Stretch James.

Through all that, though, MU has kept plugging away. The Tigers lost to the Jayhawks 63-61 in Lawrence and 60-42 in Columbia. After that latter game, Stein said she was disgusted. How did she feel after beating the Jayhawks?

"I'm excited - we're still playing, and that's all that matters right now," Stein said. "All the games you lost before don't matter."

What did matter a great deal Tuesday was rebounding: MU had a 40-34 edge. The Tigers' 11 offensive boards in the first half were key in allowing them to rally from a nine-point deficit.

Kansas looked loose, relaxed and in good form offensively in the first half, hitting 10 of its first 15 shots. Then MU got to within 22-19 when it had a possession where the work on the offensive glass really stood out.

The Tigers missed three shots, were fouled on the fourth, missed the free-throw front end, got the rebound, missed two more shots and then were fouled again. Christelle N'Garsanet made just one free throw, but the tone was set for how hard MU was fighting. "I think the most telling statistic as far as intensity, this time of year, is we give up 11 offensive rebounds in the first half," KU coach Bonnie Henrickson said.

The second half was more frustrating offensively for the Jayhawks. They started cold and soon trailed 40-33. Still, KU came back and took the lead 46-45 with two free throws from Crystal Kemp with 12 minutes, 21 seconds left.

After that, the lead went back and forth, and the Jayhawks were up by as much as four with 6:50 left. Then, KU's offense went totally cold, and the Jayhawks scored only once more. KU shot just 25.7 percent in the second half.

"We just knew we had to put great pressure on and try to get a whole bunch of stops," Bond said.

KU guard Erica Hallman, who finished with 19 points, said: "I thought it got away from us. We got some open looks, but we didn't knock them down. We just weren't as efficient as we were in the first half, particularly down the stretch."

FROM THE KANSAS CITY STAR, FEBRUARY 15, 2003

MU-KU WOMEN'S 'BORDER WAR' SERIES HAS HAD ITS MOMENTS TOO

BY MECHELLE VOEPEL
THE KANSAS CITY STAR

The "Border War" on the women's basketball side doesn't have a history that's been well-documented. But there have been some barnburners.

Our pick for the best? Go back two decades to January 1983. The Tigers were ranked No. 13 in the country, and that season had five players who ended up with more than 1,000 points in their careers, including all-time leading scorer Joni Davis with 2,126.

MU would win the Big Eight tournament and then fall in the NCAA first round to Auburn, finishing the season 25-6 and ranked No. 15.

But ... KU got the best of the Tigers on Jan. 29, 1983, winning 118-111 in triple overtime in Lawrence. It's the third-most points KU has ever scored - the Jayhawks have gotten 122 twice - and the most vs. a conference foe.

KU's leading scorer that season was Angie Snider of Roeland Park and Bishop Miege; she led the Jayhawks in that game with a career-high 38 points.

In 1982-83, KU had a very difficult non-league schedule and was 2-9 entering Big Eight play. In the league, the Jayhawks went 9-5 and finished third. But MU got revenge and ended KU's season in the Big Eight tournament, 75-74.

One coach who has a good perspective on the rivalry is Colorado's Ceal Barry, who's been with the Buffaloes since the 1983-84 season.

"Back then in the '80s ... Missouri was the dominant team, winning championships. It was a literal tiger's den at Hearnes to go in there and play," she said. "Kansas had some very good players then, too. When I first came into the Big Eight, it was a question of which of those two teams was going to win."

A COACH, AND A PIONEER

WASHINGTON BLAZED A TRAIL FOR WOMEN'S BASKETBALL

BY MECHELLE VOEPEL
THE KANSAS CITY STAR

Her first office was about as small as a closet, but her vision was as large as the plains of the Sunflower State. Marian Washington came to Kansas in 1972, months after Title IX was signed into law and while everyone was still trying to grasp just what it meant.

She became KU's women's basketball coach in 1973. As she now steps away after 31 years in that pivotal role in the athletic department, it's instructive in defining her legacy to also define the tenor of the times when she began. And what led her to Lawrence.

Washington was ready for the hopeful uncertainty and the range of possibilities that Title IX presented. She was ahead of the curve for several reasons. One, she was part of the baby-boom generation that saw the civil rights movement change the course of American history.

Born in 1946, she grew up in greater Philadelphia and witnessed how the frustration and desperation of black people were channeled into a force of social change.

As a young black girl in the 1950s, she knew racism at its loudest and ugliest level ... and at its quietest, most insid-

ious level. It was the latter that was actually the worst. Bigots' taunts could not do the long-lasting damage that condescension and instant dismissal did.

Exterior hate became internalized self-doubt, a horrific enemy from within.

"As I got older," Washington once said, "I realized you had to unlearn so many things you had always been taught. Things that had made us really think so much less of ourselves and feel like we inherently were inferior."

But there were two other movements that she both partook in and was shaped by. One was the elevation of women and the other, more specifically, was the development of women's and girls' athletics.

She was in just the right place geographically for that: West Chester State, in a suburb of Philadelphia, held the first national intercollegiate basketball tournament for women, in 1969.

Washington was a senior star player that season for West Chester, and her performance in that tournament garnered her an invitation to the national-team trials in Arkansas.

Wary and uncertain of what she was getting into, Washington came west to the trials, first stopping at a tryout camp in Iowa. She was at first intimidated by Alberta Cox, the national-team

coach who seemed "a godlike figure."

But Cox became both mentor and friend, and soon the Midwest was Washington's home. She played AAU ball for Cox's Raytown Piperettes and was on the U.S. team that competed in the 1971 World Championships.

She was to be part of the first Olympic team for women's basketball, at the 1972 Munich Games. But then it was decided the Olympics had gotten a bit too big too quickly, and the debut of women's basketball was delayed to 1976.

It was a crushing blow for Washington, leaving her with a searing memory of how easily it seemed to her that bureaucrats could toss aside some people's dearest dreams.

And she vowed as she began her coaching career that she would try to keep that kind of disappointment from happening to new generations of athletes.

Washington first taught physical education at a junior high in Kansas City. Then, with no Olympics to go to in the fall of 1972, she instead went to work as a graduate assistant in the health and physical-education department at KU.

KU had a women's basketball team - although it had no scholarships - beginning in 1968-69. Some records exist from those first five years, but many don't, not even some game scores.

WOMEN ON THE COURT

242

In her first season, 1973-74, KU played 19 games, all in Kansas and Missouri. In the spring of '74, she started a women's track and field program at a school that, on the men's side, had legendary status in that sport as well as basketball.

Her second season, doing administrative work - she was KU's women's athletic director during 1974-79 - looking after two programs and finishing her masters degree, Washington had to battle through the feeling of being overwhelmed ... and very alone.

"Coaches in women's sports today have the opportunity to go into situations where they don't have to build from the ground up," Washington said. "They're not having to bang the drum as much as some of us that started some time ago.

"When you talk about paving the way, there was great clearance by those who came before me. But it was about perseverance for me, too. I can't say I always felt a lot of encouragement."

Yet the energy she got from the players, the certainty of knowing she could impact them, got her through the early years. And then one of the best women's players ever came into Washington's life.

Cox, who was a visionary herself, recalls how Washington as a player was obsessed with trying to find some way to do something better every day.

So when Washington first saw this kid from Wichita, Lynette Woodard, play ball ... there was an instant connection. Here was a player who saw no limit to how good she could be.

Woodard was an ebullient talent, the player of a lifetime for a coach. The

only bad thing: She's been the toughest of all acts to follow. She scored more points than anyone in collegiate women's basketball history, 3,649.

KU won 108 games and three Big Eight titles in Woodard's career, from 1977-81. She was a four-time Kodak All-American. In an eerie twist that pained Washington, Woodard was denied an Olympic chance, too, when she made the 1980 team but the United States boycotted the Moscow Games.

Woodard got another opportunity and won Olympic gold in 1984.

The pair has stayed close throughout the years. Woodard, in fact, has been serving as interim head coach since Washington stepped away for health reasons on Jan. 29.

Replacing Woodard on the court wasn't as easy.

Washington recruited a series of talented players, including Vickie Adkins, Angela Aycock, Charisse Sampson, Tamecka Dixon and Lynn Pride. All were from large cities and came to KU specifically to play for Washington.

Dixon once summed up exactly what Washington offered.

"I knew she was going to be more than just my coach," said Dixon, the 1997 Big 12 player of the year who's won two WNBA titles as a starter with the Los Angeles Sparks. "She would be there for me for the rest of my life. And she has been."

As a teen-ager, Washington had a daughter, Josie, who graduated from KU in 1984. Washington is very guarded about her private life, but she acknowledges she has always felt a special need to

reach out to the girl who might be looking over the ledge at a lifetime of hardship - the girl for whom athletics is an escape hatch to a better world.

It bothers Washington that relatively few black women have joined the women's basketball coaching ranks.

Washington was the only black women's coach in the history of the Big Eight, which ended in 1996. And there has been only one other coach in Big 12 history, Peggie Gillom, who coached at Texas A&M during 1999-2003.

Nationally, only two black women have taken teams to the NCAA Final Four: C. Vivian Stringer with Cheyney, Iowa and Rutgers, and Carolyn Peck, who won the 1999 NCAA title with Purdue.

"It's like anything else," said Washington, who will be inducted into the Women's Basketball Hall of Fame in Knoxville, Tenn., this spring. "If you don't see a lot of examples, it doesn't seem real. That's why if there's significance to my career, it has to be that I was around and anybody who wanted any guidance could call me."

What's stung Washington more

than anything, though, is when black players have told her - not in so many words, but the meaning is unmistakable – that they have more confidence in white coaches.

"They believe the myths that black people have always had to fight," Washington said.

But she has had other difficult hurdles. KU men's basketball is worshipped; it has been hard for the KU women to gain any foothold in fans' esteem - despite 11 consecutive 20-plus victory seasons from 1989-90 to 1999-2000 - including nine NCAA Tournament appearances and two trips to the Sweet 16.

Pride, who finished her career in 2000, was Washington's last superstar. The program is 37-76 since Pride left. The Jayhawks had a disastrous 2001-2002 season, in which they finished 5-25 and 0-16 in the Big 12. It coincided with Kansas State's elevation to a national power behind three Kansas-native players.

For Washington, it has been maddening to hear people complain about the Jayhawks' lack of success the last three seasons compared with K-State - because where were those people in the entire decade before when the situation was the opposite? Certainly, they were not filling up Allen Fieldhouse to support Washington's team.

This season, Washington was again trying to get a young group to jell in what many regard as the most difficult conference in the country. When the

Jayhawks did get a potential breakthrough win, at Missouri on Jan. 10, the overzealous actions of a few players triggered a post-game scuffle with the Tigers that marred the victory and added even more stress for Washington.

On Jan. 29, she announced she was taking a medical leave of absence.

"I think all of us have had thoughts about doing that: 'I need to step back and regroup,' " said Texas' Jody Conradt, who began her college coaching career in 1969. "And I've found the older I get, I don't recover quite as quickly - the travel, the ups and downs, and how that impacts you. Part of the message to athletes is to push through things. Coaches are reluctant to honestly access where they are, for fear that's in conflict with what you try to instill in your players. But you reach a point where you have to take care of yourself." Washington acknowledges she has never had close friends in the coaching profession. But she considers someone such as Conradt to be a trusted and supportive colleague.

"I think Jody and Marsha Sharp (of Texas Tech) are people I have a lot of respect for as professionals," Washington said. "That word means a lot to me. I watch from afar. I know a lot of history."

And she has been part of so much of it.

"When you think about what she's meant to the game," Sharp said, "it will seem very strange to see Kansas and not see her."

"Me" kicks goal.
Missouri 3 Kansas 0

RIVALS!
MU VS. KU

A CLASSIC SPORTS MATCH-UP, SINCE 1891